ALL · IN · ONE

SCSP

SNIA™ Certified Storage Professional

EXAM GUIDE

(Exam S10-110)

ABOUT THE AUTHOR

Eric Vanderburg directs IT and cybersecurity consulting teams at TCDI and serves as the vice-chairman of the board for the Technology Ministry Network. He has spent the last 20 years in the information technology and security field, specializing in complex storage systems, database management systems, e-commerce, cloud computing, and big data projects. He is also a licensed private investigator with undergraduate degrees in computer information systems and technology and a graduate degree in business administration. He is a continual learner and has earned over 40 technology certifications from Microsoft, Cisco, CompTIA, (ISC)², Rapid7, EMC, CWNP, and Hitachi Data Systems.

Vanderburg has deployed numerous large enterprise storage and information systems for clients around the world. He has served as an expert witness in security, databases, and storage and is a trusted adviser and subject matter expert for his clients. He has worked closely with Dell/EMC in storage and security initiatives and has partnered with Hitachi Data Systems to test their Essential NAS. He has been interviewed on radio and television programs and is regularly invited to present on technology topics. Eric currently lives in Cleveland, Ohio, with his wife, Aimee, and two children, Faith and Jacob. He can be followed via the following social networks:

Twitter: @evanderburg
LinkedIn: https://www.linkedin.com/in/evanderburg
Facebook: https://www.facebook.com/VanderburgE

About the Technical Editor

Glen E. Clarke, CCNA, MCITP, MCT, CEH, CHFI, SCNP, CISSO, CompTIA Security+, CompTIA Network+, CompTIA A+, is an independent trainer and consultant, focusing on network security and security auditing services. Glen spends most of his time delivering certified courses on Windows Server, SQL Server, Exchange Server, SharePoint, Visual Basic .NET, and ASP.NET. Glen also teaches a number of security-related courses covering topics such as ethical hacking and countermeasures, computer forensics and investigation, information systems security officers, vulnerability testing, firewall design, and packet analysis.

Glen is an experienced author and technical editor whose published work was nominated for a Referenceware Excellence Award in 2003 and 2004. Glen has worked on a number of certification books, including topics on A+ certification, Windows Server certification, Cisco's CCENT and CCNA certifications, Network+ certification, and Security+ certification.

When he's not working, Glen loves to spend quality time with his wife, Tanya, and their four children, Sara, Brendon, Ashlyn, and Rebecca. He is an active member of the High Technology Crime Investigation Association (HTCIA). You can visit Glen online at www.gleneclarke.com or contact him at glenclarke@accesswave.ca.

ALL ■ IN ■ ONE

SCSP

SNIA™ Certified Storage Professional

EXAM GUIDE
(Exam S10-110)

Eric Vanderburg

New York   Chicago   San Francisco
Athens   London   Madrid   Mexico City
Milan   New Delhi   Singapore   Sydney   Toronto

Cataloging-in-Publication Data is on file with the Library of Congress

McGraw-Hill Education books are available at special quantity discounts to use as premiums and sales promotions, or for use in corporate training programs. To contact a representative, please visit the Contact Us pages at www.mhprofessional.com.

SCSP SNIA™ Certified Storage Professional All-In-One Exam Guide (Exam S10-110)

1 2 3 4 5 6 7 8 9   QFR   21 20 19 18 17

ISBN   978-1-260-01107-4
MHID   1-260-01107-0

Sponsoring Editor	**Copy Editors**	**Composition**
Timothy Green	Bart Reed and Kim Wimpsett	Cenveo® Publisher Services
Editorial Supervisor	**Proofreader**	**Illustration**
Janet Walden	Rick Camp	Cenveo Publisher Services
Acquisitions Coordinator	**Indexer**	**Art Director, Cover**
Claire Yee	Claire Splan	Jeff Weeks
Technical Editor	**Production Supervisor**	
Glen E. Clarke	James Kussow	

To my parents, Keith and Lynda Vanderburg,
for their encouragement, support, and love.

CONTENTS AT A GLANCE

Chapter 1   Storage Essentials 1

Chapter 2   Storage Infrastructure... 41

Chapter 3   Storage Networking... 71

Chapter 4   Storage Hardware 111

Chapter 5   Virtualization... 143

Chapter 6   Storage Management... 171

Chapter 7   Business Continuity 205

Chapter 8   Security... 233

Chapter 9   Design 263

Chapter 10 Environment 291

Chapter 11 Advanced Topics... 311

Chapter 12 Performance and Troubleshooting 327

Appendix   Practice Exam 383

                Index.. 433

CONTENTS

Acknowledgments xvii

Introduction xix

Chapter 1   Storage Essentials 1

How Disk Storage Systems Work 1

Physical Components 1

Solid-State Drive 7

Electrical and Mechanical Differences 8

I/O vs. Throughput 11

Capacity vs. Speed 12

Available Disk Interfaces and Their Characteristics 13

ATA 13

SCSI 17

Fibre Channel 18

SAS 18

PCI Versions 18

Multiple Disks for Larger Storage and Fault Tolerance 24

RAID Levels 24

JBOD 31

Hardware, Host-Based, and Software Implementations 31

Hosts Interaction with Disks 32

File Systems 33

Chapter Summary 34

Chapter Review Questions 36

Chapter Review Answers 38

Chapter 2   Storage Infrastructure 41

Storage Arrays 42

Controller Head 44

Disk Enclosure 49

Hot-Swap 52

Storage Area Networks 52

Fibre Channel 52

Fabric 53

FC or iSCSI Protocol 53

Block Mode 53

File System on Host 53

Direct Attached Storage 54
SCSI 54
SAS 55
eSATA 55
FC 55
Network Attached Storage 55
Components 57
UNC-Addressable Storage 57
TCP/IP-Based Storage 58
NAS File System Protocols 58
Ethernet-Based Storage 60
Cloud Storage 60
Cloud Storage Types 61
Cloud Storage Methods 62
Chapter Summary 65
Chapter Review Questions 66
Chapter Review Answers 68

Chapter 3   Storage Networking 71
Fibre Channel Storage Network 71
Components 71
Protocols 76
Topologies 81
ISL 85
Port Channel 85
Trunking 86
Port Types 86
Tools 88
iSCSI Storage Network 93
Block Mode 93
Initiator 93
Target 93
Ethernet Switching 94
Ethernet Features 96
Tools 99
Storage over a WAN 102
Bandwidth 102
Latency 103
Flow Control 104
Chapter Summary 105
Chapter Review Questions 107
Chapter Review Answers 109

Chapter 4   Storage Hardware   111

Cables   111

Optical Cables   113

Copper Cables   116

Storage Networking Devices   121

HBA   122

NIC   122

CNA   123

Repeaters and Amplifiers   123

Ethernet Switch   123

Fiber Hub   124

Fiber Switch   125

Director   126

Router   126

Hot-Swappable Network Components   126

Removable Storage   127

Tape Media   127

Optical Media   132

Flash Media   136

Chapter Summary   137

Chapter Review Questions   138

Chapter Review Answers   140

Chapter 5   Virtualization   143

Types of Storage Virtualization   144

Tape Virtualization   146

Disk Virtualization   149

Block Virtualization   150

File Virtualization   151

Host Virtualization   154

LVM   154

Virtual Provisioning   156

Implementing Host Virtualization   156

Array-Based Virtualization   157

Virtual Provisioning of the Array   158

Implementing Array-Based Virtualization   158

Network Virtualization   159

Concepts   159

Methods   159

Provisioning the Logical Fabric   164

Chapter Summary   165

Chapter Review Questions   166

Chapter Review Answers   168

Chapter 6	Storage Management	171
	Storage Provisioning	171
	LUN Provisioning	172
	Thick Provisioning	173
	Thin Provisioning	174
	Thin Provisioning Woes	176
	Best Practices for Disk Provisioning	176
	Oversubscription	177
	Management Protocols	177
	SNMP	177
	WBEM	179
	SMI-S	180
	In-Band vs. Out-of-Band Management	180
	Storage Administration	181
	GUI	181
	CLI	181
	Configuration Management	185
	Information Technology Infrastructure Library	186
	Storage Monitoring, Alerting, and Reporting	187
	Settings Thresholds	188
	Trending	189
	Forecasting and Capacity Planning	189
	Recording a Baseline	190
	Setting Alerts	191
	Displaying Performance Data in Windows with Performance Monitor	192
	Auditing Log Files	193
	Backup Logs	194
	Alerting Methods	194
	Software-Defined Storage	196
	SDS Caveats	197
	Chapter Summary	198
	Chapter Review Questions	200
	Chapter Review Answers	202
Chapter 7	Business Continuity	205
	Business Continuity Objectives	206
	Integrity	207
	Availability	207
	Reliability	207
	Data Value and Risk	208
	Recovery Point Objective	209
	Recovery Time Objective	210
	Mean Time Between Failures	210
	Mean Time to Failure	210

Backup Frequency 210
    Rotation Schemes 211
    Continuous Data Protection 212
    Contention of Media 213
    Impact on Production 214
Backup Reliability 214
    Backup and Restore Methods 216
    Backup Implementation Methods 219
    Backup Reliability Methods 220
Backup Locations 222
    Disk-to-Disk 222
    Disk-to-Tape 223
    VTL 223
    Disk-to-Disk-to-Tape 224
    Vaulting and E-vaulting 224
    Offsite Tape Storage 225
    Array-Based Backups 227
Chapter Summary 228
Chapter Review Questions 230
Chapter Review Answers 231

Chapter 8 Security 233

Access Control 234
    Authentication 234
    Authorization 235
    Interoperability 240
Encryption 241
    Encryption Keys 242
    Data at Rest 243
    Data in Motion 246
    Host Encryption 249
Storage Visibility 249
    LUN Security 250
    Zoning 252
    iSCSI Security 253
    Storage Segmentation 255
Chapter Summary 256
Chapter Review Questions 258
Chapter Review Answers 260

Chapter 9 Design 263

Storage Architecture Components 263
    Types of Storage Architecture 264
    High Availability 265
    Online Transaction Processing 267
    Cloud Services 267

Redundancy 271
    Clustering 271
    Power Supply 273
    Controller 273
    Redundant Paths to Disks 274
    Hot Spare 275
    Multipath I/O 276
    Hot-Swap 276
    Path/Bus 277
    Switch 278
    HBA 278
    NIC 278
    Link Aggregation 278
    Array 278
    Cache Redundancy 278
Replication 279
    Point-in-Time Replication 280
    Continuous Replication 280
    Scope 282
    Site Redundancy 283
    Consistency 284
Chapter Summary 284
Chapter Review Questions 286
Chapter Review Answers 288

Chapter 10 Environment 291
Facilities 291
    Cable Management 293
    Cooling 294
    Humidity Control 295
    Fire Suppression 295
Storage Power Requirements 298
    AC 298
    DC 299
    Grounding 299
    Sufficient Capacity 299
    Division of Circuits 301
    Uninterruptable Power Supply 301
Safety 304
    Weight Considerations 304
    Antistatic Devices 306
Chapter Summary 306
Chapter Review Questions 307
Chapter Review Answers 309

Chapter 11 Advanced Topics 311

Information Lifecycle Management 311
Value of Data Based on Frequency of Access 313
HSM 313
Storage Tiers 314
Compliance 316
Retention Policy 316
Archiving and Purging 317
Preservation and Litigation Holds 317
Advanced Storage Methods 318
Content-Addressable Storage 318
Object-Oriented Storage 319
Deduplication and Compression 319
Deduplication Levels 319
Inline and Postprocess Deduplication 320
Source and Target Deduplication 320
Deduplication Software and Appliances 320
Performance and Capacity Implications 321
Reduction Ratios for Data Types 321
Chapter Summary 321
Chapter Review Questions 323
Chapter Review Answers 325

Chapter 12 Performance and Troubleshooting 327

Optimize Performance 327
Necessary IOPS 328
Random vs. Sequential I/O 329
RAID Performance 330
Defragmentation 333
Cache 335
Impact of Replication 337
Partition Alignment 340
Queue Depth 341
Storage Device Bandwidth 342
Network Device Bandwidth 347
Adequate Share Capacity 349
Performance Metrics and Tools 349
Switch 350
Array 353
Host Tools 357
Network Troubleshooting 360
Connectivity Issues 361
VLAN Issues 363
Zoning Issues 363
Interoperability Issues 364

Host Troubleshooting 364
    Hardware or Software Incompatibility 365
    Outdated Firmware or Drivers 365
    Incorrect NIC Configuration 365
    Bad Connector 365
    Bad Cable 367
    Bad Port 367
    Bad NIC 368
    NIC Improperly Connected 369
    Incorrect Firewall Settings 369
    Incorrect Cluster or Multipath Settings 369
Backup Troubleshooting 370
    Space Limitations 371
    Open Files 372
    Virus Scanning 373
    Permissions 374
Chapter Summary 376
Software References 376
Chapter Review Questions 378
Chapter Review Answers 379

Appendix   Practice Exam 383
Questions 383
Quick Answer Key 407
In-Depth Answers 408
Analyzing Your Results 431

Index 433

ACKNOWLEDGMENTS

I would first like to thank my wife, Aimee, for encouraging me and giving me the time and freedom to write this book. Her tireless efforts and sacrifices were an outpouring of her amazing love. I thank my parents for the example they set of working hard to accomplish great things, for modeling excellence and integrity, and for giving me the freedom to fail enough to succeed.

No matter the size, each book is a long-term effort. It has been a real pleasure to work with the professional editors at McGraw-Hill, especially executive editor Timothy Green. Thank you for your patience, guidance, and honest feedback. Glen Clarke deserves special mention for his remarkable contributions as technical editor. His comments, questions, and clarifying notes brought polish and refinement to this work. I also want to thank Janet Walden and Claire Yee for their attention to detail, feedback, and patient reminders. It has been a blessing to work with such a great editorial team.

Thank you all so much. May this book be a testimony to your efforts, assistance, and guidance.

INTRODUCTION

Organizations today are overwhelmed with data. Besides user-created data such as spreadsheets, documents, videos, audio recordings, presentation files, computer-aided design files, schematics, and health and regulatory data, as part of its ongoing management the system creates its own data. Servers and other networking equipment keep logs of activity and events; data is created in aggregate for statistics and reporting, and databases support the applications used by employees every day. Some of this data must be kept confidential, but some of it needs to be available at all times to keep the business running. You, or someone like you, will likely be asked to keep it running.

The Importance of Storage

As more and more data is collected, organizations realize the importance of knowing how to properly manage their data and the systems housing it. Although this skill is not covered in networking or computer hardware courses, it builds upon those disciplines. As shown in Chapter 1, at their most basic level, storage systems consist of storage media, such as a hard drive containing bits and bytes represented by 0s and 1s. This media is connected to the computer through an interface or expansion bus, or from a network resource.

Disk drives have a limited life span measured by metrics such as mean time between failures (MTBF) and annualized failure rate (AFR). Your choice of drive matters because some are less expensive but more prone to failure, whereas others are more costly but more reliable. Drives also differ in their ability to handle concurrent I/O. Chapter 1 describes the electrical and mechanical differences in these drive types so you can make an informed decision on the best drive for your application. Chapter 1 also introduces various forms of combining multiple drives into a RAID set in order to provide higher speeds and protection against drive failure.

To have real value, data on a disk must be accessible when needed. Moreover, in order for data to be accessible, it must be available to the authorized user wherever they are located, including in remote offices and on the road via a smartphone or another mobile device. This is accomplished by attaching storage media to computer systems and networks or by mapping remote, network, or cloud storage to the target. Chapter 2, "Storage Infrastructure," introduces components that store data on a network or cloud, while Chapter 3, "Storage Networking," explains the protocols, topologies, and tools used to connect storage devices together to make the data available to a broad range of computers, applications, and users. The topic of storage networking is divided into two sections corresponding with the two storage networking technologies that dominate the market—fibre channel and iSCSI. Chapter 4 builds on this by introducing the cables and devices, such as host bus adapters, network interface cards, switches, directors, and routers, that are used in storage networking. This chapter also explains the available removable storage options including tape, optical, and flash media.

Storage today must be made available to many different types of systems and applications. Chapters 1 through 4 provide the understanding of the underlying storage technologies. Chapter 5 explains how virtualization is used to present storage to systems and applications without the need for applications to understand the underlying technologies. This allows for more flexibility in assigning and managing storage resources. Chapter 6 introduces a way to automate many storage management tasks and a method for granting applications control over their own storage. This concept is known as software-defined storage (SDS). Chapter 6 goes on to explain storage management tasks such as storage provisioning, trending, forecasting, capacity planning, reporting, and alerting. Essentially, it shows how to organize and present storage so that it can be used effectively and how to monitor it so that it performs consistently. As a case in point, a client I worked with deployed a document repository to utilize its searching features in finding process documents. Users saved files wherever they wanted and, shortly after that, searches for documents resulted in many different documents with the same name. Users did not know which version to update, and others followed the wrong process, causing inconsistent results and a higher number of errors.

Configuration management is introduced in Chapter 6 as a way to control the changes made to organizational equipment. Configuration management often results in much greater availability for key systems because modifications to the systems are better evaluated, coordinated, and tested. Furthermore, when problems do arise, technicians and engineers know which changes were made and can use that information to reverse changes and get systems operational faster.

Next, when data is lost, there must be a way to recover it. Effective recovery requires regular backups as well as deliberate and strategic planning. It is important to know that your data can be retrieved in a crisis and within a reasonable timeframe. The backup and recovery planning process identifies the maximum amount of time data can be unavailable, as well as the maximum amount of data that can be lost, along with other business goals and compliance requirements related to data availability. Chapter 7 covers backup and recovery. Based on this, storage professionals can implement backup methods to capture the data and make it available for restoration.

Data must be available, but it also must be secure and this presents a complex balancing act for storage professionals. Chapter 8 explains access control, encryption, and storage visibility concepts that can be used to verify identify, grant access to resources, secure data in transit or at rest, and segment storage.

The connectivity, accessibility, and security needs of data and applications must be addressed in designing storage solutions. This is discussed in Chapter 9. For example, accessibility also relies upon a reasonable response time. The speed of both broadband at home and data plans on cell phones has increased to such a point that most people now expect data to be at their fingertips regardless of where they are presently located. Most users will not wait five minutes to retrieve a document from the company intranet, nor will they be pleased when a shared calendar fails to load. High-speed, on-access response to data requests requires a robust infrastructure capable of retrieving and sending information to users and applications whenever with little latency. These are the business requirements that must be addressed in an effective design. Storage professionals will also need to understand the business value of information and how to manage information over its life span. Some storage may achieve great cost savings through data compression or deduplication while other solutions may utilize content-addressable storage or object-oriented storage. Storage processionals must also manage data so that the organization complies with relevant regulatory and legal requirements such as data retention or preservation for litigation holds.

Storage solutions may require many devices and components that are often housed in server rooms or data centers. These storage devices require sufficient cooling and power as well as ongoing maintenance to function efficiently. Chapter 10 discusses how to provide for such requirements as well as how to safely install storage equipment. Chapter 11 covers advanced topics such as information lifecycle management, compliance, advanced storage methods, and deduplication and compression. And last, Chapter 12 covers how to troubleshoot common problems with storage networks, hosts, and devices.

Uses of Storage

Enormous amounts of data are created as you go about your day. Just browsing the Internet creates data on your computer as well as various servers around the world. Performing a few searches results in the collection of the search terms used by the search engine along with other data on your connection, while your browser stores the pages in history, caching some of the content. Additionally, some of the content may be cached by servers at your Internet service provider (ISP) or workplace. You may snap pictures with your phone, or record video with a mobile device or webcam, and these may be uploaded to social networking sites where others can view them and make comments. Then there are the most obvious pieces of data you create: documents, spreadsheets, schematics, presentation files, and a host of other content that resides on your computer, in department network shares, attached to e-mails, and within document management systems.

Organizations generally have trouble deleting data for fear that it might prove useful sometime in the future. Moreover, we have found new ways of making use of data by mining it for still more data so others hold onto their data so that they can mine it. Organizations hoard data like a dragon with its gold, while it piles up by the terabytes. Unfortunately, the very existence of so much data creates a host of problems that can diminish its value for organizations, and far too many organizations struggle to manage islands of information, each stored, secured, and managed in different ways. The cost of managing this data must be understood so that it can be associated with the data value. So much business value and day-to-day operations rely on the availability of data that systems must be highly available and have timely backups. Clusters and high-performance systems require increasingly complex storage systems that must meet high demands while being flexible enough to support growing business needs and changing applications.

This is where storage networking professionals enter into the picture. Organizations are in dire need of technologists with a firm grasp on how to implement reliable storage systems that will meet current organizational needs and grow with changing technologies and objectives. This book will help you refine those skills in preparation for the Storage

Networking Industry Association's storage networking foundations exam number S10-100. Passing this exam earns you the SNIA Certified Storage Professional (SCSP) certification, which can be used to validate your skills as a storage professional.

The Storage Networking Industry Association

The Storage Networking Industry Association (SNIA) is a nonprofit standards and certification organization that works to establish standards and best practices, foster innovation in vendor-neutral technologies, educate, and validate skills through certification. SNIA describes their vision as follows:

> *Be the globally recognized and trusted authority for storage leadership, standards, and technology expertise.*

You can find out more at www.snia.org/about/vision-mission.

The SNIA Certified Storage Professional (SCSP) certification is the first of four certifications from SNIA. SNIA organizes its certifications into three tiers. The first tier is called *concepts*, and this is where the SCSP falls. The next tier is called *standards*, and there is one certification in this tier called the SNIA Certified Storage Engineer (SCSE). Candidates for the SCSE must first obtain the SCSP. The third and highest tier is called *solutions*, and SNIA has two certifications in this tier: the SNIA Certified Storage Architect (SCSA) and the SNIA Certified Storage Networking Expert (SCSN-E). The SCSP is the only prerequisite for the SCSA, but the SCSN-E requires both the SCSP and the SCSE before candidates can take it.

SNIA partnered with CompTIA for several years to offer a joint certification known as the Storage+. This certification is no longer offered, but those who hold the certification can use it to fulfill the requirement for the SCSP prerequisite for the SCSE and SCSA exams up until three years from their Storage+ certification date.

The hallmark of SNIA's certifications is that they are *vendor neutral*, meaning that they do not teach to a specific vendor's technology or methodology. The advantage to this approach is that the skills measured by a SNIA exam are useful across a wide variety of technologies and platforms produced by different vendors.

The Examination

The storage networking foundations exam lasts 90 minutes and consists of 65 multiple-choice questions. Candidates must answer 66 percent of the questions correctly in order to pass. The exam costs $200 and is available in both English and Japanese. The SCSP is designed to validate the skill set of individuals filling roles such as storage administrator, storage engineer, cloud storage administrator, backup administrator, system administrator, and IT operations.

Once you have completed this book and are passing the practice test with a comfortable margin, it will be time to schedule the test. I find a comfortable margin to be about 15 percent above the passing score, so I recommend that you score at least 80 percent

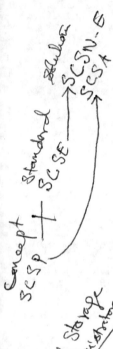

on the practice test before scheduling the exam, because a new environment, distractions, temperature differences, and nervousness can all have an impact on your exam performance.

The exam can be taken at a Prometric testing center near you. Use the Prometric web site (www.prometric.com) to find local testing locations and to schedule an exam. The exam code will be S10-110. Bring two forms of identification, including at least one photo ID, such as a driver's license.

You will not be permitted to bring electronic devices such as smartphones and smartwatches or any recording equipment into the testing area. Some testing centers have lockers or a zone where personal devices can be stored while you are taking the exam, but I find it easier to not even bring personal electronics into the testing center so as to not possibly forget them.

You will need to sign in when presenting your identification, and then the test administrator will show you the testing center rules and require you to sign that you have read the rules, including the SNIA exam security and cheating policy. The testing administrator will then lead you to a room where you can take the exam on a computer. There may be others in the room as well. They may be taking completely different tests than the one you are taking since Prometric centers are used for a variety of tests. The testing administrator will sign into the computer and then you will be allowed to sit for the test.

Verify that your name is displayed on the screen and that the exam number is correct before initiating the exam. You will then be presented with additional exam rules that you must read and accept, and you may see a survey as well. The survey and any instructions do not take away from the 90 minutes of testing time.

Your exam will be recorded, and data on how you take the test is used to identify potential cheating. You will not be allowed to bring in your own writing utensils or paper. However, the testing administrator will give you an erasable sheet and a marker that you will need to return when you complete the exam.

You will have the chance to review questions that you have marked along the way before ending the exam, and then you will have the opportunity to comment on the questions. Comments do not affect your score, but they may be used to improve the exam. Your score will be computed at the conclusion of the test. Your score will also print at the testing administrator station, and you will receive it when you sign out of the testing center.

If you did not pass, find a quiet place and think through the exam immediately and consider the areas where you were less than confident about your answers, and then write down the concept or concepts each question was related to. Do not try to write the question word for word, as this is a violation of the ethical rules. You are simply trying to identify your areas for improvement before the distractions of daily life creep in. You can reference the list you make later as you prepare to retake the exam. Look up each area in this book and focus on those areas, but don't neglect the other areas. Many certification candidates study the areas they were weak in and then take the test again, only to find that they fail again but in different areas. Your mind will forget information quickly, so it is best to concentrate on your areas of weakness, but also take a general refresher of all the remaining content. Lastly, don't wait too long before taking the test again. Create an aggressive study plan to address your weaknesses and then try again while the knowledge is still fresh. A week is generally a good time frame, but the timing really depends on how much time you will be able to dedicate to studying between exam dates.

I find it is best to schedule the retake of the exam quickly so that you have a definite target date. Too many candidates study and prepare following a failed exam but never get around to taking the exam again, or they wait too long and realize they forgot some essential elements of what they studied. Keep your momentum and don't let too much time pass between the test and the retake exam. However, there are some minimum wait times before you can retake the exam. You cannot simply sit back down and take the exam a second time in the same day. You must wait at least 24 hours before retaking the exam the first time, or seven days if you are retaking the exam a second time. After that, candidates must wait 30 days before retaking the exam.

Welcome to this journey toward certification. I am confident that this book will give you the information needed to prepare for the SCSP exam as well as a great deal of knowledge useful for those involved in storage, IT, and other technology roles.

How to Use This Book

The structure of this book follows the SCSP exam objectives from SNIA. It has been organized into 12 chapters, starting with the most conceptual area in the first five chapters, and then focusing on the practical elements that build on these concepts in the remaining chapters.

Each chapter has several components designed to effectively communicate the information you'll need for the exam.

- The certification objectives covered in each chapter are listed first, right off the bat. These identify the major topics within the chapter and help you to map out your study.

- Sidebars are included in some places to expand upon a topic and are designed to point out information, tips, and stories that will be helpful in your day-today responsibilities. Please note, though, that although these entries provide real-world accounts of interesting pieces of information, they are sometimes used to reinforce testable material. Don't just discount them as simply "neat"—some of the circumstances and tools described in these sidebars may prove the difference in correctly answering a question or two on the exam.

- Exam Tips are exactly what they sound like. These are included to point out a focus area you need to concentrate on for the exam. No, they are not explicit test answers. Yes, they will help you focus your study.

- Specially called-out Notes are part of this book too. These are interesting tidbits of information that are relevant to the discussion and point out extra information. Just as with the sidebars, don't discount them.

- The Chapter Review Questions are similar to those found on the actual exam. The answers to these questions, as well as explanations of the correct answer choices, can be found at the end of each chapter. By answering the Chapter Review Questions after completing each chapter, you'll reinforce what you've learned from that chapter while becoming familiar with the structure of the exam questions.

Following Chapter 12, you will find the Appendix, which consists of a practice exam, an answer key, and detailed answer explanations to allow you to gauge your level of readiness for the exam and to provide you with the opportunity to practice what you've learned throughout the course of this book.

Objective Map: Exam S10-110

The following table has been constructed to allow you to cross-reference the official exam objectives with the objectives as they are presented and covered in this book. References have been provided for the objective exactly as the exam vendor presents it, the section of the exam guide that covers that objective, and a chapter and page reference. There are also three check boxes labeled Beginner, Intermediate, and Expert. Use these to rate your beginning knowledge of each objective. This assessment will help guide you to the areas in which you need to spend more time studying for the exams.

Official Exam Objective	Ch #	All-in-One Coverage	Pg #	Beginner	Intermediate	Expert
1.0 Host Elements						
1.1: Identify host connectivity components used in a support matrix	4 1 4 10	Storage Hardware How Disk Storage Systems Work Cables Safety	111 1 111 304			
1.2: Describe host-based functions for storage	1	Hosts Interaction with Disks	32			
1.3: Identify storage mapping elements	6 8	Storage Provisioning Storage Visibility	171 249			
1.4: Describe virtualization concepts and techniques	5 5 5 5	Types of Storage Virtualization Host Virtualization Array-Based Virtualization Network Virtualization	144 154 157 159			
1.5: Describe data storage planning for various business applications	6 10 10 9 11	Storage Management Facilities Storage Power Requirements Replication Compliance	171 291 298 279 316			

Official Exam Objective	Ch #	All-in-One Coverage	Pg #	Beginner	Intermediate	Expert
1.6: Describe how to improve performance for host applications	12	Optimize Performance	327			
	12	Performance and Troubleshooting	327			
	12	Performance Metrics and Tools	349			
2.0 Storage Protocol Concepts						
2.1: Identify NAS components	2	Network Attached Storage	55			
2.2: Identify Fibre Channel SAN components	3	Fibre Channel Storage Network	71			
	4	Storage Networking Devices	121			
2.3: Identify Ethernet/IP SAN components	3	Ethernet Switching	94			
	3	iSCSI Storage Network	93			
	4	Storage Networking Devices	121			
2.4: Describe DCBX switching technology	3	Data Center Bridging	98			
2.5: Identify the software storage model	6	Software-Defined Storage	196			
3.0 Storage Hardware						
3.1: Identify host to SAN components	4	Storage Hardware	111			
	2	Storage Area Networks	52			
3.2: Identify Flash technology for enhancing applications	1	Solid-State Drive	7			
3.3: Describe the different RAID levels	1	Multiple Disks for Larger Storage and Fault Tolerance	24			
3.4: Describe disk technologies	1	Available Disk Interfaces and Their Characteristics	13			
	7	Mean Time Between Failures	210			
	7	Mean Time to Failure	210			
	2	Storage Arrays	42			
3.5: Identify DAS technology	2	Direct Attached Storage	54			
4.0 Disaster Recovery						
4.1: Identify backup technologies	4	Removable Storage	127			
	7	Business Continuity	205			
	12	Backup Troubleshooting	370			
4.2: Describe backup types	7	Backup Frequency	210			
	7	Backup Reliability	214			
	7	Backup Locations	222			

Official Exam Objective	Ch #	All-in-One Coverage	Pg #	Beginner	Intermediate	Expert
4.3: Describe disaster recovery concepts	7	Data Value and Risk	208			
	7	Recovery Point Objective	209			
	7	Recovery Time Objective	210			
	9	Redundancy	271			
	9	High Availability	265			
5.0 Storage Functions						
5.1: Describe storage security methods	8	Security	233			
5.2: Identify storage management technologies	11	Information Lifecycle Management	311			
	6	Management Protocols	177			
	6	Storage Administration	181			
	6	Storage Monitoring, Alerting, and Reporting	187			
	6	Configuration Management	185			
5.3: Describe data reduction techniques	11	Deduplication and Compression	319			
6.0 Cloud Storage						
6.1: Identify cloud storage methods	2	Cloud Storage Methods	62			
6.2: Identify cloud storage types	2	Cloud Storage Types	61			
	9	Cloud Services	267			

CHAPTER 1

Storage Essentials

In this chapter, you will learn how to
- Explain how drive storage systems work
- Describe the types of disk interfaces and their characteristics
- Combine multiple disks to achieve larger storage and fault tolerance
- Classify the way hosts interact with disks

At its most basic level, storage starts with a disk. These disks, connected either internally or externally to systems via interfaces, can be accessed by systems to read or write data. Disks can also be combined to achieve greater speed than each disk could individually provide, or they can be combined to protect against one or more disk failures. One or more disks are then presented to a host, enabling it and its applications to work with the storage.

How Disk Storage Systems Work

The hard disk drive (HDD) or hard drive is a good place to begin a discussion on storage. HDDs have been in use in computer systems for decades, and the principles behind their basic operation remain largely unchanged. The solid-state drive (SSD) is a more recent introduction, and although it uses different principles for storing data, it has not replaced the HDD. SSD and HDD both have their uses in storage systems today, which will be explained in this section.

Physical Components

Originally, the term *hard disk drive* was used to differentiate the rigid, inflexible metal drive from floppy disks, which could be easily bent. While floppy disks are mostly a thing of the past, the *hard disk drive* term remains. HDDs are physically composed of platters, heads, a spindle, and an actuator arm all sealed within a rectangular container that is 3.5 or 2.5 inches wide called the *head disk assembly* (HDA). This is pictured in Figure 1-1. Higher capacity can be obtained from 3.5-inch drives because they have a larger surface area. These 3.5-inch drives are typically installed in desktops and servers, while 2.5-inch drives are commonly found in laptops. Some servers use 2.5-inch drives in cases where an increased number of drives is preferred over increased capacity. Beginning with the platter,

1

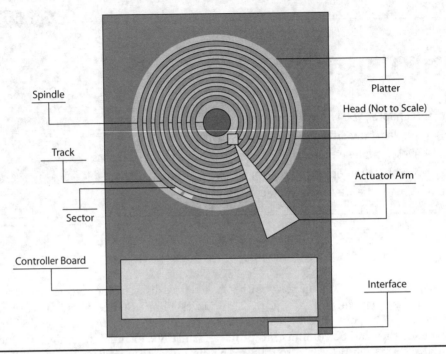

Figure 1-1 HDD components

each of these components is discussed in more detail, and key performance metrics are introduced for several components.

Platter

If you open an HDD, the first thing you notice is a stack of round flat surfaces known as *platters*. Platters are made of thin but rigid sheets of aluminum, glass, or ceramic. The platters are covered on both the top and the bottom with a thin coating of substrate filled with small bits of metal. The majority of drives contain two or three platters providing four or six usable surfaces for storing data.

Spindle

An HDD has multiple platters connected to a rod called a *spindle*. The spindle and all the platters are rotated at a consistent rate by the spindle motor. Spindles commonly spin at 7,200 or 10,000 or 15,000 rotations per minute (rpm). Disk rpm is the determining factor in the rotational latency, an important disk performance metric.

Rotational latency is the amount of time it takes to move the platter to the desired location, measured in milliseconds (ms). Full rotational latency is the amount of time it takes to turn the platter 360 degrees. Average rotational latency is roughly half the full rotational latency. Average rotational latency is a significant metric in determining the time it takes to read random data. Rotational latency is directly related to rotational speed, with faster disks (higher rpm) providing lower rotational latency. Average rotational latency can be computed using the following formula:

Average rotational latency = 0.5 / (rpm/60) × 1,000

With this formula, a disk with 10k (10,000) rpm would have a rotational latency of 3 ms.

Cylinder

HDDs are organized into a series of concentric rings similar to the rings on a tree. Each ring—called a *cylinder*—is numbered, starting at 0 with the outermost cylinder. Cylinders provide a precise location where data is located relative to the platter's center. Each cylinder consists of sections from the platters located directly above and below it. These cylinder sections on each platter start and stop at the same relative location. The cylinder area on an individual platter is called a *track*, so cylinder 0 would comprise track 0 on the top and bottom of all platters in the disk. Figure 1-2 shows hard disk platters and the tracks that make up cylinder 0. A physical demarcation, delineating the tracks on the platter, enables the head (discussed next) to follow and remain in proper alignment.

Tracks are organized into sectors, each of a fixed length. A process, often performed by the disk manufacturer, called *low-level formatting* creates the sectors on the disk and marks the areas before and after each sector with an ID, making them ready for use. These sectors make it easier to more precisely locate data on the disk, and they are more manageable because of their consistent size. Disks used a sector size of 512 bytes until 2009, when advanced format drives were released that use 4,096 bytes, or 4 kilobytes (4KB), per sector. Advanced format drives are the most common ones in use today.

Earlier HDD designs stored the same amount of data on each track even though the inner tracks were much smaller physically than the outer tracks. Later designs incorporated zone bit recording to divide the tracks into zones, with some zones having more sectors than others. Each track in a zone has the same number of sectors

Figure 1-2

Cylinder 0 and the tracks comprising it

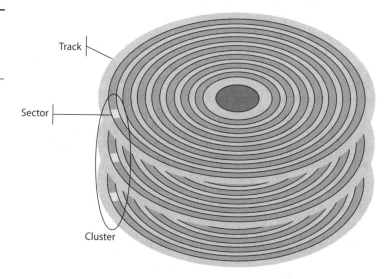

Track

Sector

Cluster

in it, with the zone closest to the center having the fewest sectors. In this way, more data could be written to the outside tracks to make use of much more space on the platters. However, with zone bit recording, the disk still spins at a constant rate, so the data stored on the outside zones is read much quicker than data on inside zones. Since performance is partially determined by where benchmarking data is stored, this can lead to inconsistent results. A better result can be achieved when the benchmark is performed on the outer zones for all disks that need to be compared.

Head

HDDs contain small electromagnets called *heads*. These heads, one for both the top and bottom sides of each platter in the disk, are attached to an actuator arm. All heads are attached to the same actuator arm, so they move together back and forth across the platter. The actuator arm can move the heads across the radius of the platters to a specific cylinder. To locate a specific section of the disk, the actuator will move the head to the appropriate cylinder, and then the head must wait for the platter to rotate to the desired sector. The actuator arm and platter rotation thus allow the heads to access a point almost anywhere on the platter surface.

A common disk metric associated with the head is seek time, which is the time it takes to move the head, measured in milliseconds. There are three types of seek times. Full stroke seek time is the time it takes to move from the head to the first to last cylinder. Average seek time is usually one-third of the full stroke time, and it represents the average amount of time it takes to move from one cylinder to another. Average seek time is an important metric in determining the time it takes to read random data. The last type of seek time is track-to-track, which is the time it takes to move to the next track or cylinder. Track-to-track seek time is a useful metric for determining the seek time for reading or writing sequential data.

 EXAM TIP If a question asks about random reads, look for an answer that contains average seek time, but if the question asks about sequential reads, look for track-to-track seek time.

When a disk is not in use or powered down, heads are parked in a special area of the platter known as the *landing zone*. This landing zone is typically located on the innermost area of the platter. As the platters rotate, the disk heads float on a cushion of air nanometers above the platter surface. The actuator arm moves the heads back to the landing zone when the disk spins down again. Normally, heads should not come in contact with the platter in any area but the landing zone because contact can cause damage to both the head and the platter. This is known as a *head crash*, and it is important to avoid because it can lead to data loss.

Head crashes can be avoided by following these best practices:

- Secure hard disks into mountings or disk caddies using four screws, two on each side.
- Wait for disks to spin down and park heads before removing them from a bay.

- Transport hard disks in impact-resistant packaging such as bubble wrap or foam.
- Do not place heavy objects on top of hard disks to avoid warping the casing.
- Give disks time to acclimate to a warmer or cooler environment before powering them on.
- Replace hard disks that are nearing their expected life span.
- Connect disks to reliable power supplies to avoid power surges or power loss during operation.
- Shut down servers and equipment containing hard disks properly to give disks time to spin down and park heads.

The head is shaped like a horseshoe where current can be passed through in one of two directions. When current passes through the head, an electromagnetic field is generated, and the metallic particles in the substrate are polarized, aligning them with the field. These polarized particles are described as being in magnetic flux. Polarization can occur in one of two directions depending on the direction the current is flowing through the head. At first glance, it might seem logical to assume that the polarities are associated with a binary 1 or 0, but the reality is more complex. When polarity is positive, a transition will always be to a negative polarity, and vice versa, meaning it is impossible to represent multiple identical transitions in sequence simply by encoding a different polarity because the polarity would always have to switch back and forth, indicating only that a transition had occurred, not what that transition represents.

The disk head can detect changes in polarity known as *flux transition* only when performing read operations, so write operations are designed to create transitions from positive to negative or from negative to positive. When the head passes over an area of the platter that has a flux transition, a current will be generated in the head corresponding to the direction of the flux transition. Here are some examples:

- The head generates negative voltage when the flux transition goes from positive to negative.
- The head generates positive voltage when the flux transition goes from negative to positive.

Each flux transition takes up space on the platter. Disk designers want to minimize the number of transitions necessary to represent binary numbers on the disk, and this is where encoding methods come in. HDDs utilize an encoding method, consisting of a pattern of flux transitions, to represent one or more binary numbers. The method currently in use today is known as *run length limited* (RLL), and it has been in use since the 1980s. The method represents groups of bits in several flux transitions.

NOTE RLL is not specific to disks. It is used in many situations where binary numbers need to be represented on a physical medium such as cable passing light or current.

Controller Board

A controller board mounted to the bottom of the disk controls the physical components in the disk and contains an interface port for sending and receiving data to and from a connected device. The controller board consists of a processor, cache, connecting circuits, and read-only memory (ROM) containing firmware that includes instructions for how the disk components are controlled. Data that comes in from the interface and data that is waiting to be transmitted on the interface reside in cache.

All of these components in the disk work together to store data on the disk. Disks receive data over an interface and place this data into cache until it can be written to the disk. Depending on the cache method, an acknowledgment may immediately be sent back over the interface once the data is written to cache, or it may wait until the data is written to the disk. The data in cache is marked as dirty so that the controller board knows that the data has not been written to disk yet. The data is then flushed to the disk. In this write operation example, the controller board will look up the closest available sector to the head's current position and instruct the actuator arm to move and the platters to rotate to that location.

Once the head is positioned at the correct location, a current passes through the head to polarize the platter substrate. Sections of the substrate are polarized in a pattern determined by the disk's encoding method to represent the binary numbers that make up the data to be written. This will continue until the sector is full. The disk head will continue writing in the next sector if it is also available. If it is not available, the controller board will send instructions to move to the next available location and continue the process of writing data until complete.

The controller locates data based on cylinder, head, and sector (CHS). The head information describes which platter and side the data resides on, while the cylinder information locates the track on that platter. Lastly, the sector addresses the area within that track so that the head can be positioned to read or write data to that location.

When the data has been fully written to the disk, the disk may send an acknowledgment back to the unit if it did not do so upon writing the data to cache. The controller will then reset the dirty bit in cache to show that the data has been successfully written to the disk. Additionally, the data may be removed from cache if the space is needed for another operation.

 EXAM TIP   If a question asks about controller performance metrics, look for an answer with the words *transfer rate*.

The disk metric often associated with the controller is transfer rate. This is the amount of time it takes to move data and comprises two metrics. Internal transfer rate is the amount of time it takes to move data between the disk controller buffer and a physical sector. External transfer rate is the amount of time it takes to move data over the disk interface. External transfer rates will be discussed in the "Available Disk Interfaces and Their Characteristics" section.

Solid-State Drive

The solid-state drive is a form of data storage device far different from a hard disk drive. The only real similarities between SSD and HDD are that both store data, come in a similar 2.5-inch size, and share the SATA and SAS interfaces discussed in the next section. SSD does not have platters, spindles, or heads. In fact, there are no moving parts at all in SSD. Because of this, SSD uses far less power than HDD. SSDs do have a controller board and cache that operate similarly to their HDD counterparts. In addition to the controller board and cache, SSD consists of solid-state memory chips and an interface. Internal circuitry connects the solid-state memory chips to the controller board. Each circuit over which data can pass is called a *channel*, and the number of channels in a drive determines how much data can be read or written at once. The speed of SSD is far superior to HDD.

SSD organizes data into blocks and pages instead of tracks and sectors. A block consists of multiple pages and is not the same size as a block in HDD. Pages are typically 128 bytes. A block may be as small as 4KB (4,096 bytes) made up of 32 pages, or it could be as large as 16KB (16,385 bytes) made up of 128 pages. SSD disks support logical block addressing (LBA). LBA is a way of referencing a location on a disk without a device having knowledge of the physical disk geometry; the SSD page is presented to a system as a series of 512-byte blocks, and the controller board converts the LBA block address to the corresponding SSD block and page. This allows systems to reference SSD just as they would HDD.

SSD has a shorter shelf life than HDD because its cells wear out. SSD disks will deteriorate over time, resulting in longer access times, until they will eventually need to be replaced. Enterprise SSD is often equipped with write leveling techniques that store data evenly across cells. Data writes and changes are written to the block with the least use so that solid-state cells age at roughly the same rate.

SSD gets its name from the solid-state memory it uses to store and retrieve data. This memory consists of transistors and circuits similar to the memory in a computer, except that it is nonvolatile—meaning that the data stored on solid state does not need to be refreshed, nor does it require power to remain in memory. This technology is also called negated AND (NAND) flash; thus, the alternative name for SSD is flash drive. NAND chips come in two types, as discussed next: single-level cell (SLC) and multiple-level cell (MLC).

 NOTE This book will use the acronym SSD instead of the term *flash drive* to differentiate SSD from USB-based flash media also known as flash drives.

Single-Level Cell

Single-level cell NAND flash is arranged in rows and columns, and current can be passed or blocked to cells. Each intersection of a row and column is referred to as a *cell*, similar to the cells in a table. Two transistors in the cell control whether the cell represents a binary 0 or 1. Those with current are a 1, and those without are a 0. A transistor called the *floating gate* is surrounded by an oxide layer that is normally nonconductive except when subjected to a significant electric field. The control gate charges the floating gate by creating an electric field to make the oxide layer conductive, thus allowing current to flow into the floating gate. Once the floating gate is charged, it will remain so until the control gate drains it. In this way, the charge remains even when power is disconnected from the disk. The threshold voltage of the cell can be measured to read whether the cell is a 1 or a 0 without having to open the control gate.

The control gate can make the oxide layer conductive only so many times before it breaks down. This change in conductivity happens each time there is a write or erase, so the life span of the disk is tracked based on write/erase cycles. The average rating for SLC is 100,000 write/erase cycles. This is much better than the write/erase rating for MLC of 10,000 but much less than a standard HDD, which does not have a write/erase limit.

Multiple-Level Cell

Multiple-level cell technology stores two or more bits per cell, greatly increasing the storage density and overall capacity of SSD disks using MLC. MLC NAND flash is also organized like SLC NAND flash, but MLC control gates can regulate the amount of charge given to a floating gate. Different voltages can represent different bit combinations. To store two bits of information, the MLC cell must be able to hold four different charges, mapping two of the four combinations of two binary digits, 00, 01, 10, and 11. Likewise, the MLC cell would need to hold eight different charges to store three bits of information. More of the oxide layer breaks down in each write or erase cycle on MLC cells, resulting in a much lower life span than SLC cells. The average rating for MLC is 10,000 write/erase cycles, which is one-tenth the rating for SLC. MLC cells also have lower performance than SLC since it takes longer for them to store and measure voltage.

SLC's higher performance and write/erase rating over MLC makes it the primary technology used in enterprise SSD, whereas MLC is most commonly seen in USB flash drives and flash media cards such as SD, MMC, Compact Flash, and xD.

 EXAM TIP   Choose SLC if an exam question lists high performance or longevity as the primary concern, but choose MLC if cost is the primary concern.

Electrical and Mechanical Differences

The choice of whether to put enterprise, midrange, or entry-level drives in equipment in a storage array or server is not often one you will be allowed to make. Server and storage vendors generally build their systems to only recognize drives that contain proprietary firmware. This allows them to mark up the drives they sell, and it ensures that the drives used in their systems are compatible and capable of meeting their published performance and reliability metrics. However, there will be cases where you will have a choice of which drive to put in a system. You will likely be able to choose which drives to place in single-shelf NAS devices, custom servers, and equipment made by manufacturers not large enough to justify developing their own drive firmware and quality-testing procedures.

Your choice of drive falls into three categories—enterprise, midrange, and consumer—with enterprise drives offering the greatest performance and reliability at the highest price and consumer drives the lowest performance and reliability at the lowest price. You should select a drive type that meets the performance and reliability requirements of your application and the server or storage device's operating environment. You might then adjust your selection upward to factor in higher utilization down the road. However, be careful to understand (and be able to explain) the impact of adjusting downward to meet cost requirements because application performance or reliability will likely be impacted.

Performance

Consumer drives, also called desktop or entry-level drives, are made for a single user who only occasionally needs to access information. Midrange drives offer somewhat higher performance than consumer drives but not the performance of an enterprise drive. Midrange drives are intended for small office NAS devices and servers with low I/O and utilization. An enterprise-grade drive is made to access data for many different users and run many different applications at the same time, which makes the drive work continuously.

Enterprise drives will perform better than consumer drives in a multiuser environment because the internal components are usually made to access the data faster. These mechanisms include faster spindle speeds, denser disks, and more cache. They usually have much more on-board cache, which is used to increase cache hits for reads and send write acknowledgements sooner.

Reliability

Enterprise-class drives are made with at least an estimated mean time between failures (MTBF) of 1.2 million hours. Consumer drives, on the other hand, only have an estimated MTBF of 700,000 hours. While these numbers may seem close at first, remember that consumer drives have an average utilization of 10–20 percent, whereas enterprise drives have 74–90 percent utilization. If both drives were at 50 percent utilization, the MTBF might be 350,000 for the consumer drive and 1.8 million for the enterprise drive. In short, using a drive for an unintended purpose can drastically affect the MTBF.

If you look at these numbers rationally, they will immediately seem implausible, because 1.2 million hours is roughly 137 years. However, let me add some clarity to these reliability numbers before you add that shiny new drive to your last will and testament. It is impossible to test drives for decades before releasing them, so statistical formulas are used and unit testing is performed to obtain these estimates. It is important to note that the accuracy of these metrics is limited to first-year operation only. The drive manufacturers gained these numbers by running a large number of drives for a shorter period of time and then computed an annualized failure rate (AFR). They then divided one year by the AFR to get the MTBF. The MTBF can be converted to the AFR by dividing the number of hours in a year by the MTBF. Thus, the enterprise drives with the 1.2 million MTBF have an AFR of 0.73 percent, whereas the consumer drives would have an AFR of 1.25 percent. The following computations are used to convert the MTBF to AFR for the enterprise drive:

- Hours in a year / MTBF = AFR
- Hours in a year: 24 × 365 = 8,760
- 8,760 / 1,200,000 = .0073, or 0.73%

If we take this a step further, we can see how many drives a storage administrator could expect to replace in the first year of a storage system if the storage system had 400 drives. Four hundred drives multiplied by the AFR of 0.0073 is 2.92, so the storage administrator could expect to replace about three drives the first year.

Also, the AFR metric is for the first year of life. The likelihood of failure increases exponentially each consecutive year. By the third year, the AFR is about five times what it was in the first year. For this reason, even enterprise drives are often warrantied only three years.

Enterprise drives have more components in them that detect read errors. When a consumer-grade drive tries to read a bad sector, it tries to read that sector over and over again, and there might be a long wait period before the user realizes that the data cannot be accessed. An enterprise environment does not have the tolerance to wait around for one drive to fix the issue. The data needs to be available at all times. Because most enterprise drives are in a RAID configuration, the computer can immediately go to another backup drive that is a clone of the drive with a bad sector and read the data from that one. After the data has been given to the user, the computer can then try to fix the bad portion of the drive that failed. Using consumer drives in such an environment would increase the likelihood of being marked "offline" and result in kernel panics and system crashes.

Enterprise-class drives use checksums when data is transmitted to make sure that the data has not been tampered with or corrupted. If the checksum does not match the data provided, the computer can make another request for the data until it does not detect that an error occurred. Enterprise drives often include error-correction techniques that are not used on consumer drives. Each sector in an enterprise-class drive has enough information to store a checksum of the sector and restore information if the sector is damaged. Consumer drives may have error-detecting checksums in them that detect that an error has occurred, but these sectors do not carry enough data to rebuild a corrupted area of the disk if something goes wrong. Enterprise-class hard drives are recommended by the manufacturers because when a consumer-class drive detects an error, it will go into a deep sleep to repeatedly try to recover from the error. This process can take so long that a RAID controller will often mark the entire drive as unusable, even though only one sector went bad, which can then take the whole array offline. Enterprise-class drives use time-limited error recovery to prevent this from occurring. This problem will progressively get worse for desktop-class drives as they age and may result in data loss. Enterprise-class drives are designed to have the RAID controller decide how the sector will be recovered.

Enterprise-grade hard disks are manufactured to be more reliable than the consumer models. Consumer drives are designed to operate at 10–20 percent average utilization. This is the type of utilization that would occur with one primary user of the device and possibly some shared access to media over a home or office network. In contrast, enterprise drives are designed for 75–90 percent utilization. They are designed to be utilized for a significant portion of the day, with multiple users or applications reading from them and writing to them concurrently. The higher workload requires greater reliability because the drive must be able to withstand a consistently higher level of read and write I/O than a consumer drive.

The cycle of a drive spinning up to read or write data and then stopping after it is done is known as a *load/unload cycle*. An enterprise-level drive is usually rated to have about twice as many of these cycles as an entry-level drive. This is an important point to think about when deciding which drive to use in a system that will be constantly spinning up and down the disks. A business wants to have as little latency as possible when performing a new read, and the spin-up time can significantly add to that latency.

Operating Environment

Drives differ in the operating environments, just like they differ in use cases. Enterprise drives are typically installed in high-density storage devices or servers. Today's high-density servers can equip up to 24 2.5" drives in a 2U chassis or 24 3.5" drives in a 3U chassis, whereas high-density storage array shelves can equip 48 2.5" drives in a 2U chassis or 48 3.5" drives in a 3U chassis. Midrange systems might have six or ten drives in them, and the drives have more space for air flow and heat dissipation. Desktop systems are usually built with only one or two drives that are located away from many of the other computer components.

High-density enterprise environments need to be able to run hotter and withstand more rotational vibration. Spinning platters in the hard drives might cause vibrations back into the computer case, which can then cause the drives in close proximity to vibrate reciprocally. Consistent vibrations can cause stress on a drive, eventually leading to the breakdown of components such as the actuator arm or read/write heads. Enterprise drives have a much greater tolerance for these vibrations and are often equipped with sensors that track vibration and the Rotational Vibration Feed Forward (RVFF), which determines the correction to the voice coil motor actuator to keep it in the right position based on the vibrations detected. Instead of RVFF and sensors, midrange drives come equipped with dual-plane balance control. Imbalance of the platters can produce excessive vibration. A dual-plane balance control stabilizes this imbalance to reduce internal vibration.

Enterprise-class drives are designed for continuous operation at 45°C with a maximum operating temperature around 60°C. Consumer-grade hard drives, on the other hand, are designed to operate at 25°C with a maximum operating temperature around 40°C.

I/O vs. Throughput

Throughput is the amount of data transferred over a medium in a measurable time interval. The throughput of disks and RAID sets are often measured in terms of I/O operations per second (IOPS). IOPS is often calculated for different types of data usage patterns as follows:

- **Sequential read IOPS**   The number of read operations performed on data that resides in contiguous locations on the disk per second
- **Random read IOPS**   The number of read operations performed on data spread across the disk (random) per second
- **Sequential write IOPS**   The number of write operations performed on data that resides in contiguous locations on the disk per second
- **Random write IOPS**   The number of write operations performed on data spread across the disk (random) per second

IOPS is an important metric because it can be calculated at differing levels of abstraction from the storage. For example, IOPS can be calculated from the operating system or from the application or even the storage array, usually with built-in tools. Each calculation reflects additional factors as you move further away from the disks themselves. IOPS is calculated end-to-end, so it can comprise many factors such as seek time and rotational latency of disk, transfer rates of interfaces and cables between source and destination, and application latency or load in a single metric. IOPS is fairly consistent for HDD, but SSDs are heavily customized by manufacturers, so their IOPS values will be specified per disk. SSD IOPS can range from as low as 5,000 to 1,000,000 IOPS, so it pays to know which disks are in a system. Table 1-1 shows standard IOPS ratings for common SATA, SAS, and SSD disks.

Capacity vs. Speed

Determining the right storage for the job starts with determining the requirements of capacity and speed. Capacity involves how much space the system or application requires, and speed is how fast the storage needs to be. I/O and throughput were discussed in the previous section, providing an understanding of how to measure the speed of a device. An application may also have a speed requirement, which is often represented in IOPS.

Table 1-1 Standard IOPS Ratings for SATA, SAS, and SSD Disks	Disk Type	RPM	Interface	IOPS
	SATA	5,400	3 Gbps SATA	50–80
	SATA	7,200	3 Gbps SATA	75–100
	SAS	10,000	6 Gbps SAS	125–150
	SAS	15,000	6 Gbps SAS	175–210
	SSD	N/A	3 Gbps SATA	5,000–50,000
	SSD	N/A	6 Gbps SATA	60,000–120,000
	SSD	N/A	PCI Express (PCIe)	120,000–1,200,000
	SSD	N/A	Fibre Channel (FC)	250,000–1,000,000

Disks may need to be combined to obtain the necessary capacity and speed for the application. For example, an application requires 5,000 IOPS and 2TB capacity; 600GB 15,000 rpm SAS disks that get 175 IOPS and 200GB SSD disks that get 4,000 IOPS are available for use. Twenty-nine SAS disks would be necessary to get 5,000 IOPS, and this would provide more than enough capacity (17.4TB). Alternatively, two SSD disks would provide the necessary IOPS but not the required capacity. It would take ten SSD disks to reach the required 2TB capacity, which would be more than enough IOPS at this point. These rough calculations assume that all disks would be able to be used concurrently to store and retrieve data, which would offer the most ideal performance circumstances. The "RAID Levels" section will show different methods for combining multiple disks and how they can be used to gain additional speed and prevent against data loss when one or more disks fail.

Available Disk Interfaces and Their Characteristics

Interfaces are the connection between data storage devices and other devices such as computers, networks, or enterprise storage equipment. Internal interfaces connect storage devices within a computer or storage system, while external interfaces connect to stand-alone storage equipment such as disk enclosures, tape libraries, or compact disc jukeboxes.

A variety of interfaces have been introduced over the years, some designed for high cost and high performance with a large amount of throughput and others designed for lower cost and lower performance.

ATA

Versions of Advanced Technology Attachment (ATA) provide a low-cost, low-performance option and are ideal when a large amount of storage is needed but does not have to be accessed directly by end users or applications. Examples of good uses of ATA include backup storage or storage for infrequently used data.

PATA

Parallel ATA (PATA), also known as Integrated Drive Electronics (IDE), was introduced in 1986 and standardized in 1988. It was the dominant interface used for HDDs and CD-ROM drives until 2003. PATA disks were originally referred to only as ATA disks, but the acronym PATA now differentiates these disks from SATA disks. The IDE name is derived from the fact that PATA disks have a controller integrated onto the disks instead of requiring a separate controller on the motherboard or expansion card. The integrated controller handles commands such as moving the actuator arm, spinning the disk up, and parking the heads.

A PATA cable, depicted in Figure 1-3, has 40 or 80 wires that make contact with the connectors on the disk and the motherboard. PATA cables also have a maximum length of 18 inches. Data is transferred in parallel, meaning that multiple bits of data are transferred at once. The number of bits transferred in a single operation is called the *data bus width*; in the case of PATA, it is 16.

Figure 1-3
A PATA cable

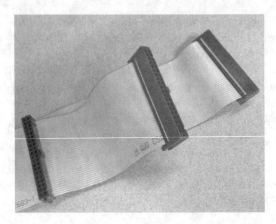

Up to two devices may be attached, but in order for both to share the same cable, one device must be configured as the master (device 0) and the other as the slave (device 1). The master or slave setting is configured by a jumper on the back of the PATA device, depicted in Figure 1-4. Some devices support a mode called *cable select*, whereby the device automatically configures itself as master or slave depending on its location on the cable.

Figure 1-4
A jumper for the
master, slave,
or cable select
setting

Standard	Alternative Name	Transfer Rate	Year Standardized
ATA-1	IDE	8.3 MBps (66 Mbps)	1988
ATA-2	Ultra ATA, Fast ATA	16.7 MBps (133 Mbps)	1993
ATA-3	EIDE	25 MBps (200 Mbps)	1995
ATA-4	Ultra ATA/33, Ultra DMA/33	33 MBps (264 Mbps)	1996
ATA-5	Ultra ATA/66, Ultra DMA/66	66 MBps (528 Mbps)	1998
ATA-6	Ultra ATA/100, Ultra DMA/100	100 MBps (800 Mbps)	2000
ATA-7	Ultra ATA/133, Ultra DMA/133	133 MBps (1 Gbps)	2001

Table 1-2   PATA Versions

PATA cables are a shared medium allowing only one device to communicate over the cable at a time. Connecting multiple devices to a single connector can impact the performance of the devices if disk operations execute on both disks at once, as is common when transferring files between disks or when installing software from a CD-ROM attached to the same cable. While earlier computers typically were equipped with two connectors on the motherboard, supporting up to four PATA devices, most computers today do not even include a PATA port on the motherboard. The best practice in this case is to place highly used devices on separate cables and pair lesser used devices with highly used ones so as to give each device maximum time on the cable.

PATA disks are powered by a plug with four pins and four wires known as a *molex connector*. The molex connector has one yellow 12-volt wire, one 5-volt red wire, and two black ground wires.

The last version of PATA, called Ultra ATA/133, had a maximum theoretical transfer rate of 133 MBps that was quickly eclipsed by SATA. Table 1-2 lists the PATA versions and their significant properties. Note that megabytes per second (MBps) is different from megabits per second (Mbps). There are 8 bits in a byte, so the megabit transfer speed is 8 times the megabyte transfer speed.

SATA

Serial ATA (SATA) was introduced in 2003 to replace the aging PATA. The parallel architecture of PATA created difficulties for exceeding the 133-MBps limit because its parallel transmissions were susceptible to electromagnetic interference (EMI) among the wires in the bus. SATA, however, runs on lower voltages and uses a serial bus, so data is sent one bit at a time. These enhancements bypassed some of the problems faced with PATA and allowed for higher transfer rates. SATA utilized the ATA command set, making it easier for equipment to include SATA ports since ATA was already supported on a wide variety of systems and BIOSs. SATA disks can also be connected as an external disk using an eSATA cable and enclosure, which offers faster speeds than external disks connected over USB or IEEE 1394 FireWire. Table 1-3 provides the speeds of each of these external disk technologies.

Table 1-3	External Disk Type	Speed
External Disk Speeds by Type	USB 1.1	12 Mbps
	USB 2.0	480 Mbps
	USB 3.0	5 Gbps
	FireWire 400	400 Mbps
	FireWire 800	786 Mbps
	FireWire S1600	1.6 Gbps
	FireWire S3200	3.2 Gbps
	eSATA	6 Gbps

SATA cables have seven connectors and a maximum length of 39 inches. SATA disks do not use a molex connector. Instead, the SATA power connector is smaller with 15 pins. Only one device can be connected to a cable, meaning the issue of a shared bus with master and slave designations does not exist with SATA disks. There have been multiple generations of SATA, depicted in Table 1-4. It should be noted that the bit per second transfer rates are not what one would expect since they are ten times the megabyte rate. This is intentional because SATA uses 8b/10b encoding. This form of encoding uses ten bits to represent one byte. The extra two bits are used to keep the clock rate the same on the sending and receiving ends.

What really differentiates SATA from previous interfaces is the host of new features added along the way. Some of the features include

- **Command queuing** Command queuing optimizes the order in which operations are executed in a disk, based on the location of data. Without command queuing, operations are processed in the order they are received. Command queuing reorders the operations so that the data can be fetched with minimal actuator and platter movement.

- **Hot-pluggable/hot-swappable** This option allows a disk to be plugged or unplugged from a system while the system is running. Systems without hot-plug interfaces will need to be restarted before disks can be added or removed.

- **Hard disk passwords** SATA devices supporting this feature allow disks to be password protected by setting a user and a master password in the BIOS. User passwords are designed to be given to the primary user of a machine, while the

Table 1-4	Version	Transfer Rate	Year Standardized
SATA Versions	SATA 1.0	187 MBps (1.5 Gbps)	2003
	SATA 2.0	375 MBps (3 Gbps)	2004
	SATA 3.0	750 MBps (6 Gbps)	2008

master password can be retained by IT administrators. In this way, should an individual leave or forget their password, IT administrators can still unlock the disk. Once the disk is password-protected, each time the machine is started up, a prompt appears requiring the password to be entered. This password will be required even if the hard disk is moved to another machine. Hard disk passwords can also be synchronized with BIOS system passwords for ease of administration.

- **Host protected area (HPA)**   HPA reserves space on the hard disk so that the system can be reset to factory defaults, including the original operating system, applications, and configuration that shipped with the machine. HPA space is hidden from the operating system and most partitioning tools so that it is not accidentally overwritten.

SCSI

Small Computer System Interface (SCSI) was standardized in 1986 and was the predominant format for high-performance disks for almost 30 years. There have been many versions of SCSI along with different cable types and speeds, as shown in Table 1-5. Internal SCSI uses ribbon cables similar to PATA. Over the years, 50-, 68-, and 80-pin connectors have been used. The last few versions of SCSI to be used shared much in common; and despite so many variations, expect to find the SCSI that uses a 16-bit bus supporting 16 devices and the connection types of 68 and 80 pin. SCSI's max speed is 640 MBps, or 5,120 Mbps. You will typically find 68-pin cables connecting SCSI devices within a server, such as the connection between a SCSI controller card and the disk backplane; but the connection between disks and the backplane most often uses the hot-pluggable 80-pin connector known as Single Connector Attachment (SCA).

Devices on a SCSI bus are given an ID number unique to them on the bus. This was originally performed using jumpers on the back of SCSI devices similar to the master slave configuration on PATA, but more recent disks allow for the SCSI ID to be

Standard	Alternative Name	Connector	Transfer Rate	Year Standardized
SCSI-1	Narrow SCSI	Centronics C50	40 Mbps	1986
Fast SCSI		Centronics C50	80 Mbps	1994
Fast-Wide SCSI		50 or 68 pin	160 Mbps	2003
Ultra SCSI	Fast-20	Centronics C50	160 Mbps	2003
Ultra Wide SCSI		68 pin	320 Mbps	2003
Ultra2 SCSI	Fast-40	50 pin	320 Mbps	2003
Ultra2 Wide SCSI		68 or 80 pin	640 Mbps	2003
Ultra3 SCSI	Ultra-160 or Fast-80 wide	68 or 80 pin	1,280 Mbps	2003
Ultra-320 SCSI	Ultra-4 or Fast-160	68 or 80 pin	2,560 Mbps	2003
Ultra-64	Ultra-5 or Fast-320	68 or 80 pin	5,120 Mbps	2003

Table 1-5   SCSI Versions

configured automatically by software or the SCSI adapter BIOS. Up to 16 devices can exist on a single bus.

Each device on a SCSI bus can have multiple addressable storage units, and these units are called *logical units* (LUs). Each LU has a logical unit number (LUN). You will not find a new machine today equipped with SCSI, but the command set and architecture are present in many current technologies, including SAS, Fibre Channel, and iSCSI.

Fibre Channel

Fibre Channel (FC) picks up in enterprise storage where SCSI left off. It is a serial disk interface with transfer speeds of 2, 4, or 8 Gbps. The latest versions of FC disks use a 40-pin Enhanced SCA-2 connector that is SFF-8454 compliant, and they are hot-pluggable, so they can be added or removed while the system is powered on without interrupting operations. They utilize the SCSI command set and are commonly found in enterprise storage arrays. FC disks are expensive compared to other disk types.

SAS

Serial Attached SCSI (SAS) is a high-speed interface used in a broad range of storage systems. SAS interfaces are less expensive than FC, and they offer transfer speeds up to 1.5 GBps (12 Gbps). The SAS interface uses the same 8b/10b encoding that SATA uses. Thus, converting from bits per second to bytes per second requires dividing by ten instead of eight. SAS can take advantage of redundant paths to the storage to increase speed and fault tolerance. SAS expanders are used to connect up to 65,535 devices to a single channel. SAS cables can be a maximum of 33 feet long. The SAS connector is similar to the SATA connector except that it has a plastic bridge between the power and interface cables. This allows for SATA disks to be connected to a SAS port, but SAS disks cannot be connected to a SATA port because there is no place for the bridge piece to fit.

SAS version 1 (SAS1) was limited to transfer speeds of 375 MBps (3 Gbps), but SAS version 2 (SAS2) achieves transfer speeds of 750 MBps (6 Gbps), with the latest SAS3 disks released in late 2013 reaching speeds of 1.5 GBps (12 Gbps). SAS2 and SAS3 are backward compatible with SAS1, so SAS1 and SAS2 drives can coexist on a SAS2 or SAS3 controller or in a SAS2 or SAS3 storage array, and SAS2 drives can likewise coexist with SAS3 drives on SAS3 arrays or controllers. However, it is not wise to mix SAS1, SAS2, and SAS3 drives in the same RAID array because the slower drives will reduce the performance of the array.

PCI Versions

Peripheral Component Interconnect (PCI) is a standard used for computer expansion cards and slots. PCI replaced the older ISA standard. As a standard, it can be used by any manufacturer. This led to easy adoption of PCI on computer and server motherboards and the creation of numerous PCI devices, such as graphics cards, sound cards, modems, network interface cards (NICs), host bus adapters (HBAs), and drive controllers. The initial PCI standard set the stage for two other standards: PCI-X and PCIe. Figure 1-5 shows a PCI Ethernet card.

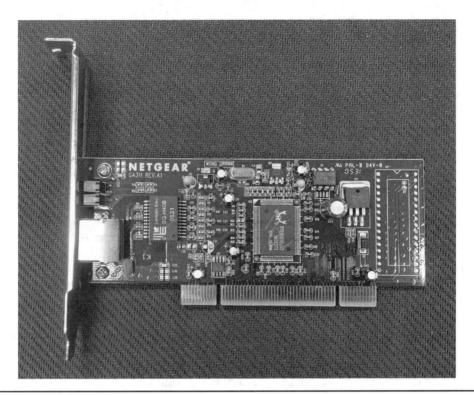

Figure 1-5 PCI Ethernet card

As you install HBAs, NICs, and other expansion cards mentioned in this book, consider which technology you will use to ensure that the card provides the required throughput. Modern servers will likely use PCIe, but you may run into some that use PCI-X. PCI is described here so that you can understand PCI-X better and the limitations of utilizing a PCI card in a PCI-X slot. It is important that you choose a technology that provides the performance necessary and does not impact the ability of other devices to function properly.

PCI

The original PCI specification was standardized in 1992. It defined a method to expand the capabilities of a computer system through the addition of cards that plugged into slots on a motherboard using a parallel 32-bit bus. Parallel busses have multiple paths, and bits travel down all the paths simultaneously. This is in contrast to serial technologies where a single path is used and data is transmitted sequentially. The number of bits transferred in a single parallel operation is called the *data bus width*. PCI's 32-bit bus allows for 32 bits of data to be transferred at once.

PCI initially had a clock speed of 33 MHz in version 1.0. This means that there were 33,000 hertz (or operations per second). Transfer rate is a measurement of how much data can be transferred in a second, and it is calculated by multiplying the clock speed by

PCI Version	Transfer Rate	Clock Speed	Year Standardized
1.0	132 MBps	33 MHz	1992
2.1	264 MBps	66 MHz	1995
3.0	512 MBps	266 MHz	2004

Table 1-6　PCI Versions

the data bus width. The bus can perform 66,000 operations per second, and each operation sends 32 bits of data over the parallel bus. We multiply the clock speed by the data bus width to get the transfer rate in bits. We divide that by 8 to turn our bits into bytes. Therefore, $33,000 \times 32 = 1,056,000$ bits, which divided by 8 produces 132,000 bytes, or 132MB. Because the operations are per second, we write these numbers as megabytes per second, or MBps. Therefore, PCI 1.0 has a transfer rate of 132 MBps.

PCI had several revisions. Version 3.0 increased the clock speed to 266 MHz, which increased the transfer rate to 512 MBps, as shown in Table 1-6. PCI 3.0 was widely adopted, so most implementations you will see run at 33 or 66 MHz.

PCI is a shared bus, so only one device can communicate over the bus at a time. Devices must contend for time on the PCI bus. This also means that some cards can be choked for speed. Imagine a server with a SCSI controller and an Ethernet card on a PCI bus. If the server hosts files for the network, user requests will be received over the Ethernet adapter, and then the SCSI controller will need to obtain the data and send it to the motherboard to be sent to the Ethernet card. The transmission of the data over the Ethernet card and obtaining the data from disk cannot occur at the same time over PCI, so one would constantly be waiting for the other in order to serve the data to network users.

PCI-X

PCI-eXtended (PCI-X) was the immediate successor to PCI. PCI-X's major differentiation from PCI is its 64-bit data bus width. It has a clock speed of 133 MHz, resulting in a 1.06-GBps transfer rate. Later versions of PCI-X utilize the Double Data Rate (DDR) and Quad Data Rate (QDR) technologies to transfer 2 or 4 bits per operation. This effectively doubles or quadruples the transfer rate. DDR sends data on both the upbeat and downbeat of a cycle, or Hertz (Hz), whereas QDR sends data at four points within the cycle. These versions are depicted in Table 1-7.

PCI-X is fully backward compatible with PCI cards. PCI-X achieves this backward compatibility by taking a PCI slot and adding an extension bus to the rear of the slot.

PCI-X Name	Version	Transfer Rate	Clock Speed	Data Rate	Year Introduced
PCI-X 133	1.0	1.06 GBps	133 MHz	Single Data Rate	1998
PCI-X 266	2.0	2.13 GBps	133 MHz	Double Data Rate	2003
PCI-X 533	2.0	4.27 GBps	133 MHz	Quad Data Rate	2003

Table 1-7　PCI-X Versions

However, although PCI devices can connect to a PCI-X slot and have full PCI functionality, they will only utilize 32 bits of the available 64-bit PCI-X data bus width, so there is no advantage to plugging a PCI card into a PCI-X slot. This extension means that the bus requires more room on a motherboard than both PCI and PCIe. Figure 1-6 shows a PCI-X Ethernet card.

One unfortunate carryover from PCI is the shared bus. PCI-X still allows for only one device to communicate over the bus at a time. Furthermore, if a PCI expansion card is plugged into a PCI-X slot, all devices on the PCI-X bus will be reduced to PCI speeds in order to maintain compatibility. This can have a very serious impact on system performance.

I had a situation where one of my clients could not figure out why his HBAs did not come close to the manufacturer's stated performance benchmarks, and he was getting very low throughput from his servers. He tried multiple HBAs, and each provided the same dismal performance. After talking through theories for an hour in his office, we went to lunch. On the way back we stopped by the data center, and the problem became immediately apparent once I saw the back of the server. He had installed PCI VGA graphics cards in the servers just in case the onboard graphics would fail. He had a bad experience once and was determined not to repeat it. However, this was causing the PCI-X cards to run at PCI speeds. Once the PCI cards were removed, performance increased dramatically. He still kept a few PCI cards tucked away in his toolbox, but he stopped putting them in servers.

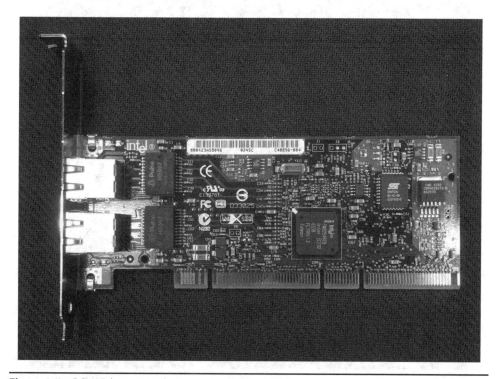

Figure 1-6   PCI-X Ethernet card

PCIe

PCI Express (PCIe) is the current standard for devices. The older PCI and PCI-X devices do not function in the newer PCIe slots. Each slot for PCIe is independently accessed, so it does not have the bottleneck issue of being dragged down to the lowest device speed. It also has the benefit that each slot can work with other slots up to 16 times and provide much better throughput than just one slot could provide. The slots are also very compact; you can fit a 16-lane slot into less space than a single PCI-X slot. Figure 1-7 shows a PCIe Ethernet card.

Parallel busses can transmit more data in a single operation, but the timing required to ensure that the data over each path arrives at the same time demands greater precision and often results in lower clock speeds. Serial busses, on the other hand, send only one bit of data for each operation, but they do not need to break apart, synchronize, and reassemble data from multiple paths, so they can run at a much higher clock speed.

PCIe is a bus that is divided into lanes, each capable of supporting an equal bandwidth concurrently. This is a significant departure from the PCI and PCI-X architectures, which use a shared bus for all slots on a mainboard. Because each PCIe

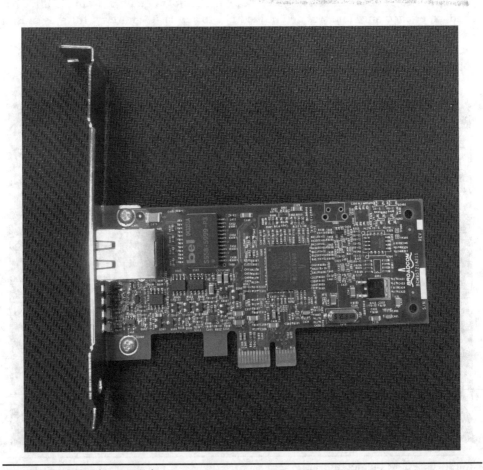

Figure 1-7   PCIe Ethernet card

Version	x1 Slot	x4 Slot	x8 Slot	x16 Slot	Year
1.0	250 MBps	1 GBps	2 GBps	4 GBps	2003
2.0	500 MBps	2 GBps	4 GBps	8 GBps	2007
3.0	1 GBps	4 GBps	8 GBps	16 GBps	2010

Table 1-8   PCIe Bandwidth by Slot Type and Version

bus is independent, each card can perform at full speed, which starts off at 250 MBps in version 1 and increases to 500 and 984.6 MBps in versions 2 and 3. PCIe slots are sized to take advantage of one or more lanes, as described by their name. The x1 slot has one lane, whereas the x16 slot has 16 lanes and 16 times the bandwidth of the x1 slot. The slot bandwidth provided by each slot type and version is shown in Table 1-8. The architecture of PCIe is drastically different from PCI and PCI-X, so it is not backward compatible with older PCI devices.

PCIe devices can be plugged into any PCIe slot, regardless of lane size. It will slow down the connected device to the maximum speed that the attached lanes provide. This means that a PCIe x4 card can be connected to a PCIe x1 slot with reduced device performance. Smaller PCIe cards can also be placed in slots that have many more lanes than the device needs and still function. If a PCIe x1 expansion card is needed and there are no x1 slots available, the card can be plugged into an x4, x8, or even an x16 slot, but it will still be limited to the maximum number of lanes supported by its connector. Figure 1-8 shows the different PCIe card types. PCIe x1 is in the upper left, x4 in the lower left, x8 in the upper right, and x16 in the lower right.

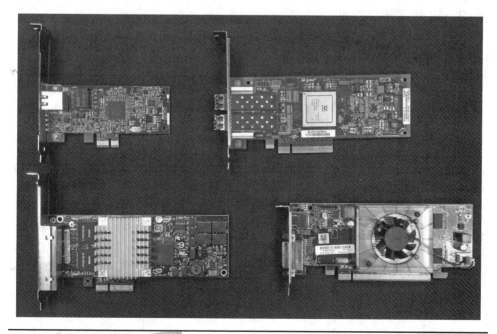

Figure 1-8   PCIe card connectors

Multiple Disks for Larger Storage and Fault Tolerance

Storage professionals are often called on to create groups of disks for data storage. Grouping disks together allows for the creation of a larger logical drive, and disks in the group can be used to protect against the failure of one or more disks. Most groupings are performed by creating a Redundant Array of Independent Disks (RAID). To create a RAID, multiple disks must be connected to a compatible RAID controller, and controllers may support one or more types of RAID known as RAID *levels*. There are two designations for capacity. Raw capacity is the total capacity of disks when not configured in a RAID. For example, five 100GB disks would have a raw capacity of 500GB. Usable capacity is the amount of storage available once the RAID has been configured.

RAID Levels

Several RAID specifications have been made. These levels define how multiple disks can be used together to provide increased storage space, increased reliability, increased speed, or some combination of the three. Although not covered here, RAID levels 2 to 4 were specified but never adopted in the industry, so you will not see them in the field. When a RAID is created, the collection of disks is referred to as a *group*. It is always best to use identical disks when creating a RAID group. However, if different disks are used, the capacity and speed will be limited by the smallest and slowest disk in the group. RAID 0, 1, 5, and 6 are basic RAID groups introduced in the following sections. RAID 10 and 0+1 are nested RAID groups because they are made up of multiple basic RAID groups. Nested RAID groups require more disks than basic RAID groups and are more commonly seen in networked or direct attached storage groups that contain many disks.

RAID 0 → striping

RAID 0 writes a portion of data to all disks in the group in a process known as *striping*. At least two identical disks are required to create a RAID 0 group, and these disks make up the stripe set. Figure 1-9 shows how a file would be written to a RAID 0 consisting of four disks. The file is broken into pieces and then written to multiple disks at the same time. This increases both read and write speeds because the work of reading or writing a file is evenly distributed among the disks in the group. RAID 0 usable capacity is the total capacity of all disks in the stripe set and thus the same as the raw capacity. The main drawback to RAID 0 is its lack of redundancy. If one disk fails, all the data in the group is lost.

RAID 1 → Mirroring

RAID 1 writes the data being saved to two disks at the same time. If a single disk fails, no data is lost, since all the data is contained on the other disk or disks. RAID 1 is also known as *mirroring*. Figure 1-10 depicts how a file would be stored on a two-disk RAID 1.

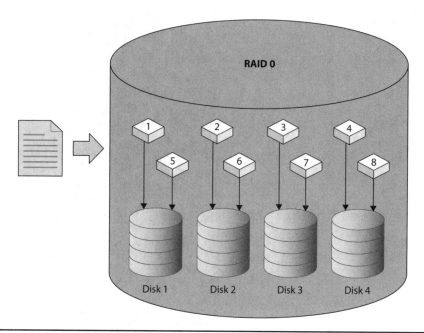

Figure 1-9   Writing a file to RAID 0

The usable capacity of the mirror is the same as the capacity for one disk in the group, but because data can be retrieved from both disks simultaneously, mirroring results in a slight boost to read performance. When a failed disk is replaced in a RAID 1 group, the mirror is rebuilt by copying data from the existing disk to the new disk. This rebuild time has significant impact on group performance, even though it takes significantly less time to perform a rebuild on a RAID 1 than on a RAID 5. RAID 1 is good for high read situations since it can read data at twice the speed of single disks. However, it is not best for high write situations because each write must take place on both disks requiring the same time as a single disk.

RAID 5 → striping + parity

RAID 5 stripes data across the disks in the group, and because it also computes parity data and spreads this across the disks, if one disk in the group is lost, the other disks can use their parity data to rebuild the data on a new disk. RAID 5 requires at least three disks and, because of its speed, is popular. Figure 1-11 shows a file write to a RAID 5 array of four disks. Since parity data needs to be computed each time data is written, it suffers from a write penalty. Additionally, the parity data also takes up space on the group. The amount of space required diminishes as the number of disks in the group increases, but it takes more time to compute parity for larger RAID 5 groups. The equivalent of one disk in the group is used for parity, which means the usable capacity

Figure 1-10
Writing a file to
RAID 1

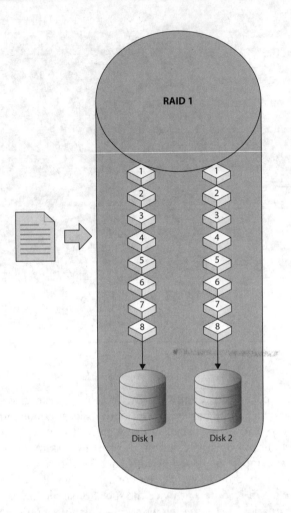

of a RAID 5 group can be computed by subtracting one from the number of disks in the group and multiplying that by the capacity of a single disk. For example, if six 1TB disks are placed into a RAID 5 group, the total capacity will be 5,000GB (5TB). We thus describe a RAID 5 group by listing the number of disks upon which the capacity is based and then the number of parity disks. Accordingly, making a six-disk RAID 5 group would be described as a 5+1.

A RAID 5 group goes into a degraded state if a disk within the group is lost. Once that disk is replaced, the group begins rebuilding the data to the replaced disk. Group performance is significantly impacted while the group rebuilds, and a loss of any disks in the group, prior to completion of the rebuild, will result in a complete loss of data. Additionally, the increased load on the remaining disks in the group makes these disks more susceptible to a disk failure. Rebuild time increases with an increase in the capacity or number of disks in the group. Thus, a four-disk group takes longer to rebuild than a three-disk group, and a group of 3TB disks takes longer to rebuild than one made up of 1TB disks.

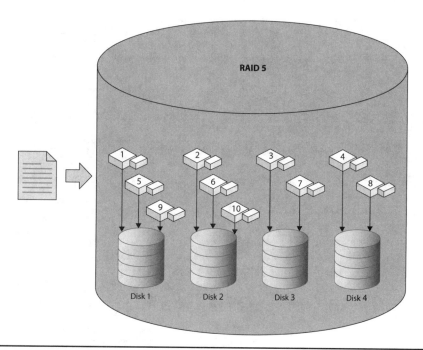

Figure 1-11   Writing a file to RAID 5

RAID 5 has good performance in high read situations because of its use of striping, and it has decent performance in high read situations but not as good as RAID 10 or RAID 1 because of the need for parity computations.

RAID 6

Although RAID 6 is similar to RAID 5, it computes even more parity data, and up to two disks can fail in the group before data is lost. RAID 6 requires at least four disks and suffers from an even greater write penalty than RAID 5. Consequently, the additional parity data of RAID 6 consumes the equivalent of two disks in the RAID group. Therefore, the usable capacity of the RAID group is the total disks in the group minus two. Figure 1-12 shows a file write to a RAID 6 array consisting of four disks. Similar to RAID 5 groups, RAID 6 groups can be described using the data and parity disks. This way, if a RAID 6 group is created from eight disks, it would be described as 6+2. A RAID 6 set made up of eight 500GB disks would have a usable capacity of 3,000GB (3TB). In spite of RAID 6 suffering from an even greater rebuild time, the group is not at risk for a total loss of data if another disk fails during the rebuild period.

RAID 10 (1+0)

RAID 10 is a stripe made up of many mirrors. RAID 10 requires an even number of at least four disks to operate. Pairs of disks in the group are mirrored, and those mirrored

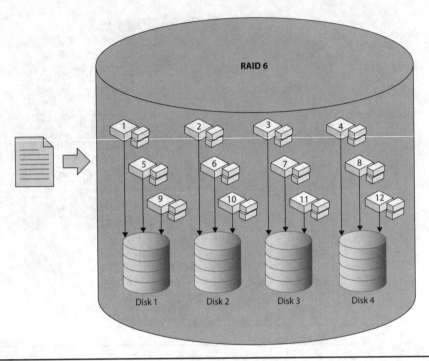

Figure 1-12 Writing a file to RAID 6

sets are striped. RAID 10 offers the closest performance to RAID 0 and offers extremely high reliability as well since a disk from each of the mirrored pairs could fail before loss of data occurs. Figure 1-13 shows how a file would be written to a RAID 10 array of eight disks. The main drawback of RAID 10 is its total capacity. Since RAID 10 consists of many mirror sets, the usable capacity is half the raw capacity. A ten-disk RAID 10 group made up of 100GB disks would have a usable capacity of 500GB and a raw capacity of 1TB (1000GB). This disk configuration would be described as 5+5. RAID 10 rebuild times are comparable to those of RAID 1, and the performance impact of a failed disk will be much shorter in duration than had it occurred on a RAID 5 or RAID 50. RAID 10 is best for high read situations since it can read from the stripes and mirrors of all the disks in the RAID set. It is good for high write situations since it uses striping and there is no parity computation.

RAID 0+1

RAID 0+1 is a mirror of stripes—the opposite of RAID 10. RAID 0+1 does not have the same reliability as RAID 10 because a loss of a disk from both mirrors would result in a total loss of data. RAID 0+1 can, however, sustain a multiple-disk failure if the failures occur within one of the stripe sets. RAID 0+1 is less commonly implemented because most implementations favor RAID 10. RAID 0+1 has fast rebuild times similar

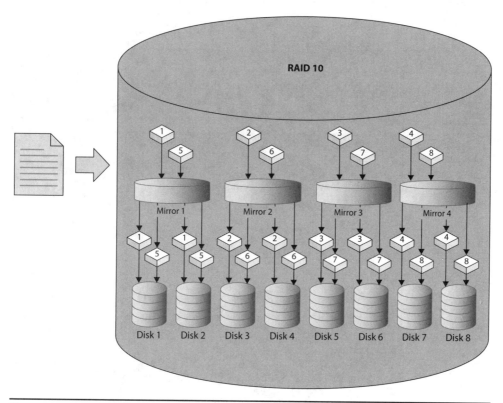

Figure 1-13   Writing a file to RAID 10

to RAID 10. Figure 1-14 shows how a file would be written to a RAID 0+1 array of eight disks.

RAID 50

RAID 50 is a stripe made up of multiple RAID 5 groups. A RAID 50 can be created from at least six drives. RAID 50 offers better performance and reliability than a single RAID 5 but not as much as a RAID 10. However, RAID 50 offers greater capacity than a RAID 10, so it is often used when performance requirements fall in between RAID 5 and RAID 10. One drive from each RAID 5 group in the RAID 50 can fail before loss of data occurs. The usable capacity for a RAID 50 depends on how many RAID 5 sets are used in the construction of the RAID 50.

Similar to a RAID 5, rebuild times increase with an increase in the capacity or number of drives in the group. However, the rebuild time for a loss of a single drive in a RAID 50 group would be much faster than a single drive loss in a RAID 5 group with a similar number of disks because the rebuild effort would be isolated to one RAID 5 within the RAID 50. Performance would still be degraded because the degraded RAID 5 is within

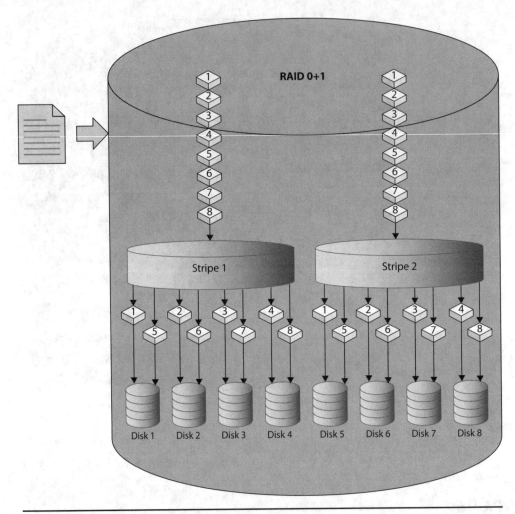

Figure 1-14   Writing a file to RAID 0+1

the overall stripe set for the RAID 50 group, so each new data operation would need to access the degraded RAID 5.

RAID 51

RAID 51 is a mirror of RAID 5 groups. This provides more reliability than RAID 5 and RAID 50, and the usable capacity of the set is half the total number of drives minus one; therefore, if there were ten 100GB drives in a RAID 51, the total capacity would be 400GB because five drives are used in the second RAID 5 set that is mirrored and one drive is used in each of the RAID 5 sets for parity. The parity drive in the mirrored set is already accounted for, so you subtract out the parity drive from the first set to get the usable capacity. RAID 51 can sustain a loss of multiple drives up to an entire RAID set as long as not more than one drive has failed on the other mirrored RAID 5 set.

RAID 51 rebuild times can be quite short because the data from the identical unit in the mirrored RAID 5 can be used to build the faulty drive. However, some implementations of RAID 51 use multiple controllers to protect against RAID controller failure. If this is the case, RAID 51 rebuild times will be comparable to RAID 5 because rebuilds take place within the controller, so the data from the mirror set cannot be used to rebuild individual drives on another controller.

RAID 51 is often used with two RAID controllers. Both controllers host a RAID 5 array, and the arrays are mirrored. If an entire controller fails, the RAID 51 is still accessible because it can operate in failover mode on the other RAID 5 set and controller until the controller and/or drives are replaced in the other RAID 5 set.

JBOD

Just a Bunch of Disks (JBOD) is not a RAID set, but it is a way to group drives to achieve greater capacity. JBOD uses a concatenation method to group disks, and data is written to a disk until it is full; then data is written to the next disk in the group. JBOD does not offer higher availability because the loss of a single drive in the group will result in a loss of all data. JBOD, however, is simple to implement, and it results in a usable capacity that is the same as its raw capacity. Use JBOD when you need the maximum usable capacity and when the reliability of the data is not a concern.

Hardware, Host-Based, and Software Implementations

RAID can be configured on a hardware RAID controller, on a host-based disk controller with RAID firmware, or in software. A hardware RAID controller can exist on an expansion card or be built onto the motherboard. Hardware RAID controllers perform all RAID functions on the controller and do not place additional burden on the computer processor. Hardware RAID is best when high performance is required for disks.

Host-based implementations utilize a dedicated drive controller, which usually contains custom firmware to understand how to group drives into a RAID. However, the host-based implementation relies on the computer processor to perform RAID computations. Host-based RAID is a low-cost way to add RAID to existing hardware when excess processor cycles are available for RAID operations.

Software-based RAID is implemented at the operating system level. Software RAID is the easiest to implement because it can be implemented on any hardware. No hardware needs to be purchased for a software RAID, so it is also the least expensive option. However, it suffers from reduced performance because RAID operations must pass through the operating system before being processed. It also places a burden on the computer processor. Software RAID systems usually cannot be used for boot drives because the operating system must first be available before RAID operations can begin. Some operating systems allow for a RAID 1 mirror of the operating system but no other forms of RAID.

RAID operations include parity computations, rebuilds, disk health tracking, and swapping out hot spares. However, the operation that is of main concern is parity computations. Parity is used for writing data to disks and for disk rebuild operations, and it can result in a lot of processing in write-intensive applications.

RAID controllers need to compute parity for each write to a RAID array that uses parity. As a reminder, RAID 5, RAID 6, RAID 50, and RAID 51 use parity. Parity is a value computed for a bit string in a stripe set that indicates whether the bit string is even or odd. Even-bit strings will have a 0 for parity, and odd-bit strings will have a 1 for parity. For example, consider a five-disk RAID 5, which can also be referenced as 4+1, with four drives for data and one for parity. If the bit string in the first stripe is 1, 0, 1, 0, then the parity bit would be 0 because the bits are even. However, if the bit string in the stripe was 0, 0, 0, 1, the parity bit would be 1 because the bits are odd.

The RAID controller goes through a process called "read, modify, write," where it first reads the data present on the disks and then reads the current parity. It performs an XOR operation on the old and new bit strings to determine if new parity data needs to be written. It then writes the new bits to each of the bit strings in the RAID stripe and writes parity to the stripe if the parity has changed due to the new bits.

The second function a RAID controller performs is a rebuild. If a drive in a parity RAID set fails, the parity bit can be used to rewrite the data to a new drive. In the previous example, the first bit string has 1, 0, 1, 0, with a parity of 0, so disk 0 has a 1, disk 1 has a 0, disk 2 has a 1, disk 3 has a 0, and disk 4 (the parity disk) has a 0 in its first location. If disk 1 fails, then the parity on disk 4 would be used to reconstruct the bits on disk 1. Disk 4 has a 0, so the result of the bits must be even. Our remaining disks, 0, 2, and 3, have the values 1, 1, and 0, respectively. This is even, and our parity is even, so the missing bit on disk 1 must be a 0 so that the value of the bit string remains 0.

Our example computed parity and used parity to reconstruct the data for the first bit striped to the disks in this RAID 5 set. If you want to store 4MB of data on the RAID set, this data would be striped across four disks, so each disk would get 1MB, which is equivalent to 8 million bits, because each byte has 8 bits in it and a megabyte (MB) has 1 million bytes in it. This 4MB file results in 8 million parity computations. As you can see, parity computations can take up a lot of processing cycles, and this is where a dedicated hardware solution pays off. Both the host-based and software solutions utilize the main central processing unit (CPU) to perform these computations. The CPU already has to process data for the rest of the systems on the server, so this can place a burden on the CPU and slow down other operations.

Hosts Interaction with Disks

To be used, storage must be made available to hosts. Hosts store and organize data in a directory structure known as a *file system*, and file systems exist on logical volumes that can be made up of one or more physical volumes.

A physical volume is a hard disk; a portion of a hard disk, called a *partition*; or, if the storage is remote, a LUN. One or more physical volumes can be combined on the host into a volume group. The volume group can then be divided into manageable sections known as *logical volumes*. Thus, a physical disk may have multiple logical volumes, and a logical volume may have multiple physical disks. Figure 1-15 depicts the relationship between these concepts.

Figure 1-15
Physical disks,
volume groups,
and logical
volumes

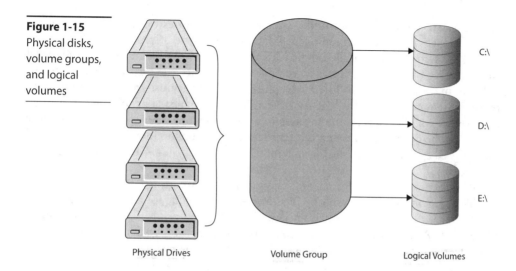

Physical Drives   Volume Group   Logical Volumes

For a system to use a logical volume, it must be mounted and formatted. Mounting the volume establishes the location where it can be referenced by the system. In Unix and Linux, this location is often a directory path. In Windows, mount points are usually given a drive letter, which is referenced with a colon and a forward slash such as C:\. Windows also allows drives to be given directory mount points similar to Linux and Unix systems.

The formatting process establishes a file system on the logical volume and sets a cluster size. The cluster size is how large of chunks the file system will divide the available disk space into. Larger cluster sizes result in fewer chunks of larger size, and this makes it faster for the system to read large data files into memory. However, if many small files are stored on the system with large cluster sizes, clusters will be padded to fill up the remaining space in the cluster, which will decrease available space and performance. Understand the size of files that will be stored on a system before configuring the cluster size. Additionally, the stripe size on RAID 0, RAID 5, and RAID 6 volumes is often a configurable option on the RAID controller. The stripe size is the size of each chunk that is placed on the disks when files are split into pieces. Select a stripe size that is a multiple of the cluster size you will use when formatting the logical drive. You can take the number of disks in the stripe and divide by the cluster size to find an optimal number. Stripe and cluster size selections are powers of 2, so a four-disk stripe for a 512KB cluster might use 64KB or 128KB stripes since these numbers divide evenly into 512. This will ensure that file reads and writes will be distributed evenly across the stripe set.

File Systems

File systems are used to organize data on a logical drive. File systems track the location of files on the disk and file metadata. Metadata is data about the file such as creation date, last modified date, author, and permissions. File systems are structured hierarchically, beginning with a root directory under which other directories can be created. File systems also collect information used to track faulty areas of the drive.

Some file systems are journaled. Journaled file systems write file metadata to a journal before creating or modifying a file on the file system. Once the file has been created or modified, metadata is also modified. The journal protects against corruption should the drive or system go offline while the file operation is in progress. The journal can be used to determine whether files on the file system are in an inconsistent state, and sometimes the files can be corrected by using the journal data. Journaling increases the amount of time required to write files to the file system, but many file systems today use it to protect data integrity.

A file system is created by formatting a logical drive. Formatting consumes some of the available space on the drive, resulting in a lower-capacity value for a formatted disk than an unformatted one. However, it is an essential step in order to use the available space on the drive. A file system type can depend on the operating system being used when beginning the formatting process.

Whereas a controller identifies data based on CHS, logical volumes map blocks using logical block addressing (LBA). LBA is a way of referencing a location on a disk without a device having knowledge of the physical disk geometry. LBA provides a system with the number of blocks contained on the drive while the system keeps track of the data contained on each block. It requests the data by block number, and the drive then maps the block to a CHS and retrieves the data. Blocks are numbered starting with cylinder 0, head 0, and sector 1 and continuing until all sectors on that cylinder and head are read. The numbering starts again with head 1, which would be the bottom of the first platter, and continues along cylinder 0. This progresses until sectors for all heads in cylinder 0 are counted, at which time the process begins again for cylinder 1. The block count continues until all sectors for all heads and cylinders are accounted for.

Chapter Summary

A hard disk drive (HDD) is a component of storage systems, computers, and servers that is used to store data. HDDs consist of round flat surfaces known as platters that rotate on a spindle. The platters are organized into cylinders and sectors. Disk heads write data to the platters by aligning a substrate on the platters using an electromagnetic field. Solid-state drives (SSDs) store data by retaining an electrical current in a gate. Control gates allow current to be placed into floating gates. These floating gates can hold one or more binary numbers depending on the type of solid-state cell in use. MLC disks can hold more than one binary number per cell to achieve a greater capacity than SLC disks, which hold only one binary number per cell. However, MLC disks do not last as long as SLC disks, and they have lower performance. Both HDDs and SSDs can be purchased in different classes for certain use cases. Entry-level or consumer drives are the least expensive but offer the lowest performance and reliability while enterprise drives are the most expensive with the highest performance and reliability. Midrange drives fall inbetween entry level and enterprise drives. Entry-level drives are best for end user machines and very light workloads. Midrange drives are best for servers or shared systems that have low I/O requirements, and enterprise drives are best for servers with high I/O requirements, such as servers that have continual use and frequent disk reads and writes.

Interfaces are used to connect disks to other components in a computer or storage system. The ATA interfaces PATA and SATA offer a low-cost interface for lower performance needs, while SCSI, FC, and SAS disks are used for high-performance storage. Disks may also be connected using expansion cards. The PCI bus and its successor, PCI-X, are both older standards that have been largely eclipsed by PCIe. However, you may need to work on these interfaces. PCIe is the only bus that has dedicated bandwidth to each slot, whereas PCI and PCI-X use a shared bus.

A single disk often does not provide enough speed and resiliency for business applications, so disks are grouped together into a RAID set. RAID 0 writes pieces of data to multiple disks to improve speed in a process known as striping. Read and write operations are divided among the disks in the set, but a loss of a single disk causes a loss of data on all disks in the stripe set. RAID 1 stores identical data on two disks in a process called mirroring. RAID 5 uses striping to achieve high-data speeds while using parity data to protect against the loss of a single disk in the set. RAID 6 operates similarly to RAID 5, but it calculates additional parity to protect against the loss of two disks in the set. RAID 10 and RAID 0+1 combine striping and mirroring to achieve higher performance and resiliency than RAID 5 or 6. RAID 10 and RAID 0+1 can lose up to half the disks in a set before data is lost.

RAID can be configured on a hardware RAID controller, on a host-based disk controller with RAID firmware, or in software. Hardware RAID controllers perform all RAID functions on the controller and do not place additional burden on the computer processor, but that requires dedicated RAID controller hardware. Host-based implementations utilize a dedicated drive controller, which usually contains custom firmware to understand how to group drives into a RAID. However, the host-based implementation relies on the computer processor to perform RAID computations. Software-based RAID is implemented at the operating system level. No hardware needs to be purchased for a software RAID, so it is also the least expensive option. However, it suffers from reduced performance because RAID operations must pass through the operating system before being processed and it uses the computer processor to perform RAID computations.

Hosts interface with storage by using logical volumes. A logical volume can be a portion of a single disk, or it can be multiple physical disks together. The host uses a file system to organize the data on the logical volume. Hosts format a logical volume to create the initial file system and make the volume ready for use. The logical volume is then mounted into a directory or as a drive letter.

RAID 0 → striping
RAID 1 → mirroring
RAID 5 → striping + parity
{ RAID 10
{ RAID 0+1 } striping + mirroring

Chapter Review Questions

1. Which of the following components would not be found in a solid-state drive?

   A. Controller board

   B. Cache

   C. Spindle

   D. Interface

2. You are configuring a server that will store large database backups once a day. Which interface would give you the greatest capacity at the lowest price?

   A. SAS

   B. FC

   C. SATA

   D. SCSI

3. A head does which of the following?

   A. Controls the flow of data to and from a hard drive

   B. Aligns tiny pieces of metal using an electromagnetic field

   C. Serves as the starting point in a file system under which files are created

   D. Connects platters in a hard drive and spins them at a consistent rate

4. Which of the following statements is true about RAID types?

   A. RAID 1 is known as striping, and it writes the same data to all disks.

   B. RAID 0 is known as mirroring, and it writes pieces of data across all disks in the set.

   C. RAID 5 uses mirroring and parity to achieve high performance and resiliency.

   D. RAID 1 is known as mirroring, and it writes the same data to all disks.

5. You have created a RAID set from disks on a server, and you would like to make the disks available for use. Which order of steps would you perform?

   A. Create a logical volume, mount the logical volume, and format the logical volume.

   B. Format the logical volume, mount the logical volume, and create a directory structure.

   C. Create a directory structure, mount the logical volume, and format the logical volume.

   D. Create a logical volume from the RAID set, format the logical volume, and mount the logical volume.

6. Which interface can transmit at 6 Gbps?

  A. SATA and SAS

  B. Fibre Channel

  C. SCSI

  D. PATA

7. Which of the following is an advantage of IOPS versus other metrics such as seek time or rotational latency?

  A. IOPS identifies whether an individual component in a system is exhibiting acceptable performance.

  B. IOPS measures end-to-end transfer to provide a single metric for transmission.

  C. The IOPS metric is specified by the IEEE 802.24, so it is implemented consistently across all hardware and software that is IEEE 802.24 compliant.

  D. IOPS eliminates the need to run further benchmarking or performance tests on equipment.

8. A customer needs 250GB of storage for a high-performance database server requiring 2,000 IOPS. They want to minimize the number of disks but still provide for redundancy if one disk fails. Which solution would best meet the customer's requirements?

  A. RAID 1 with two 3,000 IOPS 128GB solid-state drives

  B. RAID 5 with three 3,000 IOPS 128GB solid-state drives

  C. RAID 5 with seven 350 IOPS 300GB SAS drives

  D. RAID 0 with two 3,000 IOPS 128GB solid-state drives

9. You plug a PCI card into a PCI-X slot. What will the maximum transfer rate be?

  A. 132 MBps

  B. 264 MBps

  C. 512 MBps

  D. 1.06 GBps

10. What is the primary advantage of a hardware RAID versus a software RAID?

  A. Hardware RAID costs less to implement.

  B. Hardware RAID can support more drives than software RAID.

  C. Hardware RAID has a dedicated processor for performing parity computations.

  D. Hardware RAID has its own I/O interrupt to communicate with the processor.

Chapter Review Answers

1. **C** is correct. The spindle would not be found in an SSD because SSDs do not have moving parts.

   A, **B**, and **D** are incorrect because SSDs consist of flash memory cells, a controller board, a cache, and an interface.

2. **C** is correct. Performance was not a concern in this question. The only requirement was for capacity and lowest cost, so SATA disks would be the best fit.

   A, **B**, and **D** are incorrect because SATA disks are less expensive per gigabyte than SAS, FC, or SCSI. Additionally, SATA disks come in larger capacities than SCSI disks.

3. **B** is correct. The head is a small electromagnet that moves back and forth on an actuator arm across a platter. The head generates an electromagnetic field that aligns the substrate on the platter in the direction of the field. The field direction is determined based on the flow of current in the head. Current can flow in one of two directions in the head.

   A, **C**, and **D** are incorrect. Data flow is controlled by the drive controller, so **A** is incorrect. **C** is incorrect because the starting point in a file system is the root. **D** is incorrect because the spindle connects platters in a hard drive and spins them at a consistent rate.

4. **D** is correct. RAID 1 is mirroring. The mirroring process writes identical data to both disks in the mirror set.

   A, **B**, and **C** are incorrect. **A** is incorrect because RAID 1 is not known as striping. RAID 0 is known as striping. **B** is incorrect because it is not known as striping. The rest of the statement is true about RAID 0. **C** is incorrect because RAID 5 uses striping and parity, not mirroring and parity. Mirroring is used in any of the RAID implementations that have a 1 in them, such as RAID 1, RAID 10, and RAID 0+1.

5. **D** is correct. A logical volume must be created from the RAID set before the volume can be formatted. Mounting occurs last. The step of creating a directory structure is not required for the disk to be made available.

   A, **B**, and **C** are incorrect because they are either not in the right order or they do not contain the correct steps. It is not necessary to create a directory structure, as this is performed during the format process.

6. **A** is correct. SATA version 3 and SAS both support 6-Gbps speeds.

   B, **C**, and **D** are incorrect. Fibre Channel supports speeds of 2, 4, or 8 Gbps. SCSI has a max speed of 5,120 Mbps, while PATA has a max speed of 133 Mbps.

7. **B** is correct. IOPS measures the transfer rate from the point at which the IOPS metric is initiated to the storage device.

   A, **C**, and **D** are incorrect. **A** is incorrect because IOPS does not identify an individual component. **C** is incorrect because the IOPS metric is not standardized by the IEEE. The 802.24 deals with smart grids and has nothing to do with IOPS. **D** is incorrect because other metrics may be needed to diagnose where performance issues lie or to document granular metrics on individual components.

8. **A** is correct. Two SSD disks would achieve the required IOPS and still provide for redundancy if one disk fails.

   B, **C**, and **D** are incorrect. Options **B** and **C** use more disks than option **A**, so they are not ideal, and option **D** does not provide redundancy in the case of disk failure.

9. **B** is correct. The PCI card in the PCI-X 1.0 slot will run at the maximum PCI speed. Because this is a PCI-X slot and has a maximum clock rate of 133 MHz, the highest PCI standard supported will be 2.1 running at 66 MHz. It will only be able to use 32 bits of the 64-bit data bus width, so we take 32×66 to get 2,112 and then divide by 8 to convert megabits to megabytes. Thus, we get 264 MBps.

   A, **C**, and **D** are incorrect. **A** is incorrect because the device plugged into the PCI-X slot would be able to perform at 66 MHz, above the initial 33 MHz specification for PCI that results in 132 MBps. **C** is incorrect because it assumes that later standards of PCI would be possible, but PCI-X is limited to 133 MHz, so it would not be capable of providing the 266 MHz required for PCI 2.3 speeds. **D** is incorrect because this is the base speed of PCI-X and would require a PCI-X card to achieve it.

10. **C** is correct. The primary benefit of hardware RAID over software RAID is that it has a dedicated processor for performing parity computations. Parity computations can place a great burden on the CPU when applications are write intensive.

    A, **B**, and **D** are incorrect. **A** is incorrect because a hardware RAID is more expensive than a software RAID because it requires additional hardware. **B** is incorrect because both systems can support a large number of drives. **D** is incorrect because the RAID controller does not have a dedicated interrupt. It uses the interrupt of the bus it is attached to, such as PCI, PCI-X, or PCIe.

Storage Infrastructure

In this chapter, you will learn how to

- Outline how a SAN works
- Explain how a storage array works
- Identify DAS technologies
- Describe the types of NAS and how they are used
- Identify cloud storage types and storage methods

With the amount of data organizations are managing these days, it is quite easy to outgrow the capacity of a local server or desktop. Storage arrays, network attached storage (NAS), direct attached storage (DAS), and cloud storage offer organizations a way to expand storage depending on the organization's needs. In some cases, a combination of each of these may be used to provide users and applications with access to information. Storage has become so essential to the continuing operation of a business that the loss of a key application or a storage device would have disastrous consequences, so these devices can be equipped with much more component redundancy to protect against the failure of individual parts or loss of power or network connectivity.

Managing storage on many devices can be complex and costly. Storage can be centralized to more efficiently allocate storage and to more effectively administer storage systems. Centralizing storage has created the need for many devices to connect to the storage.

Storage area networks (SANs) are used to connect many devices to one or more storage arrays. Storage arrays separate storage from individual hosts and consolidate storage for easier manageability. Direct attached storage can refer to storage that is internal to hosts or storage that is connected to a host using an external interface such as SCSI or FC. DAS is usually connected to only one device, but multiple devices can be connected to a DAS; however, DAS differs from a storage array on a SAN in that there are no other network devices in between the hosts and their storage. The devices are directly attached, which is the reason for its name. Network attached storage presents storage to other devices on the network as a network share. These devices can concurrently read and write data from the NAS, and the NAS handles storing and retrieving data from the storage itself. NAS devices are often much faster than server-based file servers, and they are usually built with far more component redundancy. Figure 2-1 shows a storage array connected to several servers and a workstation through a storage network. These servers and the workstation are connected over an Ethernet network to other workstations.

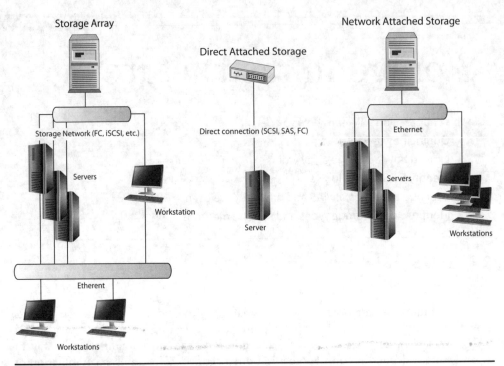

Figure 2-1   Storage array, DAS, and NAS

In the middle, a DAS is connected to a single server, and on the right, a NAS is connected to several servers and workstations over an Ethernet network.

The SAN, storage array, DAS, or NAS could be augmented or replaced with cloud storage. Those organizations that choose not to centralize data storage in their own data center or that are too small to justify their own data center often move their storage to the public cloud. Others create their own cloud for sharing storage with departments or other internal groups, or they join forces with other organizations to form a community cloud of shared storage and resources. Public and private cloud strategies can also be merged into a hybrid cloud to gain some of the benefits of both storage architectures.

Storage Arrays

Storage arrays are used to provide multiple devices with access to storage. These devices can interface with the storage in the same way they would interface with local storage. This is important because some resource-intensive applications such as database management systems (DBMSs) will require local access to storage resources. The storage array can boost disk performance and often lower costs. Consider a scenario with five database servers, as depicted in Figure 2-2. Each server needs several logical drives, and those logical drives must be separate in order to prevent I/O, such as the writing of a transaction log from interfering with I/O from a database table modification. A standard drive

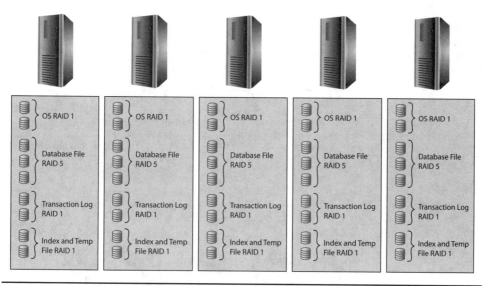

Figure 2-2   Five database servers, each with local storage

implementation might include a two-drive mirror for the operating system, three disks in a RAID 5 for the database files, two disks in a mirror for the log files, and another two-disk mirror for the temp files and indexes. So, in the end, this server requires nine disks, and the RAID 5 array is using only three spindles. Five large servers would be needed to house this many disks. Some of the space on the system may be underutilized because temp files and indexes may take up only 25GB to 50GB, whereas the disk size in the server may be 300GB to 600GB.

Storage arrays can contain hundreds or even thousands of disks with the use of many disk enclosures. These disks can be configured in different RAID types to support application needs, and multiple logical drives can be created from the RAID groups to be allocated to servers. In the database server example described previously, instead of buying five large database servers, you might purchase five smaller machines with the same processing power and memory but only two disks for the operating system. The storage array configured with a six-disk RAID 5 and two four-disk RAID 10 sets depicted in Figure 2-3 could offer storage to all five servers, and the storage would utilize more spindles, offering greater performance. However, if all five servers heavily access the disk, there could be resource contention, so a real-world scenario might include many more servers with different data needs; therefore, the logical drive would be allocated in such a way as to combine low- and high-impact storage on the RAID set, thus balancing contention on the disks.

Another problem seen with local disks is the difficulty of expanding storage. Consider a file server with a logical drive made from a five-disk RAID set. If the storage needs exceed the current capacity, the entire RAID set must be re-created and a new logical drive created. One option would be to add another physical disk and make it a six-disk RAID set. Another option would be to replace the five disks with larger-capacity disks. Either option would require the organization to back up the data on the logical

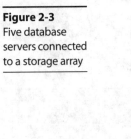

Figure 2-3
Five database
servers connected
to a storage array

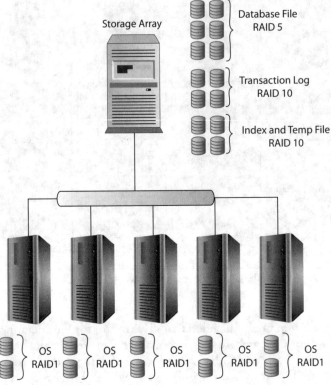

drive and then restore it once the new logical drive was created. This would result in significant downtime to the users of the file server—which should be avoided as much as possible. This scenario is different when using a storage array. For one thing, many storage arrays allow logical drives to be expanded when more space is needed. If this option is not available, a new drive can be provisioned in the storage array, and the data can be migrated using built-in tools to minimize downtime and expense.

The storage array is modular, so it can consist of one or more pieces that are connected together. The main unit contains one or more controllers and possibly some disk drives. The storage array may contain disk enclosures that house many more disks connected back to the storage array. Figure 2-4 shows the elements of a storage array.

Controller Head

The controller head manages the disks, cache, and front-end and back-end ports in the storage array. It keeps track of the RAID arrays and logical volumes, and it maps logical volumes to hosts, places data in or out of cache, and writes data to disks. The controller does exactly what its name says: It controls the storage array. Controllers can be configured as a single unit, as dual units, or in a grid.

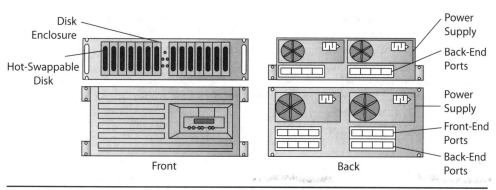

Figure 2-4 Elements of a storage array

Single

Single-controller storage arrays can be implemented at a lower cost than dual-controller units because single units minimize the number of front-end connections and ports to hosts or the fabric as well as the number of back-end ports to disk enclosures. Both front-end and back-end components need to connect only to a single device. Single-controller storage arrays typically cost less than a dual unit. This, coupled with the requirement of fewer cables, makes the solution less expensive than a dual unit. The disadvantage of this cost savings is that the controller is a single point of failure. The storage array will become unavailable if the controller fails because all I/O operations for the storage array are handled by this one controller.

EXAM TIP   Questions asking for the least expensive solution could use single controllers, but do not choose single controllers for questions requiring redundancy.

Dual

Dual-controller storage arrays are standard in enterprise storage arrays where most components are configured in a redundant fashion. Dual controller units are equipped with two identical controller heads that are each capable of operating the entire storage array. Disk enclosures must have at least one back-end connection to each controller in a dual-controller unit, and each front-end path to a host or switch needs to be cabled to both controllers. Twice as many cables and ports are required to implement a dual-controller unit, and this increases the cost. Dual-controller units are a bit more complex in design than single-controller units because the controllers must be kept in sync so that one can take over the other's operations in the case of a controller failure.

Dual controllers can be configured in one of two ways. Active/passive configurations route all I/O through a single controller, while the second controller simply stays aware of all I/O. If the active controller fails, the passive controller becomes active and assumes all the duties that were being performed on the failed controller. Active/passive solutions result in consistent performance even when a single controller has failed, but the maximum performance of the unit is equivalent to that of a single controller unit.

Active/active controllers distribute the I/O between both controllers to achieve higher performance. Both controllers stay aware of their counterpart's operations and will assume those operations if the other device fails. Controller failure does result in a loss of performance while the storage array is operating on a single controller. Keeping the two controllers in sync while both are performing work requires more complexity, leading to a higher cost for active/active controllers.

Grid

Grid storage, also known as scale-out storage, is a group of low-cost storage arrays or servers that operate together to provide fast and reliable access to data.

Grid implementations can either store entire files on a node or break up the files into segments to be stored on multiple nodes in a process known as *encoding*. Storing an entire file on a single grid node is simpler to implement, but retrieving the data relies upon a single node in the grid, so the performance is limited to the capabilities of that node. File writes are spread across the nodes in the cluster to aid in balancing the load, but reads must be directed at the node that contains the file, so it is possible for the grid to be unbalanced if some nodes contain data that is frequently accessed. Files are typically replicated to other nodes in the cluster to protect against node failure.

The grid encoding process breaks files into blocks that are spread across multiple nodes in the grid. Parity blocks are computed and stored to protect against node failures. The process is similar to RAID striping and parity. Grid file systems can be assigned a protection level that governs the maximum number of nodes that can fail before data loss occurs. Additional parity data is computed for higher protection levels, and a grid can support many different protection levels. Encoding results in better performance because more nodes can be used to retrieve files, but this increases grid management complexity.

Front-end nodes manage the I/O on the grid by identifying the nodes on which to write files or encode blocks. They keep a table mapping files to their locations within the grid to service read requests and track file locks and metadata. Grids require multiple front-end nodes for reliability, and these nodes require more processing power than other nodes in the grid. Some grid implementations spread the front-end management across all nodes in the grid, while others dedicate several powerful machines for the task. A back-end network connects the grid nodes, and this network must support high throughput and be separate from the front-end network. A write of a single file to the grid results in at least two writes for file grids and many more for encoded grids, and each frame on the network results in overhead that the network will need to absorb.

Both the front-end and distributed grid management models require a node in the grid to perform work before the data can be stored on the grid, which can increase latency. A third option has been developed to address this issue by installing a virtual controller on each host that needs to connect to the grid. The processing of management tasks is pushed to the client system. The virtual controller determines where to encode the data in the grid and keeps track of file mapping, locks, and metadata so that files can be written directly to the grid nodes that will store the data.

Cache

Cache is high-speed memory that can be used to service I/O requests faster than accessing a disk. Controller head cache is used for storing data that is waiting to be sent over the interface in response to a read request or data that is waiting to be written, or flushed, to the disks in response to a write request. Data may also remain in cache when the controller head considers it likely that the data will be requested for further read or write operations. When a request is made for data that exists in cache, it is known as a *cache read hit*. The storage array can immediately service the request by sending the data over its interface without retrieving the data from disk. Cache read hits result in the fastest response time. When requested data does not exist in cache, it is known as a *read miss*.

 EXAM TIP Having more cache read hits results in better performance. Optimize cache to maximize cache read hits.

Cache is referenced and organized by pages. Pages store data as well as a link to the location of the data on disk and a value called a *dirty bit*. The dirty bit is set to on when data is new or changed in cache, and this tells the controller head that the data needs to be flushed to disk.

- **Read ahead**   Read-ahead cache retrieves the next few sectors of data following what was requested and places that into cache in anticipation that future requests will reference this data. The read-ahead cache results in the best performance increase with sequential data requests, such as when watching videos, copying large files, or restoring files.

- **Write back**   Write-back cache sends an acknowledgment that data has been successfully written to disk once the data has been stored in cache but has not actually made it to disk yet. The data in cache is written to disk when resources are available. Write-back cache results in the best performance because the device is able to accept additional I/O immediately following the write acknowledgment. However, write back is riskier because cache failures or a loss of power to the disk could result in a loss of pending writes that have not been flushed to disk.

- **Write through**   Write-through cache waits to send an acknowledgment until a pending write has been flushed to disk. Write-through cache is slower than write back, but it is more reliable.

Cache is much more expensive per gigabyte than hard disks, and it is typically volatile, meaning that the data remains in cache only when power is provided to the device. A loss of power results in a loss of data in cache. Because of this, storage array controller heads must manage cache by flushing pending writes (dirty data) out to disk and freeing up space for new reads and writes. If cache is full when a new write is received by the controller, some data will need to be removed before the controller can cache the new write. This causes a write delay, so controller heads try to manage cache so that there is a healthy amount of free space available for new requests. The high watermark is a threshold where too much data resides in cache.

There are two methods used for freeing up cache space, and they operate based on opposite assumptions. The first method known as *most recently used* (MRU) assumes that applications are least likely to need the data they just requested, so it frees up pages with the most recent access dates. Conversely, *least recently used* (LRU) assumes that data that has been in cache for a long time since its last access least likely to be requested, so it frees up pages beginning with the oldest access dates. Thus, MRU releases the data that was accessed from cache most recently, while LRU releases the data that has remained unused in cache the longest.

Expansion Adapters

Storage arrays are often modular units that can be upgraded much like a workstation or server by using expansion adapters. Upgrades include adding more front-end or back-end ports, additional cache modules, or NAS ports. Unless you are using a server with a storage operating system on it, these expansion adapters will need to be purchased from the vendor.

Array Port Types and Cabling

Front-end ports are used for host connectivity. Figure 2-5 shows the front-end and back-end ports connected to a storage array and how they connect to disk shelves and a switch. Hosts will directly connect to these ports or, more commonly, connect through a SAN via a switch. The front-end ports need to be configured to work with the transport protocol that is in use on the network such as FC, Internet Small Computer System Interface (iSCSI), or Fibre Channel over Ethernet (FCoE). Back-end connections will use whichever technology is specified by the array such as FC or Serial Attached SCSI (SAS). Protocols are covered in more detail in Chapter 3.

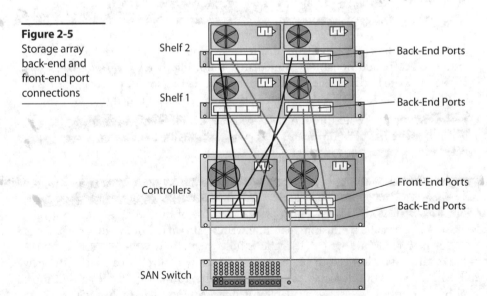

Figure 2-5
Storage array back-end and front-end port connections

Shelf 2 — Back-End Ports

Shelf 1 — Back-End Ports

Controllers — Front-End Ports / Back-End Ports

SAN Switch

The key to installing a storage array is to cable it redundantly. If the storage array is using more than one controller, both controllers should be cabled to disk enclosures. However, controllers may not be connected to all of the disk enclosures because some back-end connections can be chained from one disk enclosure to another.

Likewise, front-end ports should also be cabled redundantly. The storage array should have a front-end port from each controller connected to a redundant link on a host or fabric so that either controller can take on the load of the array if one controller fails. Single-controller units may also be cabled redundantly, but the redundancy will protect only against cable or port failure, not controller failure.

Disk Enclosure

Disk enclosures are used to hold additional disks in a storage array. Storage arrays can be expanded with many disk enclosures. Some support so many enclosures that it takes several racks to house them all. The number of supported disk enclosures is primarily determined by the controller capabilities, including the number of back-end ports.

Disk enclosures vary based on the following factors:

- Number of supported disks
- Size of supported disks (2.5 inch or 3.5 inch)
- Interface

The number of disks an enclosure can support is often a critical factor for expansion. Each enclosure takes up valuable space in a rack, but this can be minimized through the use of high-density enclosures. These enclosures come at a higher cost than low-density enclosures. There is no one standard for the number of disks in a low- or high-density enclosure, but low-density enclosures typically have between 12 and 15 disks in them, and high-density enclosures will typically have between 40 and 60 disks. Disks are loaded into low-density enclosures through the front of the enclosure, as shown in Figure 2-6. This makes it easy to swap out or add a failed disk.

To swap out a failed disk in a low-density enclosure, follow these steps:

1. Identify the disk to swap out. In the case of a disk failure, this would be indicated in the management software for the array, and the disk usually has a light to indicate its status. Green is good; an amber or red light indicates a problem.

2. Unlock and remove the front bezel from the disk enclosure with the failed disk.

3. Put on an electrostatic wrist strap and attach it to a ground.

Figure 2-6
Low-density
enclosure

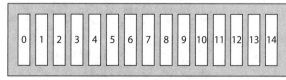

Front

4. Pull the tab on the failed disk tray to release it. Firmly pull on the exposed part of the tray to remove the disk. Do not pull on the tab to remove it because this could break off the tab or misalign it.

5. Wait 30 seconds for the disk to stop spinning and for the heads to land in their landing zones.

6. If the replacement disk did not come with a tray, remove the failed hard disk from the tray and mount the replacement disk in the same tray. Skip this step if the replacement disk came with a tray.

7. Open the tab on the disk tray and then insert the tray with the replacement disk into the enclosure with the tab facing the same direction as the other disks in the enclosure. Slide the disk in until the tab is against the enclosure and then close the tab until it snaps into place. The tab should pull the disk in a little more so that it is snug with the enclosure and level with the other disks. If the disk is not level, pull the tab and repeat so that it is seated properly.

Disks in high-density enclosures are accessed from the top of the enclosure, as shown in Figure 2-7. The enclosure slides away from the rack to expose the top of the unit for disk additions, removals, and replacements.

Figure 2-7
High-density
enclosure

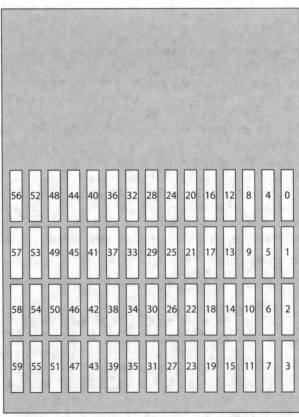

Top

Follow this procedure to replace a disk in a high-density enclosure:

1. Identify the disk to swap out. In the case of a disk failure, this would be indicated in the management software for the array, and the disk usually has a light to indicate its status. Green is good; an amber or red light indicates a problem.

2. Unlock and remove the front bezel from the disk enclosure with the failed disk.

3. Put on an electrostatic wrist strap and attach it to a ground.

4. Release the enclosure top cover by pressing a release button or by removing top screws.

5. Pull the tab on the failed disk tray to release it. Firmly pull upward on the exposed part of the tray to remove the disk. Do not pull on the tab to remove it because this could break off the tab or misalign it.

6. Wait 30 seconds for the disk to stop spinning and for the heads to land in their landing zones.

7. If the replacement disk did not come with a tray, remove the failed hard disk from the tray and mount the replacement disk in the same tray. Skip this step if the replacement disk came with a tray.

8. Open the tab on the disk tray and then insert the tray with the replacement disk into the enclosure with the tab facing the same direction as the other disks in the enclosure. Slide the disk down slowly until the tab is against the enclosure. Do not drop the disk tray into the enclosure because this could damage the disk or the interface connection. Close the disk tray tab until it snaps into place. The tab should pull the disk in a little more so that it is snug with the enclosure and level with the other disks. If the disk is not level, pull the tab and repeat so that it is seated properly.

Enclosure Controllers
Disk enclosures are equipped with controllers to send I/O over the back-end ports back to the storage array and to manage the disks in the enclosure. The controllers contain the intelligence to connect the enclosure to the rest of the storage array.

Monitoring Cards
Enclosures may also contain monitoring cards that track the health of enclosure components and report to the system. Alerts can be set up to track critical events such as a hard drive failure, path failure, or loss of connectivity to a device. Statistics can be calculated to obtain a performance baseline and to identify performance problems later.

Enclosure Addressing
The storage array must address each of the enclosures in order to send and receive traffic to and from it. This addressing takes place on the back end of the storage array, meaning that the addresses are used for communication inside the storage array, as compared to front-end ports, which have an addressing scheme used to communicate between the

storage array and hosts. Addressing the back end uses some of the same protocols that front-end communication does. Current enclosures use either FC or SAS connections. FC addressing uses a 64-bit World Wide Name (WWN) as an address, and SAS uses a 64-bit SAS address. The 64-bit address space for FC WWNs and SAS addresses would allow for 18,446,744,073,709,551,616 unique addresses, but FC is limited to about 15 million devices because of its use of 24-bit port IDs and area IDs. SAS is limited to 65,536 devices.

Cabling

The key to installing a storage array is to cable it redundantly. If the storage array is using more than one controller, both controllers should be cabled to disk enclosures. However, controllers may not be connected to all of the disk enclosures because some back-end connections can be chained from one disk enclosure to another.

Hot-Swap

Various parts of the storage array are hot-swappable, meaning they can be removed without powering off the device. Such devices include power supplies, interface cards, hard disks, controllers, and fan units.

Each unit in a storage array is usually configured with dual power supplies that are connected to different circuits and uninterruptable power supply (UPS) units called *A/B power*, where A and B are the different redundant circuits. Power distribution units (PDUs) within the rack or mounted close to the rack are similar to surge protectors, and each power supply for the A power will be connected to the A PDU, while the B power supplies will be connected to the B PDU. Each PDU connects back to a circuit leading to a different UPS.

Storage Area Networks

A storage area network connects one or more storage arrays with one or more hosts. This allows the storage in storage arrays to be shared among the hosts in the SAN and for hosts to access the shared storage of multiple storage arrays to meet their performance and capacity needs. SANs allow for data storage to be physically distant from the hosts that access it. SANs connect hosts and storage arrays together via protocols such as FC, iSCSI, FCP, iFCP, or FCoE. These protocols are discussed in detail in Chapter 3, but an overview of the two most common protocols, FC and iSCSI, is provided here.

Fibre Channel

Fibre Channel is a networking technology used to transmit data at high speeds. Current FC technology can transmit data at 16 Gbps (roughly 2,000 MBps), primarily over optical cables and to a lesser degree on copper cables. FC is expected to operate at 32 Gbps by 2014. At its release, FC outclassed its primary competing technology, Small Computer System Interface (SCSI), with support for many more devices on a single network and a longer range of operation.

Fabric

The most common way of connecting FC devices into a SAN is through a fabric. A fabric, discussed more in Chapter 3, is an interconnection of FC devices through FC switches. Each FC switch can handle multiple connections between devices, and each connection is isolated from other connections to improve security and to provide dedicated bandwidth to the connection. Similarly, iSCSI uses Ethernet switches that also isolate traffic. Both FC and iSCSI switches are a central point where devices can connect, and each can be expanded through connections with other switches.

FC or iSCSI Protocol

Internet Small Computer System Interface has experienced much growth because of its lower cost and ease of implementation as compared to FC. iSCSI utilizes common low-cost Ethernet equipment and cabling to connect storage devices and hosts over a SAN. The advent of 10GigE, which is Ethernet that has a maximum throughput of 10 Gbps, has allowed iSCSI to achieve speeds approaching those in FC networks (2 Gbps to 16 Gbps). The cost of 10GigE equipment currently negates much of the price advantage iSCSI has over FC; however, this may change as industry adoption of 10GigE increases.

iSCSI runs over Ethernet, which has higher overhead than FC. Ethernet can typically achieve 50 percent to 85 percent of its rated capacity, while FC can consistently achieve 90 percent of its rated capacity. This is why 10GigE iSCSI is considered roughly equivalent to 8 Gbps FC.

An FC host bus adapter (HBA) is required to connect to an FC network. The FC HBA performs the processing necessary for handling FC data. However, with iSCSI, a standard network interface card (NIC) can be used, which will create processor overhead as the CPU handles the TCP/IP stack. NICs equipped with TCP Offload Engine (TOE) can alleviate some of this, and iSCSI HBAs have even more capabilities built in to reduce processor overhead and improve response time. Both are discussed in more detail in Chapter 4.

Block Mode

Storage area networks present data to hosts as local storage appears so that hosts can interact with the storage on a block level. As mentioned in Chapter 1, hosts reference locations in storage by block. With a SAN, a host can write data to a block on storage that is allocated to it, and the storage network carries the commands from the host to the storage array located somewhere on the SAN. The storage array then writes the data out to disks within it.

File System on Host

Once storage is presented to the host by the SAN, it is up to the host to partition and format the storage for use. This was introduced in Chapter 1. Different operating systems use their own file systems to organize data on the disk. Enterprise servers commonly run versions of Microsoft Windows or Unix/Linux, and while Linux does support reading Microsoft's New Technology File System (NTFS), Linux disks commonly use the ext (extended) file system. The latest version of ext is version 4, termed ext4. Ext4 supports file systems up to 1.15 exabytes (EB) and file sizes of 17.5 terabytes (TB). An exabyte is 1,000 petabytes (PB), or 1,000,000TB. Ext4 achieves extremely fast file system checking by marking unused portions of the volume so that they can be skipped during a check. Delayed allocation buffers data writes so that they can be written to contiguous space and avoid fragmentation for new writes. However, delayed allocation increases the risk of data loss if power is lost to the computer before data is written to disk. Ext4 is backward compatible with other ext versions, and it is journaled. *Journaling* is a process where changes are tracked in a log, known as a *journal*, before saving the change to the file system. Journaling provides better protection against data loss or corruption in the case of a power failure. Without journaling, data that was partially written to a disk would be unreadable, but journaling would allow for the missing portion of the write to be completed once power was restored to the disk.

Microsoft systems formerly used the FAT and FAT32 file systems, but these have been replaced by NTFS and Microsoft's latest file system, ReFS. NTFS was introduced in Microsoft Windows NT. NTFS allows you to control which users have access to individual files and folders, whereas previous Microsoft file systems allowed access controls only when files were shared over the network. NTFS also supports compression and encryption on files and folders. ReFS was introduced in Microsoft Windows 2012, and it offers greater protection against file corruption and support for even larger file systems than NTFS.

Direct Attached Storage

Direct attached storage is an easy way to expand the available storage space for one or more computers. DAS is a storage array that is cabled to one or more hosts without any devices in between. In some cases, DAS is used to refer to the local storage on a device, but in most cases, DAS is a device external to the host. In these cases, the DAS connects to a host through one or more front-end ports such as SCSI, SAS, eSATA, or FC. The DAS may have multiple types of ports as well such as FC and SCSI. The number of hosts that can connect to the DAS is limited by the quantity of front-end ports on the DAS.

SCSI

Small Computer System Interface (SCSI) DAS connects to a SCSI HBA on a host and is assigned a SCSI ID. Each SCSI device will need to have a unique SCSI ID, including the SCSI controller. The controller is typically assigned the ID of 7, so make sure that the DAS or other devices connected to the SCSI chain do not conflict with each other. Each end of the SCSI bus needs to be terminated. This may be implemented in the DAS, or it might require a terminator to be installed on the device. There will be two SCSI connectors, one for the connection to the server and another for a connection to another device on the chain or for termination. If the DAS does not terminate itself, ensure that a terminator is connected to the device at the end of the chain.

Many different devices can be mixed in a SCSI chain, but this can introduce problems if all devices are not operating at the same speed. One slow device on the chain will require all other devices to communicate at that slower speed and can result in significant performance issues for the DAS.

SAS

Serial Attached SCSI (SAS) DAS devices are a direct connection from DAS to the host, so there are no other devices sharing the connection such as with SCSI. A host may be connected to the DAS via multiple SAS connectors to obtain greater redundancy if one link fails and to increase the throughput to the DAS. SAS offers up to 6 Gbps speeds, and each connection does not have to share this 6 Gbps with other devices as is the case with SCSI.

eSATA

eSATA DAS connects much like SAS with a single port on the eSATA DAS connecting to a single port on the host. eSATA offers up to 6 Gbps speeds, but it does not offer the features of SAS.

FC

Fibre Channel connections offer high speeds for DAS. The type of connection used is called FC point-to-point (FC-P2P) because the DAS and host are directly connected to one another. The host must have an FC HBA to connect to the DAS. These FC HBAs can be expensive compared to SCSI, SAS, and SATA, but FC DAS can be connected over longer distances.

Network Attached Storage

Network attached storage is a storage technology used to share files with many users. The previous technologies discussed in this chapter presented a portion of their available storage to a host to use as if it were local storage. With the exception of clustered nodes, each node can access only the storage that has been presented to it. However, with NAS, storage is made available to many computers at the same time over an IP network through the use of virtual directories called *shares*.

The concept of file sharing is not new. In fact, it was one of the drivers for initial network adoption in companies. Before the use of shares and the servers that shares reside on, known as *file servers*, users had to transport data from one computer to another, most commonly via floppy disk. This method of data sharing is known as *sneakernet* because people have to walk to another computer to share files. So, how does NAS differ from the shares that have become so commonplace in networks today?

NAS offers organizations a way to consolidate and increase availability. As companies create more and more data, much of the files users work with on a day-to-day basis are stored on file servers. File servers are good for storing small amounts of data that is used by a select number of users. However, as the amount of data and the number of users grows larger, file servers cease to be able to keep up with the load. Some servers utilize

DAS to access more disks at the same time. These servers may also utilize many network cards to service requests, but even with all this, the operating system that services requests must run in software, and this adds a delay to the servicing of user requests.

Network attached storage provides a flexible way to access files over a network. NAS is built from the hardware level on application-specific integrated circuits (ASICs) to service requests for files, making them much faster than general-purpose file servers. NAS can be equipped with many network interface cards, large amounts of cache, and multiple high-performance processors. As with the other storage technologies discussed thus far, NAS comes in many varieties to suit numerous organizational needs. NAS can have integrated storage on the device, or it can operate in "gateway" mode where it maps storage from one or more storage arrays on a SAN. Many NAS devices also support clustering for high availability. Clustered NAS devices operate under the same name and retain copies of the data on each NAS node or point back to a shared storage location such as a storage array. If a single NAS node becomes unavailable, client file requests will be serviced by other members of the cluster.

NAS can support multiple different protocols such as CIFS for Microsoft clients, NFS for Linux, or FTP for Internet users, making it ideal in environments where multiple operating systems are utilized. Some NAS run services that allow them to act as backup repositories, host web sites, stream audio and video, and more.

Shares are created by assigning a share name and permissions to a directory on the system. The share name can be different from the directory name, and shares do not have to be created in directories directly beneath the root. A share can be created on a subdirectory of a directory that is already shared. This may be necessary in situations where some users need access to only a subset of the information in a share. These users would be given permission to the shared subdirectory, and others who need access to the entire set of directories would be given access to the share above it. Both shares, however, will be seen with their own names at the same level underneath the NAS name when users browse to the NAS by name. For example, say marketing has the folder structure shown in Figure 2-8. Marketing managers and salespeople need access to the entire Marketing

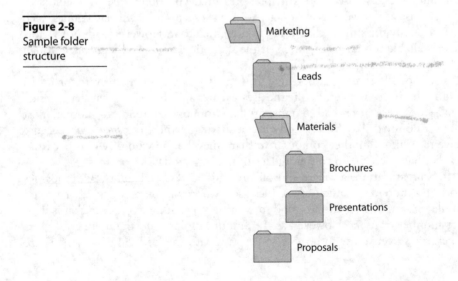

Figure 2-8
Sample folder
structure

Marketing

Leads

Materials

Brochures

Presentations

Proposals

directory, but graphic designers who create marketing materials need access only to the Materials directory underneath Marketing. The NAS administrator would create a share called marketing for the Marketing directory and give access to the marketing managers and salespeople. The administrator would then create a second share called materials that would map to the Materials directory underneath Marketing. This directory would be shared to the graphic designers.

It is important to understand the expected utilization and performance requirements for shares so that they can be provisioned appropriately. Shares with high-performance requirements or high load might need to be on a separate set of disks, whereas multiple low-performance shares or those that are infrequently used could reside on the same set of disks. Growth is also a concern for share placement. While most NAS devices allow for share expansion, it is still best to place shares in a location where they can grow naturally without the need for administrative intervention.

Components

The basic components that make up a NAS include processors, memory, NICs, power supplies, an operating system, and a management system. NAS with internal storage will also have the components mentioned in the "Storage Arrays" section, such as controllers, disks, disk enclosures, and back-end cabling. Gateway systems will have a connection to a storage array on the storage network via the storage network's transmission medium such as fiber or copper.

One or more processors perform the computations necessary for servicing I/O. Memory is used to store data that the processors are working on and to keep track of open files, metadata, and communication sessions. NICs provide the connectivity to the servers or workstations on the network. A NAS device may utilize many NICs aggregated together to obtain greater bandwidth, and NICs are usually cabled to redundant switches to avoid downtime if a switch, cable, or port fails. The NAS will have at least one power supply to provide power to the various NAS components, but NAS devices are often equipped with more than one power supply to guard against the failure of a single power supply or a loss in power to a circuit. Power supplies should be connected to different PDUs, which go to different UPS units and circuits. The operating system includes the instructions necessary for the NAS to function, and the management system allows administrators to create shares, view statistics on the NAS, join the NAS to a domain, create file systems, and perform many other tasks related to managing the device.

UNC-Addressable Storage

Resources on NAS devices can be referenced by using a uniform naming convention (UNC) path. The UNC path consists of a device name, share name, and filename. For example, to access the October2013.xls spreadsheet in the accounting share on the NAS named userfiles.sampledomain.com, you would type the following into a browser, Windows Explorer, script, or run command:

\\userfiles.sampledomain.com\accounting\October2013.xls

The path begins with \\ to tell the application that this is a UNC path. This is followed by the NAS name and a backslash and then the share name and another backslash. When the file is contained within other folders inside the share, these folders will be referenced following the share name and before the filename, such as in the following example, where the file is contained within a folder called October inside the Q3 folder in the accounting share:

\\userfiles.sampledomain.com\accounting\Q3\October\October2013.xls

Both of these examples use the fully qualified domain name (FQDN) for the NAS device, but computers that are local to the domain would be able to drop the domain suffix (sampledomain.com), so accessing the previous directory from computer1.sampledomain.com could be achieved with the following path as well:

\\userfiles\accounting\Q3\October\October2013.xls

TCP/IP-Based Storage

Data read and write requests are encapsulated into packets that are sent over the TCP/IP protocol suite to the NAS. The NAS puts together the packets to reconstruct the read or write request. This request may be CIFS or NFS (discussed in the next section) or other TCP/IP protocols such as File Transfer Protocol (FTP), Secure FTP (SFTP), or Hypertext Transfer Protocol (HTTP).

The NAS receives the read or write request and identifies the location of the data on its block-level storage, either locally or on a storage array if the NAS is operating as a gateway. Data is then written to the storage or read from the storage and sent to the requesting host via TCP/IP.

NAS File System Protocols

Both Windows and Unix systems can use a single NAS device because Common Internet File System (CIFS), the Windows file system protocol, and Network File System (NFS), the Unix file system protocol, are supported.

NFS

NFS is a protocol used for sharing files over a network. It is used on Unix and Linux systems and carries little overhead. The first NFS version was specified by Sun Microsystems in 1984 and was used only within the company. Version 2 of the protocol saw widespread use as a file system protocol. The protocol was designed to have little overhead characterized by its stateless design and User Datagram Protocol (UDP) transport mechanism.

Stateless protocols do not retain information on an overall communication session such as the current working directory or open files, so each set of requests and responses is independent. This requires that each response contain all the information necessary for processing the request rather than relying on the server to know which operation was in progress. The advantage of the stateless protocol is that the NAS does not need to retain information on sessions; in addition, it does not need to clean up information when transactions complete.

	Version	State	Transport	Year
Table 2-1 NFS Versions	NFS Version 1	Stateless	UDP	1984
	NFS Version 2	Stateless	UDP	1989
	NFS Version 3	Stateless	UDP/TCP	1995
	NFS Version 4	Stateful	TCP	2000

UDP is a connectionless transport protocol, which means it does not negotiate with a receiver or check to see whether the receiver is ready before initiating a request, nor does it keep track of packet sequence or errors in delivery. Each of these negotiation and error correction steps would require packets to be sent back and forth, so this time is reduced when using UDP. However, this comes at a cost. UDP has a higher error rate and cannot guarantee receipt of information.

The protocol remained stateless until version 4 where it was modified to become stateful, allowing the protocol to track locked files and open sessions. The protocol ran on top of the connectionless transport protocol UDP in version 2, but version 3 added support for Transmission Control Protocol (TCP), which is connection oriented. Table 2-1 compares the versions.

NFS version 4 runs only on top of TCP. Version 4 also added support for a number of other features such as parallel NFS (pNFS), data retention, and session model, but you will not find these on the SCSP exam, so they are not covered in detail here.

CIFS

Common Internet File System is an open version of Microsoft's Server Message Block (SMB) protocol that is used for sharing files over a network. The initial version of SMB/CIFS suffered from numerous problems, including high broadcast traffic, poor wide area network (WAN) performance, and weak authentication.

CIFS used NetBIOS broadcasts to announce network services. Broadcasts are messages sent to every node on the network, and these resulted in a great deal of additional traffic on the network, reducing its efficiency. This was resolved when NetBIOS was replaced with the Windows Internet Naming Service (WINS) or Domain Name System (DNS) for addressing. CIFS was also designed as a block-level protocol with a 64KB block size. This, along with small window sizes, led to poor WAN performance. Version 1.0 is an improvement on the initial version. In this version, the protocol was changed to be a streaming protocol rather than a block-level protocol, and TCP window sizing was added to achieve better performance on WAN links.

Authentication was also a problem in the initial version of CIFS. LANMan authentication used password hashes that could be reversed to determine the password. This was later replaced with NTLM; however, NTLM poorly implemented the DES encryption standard, allowing for password cracking. NTLM was replaced with NTMLv2 and then Kerberos, which is the current authentication method.

Version	Authentication	Addressing	Transport	Windows Release	Year
SMB/CIFS	LANMan, NTLM	GNS, WINS	NetBIOS, IPX	Windows 3.11, 95, NT 3.5, 4.0	1993
SMB/CIFS 1.0	NTLMv2, Kerberos	WINS, DNS	NetBIOS, TCP	Windows 2000, XP, Server 2003, 2003 R2	2000
SMB/CIFS 2.0	Kerberos	DNS	TCP	Windows Vista, Server 2008	2006
SMB/CIFS 2.1	Kerberos	DNS	TCP	Windows 7, Server 2008 R2	2009
SMB/CIFS 3.0	Kerberos	DNS	TCP	Windows 8, Server 2012	2012

Table 2-2   SMB/CIFS Versions

CIFS is a stateful protocol. This gives CIFS the ability to restore connections to shares and files after an interruption, and it can enforce locks on files to prevent users from making changes to files that are currently being modified by another client. CIFS clients can cache files locally by requesting an opportunistic lock (oplock) on the file. Most versions of SMB/CIFS use TCP as their transport protocol; however, earlier versions of SMB/CIFS used NetBIOS or NetWare's IPX. TCP is connection-oriented, so negotiation takes place between the sender and the receiver to determine capabilities. Acknowledgments are sent after requests to confirm receipt, and packets do not need to contain all the information on a transaction because the server has knowledge of the session between the client and server. Table 2-2 shows the versions of SMB/CIFS and the authentication, addressing, and transport systems used in each, along with the operating systems they were used on and their release year.

Ethernet-Based Storage

NAS devices are Ethernet-based, using twisted-pair cabling and communicating over a switched network. Ethernet devices are inexpensive compared to other storage technologies such as Fibre Channel or InfiniBand, and most organizations already have an Ethernet network in place, so adding a NAS requires little new investment.

Cloud Storage

Cloud storage is storage that can be accessed over the Internet. Users of cloud storage are distinct from those who manage and control cloud storage. This distinction makes it easier for users, because they are not required to know how the storage is configured in order to use it. Also, this distinction is useful even within organizations to streamline operations, minimize learning curves, and improve support.

Cloud storage can be part of a larger cloud service offering or it can be independent. Other cloud services are discussed in Chapter 9. In a cloud storage model, Internet-connected computers or storage devices offer their storage to users or companies on a subscription basis. Subscription models can be paid, free, subsidized, or simply tracked for accounting purposes. Let's look at cloud storage types to see how this works in practice.

Cloud Storage Types

Cloud storage types can be differentiated by who has ownership and control of the systems that house the cloud data. We describe these types as public, private, community, and hybrid.

Public Cloud

A public cloud is owned and operated by an organization and made available to customers over the Internet. The advantages of public clouds are the ability to purchase only the IT services that a company needs and the ability to increase or decrease those services extremely quickly. Companies can deploy new servers or services over the cloud in hours rather than days or weeks by using the cloud. Traditional systems would require the purchase of equipment, shipping, installation, and then initial configuration to get them to a usable state. However, the same organization could obtain a public cloud server by simply requesting another server from the cloud vendor. Public cloud resources may be offered for free, but most require a subscription that increases proportionally to usage.

Private Cloud

A private cloud is a proprietary system owned and operated by a single organization for its use. This allows the organization to centralize IT services and tightly control certain elements of IT service administration while providing services to other business groups, departments, or sites. Customers of the private cloud are internal to the organization, but they can utilize the services much like they would a public cloud. The organization may charge those business units for the service, or it may simply track usage through accounting metrics. The primary advantage of a private cloud is that the organization maintains control of the data and systems. Private clouds can reduce inefficiencies in local business group IT functions and better track IT costs, but they do require capital investment to create, and scalability is limited to the investment made into the private cloud infrastructure. Unused capacity is still a cost for the organization as a whole.

Community Cloud

A community cloud is a cloud that is owned and operated by a third party or jointly by members. Community clouds are shared between organizations to reduce IT costs for each member. Such systems are used by educational systems, research facilities, libraries, local and regional government organizations, and businesses. Some examples include county library index systems, state student reporting services, hospital anonymous statistic collection systems, and county sensor collection systems. The primary benefit of a community cloud is reduced costs for IT services to community members. The community cloud can purchase software at better rates by buying in bulk. Economies of scale can be realized because the architecture is larger than what any single community organization could deploy on its own. However, the organization must belong to a group or be associated with others who have the same need and desire to work together. The examples given here are noncompetitive examples. In the corporate world, many of the companies that have similar needs also compete with one another, so they would not want to share their services in a community and would likely utilize a public, private, or hybrid cloud instead.

Hybrid Cloud

A hybrid cloud is a combination of a public cloud and a private cloud. Hybrid clouds allow for sensitive data to be kept in private cloud storage while less sensitive data can be pushed out to public cloud storage. Other hybrid cloud solutions may utilize the public cloud for computing functions and the private cloud for storage functions. This allows the cloud to grow or shrink quickly with greater control retained over the cloud system. Hybrid clouds do require capital investment for the private cloud portion, but the public cloud portion is paid for as it is used. Hybrid clouds can improve performance because private cloud elements can be located close to the users of the system—in some cases, in the same office. This reduces latency for data stored in the private cloud portion of the hybrid cloud solution. Hybrid clouds can use the private element for highly customized user interfaces that may not be supported on existing public cloud architectures.

It is important to note that hybrid cloud architectures are often more complex than private or public cloud architectures alone, and the implementation must utilize industry frameworks for interoperability, which can limit the amount of flexibility the organization has over the application as compared with traditional hosted application models. However, the hybrid cloud model is often seen as a good solution for customers whose requirements do not neatly fit within either the public or private cloud framework alone.

Cloud Storage Methods

Just as there are several types of clouds, there are also several storage methods. One popular method is to use cloud storage for backing up the data that resides on a computer or server. Other methods use cloud storage for primary data storage through mount points, cloud synchronization, or the Web.

Cloud Backup

Cloud storage is also used as a backup destination. Typically, an agent is installed on the location computer or server, and this agent tracks changes to directories that data owners want to back up. The agent can replicate data to cloud storage on a scheduled basis, or the data can be immediately transferred whenever it changes. Cloud backup users are charged for how much storage they utilize. This is important to note because storage sizes can grow quickly depending on how many replicas the organization wants to retain. Cloud backup solutions often allow the user to specify how long data will be retained. The cloud storage vendor will then track changes to the data over that period and retain multiple copies of the data or tracked changes so that individual points in time can be recovered.

Cloud backups often make sense for companies when data growth rates are high and the cost and time to set up new equipment would impact business productivity. It can also make sense for small data sets where the cost to procure, operate, and maintain backup equipment is too significant for the relatively small amount of data that needs to be protected. Cloud backups are discussed in relation to other backup strategies in Chapter 7.

Locally Mapped Cloud Storage

Some cloud systems allow for users to interface with cloud storage just as they would with local storage. Cloud storage systems, in this model, are mounted to the file system and are provided a drive letter or a logical mount point. For example, Figure 2-9 shows that cloud storage residing on server A over the Internet is mapped to a folder called MyStorage on the user's system drive. Any files that the user stores in MyStorage will actually be stored on the cloud server.

Cloud storage can be located far away from the user which requires data transfers to traverse through many hops to reach their destination. Thus, locally mapped cloud storage systems can result in low performance due to latency. Cloud systems utilize local caching to remediate this. Files are stored in a temporary location on the local disk and then changes are flushed back to the cloud storage when permitted. In this way, writes to cloud storage do not have to wait for their writes to be sent to the cloud storage and incur that latency. Instead, they are written to local disk and sent to the cloud storage later. The disadvantage of this option is that failure of the local disk can result in a loss of data when the data has not been written to the cloud yet. Some applications will not be able to tolerate this. These applications may require that the local cache directory be located on a RAID set with adequate redundancy.

Another solution to the cloud storage latency problem is to utilize a cloud service that has cloud storage locations in many places around the world, such that connections are guaranteed a maximum latency.

 NOTE Higher latency values mean that it takes more time to travel from source to destination, so lower latency values are desired. In many cases, service level metrics provide a minimum assurance, such as a minimum of 1 Gbps of bandwidth, but with latency you want to have a maximum assurance so that latency does not exceed a specific value.

Figure 2-9
Locally mapped
cloud storage

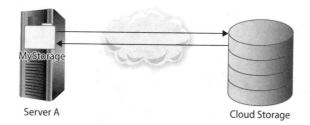

Server A   Cloud Storage

Cloud Synchronization

Cloud synchronization allocates space on the local drive of a system and replicates that data to cloud storage. New data is written to local storage so that the latency disadvantages of simply mapping to cloud storage are avoided. Furthermore, cloud synchronization can be used to create identical copies of the data at multiple locations. Whenever a write occurs at any synchronization point, the write is replicated to cloud storage and then back down to all the replica sets. Many mainstream cloud storage providers such as Dropbox, Google Drive, Amazon Drive, Microsoft OneDrive, Box, and SpiderOak all use this model.

If we use the previous example here, cloud storage residing on server A over the Internet is mapped to a folder called MyStorage on the user's system drive using cloud synchronization software. Any files that the user stores in MyStorage will be located on a local logical volume as well as a volume on the cloud server. Server B and workstation A also have the cloud synchronization software installed, and they are associated with the same corporate account. Data that is added on server A will be replicated to the cloud and then pushed down to a MyStorage folder on server B and workstation A. Likewise, files added on server B or workstation A will also be replicated to the cloud and then down to server A. This also works for changes to files and file deletions. This scenario is depicted in Figure 2-10.

Web-Based Cloud Storage

Web-based cloud storage is accessed using a browser. Users can log into the cloud storage site and then view their files. Files can be uploaded or downloaded from the site. This model is similar to traditional web storage models such as File Transfer Protocol (FTP) and Hypertext Transfer Protocol (HTTP), which allow users to browse remote storage and upload or download files to the storage location using either a web browser or client software.

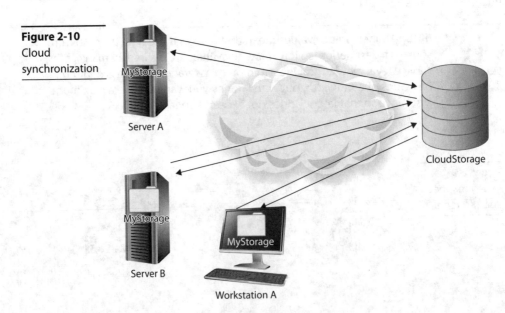

Figure 2-10
Cloud synchronization

Server A

CloudStorage

Server B

Workstation A

Chapter Summary

Storage arrays consolidate storage into a modular unit that has many redundant components. Storage arrays can contain many more disks than would fit into a single server, giving them the ability to create large RAID arrays spanning many spindles for optimal performance. Storage arrays can give hosts access to high-performance RAID arrays and just the right amount of storage for an application without overallocating, as is often the case when storage is local. Storage arrays can be expanded by adding disk enclosures when more storage is needed.

Storage arrays consist of at least one unit that contains controllers, power supplies, front-end and back-end ports, and possibly some disk drives. This main unit can be connected to disk enclosures to expand storage capacity. Controllers handle the reads and writes to the storage array, and they contain large amounts of cache to speed up the response. Cache can be used to store data that will likely be requested in future reads, or it can contain data that will be written to the disk in the future. Controllers can be configured as a single unit in a storage array or with multiple units. A single controller presents a single point of failure for the device, but it is often cheaper than dual controllers. Grids combine multiple low-cost storage arrays to form a larger storage array.

Storage area networks allow multiple storage arrays and hosts to connect together. Fibre Channel and iSCSI are the most common protocols used in SANs. FC offers high-performance storage connectivity with speeds up to 16 Gbps. iSCSI, on the other hand, operates over Ethernet, a standard computer networking medium, so it can be implemented at reduced cost. 10GigE implementations of iSCSI offer similar speeds to those of 8-Gbps FC.

Once storage has been allocated to a host on a SAN, the host will need to create a file system on the storage. Unix systems commonly use the ext file system, and Windows systems use NTFS. ReFS is a new file system introduced in Windows 2012 that is designed with greater protection against file corruption.

Direct attached storage is a storage array that is connected to one or more hosts without the use of a network. The maximum number of connections to a DAS is limited by the number of front-end ports on the DAS. Front-end DAS connections include SCSI, SAS, eSATA, and FC.

Network attached storage differs from the other technologies in that it presents data to devices on the network through shares instead of drives. Many devices can read and write to data on a share at the same time. To protect access to the data, shares are configured with permissions to define who can view the data in the share. Each share maps to a directory on the NAS, and those directories may be local to the NAS or be located on a storage array on a SAN.

NAS shares are accessed by a uniform naming convention path, which takes the following form:

\\NASname\share\folder\subfolder\file

Unix and Linux machines access shares via the Network File System, and Windows devices use the Common Internet File System, an open version of Microsoft's Server Message Block protocol. NFS began as a stateless protocol running over the connectionless UDP transport protocol, whereas CIFS was stateful, running over a connection-oriented transport protocol. The advantage to a stateless protocol is that it has less overhead, but stateful protocols can track open files and restore lost connections. NFS version 4 is now a stateful protocol running over the connection-oriented TCP protocol. CIFS has undergone many enhancements to improve performance and security.

Cloud storage is storage that can be accessed over the Internet. Users of cloud storage are distinct from those who manage and control cloud storage. Cloud storage types can be differentiated by who has ownership and control of the systems that house the cloud data. Public clouds are owned by third parties. A private cloud is a proprietary system owned and operated by a single organization for its own use. A community cloud is a cloud that is owned and operated by a third party or jointly by members. Lastly, a hybrid cloud is a combination of a public cloud and a private cloud. A third party may have ownership over the public portion of the cloud while the organization has control over the private portion. Organizations can determine which data is stored in the public or private areas and can offer a private interface to public cloud resources.

Cloud storage methods include cloud backup, locally mapped cloud storage, cloud synchronization, and web-based cloud storage. Cloud backup archives data to a cloud storage resource. Locally mapped cloud storage is storage that is available to the local machine as if it were a disk in the machine but it actually resides in the cloud. Cloud synchronization repeats file creation, modification, and deletion to a cloud storage volume and all replicas, and web-based cloud storage is storage that can be accessed via a web browser.

Chapter Review Questions

1. A NAS would be best implemented for which of the following situations?

    A. Expanding the storage of a server

    B. Creating departmental shares to be accessed by many users

    C. Connecting multiple storage arrays to a large group of hosts

    D. Interface

2. After reviewing the requirements for a new storage array, you have recommended a mid-level single controller unit. Your manager asks why you chose a single controller. What rationale could you give?

    A. High availability

    B. Redundancy

    C. Manageability

    D. Price

3. What term describes a request made for data that exists in cache?

    A. Read hit

    B. Read ahead

    C. Write back

    D. Write through

4. Which of the following is the proper way to cable a dual-controller storage array in a SAN?

   A. Cable each controller to a separate switch.

   B. Cable both controllers to both switches.

   C. Cable both controllers directly to the HBAs on a host.

   D. Cable both controllers to the WAN ports on the router.

5. In which case would iSCSI be the preferred choice over FC?

   A. The company would like to achieve the highest possible data rates.

   B. The company wants to isolate the storage traffic from network traffic on a different physical medium.

   C. The company would like to present storage to many servers from a single storage array.

   D. The company wants to use its existing Ethernet infrastructure for the SAN.

6. Which of the following would *not* be used to connect a DAS to a host?

   A. eSATA

   B. iSCSI

   C. FC

   D. SAS

7. Which address would be used to connect to a NAS share?

   A. OE:52:6B:FF:9A:8C:DE:74

   B. https://www.snia.org/guidebook.php?user=admin

   C. \\Detroitstorage\Finance\Q3\

   D. ftp://ftp.storageplus.com

8. Which protocol would be used to create a share for a group of programmers using Linux?

   A. NFS

   B. TCP

   C. CIFS

   D. NetBIOS

9. Which type of cloud would you select if you currently have small storage needs that could potentially grow rapidly?

   A. Public cloud

   B. Private cloud

   C. Community cloud

   D. Hybrid cloud

Chapter Review Answers

1. **B** is correct. A NAS would be implemented to create departmental shares to be accessed by many users. NAS devices create and manage shares. These shares can be accessed by many devices and users. This differs from storage arrays, SANs, and DAS, which allocate a chunk of storage to a host.

   A, **C**, and **D** are incorrect. **A** is incorrect because a NAS is not used to expand the storage of a server. This is a function of a storage array. **C** is incorrect because a storage area network (SAN) is used to connect multiple storage arrays to a large group of hosts. Lastly, **D** is incorrect because the choice "interface" is too ambiguous to describe the usage of a NAS.

2. **D** is correct. From these four choices, price is the only reason why you would choose a single controller over a dual controller.

   A, **B**, and **C** are incorrect. High availability and redundancy are reasons why you would choose a dual over a single controller, and manageability might be slightly less for a single controller but not as much of an advantage as price.

3. **A** is correct. When a request is made for data that is in cache, it is known as a read hit. The storage array does not need to fetch the data from disk, and it can respond with the requested data immediately.

   B, **C**, and **D** are incorrect. These choices are all methods for managing cache.

4. **B** is correct. Cable both controllers to both switches. Dual controllers provide redundancy and can be used to balance the load of the storage array, so they should be cabled to prevent a failure of any piece of equipment in the data path (path from storage array to host) from interfering with the operations of the storage array. Cabling both controllers to both switches would allow the array to operate even if a switch, cable, and controller all failed at the same time.

   A, **C**, and **D** are incorrect. **A** is incorrect because cabling each controller to a separate switch would prevent against a single controller, single switch, or single cable failure, but not all at the same time. **C** is incorrect because cabling both controllers to host HBAs would be a DAS solution, and this question states that this is a SAN. **D** is incorrect because WAN ports would not be utilized in this situation. WAN ports may be required in situations where a remote storage array is a member of a SAN, but the array would not be cabled directly to the WAN. Storage networking components would reside between the storage array and the WAN.

5. **D** is correct. iSCSI would allow the company to use its existing Ethernet infrastructure, including switches and Ethernet cables.

   A, **B**, and **C** are incorrect. Options **A** and **B** would be reasons for using FC, and option **C** is an advantage of using a SAN in general.

6. **B** is correct. iSCSI is the only one in this list that would not be used to connect a DAS; iSCSI is used in a SAN.

   A, **C**, and **D** are incorrect. eSATA, FC, and SAS can all be used to connect a DAS to a host. SCSI can also be used, but this is different from iSCSI.

7. **C** is correct. A UNC path begins with \\ followed by a NAS name and then a slash and the share name and then another slash and any directories and subdirectories.
   A, B, and **D** are incorrect. **A** is a MAC address used to uniquely identify a device on a network at OSI layer 2. **B** is an HTTP Universal Resource Locator (URL) used to connect to a web site. **D** is an FTP URL used to connect to a file transfer site.

8. **A** is correct. NFS is used with Unix and Linux hosts.
   B, C, and **D** are incorrect. **B** is incorrect because TCP is a transport protocol, not a file system protocol. **C** is incorrect because although it is a file system protocol, it is used with Windows hosts. **D** is incorrect because it is also not a file system protocol.

9. **A** is correct. You should select a public cloud because it requires that you only pay for the amount you need, and public cloud storage can be increased quickly.
   B, C, and **D** are incorrect. **B** is incorrect because the organization would need to provision equipment and make a significant capital expenditure for the small current storage needs, and given the rapid growth potential, the system would be either more than is required, costing more than is necessary, or less than is required, resulting in a lack of space when it is urgently needed. **C** is incorrect because there is no mention of other companies or entities that are also seeking to implement such a solution with this company. **D** is incorrect because the small nature of the current data would not require dedicated in-house private cloud resources. The public cloud is more cost effective.

Storage Networking

In this chapter, you will learn how to
- Describe the functions and components of a Fibre Channel storage network
- Recognize the attributes and requirements for an iSCSI storage network
- Explain how storage can be accessed over a large distance

This chapter covers the two most common storage networking technologies, Fibre Channel (FC) and iSCSI, along with several FC hybrid protocols, namely, FCIP, iFCP, and FCoE. You will learn how devices communicate on these networks, including how devices are referenced, how the network is managed, and how to give priority to certain types of traffic. The chapter finishes with a discussion on the use of storage networks over a wide area network (WAN) and how bandwidth, latency, and flow control factor into the performance of storage over a WAN.

Fibre Channel Storage Network

Fibre Channel was originally developed as a general networking technology, but it found its niche in storage networking. It has been so successful as a storage networking technology that it has almost become synonymous with the term *storage area network*. As a robust protocol, it is made up of many components.

Components

It might surprise you to know how much goes into a storage network such as Fibre Channel. As you learned in Chapter 2, a storage network needs a way to reference other devices on the network, and FC does this through a World Wide Name (WWN). Many networks, FC included, offer a way to differentiate types of traffic; FC performs this through its service classes. Finally, FC references ports and services to establish connections and physical links by using addresses.

World Wide Name

A WWN is an 8-byte (64-bit) or 16-byte (128-bit) unique identifier for a network communication port on an FC network. Devices may display the WWN in a variety of formats. The WWN is typically represented by 16 or 32 hexadecimal characters similar to Ethernet MAC addresses. Hexadecimal characters are numbered from 0 to F, as compared to the decimal system, which is numbered from 0 to 9 or the binary 0 and 1. WWNs are usually grouped into two hexadecimal character segments that are delimited by a colon or dash, so you might see WWNs represented like this:

21-01-00-E0-8B-A5-26-6A

21:01:00:E0:8B:A5:26:6A

A portion of the WWN, called the *organizationally unique identifier* (OUI), is used to identify the manufacturer.

A World Wide Node Name (WWNN) is a WWN that is assigned to an FC device such as an FC switch or director during manufacturing. WWNNs are encoded into the hardware and cannot be changed. A World Wide Port Name (WWPN) is a WWN that is used to uniquely identify ports on an FC network. These ports are generated by software on the device and are based on the WWNN. A multiport adapter may have multiple FC ports, and each one would have a WWPN. The adapter itself would have a WWNN. Similarly, an FC switch would have a single WWNN but a WWPN for each switch port.

Service Classes

FC networks define five service classes that outline different delivery requirements for types of traffic assigned to that class. A fabric is the name of an FC network, and it provides communication between many nodes, the ability to look up devices, and management and security features. Nodes and fabrics are not required to support all classes, so you will need to confirm that your equipment supports the classes of service you want to implement. Table 3-1 lists the service classes, described in more detail next.

Class 1 service establishes a dedicated connection between host and storage device ports known as *node ports* or *N-ports* so that they will have use of the maximum bandwidth until the connection is terminated. N-ports that want to use the class 1 service will request it and, if accepted by the fabric, will have their data transmitted in the order it was received without flow control or error recovery taking place. This allows the ports to achieve maximum bandwidth, but higher-layer protocols will need to conduct error recovery to ensure reliable communication. Using a class 1 service will degrade the performance for other devices if they contend with the class 1 traffic.

Class 2 is a multicast service that delivers frames to multiple N-ports from a single source N-port. Multicast traffic requires fewer frames to be sent on the wire to send

Table 3-1	Service Class	Description
FC Service Classes	Class 1	Dedicated connection (maximum bandwidth)
	Class 2	Multicast
	Class 3	Connectionless
	Class 4	Virtual circuit
	Class 5	Not fully defined
	Class 6	Multicast with grouped failure notifications

identical data to many devices. Without multicasting, a node would need to construct separate frames for each N-port it is communicating with, so if it was communicating with 100 nodes, 100 frames would be sent on the link for the first frame, severely limiting the speed at which the device could transmit to each node. Multicasting takes one frame sent on the link and retransmits it to the other ports. This does not result in saturation on a switched fabric, because each port has its own dedicated connection. Furthermore, if multiple ports on another FC switch are to receive the traffic, only one frame is sent over the interswitch link (ISL), and then the receiving FC switch replicates the frame on each destination multicast port that it supports. The fabric does not automatically redeliver failed frames, but it does notify the source of any transmission failures, and it is the responsibility of the multicast source to retransmit failed frames. N-ports can be members of multiple multicast groups, and being a member of a multicast group does not inhibit an N-port from receiving nonmulticast traffic as well.

Class 3 is a connectionless service that transmits frames without delivery confirmation. This results in faster speed, but higher-level protocols are required to ensure reliable delivery.

Class 4 establishes a virtual circuit (VC) between two N-ports. The virtual circuit has a negotiated quality of service (QoS) and a dedicated portion of the N-port's full bandwidth. This is different from class 1 where the circuit receives the entire N-port bandwidth; 254 simultaneous circuits can be created on a single N-port.

Class 5 is neither fully defined nor implemented. Class 6 is another multicast service, but it differs from class 2 in that one signed frame notifies the sending devices of a failed frame instead of each device sending a failed frame message.

Addressing

Along with a WWPN, FC ports are given a dynamic address when they log into the fabric. This FC address is 24 bits long, and it is divided into three equal 8-bit parts, as shown in Figure 3-1.

The first part is the domain ID. A principal FC switch exists in each fabric. This FC switch is the one that has the lowest switch ID number and priority number configured by the administrator. This allows for a principal FC switch to be configured automatically or set manually if a priority value is assigned. The principal FC switch assigns a unique domain ID to each FC switch to identify it within the fabric. Of the 256 combinations available to an 8-bit domain ID, 239 are usable as domain IDs and 17 are reserved for fabric services that are used to maintain the operation of the fabric. Table 3-2 shows some of the fabric service IDs. The second part of the FC address is the area ID, which is used to represent a set of switch ports such as those that exist on a single blade in an FC

Figure 3-1
FC address

Domain ID	Area ID	Port ID
23 22 21 20 19 18 17 16	15 14 13 12 11 10 9 8	7 6 5 4 3 2 1 0

	ID	Service
Table 3-2 Fabric Service IDs	FFFFF5	Multicast server
	FFFFF6	Clock synchronization server
	FFFFF7	Security key distribution server
	FFFFF8	Alias server
	FFFFF9	QoS server
	FFFFFA	Management server
	FFFFFB	Time server
	FFFFFC	Name server
	FFFFFD	Fabric controller
	FFFFFE	Login server
	FFFFFF	Broadcast address

director or those in a module on a modular FC switch. The last part of the FC address is the port ID, and this portion of the address uniquely identifies the port.

NOTE A fabric can have a maximum of 15 million devices. This limitation is based on the maximum number of FC addresses that can exist. If you take the 239 domains and multiply them by the 256 possible areas and 256 possible ports in each area, you get 15,663,104. As you can imagine, having this many devices on a fabric would require that each area have the maximum number of ports and that each FC switch have the maximum number of areas.

The multicast server (FFFFF5) directs traffic to a group of N-ports known as a *multicast group*. Multicast traffic is a more efficient way to send the same data to many devices because fewer frames must be sent on the wire. Each N-port in the multicast group receives the same frames.

The alias server (FFFFF8) registers and unregisters aliases used for creating hunt and multicast groups. Hunt groups represent the group of ports associated with a single node, and multicast groups are the groups of ports designated to receive identical traffic. Each of these hunt or multicast groups receives an alias ID so that it can be uniquely identified on the fabric. Some traffic needs to be sent to all nodes. The broadcast address (FFFFFF) sends a transmission to all N-ports and NL-ports attached to the FC hub or switch.

The clock synchronization server (FFFFF6) keeps clocks consistent among devices by using a 48-bit reference clock. Periodically, the servers will check into the clock synchronization server by sending a clock synchronization request (CSR). The period between synchronization is a value between 1 microsecond and 60 seconds that is set by the clock synchronization server. The default value is every second. The clock synchronization server will respond to CSRs with a clock synchronization update (CSU) command containing its current clock value. Nodes then reset their clock to match the clock value in the CSU. Similarly, the time server (FFFFFB) time stamps messages and synchronizes communication between devices on the fabric.

The security key distribution server (FFFFF7) assigns and manages security keys used for encrypted traffic. This server knows the keys of nodes and, when requested, can send a secret key used for secure communication to the two ports that will be communicating. The secret key is encrypted separately for each port using the port's distribution key so that only that port can read the secret key. Other ports may require a specific level of service. The QoS server (FFFFF9) manages the quality of service to ensure minimum bandwidth and guaranteed end-to-end delay for virtual channels.

The management server (FFFFFA) distributes network management information. FC uses Simple Network Management Protocol (SNMP) for collecting information on FC devices, and the management server can monitor or modify the management information base (MIB) data. See Chapter 6 for more information on SNMP. Other data is recorded by the fabric controller. The fabric controller (FFFFFD) tracks state changes in attached node ports and distributes the changes to other fabric devices using registered state change notifications (RSCNs).

The name server (FFFFFC) registers names and manages node ports. Devices register their WWN with a name server when they connect to an FC switch in a fabric. Registered devices can query the name server to locate other devices on the fabric by WWN. The name server also maintains a table of WWN-to-FC address mappings.

The logon server (FFFFFE) processes logon requests. It provides details of the N-port to the name server and communicates back to the port to tell it that it has successfully logged into the fabric. The logon server assigns an N-port ID and tracks the association of the node to its N-port IDs.

Link

A link is the physical cabling between two ports. The link is bidirectional in the point-to-point and fabric topologies, consisting of one input and one output cable, discussed later in this chapter, whereas the link in the physical ring arbitrated loop topology is unidirectional with data traveling in one direction from node to node in the ring. Bidirectional links will use cables that have the connections crossed so that each output channel is connected to the input channel on the other end.

Connection

Whereas a link is physical, a connection is logical. A connection is established for communication between two nodes on the FC network. A connection relies upon physical links on the network, but it is at a higher level conceptually because it relies upon the logic of the protocol to establish the connection, including negotiating speeds, finding addresses of communicating parties, and forwarding frames to their destination.

Physical vs. Logical Connections

Physical connections differ from logical connections. The physical connection consists of the hardware components such as ports, cards, cables, and switches that form the connection between the source and destination. The logical connection is the establishment of communication between the source and destination. A physical connection provides the potential for a logical connection, just as a water pipe would provide a physical connection, but when water flows out of your faucet, it is like a logical connection that utilizes the physical link. (This example is not perfect since water is a physical thing you can touch or feel, but it should make the concept a bit more tangible.)

The terms *physical* and *logical* are used often in computer books, including this one. Physical is related to something you can feel and touch. Often, this is a piece of computer hardware such as a cable, network interface card, host bus adapter, or hard disk drive. Logical exists on top of physical components, and it is how a component or concept is interfaced with in software.

Protocols

Protocols are established ways of communicating, and FC, like its networking counterparts, has several protocols that outline how to send and receive data over an FC network. Each of these protocols transports SCSI commands over a SAN. FC has low overhead and can typically achieve 90 percent of its rated capacity of 2, 4, 8, or 16 Gbps. Four FC protocols can be used to connect FC devices in a SAN. The first, Fibre Channel Protocol (FCP), uses FC specifications for the entire protocol stack, but others, including Fibre Channel over IP (FCIP), Internet Fibre Channel Protocol (iFCP), and Fibre Channel over Ethernet (FCoE), combine elements of FC with Ethernet.

FCP

Fibre Channel Protocol (FCP) is one of the most popular high-performance storage protocols. FCP is defined with five layers, but only four of the layers are actually implemented in the technology. The layers are depicted in Figure 3-2.

The FC layers can help you understand the process of sending or receiving data. A device works from the top layer to the bottom layer when sending data. The bottom layer, FC-0, places the data on the physical media, and the receiving end then processes the data from the bottom layer up so that the same data sent is received.

FC-4 is the upper-layer protocol mapping. It is responsible for encapsulating upper-layer protocols, including Small Computer System Interface (SCSI), Intelligent Peripheral Interface (IPI), High Performance Parallel Interface (HIPPI), Asynchronous Transfer Mode (ATM), and Single Byte Command Code Set Mapping (SBCCS), on top of FC. FC-4 encompasses the fabric logon (FLOGI) and port logon (PLOGI) procedures, state notifications, and name services.

Figure 3-2
FC layers 0
through 4

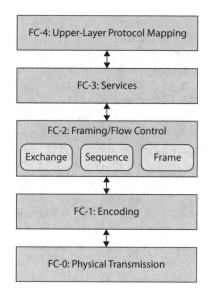

FC-4: Upper-Layer Protocol Mapping

FC-3: Services

FC-2: Framing/Flow Control

Exchange   Sequence   Frame

FC-1: Encoding

FC-0: Physical Transmission

FC-3 is known as the *services layer*, and it is designed to support striping, hunt groups, and spanning of multiple ports. Striping is a method where multiple N-ports are used to concurrently transmit data. The data is split into pieces much like striping on a disk, and each piece is sent through a different N-port. Hunt groups allow multiple ports to use the same alias address.

FC-2 breaks the data into smaller chunks called *frames* and performs flow control to ensure that devices receive data at a speed they can support. FC-2 is divided into three sublayers called *exchange*, *sequence*, and *frame*. The exchange sublayer defines a communication flow between partners that has been established but not yet terminated. For example, an exchange would be created when a host maps a file system on a remote logical unit. The partners include an Exchange Originator, which is the node that started the communication, and the Exchange Responder, which is the node that answered the originator's request. The exchanges are identified by the IDs of the originator (OX_ID) and the responder (RX_ID). The OX_ID is generated dynamically when the first frame in the exchange is sent to the responder, and the RX_ID is generated when the responder answers the first frame. Two nodes can have multiple exchanges as long as the OX_ID and RX_ID are unique.

Exchanges do not need to have data flowing through them since they can be active or passive. Active exchanges have current I/O associated with them, and passive exchanges are simply open without current I/O.

The sequence sublayer divides an exchange into smaller segments that can comprise such things as a single file or a database transaction. Sequences contain the data traveling in only one direction, from the originator to the receiver or from the receiver to the originator. A single file transfer within an exchange might have four or more sequences. The first sequence is the request for the file from the originator to the responder. This would be followed by another sequence acknowledging receipt for the request from the responder to the originator. Another sequence from the responder to the originator would contain the file, and then a last sequence from the originator to the responder would confirm the receipt of the file. All of these sequences would be contained in a single exchange. A sequence ID (SEQ_ID) is placed in each frame in the sequence, and a sequence count (SEQ_CNT) identifies individual frames within the sequence. This brings us to the third sublayer, frames.

The frame sublayer is responsible for packaging data or control information into smaller pieces called *frames*. Data frames contain a portion of the data, also known as a *payload*. Control frames contain instructions or responses such as acknowledgements (ACKs) of frame receipt, link response frames indicating that the node is too busy to receive data or that it has rejected data, and changes to the way frames are processed called *link command frames*. Figure 3-3 shows an exchange for reading a file.

FC-1 encodes the data so that it can be transmitted efficiently on the link. It uses the 8b/10b encoding method, which represents 8 bits of data as 10 bits of data. The encoding scheme ensures that a signal change from a set of 0s to a set of 1s occurs at least every 5 bits to ensure that the sending and receiving devices are synchronized; 8b/10b also has a uniform distribution of 1s and 0s that allows for lower direct currents to be used in the physical layer (FC-0).

FC-0 is responsible for the physical transmission of electrical or light impulses across a wire depending on whether copper or fiber-optic media is used. Data is sent serially to achieve high transfer rates. Distances and speeds are governed by the hardware utilized at this layer, with fiber-optic cables achieving higher speeds and distances than copper. The different types of fiber and copper cables are discussed in Chapter 4.

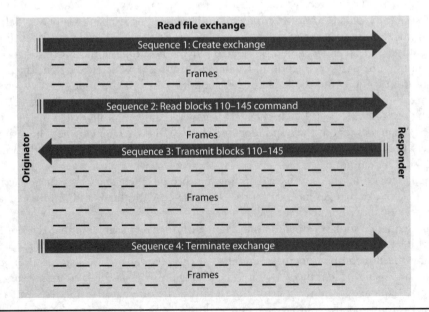

Figure 3-3   FC read file exchange

FCIP

Fibre Channel over IP (FCIP) is a protocol that sends FC protocol data over an IP network. FCIP is implemented with two or more FCIP-equipped switches that have connections to both the FCP and TCP/IP networks. The TCP/IP connection imitates the port used to connect two FC switches, known as an *E-port* or *expansion port*. FCIP calls this port a *virtual* E-port. To the FCP network, the virtual E-port can be used like any other ISL. Similar to physical E-ports, virtual E-ports are connected to a single destination, but multiple virtual E-ports can be port channeled for increased reliability and speed. Multiple virtual E-ports must be used to link multiple destination networks. FCP frames are sent to the virtual E-port that packages them inside TCP/IP packets in a process known as *encapsulation*. These packets traverse the LAN or WAN like any other TCP/IP packets. At a destination FCIP switch, the FCP frames are extracted from the TCP/IP packets and then dropped onto the destination FCP network.

 EXAM TIP FCIP is primarily used to connect remote FC SANs together over an IP wide area network.

The beauty of FCIP is that, besides the FCIP-enabled switches, other SAN devices do not need to have knowledge of FCIP to communicate with the rest of the fabric even though the fabric is separated. FCP devices see it as one big fabric, with the entire connection between SANs appearing as a single ISL even though this connection may traverse many routers and links in the process. FCIP also supports encrypting traffic using IP Security (IPSec). Figure 3-4 shows a host and storage device connected to FC

Figure 3-4
FC traffic
tunneled over
IP with FCIP

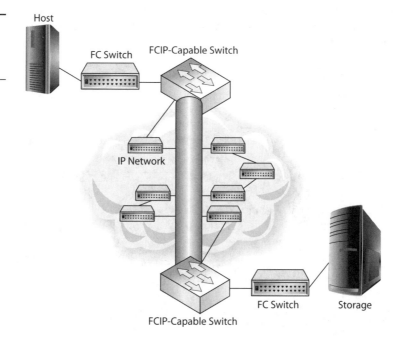

networks that are joined together over an IP network using FCIP. Note how the link between the two FCIP-capable switches would appear as one link to the FC network when it actually traverses eight links consisting of seven IP devices and two FCIP-capable switches.

iFCP

Internet Fibre Channel Protocol (iFCP) was originally designed to translate FCP traffic from end nodes onto a TCP/IP network and to use the TCP/IP network for the transmission of all storage traffic. However, iFCP equipment and FCP HBAs are more expensive than IP NICs, so iSCSI has been favored over iFCP. Figure 3-5 depicts an iFCP network. iFCP has seen practical implementation as a gateway similar to FCIP. It supports IPSec encryption for increased security, and multiple iFCP links can be grouped together to increase the bandwidth available for interswitch communication in what is known as a *port channel.*

FCoE

The Fibre Channel over Ethernet (FCoE) protocol uses the FC-4 upper-layer protocol mapping and FC-3 services layer, but Ethernet performs the FC-2 and FC-1 functions through the Data Link LLC sublayer and Data Link MAC sublayers. FCoE runs on Category 5 cabling instead of optical cabling like FCP does. FCoE is not routable, so it is suitable only on networks where the storage and hosts are on the same VLAN or network segment. FCoE is different from FCIP in that it does not use TCP/IP. Figure 3-6 compares the layers of FCP, FCIP, iFCP, FCoE, and iSCSI.

An FCoE Forwarder (FCF) is a device that has the necessary services and ports to operate as an FCoE switch. FCFs have an FCoE controller and MAC address for one FCoE port or multiple ports if FCoE bridging is used. FCFs also support FCoE VLANs. The FCoE controller creates virtual ports for FCoE VLANS using the FCoE Initialization Protocol (FIP).

Figure 3-5
iFCP network

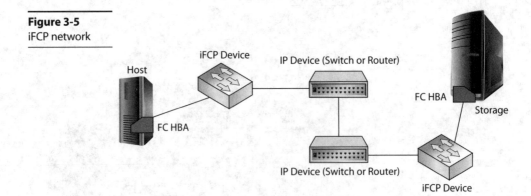

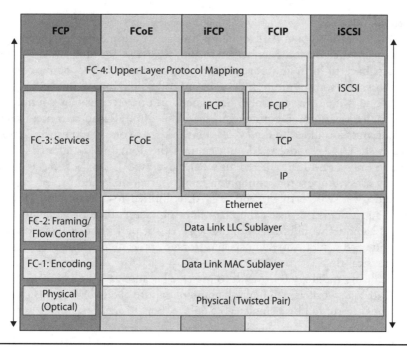

FCP	FCoE	iFCP	FCIP	iSCSI

Figure 3-6 Comparing storage networking protocol layers

Topologies

Three FC topologies define how FC devices are connected to one another. FC point-to-point is used to directly connect two devices, while FC arbitrated loop and FC switched fabric are used to connect many devices together.

Point-to-Point

The FC point-to-point (FC-P2P) topology is a connection between two devices, and it is primarily used with DAS systems as an alternative to SCSI. FC-P2P can connect two devices over a distance of 10,000 meters (10 km), whereas SCSI is limited to 25 meters. Figure 3-7 depicts a host and a storage array in an FC-P2P topology.

Figure 3-7
FC-P2P topology

Host   Storage

Arbitrated Loop

The FC arbitrated loop (FC-AL) topology connects multiple devices together using a ring. This means each device is connected to another device forming a chain that eventually connects back to form an unbroken circle. Each device in the loop is connected to two neighbors, and communication flows in only one direction, so one link is always the sender and one is the receiver. Only one sender and one receiver may communicate on the FC-AL at a time, so this is considered a shared medium. Resource contention increases as more devices are added to the FC-AL network, and you should expect performance to drop as well. FC-AL addresses do not contain the domain ID and area ID. Instead, they contain only an 8-bit number. This would give FC-AL 256 possible addresses, but FC-AL only uses numbers that contain an even number of 1s and 0s, leaving 127 with one reserved for a switch. In the end, FC-AL is limited to 126 devices. However, the number of addresses is not really the main limiting factor since an implementation approaching 126 nodes would be far from ideal given the performance loss each new node creates. Figure 3-8 depicts several hosts and storage arrays in an FC-AL topology configured as a physical ring.

A physical ring topology is difficult to manage because each link between two nodes on the FC-AL network is a potential point of failure. Network connectivity for all nodes can be interrupted by a single cable failure. For this reason, FC-AL is commonly

Figure 3-8
Physical ring
FC-AL topology

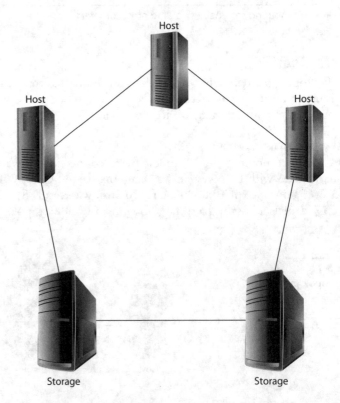

Figure 3-9
Physical star
FC-AL topology

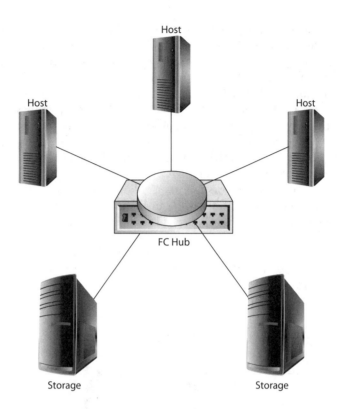

implemented using hubs. Each node on the network is cabled to a port on one or more hubs. The hubs create a loop between the ports in the switch and links between switches while bypassing ports that are not in use or in a failed state. Another description for this is physical star, logical ring. The physical cabling looks like a star with a central device and many other devices connected to it, but data flows logically like a ring with each device passing the data to the next one in the chain until it reaches its destination. Figure 3-9 depicts several hosts and storage arrays in an FC-AL topology configured as a physical star.

FC-AL is rarely used to connect hosts and storage devices, but you may encounter it within a storage array where few back-end ports are available to connect several disk enclosures or in situations where a guaranteed maximum response time is necessary for all components.

Switched Fabric
The FC fabric, also known as FC switched fabric (FC-SW), is by far the most common FC topology and the one you will want to be most familiar with. The term *fabric* is used to describe a network topology where components pass data to each other through interconnecting switches. The word *fabric* is used as a metaphor to illustrate the idea that network components and their relationships form lines that weave back and forth resembling a piece of cloth.

In a switched fabric, storage devices and hosts are connected to one another using switches. Switches are similar to hubs in that they are a physical star. Devices are connected to ports on the switches that enable communication between devices. However, FC-SW differs from FC-AL using hubs in that communication between ports is isolated from other ports. The medium is not shared among the devices, so each communication between the sender and the receiver can use the maximum available bandwidth when connecting over the same switch. FC-SW fabrics scale out by adding more switches connected together using ISLs, and thus connections that cross over ISLs will share the ISL with other communication crossing that ISL. Figure 3-10 depicts several hosts and storage arrays in an FC-SW topology.

The FC-SW topology supports millions of devices as compared to FC-AL's 126 devices. The scope of a fabric can be defined by the number of tiers it contains, which is determined by the number of ISLs between the two furthest points on the fabric. Tiers are important because they impact the amount of time it takes to complete fabric reconfiguration. Reconfiguration happens when devices are added to or removed from the fabric. FC uses registered state change notifications to inform FC devices of additions and removals. N-ports and NL-ports can register to receive state change notifications, but they are not required to do so.

Figure 3-10
FC-SW topology

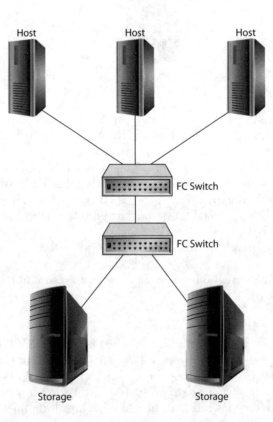

Redundant Fabric

A redundant fabric is one that has separate interconnecting devices such as switches and directors but the same end nodes. The redundant fabric is used to prevent a loss in communication because of fabric reconfiguration or a loss of an entire fabric.

 NOTE Topologies that are fully redundant, meaning that every node is connected to every other node, are known as a *mesh*.

ISL

The interswitch link is used to connect two FC switches in an FC fabric. The ports comprising the ISL need to be E-ports, a specific port designed for communication between FC switches. Communication crossing the ISL will contend for available bandwidth, so ISLs can be a primary limiting factor in FC SAN performance. You can achieve the best performance by reducing the number of ISLs that need to be crossed.

Port Channel

Multiple ISLs between FC switches can be grouped together into a port channel to increase the bandwidth available for interswitch communication. Traffic traversing the port channel is distributed among the ISLs to take advantage of the bandwidth of each ISL concurrently. Port channeling can greatly increase the performance of traffic traversing multiple FC switches at the cost of using more ports on each switch. Figure 3-11 shows four ISLs that have been combined into one port channel. The number of ISLs in a port channel should be determined by the sum of the bandwidth required by hosts that need to connect to a storage device on another FC switch. In some cases, it may be advantageous to set a bandwidth threshold on the port channel so that it does not consume more than a ceiling limit. This is typically used to reserve bandwidth so that application performance stays the same when one or more ISLs in the port channel go offline. It may be more advantageous to upgrade the FC switch to a larger capacity device if it is determined that many ISL links will be necessary to

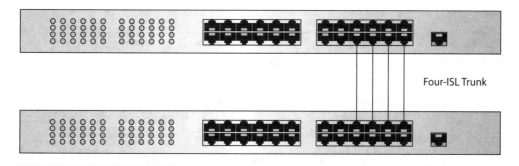

Figure 3-11 Port channel created with four ISLs

support SAN traffic patterns. Another option would be to move some hosts to the same switch as storage devices or to a switch with a larger port channel to conserve FC ports. The remaining hosts would connect to switches with smaller port channels or even a single ISL.

 EXAM TIP Port channels must be created between a single pair of devices, and each ISL in the port channel must run at the same speed.

Trunking

Trunking is used with virtual SANs (VSANs). VSANs are a subset of ports in an FC fabric that are segmented from the rest of the fabric. This is typically performed for security reasons or to reduce overall traffic on the SAN through VSAN partitioning. Trunking allows data from multiple VSANs to traverse the same ISL. Trunks may be used with port channels to provide redundancy in case a single ISL fails and to better aggregate bandwidth. If a single VSAN needs a lot of bandwidth, it can utilize multiple ISLs, but at other times it may not need that much bandwidth, so the bandwidth will be available to other VSANs. This is an improvement over mapping a single VSAN to an ISL because it offers better utilization of ISL.

Port Types

FC ports have different uses that are described by one or more letters. They are compared in Table 3-3, and each is described in more detail in the following sections.

N-port

N-ports, or "node" ports, are used on end devices such as a server, workstation, or tape disk or storage array in an FC network. If the network is a tree, the end devices would be the leaves on the tree, and in fact, sometimes end devices are referred to as *leaves*. These devices include hosts such as servers or workstations and storage devices such as storage arrays, tape drives, or network attached storage. N-ports are given an ID called the *N-port ID* by the fabric logon server when the port first becomes active on the fabric. N-ports are initialized in three steps. First, the N-port sends a fabric logon request called

Table 3-3	Type	Alternative Name	Topology
FC Port Types	N-port	Node port	FC-P2P, FC-SW
	F-port	Fabric port	FC-SW
	E-port	Expansion port	FC-SW
	NL-port	Node loop port	FC-AL
	FL-port	Fabric loop port	FC-AL
	G-port	General port	FC-SW
	U-port	Universal port	FC-AL

Figure 3-12
N-ports, F-ports,
and E-ports in
FC-SW topology

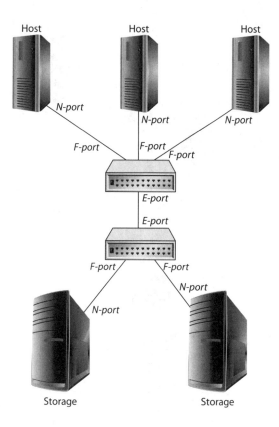

an FLOGI to the login server (address FFFFFE) to obtain a valid address. It then registers the address with the name server by sending a port logon request called a PLOGI to the name server (address FFFFFC). Finally, the N-port sends a state change registration (SCR) to the fabric controller (address FFFFFD) to register the state change notification.

F-port

F-ports, or "fabric" ports, reside on an FC switch, and they connect to N-ports. F-ports can receive frames from N-ports so that the frames can be switched to their destination, and they deliver frames addressed to the N-port ID they are connected to.

E-port

E-ports, or "expansion" ports, are used to create a connection between two switches known as an ISL. E-ports connect to other E-ports. When data is received on an F-port for a node on a different switch, the frame is sent over one or more ISLs to the switch that has the destination N-port ID. Figure 3-12 shows the location of N-ports, F-ports, and E-ports in an FC-SW topology.

NL-port

NL-ports, or "node loop" ports, are used to connect nodes that are members of an FC-AL ring. Figure 3-13 shows the location of NL-ports in an FC-AL topology.

Figure 3-13
NL-ports in
FC-AL topology

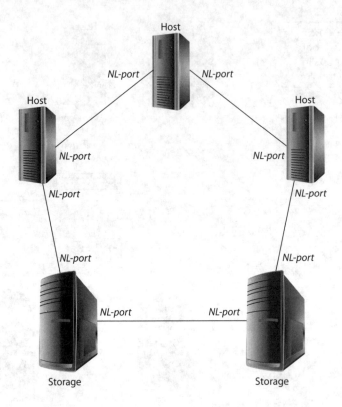

FL-port

FL-ports, or "fabric loop" ports, are used to connect to NL ports when hubs are used in the FC-AL physical star, logical ring implementation. Figure 3-14 shows the location of NL-ports and FL-ports when using a hub in a physical star implementation of the FC-AL topology.

G-port

G-ports, or "generic" ports, can function as either an F-port or an E-port in FC-SW topologies. Many modern switches are equipped with G-ports that can detect whether they are connected to a node or a switch and configure themselves automatically as an F-port to connect to nodes or an E-port to connect to another switch.

U-port

U-ports, or "universal" ports, are like generic ports in that they can function as either an NL-port or an FL-port. U-ports are used in the FC-AL topology.

Tools

Several tools such as port error counters, fcping, name servers, and rescans can help in managing, maintaining, and troubleshooting an FC network.

Figure 3-14
NL-ports and
FL-ports in
FC-AL physical
star topology

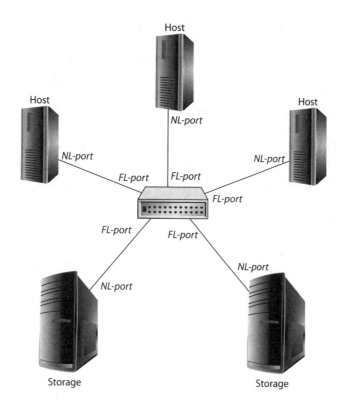

Port Error Counters

Port error counters are useful for identifying problems with FC switches, host bus adapters (HBAs), or cables and for diagnosing congestion or connectivity problems. Error counters can be viewed on devices with FC ports, but each vendor can choose to implement the counters they deem suitable for their device. More counters may be available for some equipment such as switches than for other equipment like HBAs. Counters for HBAs in storage arrays may have more counters available than those installed in a host, and those counters are typically accessed via a storage array management utility or via a command-line connection to the array such as Secure Shell (SSH). Port error counters on switches can be viewed from the switch management utility or command line. Additionally, counters may be sent to a central collection device using protocols such as Simple Network Management Protocol (SNMP). Some counters that may be available for your device are as follows:

- **Bad frames**   Some frames are received without an end of frame (EOF) or with one that is unreadable. This can be caused by a loss of synchronization on the link. Switches will add an EOF normal invalid or abort to the end of the frame, causing the destination address to drop the frame.

- **Decode errors**   FC uses the 8b/10b encoding scheme, which is organized into words made up of 8 bytes represented at 10 bits each. As discussed earlier, 8b/10b initiates a signal change from a set of 0s to a set of 1s at least every 5 bits, and the number of 0s and 1s is uniform. Words that do not have a signal change at least every 5 bits, or words that do not have uniform 0s and 1s, are invalid and result in a decode error. A high number of decode errors could point to a faulty cable or port.

- **Fabric busy**   Fabric busy events are generated when the FC fabric sends out notifications that higher-priority class traffic is using the link.

- **Invalid CRC**   The cyclic redundancy check (CRC) is a mathematical value that is computed based on the contents of the frame. It is compared when frames are received to determine whether the contents changed in transit. If the CRC differs, it is termed invalid, and this counter increases.

- **Invalid destination address**   This error occurs when an incorrect source ID or destination ID is included in a frame. Invalid source addresses are used in spoofing attacks, and invalid destination IDs are used in denial-of-service attacks.

- **Short frames**   Short frames are those that are less than the minimum frame size of 24 bytes.

fcping

The fcping command is used to issue an FC Extended Link Service (ELS) request to a port or pair of ports. Ports that receive an ELS request will respond, letting the user know that it is active and able to communicate. If a device fails to respond to fcping, it may be unavailable. This could be the result of a port or cable failure, software failure, or an administrator taking the port offline. Some devices may be configured to not respond to ELS messages, so it is important to not assume that the device is unavailable just from the result of fcping. Check the port status lights as well. You can do this by physically looking at the FC switch or HBA or by viewing the port status in a switch's command-line or web administrative console.

Running the fcping command from an FC switch to WWN 21:01:00:E0:8B:A5:26:6A would produce the following output:

```
storageplusswitch:admin> fcping 21:01:00:E0:8B:A5:26:6A
Pinging 21:01:00:E0:8B:A5:26:6A [fd1091] with 12 bytes of data:
received reply from 21:01:00:E0:8B:A5:26:6A: 12 bytes time:1194 usec
received reply from 21:01:00:E0:8B:A5:26:6A: 12 bytes time:997 usec
received reply from 21:01:00:E0:8B:A5:26:6A: 12 bytes time:1222 usec
received reply from 21:01:00:E0:8B:A5:26:6A: 12 bytes time:1035 usec
received reply from 21:01:00:E0:8B:A5:26:6A: 12 bytes time:902 usec
5 frames sent, 5 frames received, 0 frames rejected, 0 frames timeout
Round-trip min/avg/max = 902/1070/1222 usec
```

The first line shows the prompt storageplusswitch:admin>, which indicates that you are logged onto a switch called storageplusswitch under the username admin. The fcping command follows the prompt. The first line after the command confirms you are fcpinging WWN 21:01:00:E0:8B:A5:26:6A, which has an FC-ID of fd1091.

Each ELS reply is then given along with the time it took to receive a reply. The last line of the output shows the statistics beginning with the shortest (min), average (avg), and longest (max) ELS reply in the set. The output of this command shows that all five out of five pings were sent, and ELS replies were received for each of the five, with the shortest response taking 902 microseconds, the average 1,070, and the longest 1,222.

This example is given for a basic command, but fcping can include other variables as well. The syntax for the command may be implemented differently by different switch vendors or software packages, so this book will cover options but not the exact syntax. Some fcping options include specifying the number of ELS messages to send, the interval in milliseconds between ELS messages, or the ELS message size. WWN may also be substituted for the FC-ID.

Name Server

Name servers are important to the operation of an FC fabric because they map the WWN and FC port addresses. Name servers can be queried to find the WWN and port for a node on the FC network, which can be useful when troubleshooting FC network issues. Nodes are referenced by WWN often in software, but it may be necessary to view port error counters for that WWN to isolate connectivity or performance issues by querying the name server. Connectivity problems can arise if the name server does not have information on a WWN, so the name server can be used to verify that an entry exists for the troubled node.

Rescan

Hosts connected to a SAN may have storage allocated to them by storage arrays on the SAN. The provisioning process is discussed in Chapter 6. In some cases, the storage may not immediately be seen by the host, and other times storage that has been available might not be visible in the operating system. A rescan will search for storage so that it can be used on the host.

There are four steps for performing a rescan in Linux. You will need to know which HBA is connected to the SAN that contains the storage, and then you can determine the host number for that HBA by issuing the following command:

```
ls /sys/class/fc_host/
```

The result of this command will be the word *host* followed by a number that you will use in the next steps. The second step is to send a Loop Initialization Protocol (LIP) rescan on the FC bus using the following command:

```
Echo 1 > /sys/class/fc_host/HOST/issue_lip
```

The host will scan the bus looking for storage and update the system's SCSI layer with any new or removed devices. This may cause delays or timeouts in I/O operations, so use care when issuing the command. The command takes time to complete, and you may be presented with a command prompt before the scan has fully completed. Give the command 15 to 20 seconds before issuing other commands just to be safe. Use the host number obtained in the previous step in place of the word *host* in the command.

Next, perform a rescan on the HBA with this command and add any new devices found; it will not remove any devices:

```
Echo - - - > /sys/class/scsi_host/HOST/scan
```

Finally, check to see whether the storage is available with this command:

```
/proc/scsi/scsi
```

 NOTE Linux commands may vary based on distribution and version.

Microsoft Windows manages storage within the Server Manager console. Open Server Manager by clicking Start, right-clicking Computer, and selecting Manage. Expand the storage container. Right-click Disk Management, as depicted in Figure 3-15, and select Rescan Disks. New storage will appear in the bottom pane.

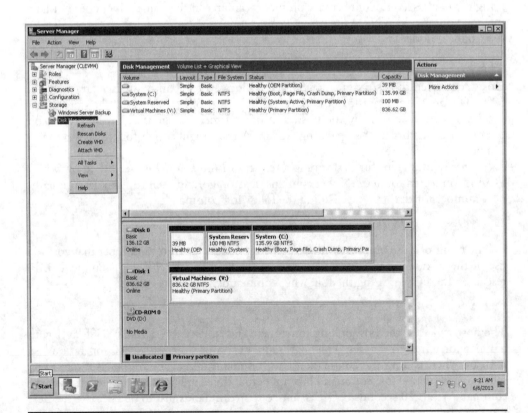

Figure 3-15 Disk Management within Server Manager

iSCSI Storage Network

Internet Small Computer System Interface (iSCSI) is a protocol that sends SCSI disk commands over an IP network. iSCSI as a storage networking technology offers cost-conscious companies an excellent solution at a much lower cost than FC. iSCSI is most commonly deployed over Gigabit Ethernet, utilizing Category 5 (Cat5) cabling, Gigabit Ethernet switches, and network interface cards (NICs) such as those used in computer networks.

Block Mode

Block mode is a method for accessing storage that is used by disk drivers such as SCSI. Block mode requires few operations to access disks as compared with protocols such as FTP or CIFS/SMB.

Initiator

An iSCSI initiator is a device that creates a session by sending commands to a target. Hosts that connect to an iSCSI network require an initiator to connect to iSCSI logical unit numbers (LUNs). Software initiators are implemented as part of an operating system such as Microsoft Windows or Linux. Hardware initiators, on the other hand, are built into iSCSI host bus adapters, and they do not rely upon the OS to structure and process iSCSI commands. This can reduce some of the load on the host system. Hardware initiators are not an option when using NICs, so this is something that will need to be considered when deciding whether to utilize NICs or iSCSI HBAs.

Target

iSCSI targets await commands from iSCSI initiators. LUNs are located on targets, and initiators interface with the LUNs by sending commands to the target. iSCSI storage arrays are equipped with software or hardware that manages targets, but there is software available for servers and workstations that allows local drives and folders to be allocated to other devices on the network as an iSCSI target.

Initiators must map targets in order to start using their storage. Targets can be located manually by IP address and port. By default, iSCSI uses TCP ports 860 and 3260. Manual target mapping may be fine for small, simple environments, but it becomes necessary to use a method of target discovery in larger and more complex environments where there may be many targets and initiators.

Service Location Protocol

The Service Location Protocol (SLP) and Internet Storage Name Server (iSNS) both provide a method for initiators to discover storage targets. These systems utilize a server that provides name-to-address resolution. SLP is a simple-to-implement client-server protocol that consists of user agents, service agents, and discovery agents. Discovery agents retain a list of targets and their resources, and they make this list available to user agents that reside on initiators. Service agents reside on targets, and they register their resources with the discovery agent or advertise their resources if a discovery agent is not present.

Security is maintained through a list of initiators that are authorized to connect to a target. This list is known as a *scope entry*. SLP resources are referenced by a service universal resource locator (URL) made up of the target IP address, port, and friendly name. For example, the resource named MainDatabaseLogs on IP address 192.168.5.56 using port 3260 would have the following service URL: 192.168.5.56:3260/MainDatabaseLogs. SLP is suitable for small iSCSI networks, but it does not scale well with larger implementations because of the large amount of administrative data such as logon requests that must traverse the iSCSI network.

Internet Storage Name Server

iSNS allows for initiators to discover iSCSI targets. iSNS can retain target information for both iSCSI- and FC-attached devices over iFCP gateways in iSNS databases. iSNS databases can reside on iSCSI switches or on software-based iSNS databases such as those bundled in Linux, Solaris, and Microsoft Windows servers. iSNS databases can be distributed among many iSCSI switches to allow for larger scalability. iSNS servers on targets register their resources and state changes with SNS databases, which initiators running iSNS clients can query to find available targets.

 EXAM TIP   iSNS is the predominant method for iSCSI target discovery.

iSNS URLs begin with iscsi:// followed by the target name, port, resource name, and then an optional WWPN that is used when connecting to FC resources. The following URL would be used to connect to an iSCSI resource called Logs on the MainDatabase .Test.com device using port 3260: iscsi://MainDatabase.Test.com:3260/Logs. If the resource was on iFCP, the URL would be structured as follows: iscsi://MainDatabase .Test.com/Logs?WWPN=F3EB56A914.

iSNS improves on SLP by adding state change notification alerts that inform initiators of target availability. iSNS databases automatically remove entries after a period of inactivity so that stale records do not remain in the database. Targets must periodically update the iSNS database to ensure that their resources are not removed because of inactivity. Security and scalability are provided through discovery domains (DDs). DDs contain targets and imitators that are allowed to connect to one another. Initiators can belong to many DDs so that they can connect to multiple resources. Initiators and targets do not belong to any zones by default, so new initiators are prevented from connecting to resources, and newly provisioned targets are prevented from being accessed until they are placed into a zone. DDs also restrict target discovery information that flows through the iSCSI network to a smaller set of initiators and targets, which allows the iSNS protocol to scale better in larger environments.

Ethernet Switching

Traffic traverses an iSCSI network via Ethernet switches. Companies can use existing Ethernet switches for iSCSI traffic if they want and avoid the cost of purchasing additional Ethernet switches. This also decreases the management cost of the SAN because another technology (and its management interfaces) does not need to be introduced into the network.

It is common to use a virtual local area network (VLAN) to separate iSCSI traffic on Ethernet switches from computer network traffic. VLANs are created by assigning a VLAN ID to each Ethernet switch that will contain ports in the VLAN. Each port is then associated with the VLAN ID. These ports will not be able to communicate with ports that have a different VLAN ID unless a router is used to route between the VLANs. iSCSI traffic can be isolated from the rest of the network with VLANs, which protects iSCSI traffic from being observed by other hosts on the network and isolates the iSCSI network cards from broadcast traffic originating from the computer network. Ports used to connect Ethernet switches together need to be configured as port channel ports in order to send VLAN traffic to another Ethernet switch. These port channel ports tag the traffic with a VLAN ID so that the receiving Ethernet switch will know which VLAN to place the traffic on when it arrives.

Jumbo Frame

Storage administrators can modify port settings on an Ethernet switch to improve the speed of iSCSI operations. Jumbo frames can boost the performance of the iSCSI network. Jumbo frames are Ethernet frames that are larger than 1,500 bytes. Jumbo frames can be as large as 9,000 bytes. Ethernet frames consist of header information and data. Headers include such things as source and destination MAC addresses, protocol information, and flags for supported settings. An Ethernet frame header consists of 38 bytes and is depicted in Figure 3-16.

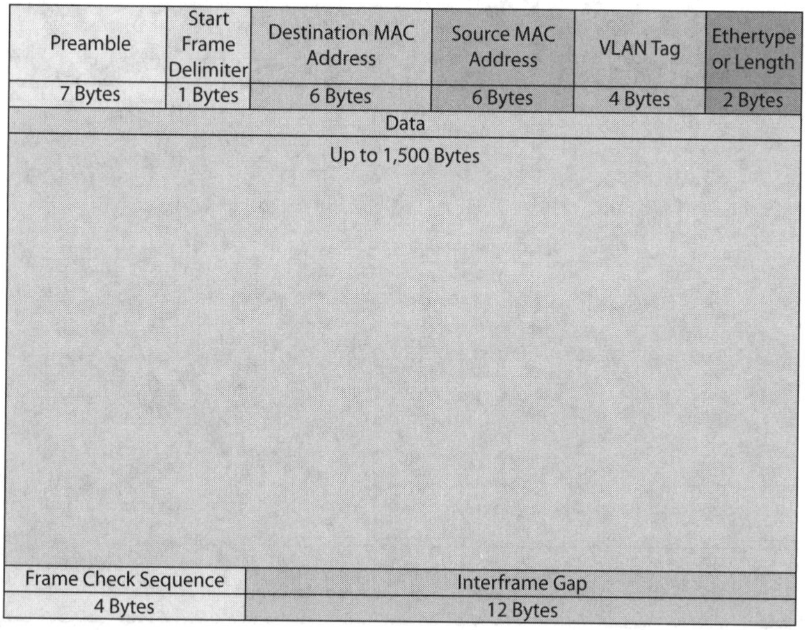

Preamble	Start Frame Delimiter	Destination MAC Address	Source MAC Address	VLAN Tag	Ethertype or Length
7 Bytes	1 Bytes	6 Bytes	6 Bytes	4 Bytes	2 Bytes
Data					
Up to 1,500 Bytes					

Frame Check Sequence	Interframe Gap
4 Bytes	12 Bytes

Figure 3-16 Ethernet frame

It would take 14 standard Ethernet frames to transfer a 20,000-byte file incurring 532 bytes of overhead, but it would take only three jumbo frames to transfer the same file incurring only 114 bytes of overhead. In this example, overhead was reduced by almost 80 percent, but the overhead consisted of only 3 percent of the total data transferred, so the total frame size savings are still rather small overall. However, each frame results in processing that must occur on the sending, receiving, and intermediary units, so a reduction in the number of frames will also reduce the amount of processing required to segment, forward, and reassemble frames. Figure 3-17 shows a jumbo frame. Jumbo frames must be supported on Ethernet switches and NICs or HBAs that are connected to the Ethernet switches in order for a connection to be maintained.

Baby-Jumbo Frame

Baby-jumbo frames, also called *baby giants*, are frames between 1,500 and 9,500 bytes. They are used for services such as the Layer 2 Tunneling Protocol (L2TP), virtual private network (VPN), Multiprotocol Label Switching (MPLS), and Tagged Quality of Service (QoS) frames.

Ethernet Features

Since iSCSI is based on Ethernet, it is good to understand how Ethernet works as a networking technology and how the local area network (LAN), metropolitan area network (MAN), and wide area network (WAN) function. iSCSI can operate over a LAN,

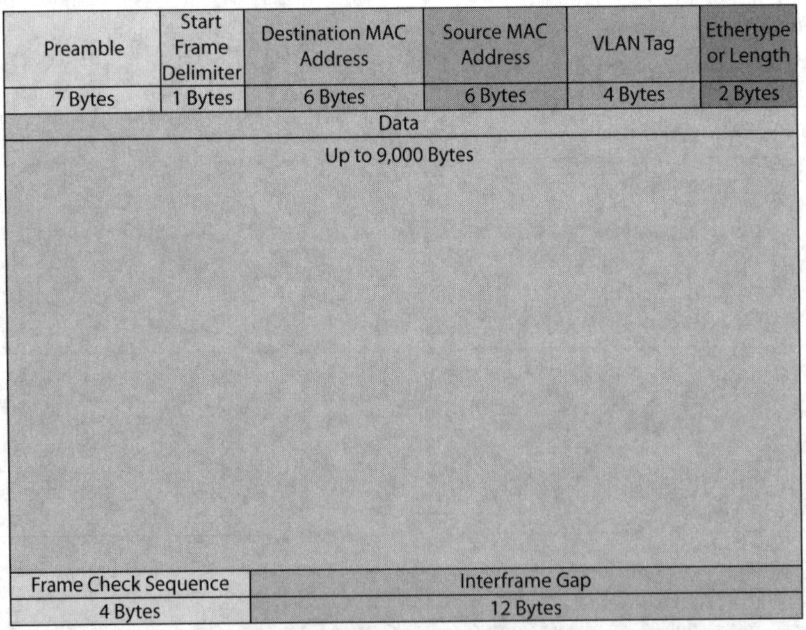

Preamble	Start Frame Delimiter	Destination MAC Address	Source MAC Address	VLAN Tag	Ethertype or Length
7 Bytes	1 Bytes	6 Bytes	6 Bytes	4 Bytes	2 Bytes

Data					
Up to 9,000 Bytes					

Frame Check Sequence	Interframe Gap
4 Bytes	12 Bytes

Figure 3-17 Ethernet jumbo frame

MAN, or WAN depending on the organization's requirements. Ethernet devices are classified based on the speed they support. For example, Ethernet runs at 10 Mbps, while 100-Mbps Ethernet networks are known as Fast Ethernet. Gigabit Ethernet runs at 1,000 Mbps and is most commonly seen today. All flavors of Ethernet have higher overhead than Fibre Channel. Ethernet can typically achieve 50 to 85 percent of its rated capacity of 10 Mbps, 100 Mbps, 1 Gbps, or 10 Gbps, while FC can consistently achieve 90 percent of its rated capacity of 2, 4, 8, or 16 Gbps.

LAN

LANs connect computers in a single site. LANs are used for file sharing, printer sharing, running applications from servers, and many more activities that may be taken for granted at a typical organization. Before LANs, data had to be transported using a disk, such as a floppy disk, to another machine in order to be shared, and printers were often connected to each machine that needed to print on a regular basis, or users transported documents to a device that could print. The same was true for scanners.

MAN

A MAN is a larger network than a LAN. MANs extend to two or more sites within a metropolitan area such as a city or county. For example, large hospitals or universities have MANs that connect their various buildings together so that applications, file servers, and network resources such as domain controllers or DHCP servers do not need to be housed and supported in each building. Each building has its own LAN, and all the buildings together form a MAN. The LAN at each location will typically contain Ethernet switches that connect the various devices together and then a high-bandwidth link to other buildings. The MAN may be hierarchical where buildings connect to a central building that houses shared resources, or they may be configured as a mesh where many buildings connect to one another so that if one link fails, multiple other redundant paths connect the buildings. Some buildings may be in different areas of the city, but they are still part of the same MAN.

WAN

A WAN is a network that connects geographically distant locations. The Internet is the most common WAN because it connects people from around the world. Organizations will set up WAN links to connect remote offices so that the resources in one office, such as file servers, applications, or storage, can be shared with other locations.

Class of Service

Class of service (CoS) is a way of prioritizing types of traffic. It is specified as part of IEEE P802.1p. As an Ethernet technology, CoS can be implemented on lower-cost Ethernet switches with CoS support rather than relying on layer 3 switches or slower and more expensive routers to prioritize traffic. CoS operates as the Data Link layer (layer 2) and is contained within Ethernet frames. The 802.1q Ethernet header contains a 3-bit field that can specify one of eight CoS levels ranging from 0 to 7, with 0 being the lowest priority and 7 being the highest. The IEEE has issued guidelines for the use of the CoS levels, but

	Name	Alternative Name	Description
Table 3-4	CS0	BK	Background
CoS Levels	CS1	BE	Best effort
According to the	CS2	EE	Excellent effort
IEEE Guidelines	CS3	CA	Critical applications
(IEEE 802.1Q-	CS4	VI	Video
2005)	CS5	VO	Voice
	CS6	IC	Internetwork control
	CS7	NC	Network control

vendors are free to implement the classes as they see fit. Table 3-4 lists the IEEE's CoS level guidelines.

Priority Tagging

Priority tagging is a way of differentiating among types of traffic that should be treated differently, with some being given priority over others. Priority tagging uses an 802.1p tag that takes up 3 bits in the Ethernet header frame.

Data Center Bridging

A data center is a facility with the primary purpose of housing computer information systems, including servers, storage arrays, NAS, DAS, switches, routers, and firewalls. Data centers are usually equipped with features such as high-powered cooling devices, redundant power, backup generators, multiple Internet connections, fire suppression systems, and advanced power and temperature monitoring systems. Data center bridging (DCB), also known as *data center Ethernet* (DCE) or *convergence enhanced Ethernet* (CCE), is a set of technologies and specifications by the Institute of Electrical and Electronics Engineers (IEEE) and Internet Engineering Task Force (IETF) intended to improve Ethernet performance and reliability for the data center. DCB is commonly used with FCoE because FC has a lower tolerance for frame loss, but DCB can benefit other storage technologies that operate over Ethernet as well. For example, clustering is improved with DCB by prioritizing cluster control messages above data transfer frames used in clusters. Cluster control messages ensure that the cluster remains operational, so it is more important for them to avoid being dropped because of Ethernet congestion. Each of the technologies that make up DCB is described briefly here:

- **IEEE 802.1AB**   Called Link Layer Discovery Protocol (LLDP), this is a method for obtaining information on the topology used and neighboring devices on an Ethernet LAN or MAN.

- **IEEE 802.1aq**   Called Shortest Path Bridging (SPB), this allows VLANs to share bridging table information that contains the MAC addresses of devices connected to ports. It also specifies 16 other multipath options such as the ability for multiple redundant links connected to core Ethernet switches to be used at the same time. Without 802.1aq, the Spanning Tree Protocol would turn off one of the redundant links to prevent broadcast messages from repeating on the network indefinitely and creating more traffic exponentially in what is known as a *broadcast storm*, but 802.1aq allows both links to work in parallel to load balance the traffic while still preventing broadcast storms.

- **IEEE 802.1Qau**   Termed Congestion Notification (CN), this allows links to reduce the transmission rate instead of dropping frames.

- **IEEE 802.1Qaz**   Called Enhanced Transmission Selection (ETS), this allows unused bandwidth assigned to classes to be reassigned to other classes until it is needed.

- **IEEE 802.1Qbb**   Also called Priority-based Flow Control (PFC), this is a method of link-level flow control that allows lower classes of service to be paused while higher classes of service are allowed through. Link-level flow control link scheduling allows a certain amount of a link's bandwidth to be assigned to a class of service, allowing for more predictable performance from Ethernet links.

- **IEEE 802.3bd**   This adds a new type of Ethernet control frame to allow for PFC.

- **IETF Transparent Interconnection of Lots of Links (TRILL)**   This defines a type of Ethernet switch called a Routing Bridge (RBridge) that can compute better paths to forward frames to Ethernet switches. RBridges can do this because they have more information on the devices that are connected to other RBridges. RBridges inform neighboring RBridges of their connections, and those connections are then shared again with neighbors similar to how routers distribute routing information.

10GigE (10GbE)

10 Gigabit Ethernet (10GigE) is the latest version of Ethernet and can run at 10 Gbps (10,000 Mbps). The IEEE standardized it in 802.3ae, and it uses Category 6 or Category 7 cables instead of the Category 5 cables used in Gigabit Ethernet. iSCSI running over 10GigE can achieve speeds relative to FC 8 Gbps links; however, at the time of this book, 10GigE devices are still quite a bit more expensive than Gigabit Ethernet.

Tools

Several tools such as ping, trace route, ipconfig, and nslookup can help in managing, maintaining, and troubleshooting an FC network.

ping

The ping tool is used to verify connectivity to a device on an IP network. Devices are referenced by name or IP address, and the command will send several Internet Control Message Protocol (ICMP) echo request messages (pings) to the node and wait for an ICMP echo reply (pong) in response.

tracert/traceroute

The trace route command displays the path a packet takes through an IP network to reach its destination. Windows devices use the command tracert, and Linux devices use the command traceroute to perform a trace route. The trace route sends messages to a destination with a time to live (TTL) starting at 1 and increasing until it reaches the destination. Each device along the path to the destination will decrease the TTL in the packet. When the TTL reaches 0, the packet is discarded, and an ICMP time exceeded message is sent back to the sender notifying them of the discarded packet. The trace route tool uses these ICMP time exceeded messages to identify each node or hop along the way to the destination.

ipconfig/ifconfig

The ipconfig command in Windows and the ifconfig command in Linux display the TCP/IP configuration for the NICs in the device. Output from an ipconfig command showing the IPv4 and IPv6 addresses, domain name, subnet mask, and default gateway is displayed here:

```
C:\Windows\system32>ipconfig
Windows IP Configuration
Ethernet adapter Gigabit Ethernet:
    Connection-specific DNS Suffix  . : TEST.com
    Link-local IPv6 Address . . . . . : fe80::311d:7e57:eae:41f1%27
    IPv4 Address. . . . . . . . . . . : 192.168.5.50
    Subnet Mask . . . . . . . . . . . : 255.255.255.0
    Default Gateway . . . . . . . . . : 192.168.5.1
```

The ipconfig /all command displays much more information than the ipconfig command alone. This information can be useful in troubleshooting or in documenting the network. Some sample output of the ipconfig /all command is given here:

```
C:\Windows\system32>ipconfig /all
Windows IP Configuration
    Host Name . . . . . . . . . . . . : TESTING
    Primary Dns Suffix  . . . . . . . : TEST.com
    Node Type . . . . . . . . . . . . : Hybrid
    IP Routing Enabled. . . . . . . . : No
    WINS Proxy Enabled. . . . . . . . : No
    DNS Suffix Search List. . . . . . : TEST.com

Ethernet adapter Gigabit Ethernet:
    Connection-specific DNS Suffix  . : TEST.com
    Description . . . . . . . . . . . : Broadcom NetXtreme Gigabit Ethernet
    Physical Address. . . . . . . . . : 00-70-18-04-34-F1
    DHCP Enabled. . . . . . . . . . . : Yes
    Autoconfiguration Enabled . . . . : Yes
    Link-local IPv6 Address . . . . . : fe80::311d:7e57:eae:41f1%27(Preferred)
    IPv4 Address. . . . . . . . . . . : 192.168.5.50(Preferred)
    Subnet Mask . . . . . . . . . . . : 255.255.255.0
    Lease Obtained. . . . . . . . . . : Sunday, June 16, 2013 2:58:04 PM
    Lease Expires . . . . . . . . . . : Sunday, June 30, 2013 2:58:05 PM
    Default Gateway . . . . . . . . . : 192.168.5.1
    DHCP Server . . . . . . . . . . . : 192.168.5.4
    DHCPv6 IAID . . . . . . . . . . . : 570454040
```

```
      DHCPv6 Client DUID. . . . . . . . : 00-01-00-01-19-24-32-B9-00-21-97-AB-
12-DE
      DNS Servers . . . . . . . . . . . : 192.168.5.10
      NetBIOS over Tcpip. . . . . . . . : Enabled
```

nslookup

The nslookup command can display information on the Domain Name System (DNS) servers that are in use on the network and query the DNS servers for IP address or DNS name mappings. Typing **nslookup** followed by the name of a computer on the network will display the IP address of that computer. The response will be authoritative if the DNS record for that computer is maintained on the DNS server, as can be seen in the following command that queries the name server for a host called testing.test.com. Non-authoritative responses are issued when the server is not managing that machine.

```
C:\Windows\system32>nslookup testing
Server:  dc2.test.com
Address:  192.168.5.10

Name:    testing.test.com
Address:  192.168.5.50
```

ARP

The Address Resolution Protocol (ARP) translates an IP address to a MAC address on Ethernet networks. IP addresses are needed in the OSI layer 3 packet, but this is encapsulated into a layer 2 frame that uses the MAC address for its source and destination. The encapsulated packet may traverse multiple switches before it reaches a router that reads the packet information. Each switch along the way will repackage the packet into a new frame that lists the switch address as the source and the next layer 2 device along the way as the destination. To determine what the MAC address is, these devices will use the ARP protocol.

The ARP command can be used to list the MAC addresses a machine knows about, modify the MAC-address-to-IP-address mappings on the local machine, or create a new MAC-address-to-IP-address map. For example, the ARP –a command shows the MAC addresses a machine knows about. This command, and its output, are shown next:

```
arp -a

Interface: 192.168.254.151 --- 0xa
  Internet Address      Physical Address      Type
  192.168.254.1         00-06-5b-00-e2-e0     dynamic
  192.168.254.4         00-15-5d-32-49-01     dynamic
  192.168.254.5         00-15-5d-d7-0b-02     dynamic
  192.168.254.6         00-15-5d-d7-0b-00     dynamic
  192.168.254.10        00-15-5d-32-49-00     dynamic
  192.168.254.11        00-15-5d-fe-2f-2a     dynamic
  192.168.254.16        00-15-5d-32-32-02     dynamic
  192.168.254.20        00-15-17-48-aa-56     dynamic
  192.168.254.21        00-15-5d-d7-0b-01     dynamic
  192.168.254.24        02-bf-c0-a8-fe-18     dynamic
  192.168.254.28        02-bf-c0-a8-fe-18     dynamic
```

```
   192.168.254.75        00-70-18-04-35-11      dynamic
   192.168.254.84        00-15-5d-32-fb-16      dynamic
   192.168.254.155       00-15-5d-32-32-07      dynamic
   192.168.254.156       6c-3b-e5-83-a3-2b      dynamic
   192.168.254.158       00-15-17-2d-8a-8b      dynamic
   192.168.254.165       00-15-17-94-d2-62      dynamic
   192.168.254.255       ff-ff-ff-ff-ff-ff      static
   224.0.0.22            01-00-5e-00-00-16      static
   224.0.0.252           01-00-5e-00-00-fc      static
   239.255.255.250       01-00-5e-7f-ff-fa      static
255.255.255.255      ff-ff-ff-ff-ff-ff     static
```

Storage over a WAN

With traditional local storage and DAS, storage was limited to disks that were installed on a host or near to a host. However, SANs allow for data to be physically separate from the hosts that use it. Some SANs utilize WANs to connect hosts and other storage arrays to storage arrays that are in remote sites. This is also known as extending the SAN over a WAN. This is usually performed for one of two reasons. First, organizations may seek to centralize storage in one location so storage arrays may reside in a regional data center, while the hosts that connect to the storage reside at branch offices connected via a WAN link. The second reason for extending a SAN over a WAN is to provide protection against the loss of a single site or of a critical site link. The data on storage arrays can be replicated to other sites over a WAN link so that if one site becomes unavailable, the data can be obtained from the alternative or backup site. True online solutions may use mirroring and synchronization to keep a copy of data online in the case of a failure, while other solutions may use another site for periodic backups. In the case of an emergency, the backups could be used to restore the data, but it may need to be restored to new hardware or to a different setup, and more configuration changes would need to be made to bring the systems up again following the failure than would be necessary when using an online copy of the data.

Hosts and storage on a SAN that is extended over a WAN communicate using their standard protocol such as FC or iSCSI and have no knowledge that their FC frames or iSCSI packets are being delivered over a WAN. FC data traverses a WAN with protocols such as FCIP and iFCP, while iSCSI uses existing TCP/IP technologies.

Applications that access storage over a WAN will expect, or demand, if you want, a minimum level of performance. Thus, SAN administrators need to know the application requirements to provide the expected level of service. Bandwidth and latency are crucial factors for determining whether existing WAN links can handle application requirements.

Bandwidth

Bandwidth is how much data can be transferred during a measured interval such as a second, as in megabits per second (Mbps). For example, streaming 1080p high-definition video at 24 frames per second might require 25 to 40 Mbps, and a business application streams a maximum of 10 concurrent videos at a time from storage over the WAN.

Name	Type	Speed	Region
T1/DS1	Copper	1.544 Mbps	North America
T3/DS3	Copper	45 Mbps	North America
E1	Copper	2.048 Mbps	Europe
E3	Copper	34 Mbps	Europe
OC-3	Optical	155 Mbps	North America
OC-12	Optical	622 Mbps	North America
OC-48	Optical	2.5 Gbps	North America
OC-192	Optical	10 Gbps	North America
Fractional Metro Ethernet	Copper	Up to 1 Gbps	World
Gigabit Metro Ethernet	Copper	1 Gbps	World
10GigE Metro Ethernet	Copper	10 Gbps	World

Table 3-5 WAN Bandwidth Options

This would require up to 400 Mbps of WAN bandwidth. Table 3-5 shows some of the WAN options and their speeds.

Latency

Latency is the time it takes to go from source to destination. In other words, it is the travel time. Electrical impulses and light have a maximum speed. It may seem like light is so fast that latency would not matter, but it can have an impact at greater distances. Light travels at 186,000 miles per second in a vacuum and approximately 100,000 miles per second in fiber-optic cables. Therefore, it would take five milliseconds for light to travel 500 miles, the distance from New York to Cleveland, over fiber-optic cabling. Five milliseconds may not feel like much time for a human, but it can feel like a long time for a computer. Modern processors operate around 3 GHz, which equates to 3 billion cycles per second or 3 million cycles per millisecond, so a processor would go through 15 million cycles while the data traveled 500 miles. Of course, sending data from one place to another is not as simple as dropping it on a wire. Devices forward or route the data to its destination along the way, and each of these devices will add latency to the equation.

EXAM TIP Know the difference between bandwidth and latency. A real-world example of latency can be seen when news anchors correspond with reporters overseas. There is a noticeable delay between when the anchor asks a question of the reporter and the reporter's response. The reporter has to wait for the anchor's question to travel from the station to a satellite and then back to his location, and then his response has to travel back to the station before it can be broadcast to the TV viewer.

Flow Control

The pace of a connection between two ports is managed through flow control to ensure that frames are not dropped by sending too much data. Two mechanisms used for flow control include buffer-to-buffer and end-to-end credits.

Buffer-to-Buffer Credits

Buffer-to-buffer credits (BB_Credits) are the number of unacknowledged frames that exist between ports. The sending device will send frames until it runs out of BB_Credits, and it will decrement the BB_Credit counter for each frame sent. Receivers return a receiver-ready (R_RDY) frame to indicate that a frame was received, and this increases the BB_Credit count so that more frames can be sent. BB_Credits are negotiated in the fabric logon (FLOGI) process. Larger BB_Credit values may be necessary on long WAN links to ensure that the WAN link is properly utilized. Since the frames travel a longer distance, it takes longer for R_RDY frames to be received by the sender. If the BB_Credits are not increased from their default setting, the sender may run out of BB_Credits while frames are still in transit to the receiver, leading to a gap where no frames are sent until R_RDY frames are received. The latency of the WAN link can be used to determine how high to set the BB_Credits to ensure that the WAN link is properly utilized. Figure 3-18 shows communication over a WAN link. Before data is sent in step 1, BB credits are at 16. BB credits drop to 12 in step 2 after four frames have been sent. Later in step 3, 16 frames have been sent and BB credits are exhausted, so the sender stops sending frames. The receiver starts sending R_RDY frames back in step 4, but the sender cannot send additional frames until it begins receiving the R-RDY frames in step 5.

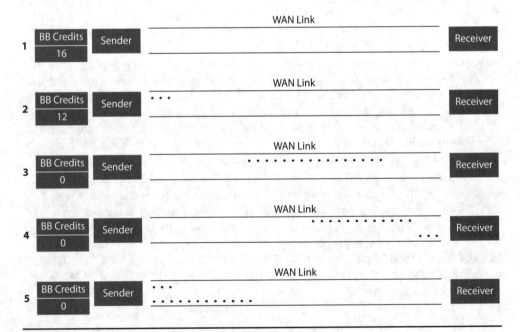

Figure 3-18   Insufficient BB_Credits on a WAN link

End-to-End Credits

End-to-end credits (EE_Credits) are similar to BB_Credits, but they are used between two connections instead of two links. If a host and a storage device were communicating over a switch, BB_Credits would be used between the host and the switch and between the switch and the storage device, while EE_Credits would be used between the host and the storage device. The host and storage device are the devices at the end of the communication stream, so the term *end-to-end* credits is an apt description.

Chapter Summary

This chapter introduced you to the Fibre Channel and iSCSI technologies used for storage networking as well as several hybrid storage protocols such as iFCP, FCIP, and FCoE. FC and iSCSI are the most popular storage protocols.

- Fibre Channel over IP is a protocol that sends FC protocol data over an IP network. FCIP is primarily used to connect remote FC SANs over an IP wide area network.

- iFCP also sends FC data over an IP network. It is not used much in favor of FCIP and iSCSI.

- FCoE sends FC data over Ethernet. FCoE is not routable.

Fibre Channel offers a robust enterprise-class solution with low overhead, consistent performance, and high scalability, while iSCSI can utilize less expensive components and integrate with existing computer networks.

- FC devices are known by their World Wide Name, a 64-bit number displayed in hexadecimal.

- FC services are used to manage the FC network, and they provide features such as time synchronization, name resolution, fabric logon, and quality of service.

- Service classes are used to prioritize different types of traffic, with class 1 providing the best performance and a dedicated connection between devices.

The Fibre Channel Protocol is broken down into five layers:

- Layer 0 is the physical layer where electrical impulses or light is transmitted over a cable.

- Layer 1 is responsible for turning physical signals into binary 1s and 0s in a process known as decoding or 1s and 0s into physical signals in a process known as encoding.

- Layer 2 assembles and disassembles frames and is responsible for managing exchanges and sequences.

- Layer 3 is known as the services layer, and it is designed to support striping, hunt groups, and spanning of multiple ports.
- Layer 4 maps upper-layer protocols such as SCSI to FC.

FC can be implemented in one of three topologies:

- The FC point-to-point topology is used for direct attached storage and direct attached tape devices.
- FC arbitrated loop is a ring topology where data is passed from one node to another until it reaches its destination.
- FC switched fabric (FC-SW) is configured as a star with each device connecting into a switch. Multiple switches can be connected to support many devices.

A link is the physical cabling between two ports, while a connection is a logical method for communicating between two devices. Many links may be traversed when data travels over a connection.

Switches are connected through interswitch links. Devices that need to communicate with other devices on a different FC switch must traverse the ISL.

FC has seven different port types. The N-port (node) is used on end devices. The F-port (fabric) is used by FC switch ports that connect to N-ports. ISLs use E-ports (expansion), and G-ports (generic) can be used as either an F-port or an E-port. G-ports can automatically sense the type of connection on the other end and configure themselves to match. The NL and FL ports are used in the FC-AL topology. The NL-port is the FC-AL node port, and the FL-port is the FC-AL fabric port. Universal ports can function as either an NL or FL port.

iSCSI is a low-cost alternative to FC and a popular storage networking technology. iSCSI uses Ethernet switches, network interface cards, and twisted-pair cabling. iSCSI sends SCSI commands over IP. The SCSI commands allow block mode access to storage across a network so that remote storage appears and functions much like local storage to a host.

- The term for a device that creates a session is an *initiator*, and initiators point to targets. Targets receive commands from initiators and are associated with remote storage on the iSCSI SAN.
- Protocols like SLP and iSNS can be used to locate storage by name rather than by IP address and port, and they make it easier to configure iSCSI.
- iSCSI devices are connected over an Ethernet network that uses Ethernet switches.
- iSCSI traffic can be prioritized by using class of service. There are eight classes ranging from 0 to 7, with 0 being the lowest priority and 7 being the highest.

LANs, MANs, and WANs describe networks based on their regional scope. LANs comprise a single site such as an office space or building. MANs are networks over a metropolitan area such as a college campus network or a factory with many buildings. WANs connect networks that are distant from one another. Bandwidth, latency, and flow control are important to the performance of storage resources over a WAN.

- Bandwidth is how much data can be transferred during a measured interval such as a second.

- Latency is the time it takes to go from source to destination, and it is controlled through buffer-to-buffer credits and end-to-end credits.

Chapter Review Questions

1. You are the storage administrator for a company network. The company uses iSCSI for storage communication and users connect to servers and the Internet over Ethernet. Programmers download large files from the Internet each day and you have noticed decreased performance of the storage network when large files are downloading. Which of the following might you implement to prevent web traffic from consuming iSCSI bandwidth?

    A. WAN

    B. VSAN

    C. Class of service

    D. VLAN

2. Which FC service assigns N-port IDs?

    A. Name server

    B. Logon server

    C. Management server

    D. Security key distribution server

3. Which of the following addresses is a WWN?

    A. A25FED

    B. 192.168.5.59

    C. 21-00-A4-55-92-A5-FB-71

    D. Host.domain1.local:3260

4. Communication over a WAN link seems to be operating in spurts. A small number of frames are sent, and then there is a long period of inactivity. Which action would resolve the issue?

    A. Adding a second ISL to the port channel on the WAN

    B. Changing the service class to class 1

    C. Increasing the speed of the WAN link

    D. Increasing the buffer-to-buffer credits

5. An application is failing to start because it cannot find the drive where its application files reside. Other critical applications that depend on other FC drives are running fine on the server. The disk is located on the SAN and attached via FC. You access the machine and confirm that the drive is not visible. Which action would you take first?

   A. Issue a rescan to detect the drive.

   B. Restart the computer.

   C. Review port error counters to identify problems with the fabric.

   D. Reinstall the HBA drivers.

6. Which service is used by initiators to locate targets?

   A. SNMP

   B. RSCN

   C. iSNS

   D. FCIP

7. Which technologies are used with an iSCSI storage network?

   A. Category 5 cables, network interface cards, N-ports

   B. Ethernet switches, Category 6 cables, network interface cards

   C. Ethernet switches, ISL, host bus adapters

   D. Ethernet switches, ISL, network interface cards

8. Which ports are usable in the FC-AL topology?

   A. N-port, F-port, and E-port

   B. U-port, FL-port, and NL-port

   C. FL-port and F-port

   D. FL-port, NL-port, and G-port

9. You work for an engineering company that recently merged with another firm. Engineers from the other firm will be relocating to your office. The other firm has a Fibre Channel storage array that attaches to two servers via FCP. They house their engineering documents on these servers and you have been tasked with integrating the device onto your company network. Your network is currently all Ethernet based with an iSCSI storage network and it resides in New York and connects to local servers only. Your manager wishes to implement the new system with the least number of changes to the network infrastructure. Which technology should you select?

   A. FCP

   B. FCIP

   C. FCoE

   D. iSCSI

10. A scheduled job shuts down a server each week once updates have been applied. Occasionally, however, backup jobs are still running on the server and these jobs fail when the server restarts. The backup administrator configured the job to autoresume, but it tries several times and then fails. She asks you how she might determine when the server is available again so that her job can resume processing. Which tool would you recommend?

   A. ping

   B. tracert

   C. ipconfig

   D. nslookup

Chapter Review Answers

1. **D** is correct. A VLAN would segment the iSCSI traffic so that it is on its own virtual LAN. Internet traffic would traverse the computer network, and iSCSI traffic would traverse its VLAN.
   A, **B**, and **C** are incorrect. **A** is incorrect because a WAN is used to connect networks over a large distance, not to separate traffic. **B** is incorrect because VSANs do segment the network, but they are used with FC. **C** is incorrect because class of service could be used to prioritize traffic, but it would not prevent the web traffic from consuming bandwidth.

2. **B** is correct. The logon server processes logon requests and assigns the N-port ID.
   A, **C**, and **D** are incorrect. **A** is incorrect because the name server registers names and ports but does not assign the IDs. **C** is incorrect because the management server distributes network management information. **D** is incorrect because the security key distribution server manages security keys.

3. **C** is correct. WWNs are represented by hexadecimal characters, numbered from 0 to F, similar to Ethernet MAC addresses. The format of this choice utilizes hexadecimal and it is the appropriate length.
   A, **B**, and **D** are incorrect. **A** is a port ID, **B** is an IP address, and **D** is a hostname and port.

4. **D** is correct. Once a set of frames is sent, the device runs out of buffer-to-buffer credits and has to wait until it receives an R_RDY frame to begin sending again.
   A, **B**, and **C** are incorrect. Adding a second ISL to the port channel would increase the available bandwidth, but it would not impact latency, which is the root cause of this problem. Similarly, choice **C** increases the speed of the WAN link, but does not address latency. Choice **B** changes the service to class 1 and would give it higher priority, but it would still have to wait due to the latency. The way to deal with latency is to increase the buffer-to-buffer credits so that more data can be present on the line before requiring an R_RDY frame.

5. **A** is correct. A rescan might detect the drive if it is still offered by the storage array.
B, **C**, and **D** are incorrect. **B** is incorrect because it may solve the problem, but it would result in downtime to the server and make the applications running on it unavailable. **C** is incorrect because there is no indication that the port has a problem yet. **D** is incorrect because other FC drives are accessible.

6. **C** is correct. Internet Storage Name Server (iSNS) is a method used to locate targets.
A, **B**, and **D** are incorrect. **A** is incorrect because SNMP is used to send network management messages. **B** is incorrect because RSCN is used to send state change notifications, and **D** is incorrect because FCIP is a protocol used to send FC protocol data over an IP network.

7. **B** is correct. iSCSI uses Ethernet switches; Category 5, 6, or 7 cables; network interface cards; or host bus adapters.
A, **C**, and **D** are incorrect. **A** is incorrect because N-ports belong to FC. **C** is incorrect because iSCSI does not use ISL. **D** is incorrect because iSCSI does not use ISL.

8. **B** is correct. FC-AL uses the NL-port, FL-port, and the U-port.
A, **C**, and **D** are incorrect. N-ports, F-ports, E-ports, and G-ports are not used with FC-AL. Rather, they are used with FC-SW.

9. **A** is correct. The servers and storage array are already configured to run over FCP. The storage device will only be connecting to the two servers, so the entire system can be moved over as is and the two servers can then be attached to the company Ethernet network.
B, **C**, and **D** are incorrect. **B** and **C** are incorrect because this would require changing hardware on the storage device and servers to support another protocol. **D** is incorrect because the storage device is Fibre based, not Ethernet based.

10. **A** is correct. Ping can be used to determine if a device is accessible over the network. The command sends an ICMP message to the network device which then responds.
B, **C**, and **D** are incorrect. **B** is incorrect because tracert shows the path from source to destination. **C** is incorrect because ipconfig is used to display interface IP settings. **D** is incorrect because nslookup displays DNS information.

Storage Hardware

In this chapter, you will learn how to
- Classify storage networking devices
- Differentiate between the types of cables used for storage
- Select removable storage options that best fit a business scenario

The previous chapters covered disks and their operation as well as the function of RAID groups. This was followed by technologies that utilize the capacity and speed of many disks together to provide storage to direct attached or networked hosts over a storage area network (SAN). Next, the methods for communicating over storage networks, called *protocols*, were discussed. This chapter builds on the previous chapters by introducing the hardware that storage networks are built upon.

Cables

Cables of all shapes, lengths, and compositions make up the networks that connect our offices, homes, schools, and the world. Cables are a medium through which data, represented as light or electromagnetic waves, travels from source to destination. Most high-performance networks are composed of physical cables that connect devices together. Cables provide faster speeds and greater security than wireless networks, and they have a long history of use. The two main types of cables used in storage networking are optical and copper cables.

Analog vs. Digital

The cables and media types discussed in this chapter will be either analog or digital, so it is important to understand the difference between these transmission and storage methods. Analog data is transmitted as a signal that varies in power level, which is called *amplitude*, and number of waves in a time period, which is called *frequency*.

(continued)

Figure 4-1 shows an analog signal. Each wave in an analog signal can represent a discrete value, of which there are many (in fact, infinite) possibilities. For example, when a person sings a note, the note is an analog sound wave that hits our ear at a certain frequency, and the loudness of the voice is determined by the amplitude. When sending data, the amplitude is used to specify the piece of data such as an *A* from a *B*. The downside to analog is that it is easily susceptible to noise and interference, which makes determining the amplitude of the wave more difficult and results in data errors and retransmission. Figure 4-2 shows a noisy analog signal. For this reason, analog communications have error detection and retransmission safeguards built in, but the addition of these safeguards results in more information that must be transmitted that consumes a portion of the available bandwidth, known as *overhead*.

Digital signals differ from analog signals in that one of only two values is specified: 1 or 0, on or off. Figure 4-3 shows a digital signal.

Nominal amplitude is interpreted as a voltage close to 0, usually 0.00 to 0.8 volts; higher amplitude, such as 2.5 to 5.0 volts, is a 1. The great difference between nominal and higher amplitude makes it easier to differentiate between a 1 and 0, so digital communications are more resistant to noise. Figure 4-4 shows a noisy digital signal. The downside to digital transmissions is that they can represent only one of two values at a time, so while a single analog waveform could represent an *A*, digital communications would need a series of eight waveforms to represent the letter *A* in ASCII as 01000001.

Analog storage, similar to analog transmissions, can store one of many possible values in a discrete location, while digital storage represents only a 0 or a 1 in each discrete location on the media.

Figure 4-1
Analog signal

Figure 4-2
Noisy analog
signal

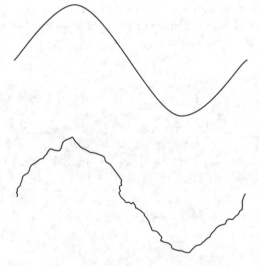

Figure 4-3
Digital signal

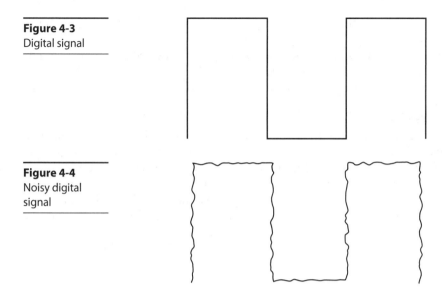

Figure 4-4
Noisy digital
signal

Optical Cables

Optical cables transmit data via light impulses. They are made of thin transparent glass or plastic core inside a protective cladding. Light travels very fast and over long distances, but the speed of light is not constant. Rather, it depends upon the medium it travels through. Light travels at 186,000 miles per second in a vacuum such as space and approximately 100,000 miles per second in fiber-optic cables. The high speed at which light travels makes optical cables a low-latency form of communication. This means that little time passes between when data is sent and when it is received.

Optical cables have several advantages over copper cables. They are not affected by interference such as electromagnetic interference (EMI) or radio frequency interference (RFI), and they are relatively small compared to copper cables, so more optical cables can be placed in the same location. Optical cables also offer the highest transmission rates and can transmit much farther than copper cables. Finally, fiber cables protect sensitive electronic equipment from damage from power spikes because they do not conduct electricity. However, optical cables are more expensive than their copper counterparts.

Optical cables can transmit multiple pieces of data at the same time by using different light wavelengths, what we might interpret with our eyes as colors, for each segment; this method is called *wavelength division multiplexing* (WDM). WDM uses a multiplexer to combine the signals and a demultiplexer at the receiving end to split them into their individual signals again.

It is much more difficult to splice optical cables than copper cables. Optical cables must be combined mechanically or fused in a process similar to soldering except at a much more delicate scale. Fiber-optic cores are about the size of a human hair, and the fusing must ensure that the light signal is not attenuated when passing through the fused portion. Once the cores of both cables are aligned, an electrical pulse is used to burn off residue, and then a larger electrical pulse fuses the two components together.

On the positive side, the difficulty of splicing optical cable makes them more resistant to unauthorized access through tapping.

There are two main types of optical cables: single-mode fiber (SMF) and multimode fiber (MMF). SMF can transmit at longer distances, but it is more expensive and transmits at lower data rates. MMF works at higher data rates but shorter distances at lower cost.

Single-Mode Fiber

Single-mode fiber uses a single beam of light generated by a high-precision laser to transmit data over a fiber-optic cable. The beam travels down the center of the core without reflecting off the edges. This allows for the signal to be sent great distances without suffering from much attenuation because the shortest distance between two points is always a straight line. SMF is more expensive than MMF, and it is harder to work with. SMF splicing has to be much more precise because of its small size and the need for precise alignment. Fiber cables are often referenced by their core and cladding sizes, such as 9/125, which has a 9-micron core and a 125-micron cladding. SMF cables will have core sizes less than 10 microns in many cases.

Multimode Fiber

Multimode fiber, as the name implies, uses multiple light beams generated by a light-emitting diode (LED) at the same time to achieve greater speeds than SMF. Each beam is emitted at a slightly different angle. The beams reflect off the inner wall of the core many times before reaching the destination, and MMF is designed with a grade index on the inside part of the cladding to bring the beams to the destination at the same time; however, there is some variation, and this does not always happen. MMF signals can arrive at different times since some will reflect off the inside edges of the cable more often than others. This is called *modal dispersion*, and higher data rates result in more pronounced modal dispersion, which reduces the maximum data rates or lengths for MMF. The core of MMF is larger in diameter than SMF. MMF's larger size allows for the use of less expensive LEDs instead of lasers. MMF cables will have a core size between 50 and 62.5 microns. Some older cables had a core of 100 microns, but they are now obsolete. An example of an MMF cable would be 50/125, which has a 50-micron core and a 125-micron cladding. The process for transmitting multiple light impulses at different wavelengths is known as *multiplexing*.

Multiplexing in Optical Cable

Multiplexing, or WDM, is the process for transmitting multiple light impulses at different wavelengths. There are two types of WDM, known as *coarse wavelength division multiplexing* (CWDM) and *dense wavelength division multiplexing* (DWDM). CWDM is used for multiplexing anywhere from two to eight wavelengths over a single optical cable, whereas DWDM is used for multiplexing more than eight wavelengths, typically 32, 64, or 128 wavelengths, but at a higher cost than CWDM. CWDM is used for short-range communications, whereas DWDM is used for long-range communications. CWDM wavelengths use wide-range frequencies that spread wavelengths far apart from one another so that they do not drift into one another and overlap, causing a loss of data.

Limitations

The maximum length of optical fiber depends on the data rate, with higher data rates reducing the maximum transmission length since higher data rates suffer greater from attenuation. Attenuation is primarily caused by scattering when light collides with atoms in the glass. SMF can transmit at 10 Gbps at a distance of several thousand kilometers and 40 Gbps at several hundred kilometers, while MMF can support speeds up to 100 Gbps but for only 150 meters. MMF's range extends to 550 meters when transmitting at 40 Gbps and 1 kilometer at 1 Gbps or 2 kilometers at 100 Mbps.

Connectors

Optical connectors join fiber cables to another piece of compatible networking equipment such as a switch or host bus adapter (HBA). There have been many fiber connections, but some of the most common fiber connectors include standard connector (SC), local connector (LC), and straight tip (ST). Many switches come without transceivers, so a compatible SC, LC, or ST transceiver, known as a small form-factor pluggable (SFP), would need to be purchased for switch ports.

The *standard connector*, also known as the *subscriber connector*, has a sending and receiving connector combined in two square ends, each containing a 2.5-mm fiber tip. Both ends plug into an SC receptacle via a push-pull latching mechanism.

The *local connector* (LC), also known as the *lucent connector*, is even smaller than the SC connector, offering greater density in switches and networking hardware. It snaps together in much the same way as SC using two smaller square ends, but a set of prongs on the top of the connector will push back when in place, and these can be used to eject the cable from the receptacle. LC uses a 1.25-mm fiber tip as compared to SC's 2.5-mm tip.

The *straight tip* (ST) connector is a round connector with a bayonet plug and socket. A connection is made once the ST connector has been pushed in place and then twisted. This locks the connector so that it will not fall out. Each ST connector is either a sending or receiving line, so two ST connectors must be used in between nodes.

Cable Care

Optical cables are expensive and sensitive pieces of equipment. If a fiber-optic cable is bent too far, the light inside the cable will be reflected and dispersed, resulting in a loss of signal until the bend is corrected. The fiber-optic core can also be damaged if bent too far and will need to be replaced. For example, one engineer decided to take up the extra slack in fiber cables by spooling them beneath the fiber switch. This created extra pressure on the cables, causing them to bend past their bend radius right after the connection point, and some started failing until the bundles were loosened and attached in proper cable runs.

Stress can occur in cables resulting in a loss of connection. The most common places where stress occurs is at the point of termination in places where cable friction or pressure may occur. Extensive vibration on a cable can potentially loosen connectors, and repeated reseating of connectors or exposure to contaminants such as oils may inhibit communication between the connector and receptacle. For this reason, fiber cables ship with a protective cap on each tip that must be removed before inserting the connector into the receptacle. These caps should be reattached if the cable is unplugged, transported, or left unused for some time to prevent damage to the tip because of foreign substances on it. When removing fiber cables, do not pull on the cable itself to unseat it. Rather, pull on the connector and make sure any unlocking tabs have been depressed first.

Fiber cables should be placed in tubes or runways to prevent their own weight from crushing or bending the cable and to protect against external impact. Do not hang anything from fiber cable strands. Cable manufacturers include small pieces of yarn or other material in cables that can be used for pulling. Use these instead of the cable itself to reduce cable stress. Keep cables straight and free from twists when installing them and maintaining them. Finally, roll cables off a spool instead of spinning it off the spool to avoid introducing twists in the cable.

Copper Cables

Copper is an excellent cheap conductor used in many situations where fiber would be too costly, especially in office wiring and connections between servers and switches at the top of the rack. Whereas fiber cables transmit light impulses to represent data, copper cables transmit electromagnetic waves. Electromagnetic waves are quite fast and can travel at the speed of light in a vacuum. However, their speed elsewhere depends on the material they travel through and how much it insulates. Copper is a good conductor, and electromagnetic waves can travel at approximately 66 percent the speed of light in a typical cable. Some copper cables you may be familiar with include coaxial cable used for cable TV and twisted pair used for telephones.

Twisted-pair cabling is a form of copper cable that has several smaller sheathed copper wires twisted together within it. The pairs help reduce EMI from other wires in the strand. This type of EMI is known as *crosstalk*, abbreviated as XT. The forms of twisted pair are given categories starting at 1. The most current twisted-pair category is 6a, labeled Cat6a. Table 4-1 lists the categories of twisted-pair cables. Twisted pair can be bent much more than optical cable, but it is still vulnerable to kinking. The twisted-pair bend radius must be at least four times the outer diameter of the cable to avoid kinking, so be careful when moving wiring.

Table 4-1 Twisted-Pair Categories	Category	Use
	Cat1/Cat2	Voice/data over modem only
	Cat3	Voice and 10 Mbps data
	Cat4	Voice and 16 Mbps data (used with token ring)
	Cat5	Data up to 100 Mbps
	Cat5e	Data up to 1 Gbps
	Cat6	Data up to 10 Gbps with some limitations
	Cat6a	Data up to 10 Gbps

Noise

Copper cables can suffer from interference from noise such as EMI or RFI. EMI is disruption in a transmission due to an electromagnetic field, such as those generated by computing equipment, cathode ray tubes, and generators, in close proximity, whereas RFI is a disruption caused by nearby radio frequencies such as cell phones, wireless signals, and other broadcasts.

Cat5

Category 5 (Cat5) cabling is made up of eight 24-gauge wires separated into four twisted pairs. Cat5 cables use the RJ-45 connector and are made up of eight 24- to 26-gauge wires arranged in one of two configurations, standardized in Telecommunications Industry Association/Electronic Industries Association (TIA/EIA) 568A and 568B. Table 4-2 depicts the cabling layout. Either standard can be used to create a Cat5 cable as long as the same standard is used on both ends. A special cable called a *crossover* cable is used to connect two devices without the use of a switch, and this cable is created by wiring one end using TIA/EIA 568A and the other end using TIA/EIA 568B.

Cat5 cable runs at 100 MHz and can support 10Base-T and 100Base-T networks running at 10 Mbps and 100 Mbps. It has a maximum length of 100 meters (325 feet).

Cat5e

Category 5 Enhanced (Cat5e) is an upgraded version of Cat5 with more tightly twisted wire pairs that reduces crosstalk to a greater degree than in Cat5. Cat5e supports 1000Base-T networks running at 1 Gbps (1,000 Mbps) as well as earlier 10Base-T and 100Base-T networks.

Cat6

Category 6 (Cat6) cable is a twisted-pair cable. Similar to Cat5, it has four pairs of wires, but the wires are 22 gauge, which is slightly larger than those used in Cat5. The TIA/EIA 568A and 568B cable layouts depicted in Table 4-2 also apply to Cat6. Cat6 differs from

Table 4-2 TIA/EIA 568A and 568B Cable Layouts	**Pin**	**TIA/EIA 568A**	**TIA/EIA 568B**
	1	White/green	White/orange
	2	Green	Orange
	3	White/orange	White/green
	4	Blue	Blue
	5	White/blue	White/blue
	6	Orange	Green
	7	White/brown	White/brown
	8	Brown	Brown

Cat5 and Cat5e in that it runs at 250 MHz and has roughly 50 percent more protection against crosstalk. Cat6 supports 10Base-T, 100Base-T, 1000Base-T, and 10GBase-T networks running at 10 Mbps, 100 Mbps, 1,000 Mbps, and 10,000 Mbps.

Cat6 cable has a maximum length of 100 meters (425 feet) when used for 10 Mbps, 100 Mbps, or 1,000 Mbps networks. However, Cat6 is limited to 55 meters (180 feet) when used in 10GigE networks (10,000 Mbps/10 Gbps). Similar to Cat5, the Cat6 bend radius must be at least four times the outer diameter of the cable to avoid kinking.

Cat6a

Category 6 Augmented (Cat6a) is an upgraded version of Cat6 that runs at 500 MHz. Additionally, Cat6a is not limited to 55 meters when used in 10GigE. It can extend to 100 meters just when used for other network speeds. This is an important point to consider, and it makes Cat6a a much better choice to avoid potential problems down the road. For example, one company replaced existing Cat5 cable with Cat6 because of its ability to support 10GigE speeds. Over the next few months, gigabit network equipment was replaced with 10GigE, but the engineers were confused when their network experienced high latency and switches showed a high number of dropped frames and frame errors. The engineers finally realized, after much troubleshooting, that their distribution switches were 75 meters away from their core switches. This was fine when they were running at 1 Gbps, but the Cat6 cable is limited to 55 meters when running at 10 Gbps. The company was left with the choice to either replace the cables between core and distribution switches with Cat6a or to add another set of 10GigE switches between the core and distribution. The company chose to replace the cables because that was the less expensive option.

Serial

Serial cables allow two devices to be connected; most commonly, this is a command-line management terminal such as a PC to a network device such as a fiber switch. Serial communication, specified in Reference Standard 232 (RS-232), operates asynchronously, meaning there is no signal or time spacing used to keep the communication in sync. There are a number of serial ports, but the most common one is shaped roughly like the letter *D* and has nine ports. This type of serial port can be referred to as DB-9. As the name suggests, serial ports send data serially, one bit at a time. Each set of bits is framed with a start signal and a stop signal. The number of bits that must be framed is specified when configuring a serial port. Serial cables can be a maximum of 50 feet.

Serial communication does not include a negotiation stage, so communication settings must be configured prior to initiating a connection. There are several settings that can be configured when connecting to a device with a serial port. These include speed, data bits, parity, stop bits, and flow control. The speed is the rate at which data can be transferred over the cable, measured in bits per second (bps). Common speeds include 1,200, 2,400, 4,800, 9,600, 19,200, 38,400, 57,600, and 115,200 bps. The data bit setting configures how many bits will be framed by a start signal and a stop signal. Most communication frames are 8 bits because this correlates to a single ASCII character, but you may encounter 5, 6, 7, or 9 as well. Parity can be set to even, odd, or off. When parity is set to on, an extra bit is added to each data bit set to make the number of 1s in the bit set either odd or even. If the receiver finds a bit set that is odd when the parity is set to even, it knows that the data was corrupted in transit. This method is still prone to error because corruption in the data could still result in the parity calculation to prove correct, so other mechanisms for error detection are usually required on top of parity calculations. The last setting is the stop bits. This setting determines how many bits will be used to show that a character stream has ended. This is usually set to 1. Serial communication does allow for flow control if this is specified in the configuration. Flow control allows for a device to pause and resume communication.

Twinax

Twinaxial, or twinax, cable has two copper wires inside a sheath that looks similar to coaxial cable (what you might have seen connected to your TV or cable modem) and can support speeds up to 10 Gbps. Twinax is a cheaper alternative to fiber; it has 15 to 25 times lower latency and uses only two watts per port rather than two to four watts used by comparable Cat6 cable. However, these power savings are somewhat mitigated by the introduction of IEEE P802.3az, which allows Ethernet to place links into a low power mode when they are not being used. Unlike Cat5, twinax cables cannot be made to a custom size onsite in a process known as *field terminating*. The cables must be purchased in preset lengths from the manufacturer, which can lead to more difficulty in cable management.

There are a number of applications for twinax, including use in display ports, drive connectors, and aviation equipment, but storage networks make use of direct attach (DA) twinax, a cable that runs at 10 Gbps. DA twinax is typically used for the connection between servers and switches in a storage area network or for storage arrays to the storage area network, including FCoE. DA twinax includes an attached SFP for use in attaching to supported switches and HBAs, but this requires the SFP component in the cable to have some intelligence built in, and not all cables are compatible with all hardware. For this reason, it is best to pair cables and equipment from the same vendor and to verify compatibility prior to purchasing.

Finally, DA twinax comes in active and passive flavors. Active twinax cables can be a maximum of 15 meters, while passive twinax cables can be a maximum of 7 meters, but fewer devices support them.

SAS

Serial attached SCSI (SAS) cables can be used for both internal and external connections to drives and storage units. There are more than five internal SAS cable types and three external cable types, as shown in Table 4-3. SAS speeds vary between 3 Gbps and 12 Gbps, with SAS1 running at 3 Gbps, SAS2 at 6 Gbps, and SAS3 at 12 Gbps. SAS cables can be a maximum of 10 meters long.

Copper Cable Care

Twisted-pair cabling must not be stretched or the twists will elongate and make it more susceptible to crosstalk. Higher categories have more twists per inch and are more sensitive to stretching than lower-category cables. This is why you can tug on a phone cable

Cable Type	Alternative Names	Internal or External	Shielded or Unshielded	Supported Devices	Pin Count	SAS Versions	Max Speed	SATA Support
SFF-8086	Internal mini-SAS, internal mSAS	Internal	Unshielded	4	26	SAS1, SAS2	6 Gbps	No
SFF-8087	Internal iSAS, internal	Internal	Unshielded	4	36	SAS1, SAS2	6 Gbps	No
SFF-8482	None	Internal	Unshielded	1	29	SAS1, SAS2	6 Gbps	Yes
SFF-8484	None	Internal	Unshielded	4	32	SAS1, SAS2	6 Gbps	Yes
SFF-8643	Internal iSAS+, internal iPass+	Internal	Unshielded	8	36	SAS1, SAS2, SAS3	12 Gbps	No
SFF-8680	None	Internal	Unshielded	2	29	SAS1, SAS2, SAS3	12 Gbps	No
SFF-8088	External iSAS, external iPass	External	Shielded	4	26	SAS1, SAS2	6 Gbps	Yes
SFF-8470	Infiniband CX4, Molex LameLink	Both	Unshielded	4	32	SAS1, SAS2, Infiniband	10 Gbps	No
SFF-8644	None	External	Unshielded	8	36	SAS1, SAS2, SAS3	12 Gbps	No

Table 4-3 SAS Interface Cables

quite a bit before losing connectivity, whereas a Cat6 cable might begin to lose data after a few good pulls. Also, don't run Ethernet cables near power lines or light fixtures because these generate EMI that can disrupt communications. If cables must be located near power or lights, consider using shielded tubes or tape to provide extra protection against EMI. The bend radius for twisted-pair cabling must be at least four times the outer diameter of the cable to avoid kinking.

Terminate cables into punchdown blocks in the server room or wiring closet and to ports in the wall. This prevents against users at workstations or administrators in the server room from inadvertently pulling on a cable, and it aids in clean cable management. It also allows for easier reconfiguration of port mappings if necessary.

TIP Use different colored cables to designate their use types. For example, in one data center I managed, we used gray cables for backup, blue for primary Ethernet, green for secondary Ethernet, yellow for remote diagnostic cards, purple for trunks, and orange for iSCSI. Cables should also be labeled. It can be difficult to identify which cable is connected to a device once they have all been bundled together for cable management. There are tools that can identify the cable such as a tone generator, but labeling will save you plenty of headaches. Just make sure to update your labels when things change.

Storage Networking Devices

Storage networks require hardware to connect to the cables running through the network. These devices include host bus adapters, network interface cards, or converged network adapters at the sending and receiving ends of the network and repeaters, amplifiers, switches, directors, and routers in between, as shown in Figure 4-5. Specifically, Figure 4-5 shows two fiber storage arrays with their controllers redundantly connected into two fiber directors using HBAs. The directors form the core of the fiber network, and two Fibre Channel (FC) switches and two FCoE switches are connected to them via an interswitch

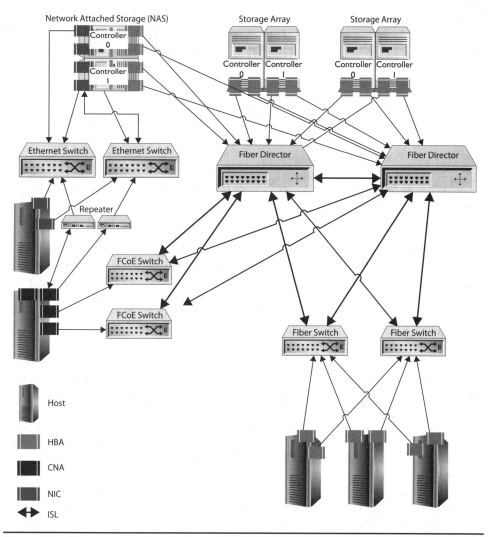

Figure 4-5 Storage networking devices

link (ISL). Three hosts reside off the two FC switches, and each has a connection to both FC switches through HBAs installed in the host. Another host is connected using redundant converged network adapters to the FCoE switches. It is also using converged network adapters to connect to the Ethernet network for access to the NAS. A NAS is connected to two Ethernet switches and also to the FC directors. It is connected to the directors to access its own storage and to the Ethernet network to provide CIFS and NFS shares to the hosts connected to the Ethernet switches. This section introduces each of these devices and how they assist in providing network services.

HBA

A host bus adapter is a device that connects a host to storage. The HBA processes I/O requests from the host and passes them to the storage. HBAs are equipped with one or more ports that provide a physical connection to storage such as copper or optical cables.

NIC

A network interface card (NIC) can be a form of HBA when it is used to connect to a storage resource, but it can also be used for communication with non-storage-related equipment such as servers or other hosts. The NIC provides the connection between a piece of equipment such as a server or storage device and the network. This will include a method for connecting to the equipment such as an interface for an internal slot such as PCI or PCIe, or it could be over USB; it will also include a port for connecting to the network such as RJ-45 for 100Base-T Ethernet.

Speeds

NICs are rated for the types of networks they can connect to, which also specifies the transmission speeds they support. The NIC will be labeled as follows: speed in megabits per second, baseband, or broadband, and the type of cabling. For example, 100Base-T is a baseband connection running at 100 Mbps over twisted-pair cabling, while 1000Base-X is a gigabit (1,000 Mbps) baseband connection running over fiber. T indicates twisted pair, and X indicates fiber.

TCP Offload Engine

The TCP Offload Engine (TOE) offloads the TCP/IP protocol processing to the network controller, alleviating the computer processor from having to perform this work. This can greatly decrease the impact high I/O network traffic has on the host system such as with the use of iSCSI or network file servers running NFS or CIFS. On average, each bit of TCP/IP data requires 1 Hz of processing power, so 500 Mbps of traffic would require 0.5 GHz of CPU time. As you can see, this is not an insignificant impact on the host system.

TOE performs the following tasks: synchronizations and acknowledgments, data verification through checksums and sequence numbers, congestion control, and connection establishment and termination.

CNA

A converged network adapter (CNA) is a multiprotocol adapter card that functions as both a NIC and an HBA. A single CNA can be used for FC, Ethernet, or twinax connections. CNAs perform onboard processing for FCoE, freeing up processor time for other tasks.

Repeaters and Amplifiers

A repeater rebroadcasts a digital signal over a cable. Repeaters can be used with optical or copper cables, and they must be installed at a point prior to the maximum distance of the cable so that the signal they receive can be correctly received and rebroadcast. Repeaters remove noise from the digital signal and then transmit the same signal that was sent at the source to the next repeater or the receiving node.

Amplifiers perform much the same role as a repeater for analog signals. The main difference, however, is that amplifiers cannot remove noise from the signal, so this is amplified along with the transmission. Analog signals do not attenuate as fast as digital signals, so fewer amplifiers are required to traverse the same distance.

Ethernet Switch

Ethernet switches are networking devices consisting of a group of RJ-45 ports for connecting twisted-pair cables in a physical star topology (see Chapter 3 for more information on topologies). Each port acts as a repeater as well, rebroadcasting the signal sent over it and extending the distance nodes can be separated by. The switch creates a dedicated connection between sending and receiving ports so that ports that are not part of the communication do not receive unnecessary traffic.

Switches will support a maximum bandwidth, meaning that while each port theoretically has full bandwidth, the overall bandwidth of the switch might be somewhat less than that. Table 4-4 lists the max speed supported by each Ethernet type. For example, a 48-port Gigabit Ethernet switch would be expected to have a bandwidth of 48 Gbps, but the vendor specifications may say that it has a bandwidth of 36 Gbps, so if all 48 ports were transmitting at the same time, the switch would not be able to give each port its full bandwidth.

Two different types of switches have been made that forward frames differently. Cut-through switches read the destination address and then immediately forward the frame to the destination port, while store-and-forward switches buffer the entire frame and then determine where to forward it. Consequently, cut-through switches are faster than

Table 4-4 Ethernet Types	Name	Speed
	Ethernet	10 Mbps
	Fast Ethernet	100 Mbps
	Gigabit Ethernet	1 Gbps (1,000 Mbps)
	10GigE	10 Gbps

store-and-forward switches, and you would be hard-pressed to find a store-and-forward switch on the market today.

Ethernet switches typically have LED lights placed around the port to indicate connection type and activity. These LEDs can change color and blink. The colors may differ based on the manufacturer, but a green light typically means that the link is running at full duplex, and amber means it is running at half duplex when the display mode is set to duplex. If the display mode is set to STAT, then the green light typically indicates a link, and a blinking light means data is being transmitted.

Full-duplex communication allows data to be sent and received at the same time. Half-duplex communication must wait for a sending or receiving action to complete before another can take place. Blinking LEDs show that data is traversing over the link. Sometimes LEDs will be placed directly above ports, but in high-density switches, this may not be possible, so a separate section may have a large bank of LEDs labeled by port number. Port numbers typically start with 0, so a 48-port switch would have ports numbered from 0 to 47.

GBIC

Some Ethernet switches are equipped with Gigabit Interface Converter (GBIC) transceivers to allow for one or more fiber connections. Fiber connections are useful for connecting a wiring closet to the main facility. GBIC transceivers have electrical connectors on the end that connects to the switch and optical connectors on the end that connects to the fiber cable. GBIC can provide the switch with information on their capabilities and performance. GBIC port numbers are usually in addition to the port count on the switch, so a 48-port switch might have four GBIC ports as well. You should verify that all GBIC ports will work in addition to the 48 Ethernet ports because some vendors link the GBIC ports to other Ethernet ports; therefore, if the four GBIC ports are in use, ports 44–47 may be inoperable.

Fiber Hub

Fiber hubs are used with the Fibre Channel arbitrated loop (FC-AL) topology (see Chapter 3 for more information on topologies). Hubs act like a loop within the device, but nodes are connected to the hub like a switch, with each device having a cable from the device to the hub. The hub creates circuits between neighboring ports to form a ring. The transmit circuit from the upstream port is connected to the receive circuit of the downstream port. Inactive ports, such as those without a cable connected, are put into bypass mode through a feature called *autobypass*. Bypass mode skips the port and sends data to the next port. This increases the speed of the ring because it can reconfigure itself to be smaller when devices are removed or larger when they are added. Since fiber hubs are built for the FC-AL topology, they are not fabric capable, so they do not support fabric features such as Internet Storage Name Server (iSNS), registered state change notifications (RSCNs), security key distribution, or fabric logon.

 NOTE Fiber hubs will allow you to create a larger network of devices, but remember that you cannot have more than 126 devices on an FC-AL network.

Fiber Hub Ports

Chapter 3 introduced the FC port types. As a reminder, fiber hubs use NL-ports to connect to FC-AL nodes and use FL-ports to connect to other fiber hubs. U-ports can be either an NL or an FL port, and it autosenses the type of port it is connected to in order to configure itself. There are some cases where autosensing does not work, and you will need to manually set the port configuration of a U-port to NL or FL on both sides for it to function. If you have cabled two fiber hubs together using U-ports and they are not communicating, check the port status on both sides to verify that each side has configured itself to be an FL-port and configure it manually if it is set to something else.

Fiber Switch

Fiber switches are networking devices consisting of a group of transceivers used for connecting fiber cables in a physical star topology (see Chapter 3 for more information on topologies). Fiber switches can be managed or unmanaged, but most of the models you will work with will be managed. Managed switches have an Ethernet interface that is used for web-based graphical user interface (GUI) or terminal-based command-line interface (CLI) administration of the switch. Some features of the managed switch include Simple Network Management Protocol (SNMP), firmware upgrades, centralized management of many switches from one console, and diagnostics. Windows or Linux servers can administer a managed switch by connecting to its IP address via HTTP for GUI management or Telnet or Secure Shell (SSH) for the CLI.

Fiber switches are capable of storing frames that cannot be delivered due to congestion on the link. This feature is known as *buffering*, and switches will measure their buffering capability in how many frames can be buffered. Modular switches have components that can be replaced if they fail. Some components such as power supplies may be hot-swappable, meaning they can be replaced without impacting the availability of the device. Other switches may be configured with banks of switch ports known as *switch blades*.

Low-end fabric switches may be configured with fixed fiber ports that will support only one type of fiber cabling and speed, but midrange and enterprise fabric switches use small form-factor pluggable transceivers.

SFP

Small form-factor pluggable (SFP) transceivers are used with fiber equipment. SFPs are used rather than building the transceiver directly onto the switch in order to support different types of media such as twinax, LC, SC, or ST connectors. SFPs also make the base switch cheaper to build, and companies can add SFPs as needed.

Fiber Switch Ports

Port types were introduced in Chapter 3, and they need to be mentioned once again in this discussion on switches. Please remember that fiber switches use F-ports to connect to FC-AL nodes and use E-ports to connect to other switches. G-ports can be either an F or E port, and the port will autosense the type of port it is connected to in order to configure itself. Similar to the U-ports on fiber hubs, there are some cases where G-port autosensing does not work and you will need to manually set the port configuration to

F or E on both sides for it to function. If you have cabled two fiber hubs together using G-ports and they are not communicating, check the port status on both sides to verify that each side has configured itself to be an E-port and configure it manually if it is set to something else. If you plugged a node into a G-port, make sure the G-port has configured itself as an F-port.

Director

Fiber directors are high-capacity modular switches that can have upward of 500 ports, usually through the use of switch blades that plug into a backplane on the director. Directors have two or more hot-swappable power supplies and redundant routing engines, pathways, and processors in the backplane to better prevent against failures. Directors may be used in the fabric core to ensure that core services have the highest redundancy. They may also be used to connect storage arrays to the fabric because of the need of storage arrays to be highly available. It would most likely cost an organization much more if a storage array were unavailable than if a single host were unavailable, so a higher priority for redundant components is given to storage arrays. When choosing a director, check to see how the modules connect. Cheaper directors may connect switch blades together with an internal ISL or ISL port channel. This will significantly limit the bandwidth available between switch blades, and it will create another hop between devices on different blades, which will reduce the number of switches that can be attached to the fabric.

Router

A router operates much like a switch, but it has a higher-level understanding of the data that passes through it. A router can differentiate between traffic from different networks so that data can be passed to the appropriate destination. Routers maintain a routing table that provides information on how to get to other networks. Various routing protocols such as Routing Information Protocol (RIP), Open Shortest Path First (OSPF), Border Gateway Protocol (BGP), and Enhanced Interior Gateway Routing Protocol (EIGRP) can be used by routers to share information on the networks they service. These routing tables are updated as links go down so that the routers in a network can send data along alternative paths. Routers determine the required hop counts or number of nodes a packet would need to traverse in a route to reach a destination. Routers will use the route with the lowest hop count unless that route becomes unavailable. This makes routers efficient for delivering data but also resilient against link failures.

Hot-Swappable Network Components

Many network components can be hot-swapped in compatible devices. For example, fiber switches or directors may include hot-swappable power supplies, banks of ports, or control boards, and SFP and GBIC are hot-swappable. Hot-swappable components can be replaced while the system is online. If a hot-swappable component fails or needs to be changed, it can be done without shutting down the device. Once the new device is inserted, the network device will recognize that it has been inserted, and storage administrators can then configure it.

Before moving on to removable storage, you may want to revisit Figure 4-5 showing how all these devices, directors, routers, switches, repeaters, HBAs, CNAs, and NICs work together.

Removable Storage

Sometimes it is important to be able to move or copy data to another location physically. The most common use of removable storage is for archiving. For example, a company may copy data onto backup tapes that can be taken offsite. If systems are destroyed at the primary site because of an incident such as a fire, the offsite tapes can be used to restore the data and bring the systems back online. Consumers and companies utilize removable storage such as USB hard drives, flash drives, or DVDs to archive data in the case of accidental deletion, corruption, or loss, so it is important for storage administrators to understand the types of removable storage hardware available and commonly in use.

Tape Media

Tapes are an efficient method for writing sequential data to a removable media and are especially well suited for backups and archiving. Tape media is relatively inexpensive compared to nearline and online storage technologies such as hard drives. Backup tapes are made up of two spools, one of which is wound with a strip made of plastic and coated with a magnetic material. Tape media is read by tape drives. Tape drives slide open an access port on the tape and advance the magnetic strip across the access port to read or write data. The second spool receives the strip that has passed by the access port. A read-write head in the tape drive can use a magnetic field to create patterns in the magnetic material on the tape, or it can read the patterns that have been placed on it before.

Tape drives read and write data sequentially. When reading data in the middle of a tape, the drive will fast-forward the tape to the desired location and then read the data. This is efficient for data that is located in adjacent areas, but inefficient for data scattered throughout the tape.

There are many cases where tapes are not the best option, and that is because tape media suffers from several limitations. First, accessing random data from a tape takes an average of 50 seconds, an extremely long time in computer terms, because the tape has to fast-forward or reverse to put the read-write head in position to read the data. The situation is one you are likely familiar with if you have listened to both cassette tapes and compact discs. If you want to find a specific song on a compact disc, you simply skip to the track number, but on a cassette tape, you have to fast-forward or rewind to the appropriate part and you must listen and wait until you get there.

Second, the reading and writing process causes much more stress to a tape than a hard drive. The read-write head makes physical contact with the tape each time data is read or written, which wears out the tape. The average tape can be written to fully about 200 times or have no more than 5,000 cartridge loads and unloads. This means that daily tapes should be replaced every six months and weekly tapes every four years.

Real-World Example

A customer I worked with archived much of its data to Data Linear Tape (DLT) and then, several years after switching to Linear Tape-Open (LTO), needed to restore data from an old DLT tape. The company, however, had already decommissioned and sold its DLT equipment, so the tapes had to be sent to another company to perform the restore onto a compatible LTO tape, which took several days. The organization's recovery time objective (RTO) was a maximum of four hours, so this created an unexpected delay. The company learned its lesson and evaluated whether all the DLT tapes it was storing were actually needed and then converted the required tapes to LTO so that they could be read if necessary.

Even tapes used purely for archival purposes should be replaced every 15 years because their archival life span is between 15 and 30 years; the general rule is to replace monthly and yearly tapes every 15 years to be safe. The replacement process when data must be preserved involves reading the data from the tape and then writing it back to a new tape. To refresh old tapes and to be able to recover data from old tapes, organizations may need to keep antiquated hardware around.

Particles can build up on tape heads, so they must be periodically cleaned. Unreadable data may be written to tape if the drive is not cleaned regularly. Fortunately, many tape libraries are equipped with sensors that can detect when a drive must be cleaned, and a cleaning tape can be permanently loaded in the library so that cleaning operations will take place automatically. This removes the risk of a loss of data integrity because of a backup operator's lack of diligence in tape cleaning. Finally, tape drives can service only one request at a time, so they are ill suited as a shared medium.

Multistreaming and Multiplexing

Multistreaming allows a backup job to be sent to multiple I/O devices such as tapes or virtual tape library (VTL) stores (see Chapter 5 for information on VTL). This is especially useful for large backups that would take an extremely long time to write to a single tape, but the recovery process may require multiple tapes to be inserted.

Multiplexing is a method for writing multiple backups at the same time to a backup tape. This can save time, and it ensures that the stream of data to the tape remains full; however, it comes at a disadvantage when recovering backups because the data associated with a single backup is fragmented on the tape, so the drive will end up reading some data and then fast-forwarding ahead to the next point where that data was written.

Shoe Shining/Backhitching

Tapes can also suffer from shoe shining, sometimes called *backhitching*, a condition where the device sending data to the tape does not send data fast enough so the tape has to repeatedly stop and rewind to put itself back into position to write the next chunk of data in sequence. This causes strain on the tape and decreases its life expectancy.

Version	Released	Raw Capacity	Encoding	Read-Write Speed (Uncompressed)	Length	Linear Density (Bits/mm)	LTFS Support
LTO1	2000	100GB	RLL 1,7	20 MBps (160 Mbps)	609m	4,880	No
LTO2	2003	200GB	PRML	40 MBps (320 Mbps)	609m	7,398	No
LTO3	2005	400GB	PRML	80 MBps (640 Mbps)	680m	9,638	No
LTO4	2007	800GB	PRML	120 MBps (960 Mbps)	820m	13,250	No
LTO5	2010	1.5TB	PRML	140 MBps (1.12 Gbps)	846m	15,142	Yes
LTO6	2012	2.5TB	NPML	160 MBps (1.28 Gbps)	846m	15,143	Yes

Table 4-5 LTO Specifications

LTO Versions

Linear Tape-Open (LTO) is a magnetic tape standardization for use in data storage to replace Quantum's Data Linear Tape (DLT) and Sony's Advanced Intelligent Tape (AIT). The LTO consortium was started by HP, IBM, and Seagate so that rather than dealing with different vendor offerings, vendors could operate off a single standard. Its first version, LTO version 1 or Ultrium, was a tape that could hold 100GB. Table 4-5 provides the specifications for the different versions of LTO.

LTO tapes must be rewound once data has been written to them. This adds approximately 80 seconds to the tape operation if the tape must be completely rewound.

Compression and Encryption

LTO compression and encryption can be implemented in hardware or software. Hardware implementations are generally faster since they eliminate the operating system processing overhead required to perform compression or encryption calculations.

Table 4-6 provides the compression and encryption specifications for each LTO type. LTO versions 1 through 5 used the Adaptive Lossless Data Compression (ALDC) method, and LTO6 uses Streaming Lossless Data Compression (SLDC). ALDC achieves a compression ratio of 2 to 1 and has been used in versions of LTO1 through LTO5. However, some data that is compressed by ALDC is actually larger than the source data when it has been compressed already with another algorithm. SLDC solves this problem by comparing the compressed size using SLDC to the size of the data without SLDC

Version	Raw Capacity	Compressed Capacity	Compression Type	Encryptable
LTO1	100GB	200GB	ALDC	No
LTO2	200GB	400GB	ALDC	No
LTO3	400GB	800GB	ALDC	No
LTO4	800GB	1.6TB	ALDC	Yes
LTO5	1.5TB	3TB	ALDC	Yes
LTO6	2.5TB	6.25TB	SLDC	Yes

Table 4-6 LTO Compression and Encryption

and then writing the smaller of the two. SLDC achieves a compression ratio of 2.5 to 1 and is used in LTO6.

LTO4 through LTO6 tapes can be encrypted using a symmetric version of the Advanced Encryption Standard (AES) that encrypts and decrypts with the same key. The encryption can be handled by the LTO drive and does not require additional software to implement.

Size vs. Speed

Data sets typically get larger rather than smaller over time, so backup strategies must be scalable. One option is to extend backups onto multiple tapes as they grow. This will increase capacity, but it will take much longer to write the backup job. Speed can be increased by adding more drives and splitting the data among the drives through backup partitions or through multistreaming. In some cases, it may be advantageous to upgrade to a newer version of LTO. The capacity of the tapes doubled between LTO specifications 1, 2, 3, and 4, and read-write speed doubled between specifications 1, 2, and 3; therefore, tape users who moved from LTO1 to LTO2 or from LTO2 to LTO3 could store twice as much data on the tape because of its double capacity, but the write operation took the same amount of time (see Table 4-4).

Tape Care

Follow these guidelines to protect backup tapes and the data they contain. The access door that covers the tape keeps foreign particles such as dirt and dust from entering the tape cartridge. Avoid opening the access door unless absolutely required for servicing. Do not touch the magnetic strip inside the tape cartridge because this can destroy data on the tape and leave residue from your fingers that can harm the read-write heads in tape drives. Place barcode labels straight in the space provided on the edge of tapes to avoid barcode read errors in tape autoloaders and libraries. Discard tapes that repeatedly show read-write errors.

Clean tape drives as needed and keep track of the number of times tape-cleaning media is used so that it can be replaced when necessary. Tape-cleaning media can be used only a certain number of times before it becomes ineffective, potentially doing more harm than good. The number of cleanings will be documented in the cleaning-tape packaging and many times on the cleaning tape itself. Store tape drives and tape media away from printers and other devices that produce dust and other contaminants.

Tapes should be stored in an environment that is kept between 41 degrees and 90 degrees Fahrenheit with a relative humidity between 20 and 60 percent. When transporting tapes, it is best to use a carrier designed for the type of tape you are using. These cases will have inserts for tapes and have plenty of padding to protect against bumps or drops. Some cases can be locked for additional security if necessary.

LTFS

Linear Tape File System (LTFS) is an Extensible Markup Language (XML)–based tape file system that allows for tape resources to be accessed much like a mounted drive. Prior to LTFS, file metadata including filenames was stored in a database, catalog, or index maintained by the backup software, so the backup software was necessary to access files and directories on the tapes. With LTFS, files and directories on the tape can be viewed within the operating system itself without the need for backup software, and files can be added, opened, or removed directly without the use of specialized backup software as long as the operating system supports LTFS. Currently, LTFS is supported on LTO5 and LTO6 tapes and the following operating systems:

- Microsoft Windows 7
- Microsoft Windows 8
- Microsoft Windows Server 2008 R2
- Microsoft Windows Server 2012
- Mac OSX 10.5.6 Leopard and newer versions
- Red Hat Enterprise Linux 5.4 and newer versions
- SUSE Linux Enterprise Server 11 SP1 and newer versions

Please note that while LTFS tapes allow for file deletion, deletions only mark the blocks where deleted files reside as unavailable. These blocks are not free to use for storing other files, so it is not possible to delete a large amount of data from the LTFS tape through the operating system in order to add different data to the tape because the deletion would not actually free up space.

NDMP

Network Data Management Protocol (NDMP) is a method for transferring backup data directly between devices on a storage area network such as a storage array and a tape library. This allows for less overhead for backup operations since a server is not required to manage the backup jobs and interface between the storage array and the backup device. NDMP backups are known as an in-band solution since communication occurs entirely within the storage network. NDMP is especially valuable for network attached storage (NAS) since the backups can occur in-band on the storage network rather than over the data network. This results in less impact to the performance of the NAS during backups. NDMP is an industry standard that is supported by many vendors, so equipment from different vendors can work together using this protocol.

Libraries and Autoloaders

Organizations may end up managing hundreds if not thousands of tapes in the course of backing up data. Libraries and autoloaders make the job of managing and changing tapes easier. Tape libraries, sometimes called *tape jukeboxes* or *active tape libraries* (ATLs), are devices that can hold many tapes in slots known as *magazines* along with several drives. Multiple-drive units can write data to multiple tapes concurrently. A robotic arm moves tapes from the magazines to drives and then back into magazines when read or write operations complete. Tape barcodes are used to identify tapes to the library. Stackable tape libraries allow for additional shelves to be placed above or underneath the main library unit to provide more tape magazines. Tape autoloaders are a smaller version of a tape library that contains only one drive, but it may contain one or more magazines with many tapes. Tape libraries and autoloaders come equipped with interfaces such as FC, SAS, or SCSI to connect to a storage network or to a host. Those that use NDMP should be connected to the storage fabric directly rather than through a host.

Optical Media

The technology behind optical media began with the LaserDisc. LaserDisc technology was created in 1958 and first used for the storage of video in 1968. The LaserDisc format, the highest-quality video available from 1978 until the release of DVD, was born as a two-sided, 12-inch-diameter optical disc made of aluminum covered in plastic with a label in the center. LaserDisc was primarily a video format, but it was also used for mass data storage, although this was rather rare. LaserDisc technology was adapted to be used in audio in 1982 as the compact disc format, and compact discs were eventually used for data storage with the release of the Compact Disc Read-Only Media (CD-ROM). As technology improved, the CD was replaced by the Digital Video Disc (DVD), which, in turn, was replaced by Blu-ray Disc.

These optical formats, LaserDisc excluded, each share some of the same technologies such as the ability to write data to discs in a process known as *burning*, use of buffer cache, and their use of pits and lands to represent binary 0s and 1s.

A large number of optical discs can be stored in a jukebox. Jukeboxes have been made for LaserDiscs, CDs, DVDs, and Blu-ray Discs. Jukeboxes keep track of the discs they house and will load a disc on demand similar to a tape library. Some jukeboxes are available for writing data to discs. These devices can take a large amount of data that spans many discs and write it out to discs sequentially with one or more CD, DVD, or Blu-ray burners. Technology such as LightScribe allows these jukeboxes to create a descriptive label for completed discs. These devices often are equipped with software to allow multiple network users to submit data to the device. Administrators can view and manage job queues, manage access to the device, and run reports.

Most optical media are write-once, read-many (WORM) media. Once they are pressed at the factory, the data cannot be changed on the disc. Naturally, scratches and smudges can make portions of a disc or an entire disc unreadable, but users cannot write new data to a disc or other WORM media as they could with a hard disk drive. Once WORM media has been written to, there is a reasonable assumption that the data has not been altered, so WORM is an effective way to prevent changes to stored data.

Burning

Disc burning technologies have come in many formats such as CD-R, CD-RW, CD+R, CD+RW, DVD-R, DVD-RW, DVD+R, DVD+RW, DVD+R DL, DVD-R DL, DVD-RAM, BD-R, BD-RE, BD-R DL, and BD-RE DL; these technologies can be easily organized into one of two feature offerings. One type can write data to a blank disc, and then the disc cannot be written to again. The second, rewritable technology allows for discs to be written to and erased over and over again.

Burning processes originally required the recorder to write continuously without disruption. If the burning process was disrupted, the disc would become worthless.

Disc burners use a buffer to stage information about to be written to disc, but if this buffer is emptied, the process will become disrupted. This is known as *buffer underrun*. I used to make sure that all other programs were closed, and I would not use my computer while burning to guard against failed burns. Manufacturers introduced buffer underrun protection technologies such as BURN-proof, Safeburn, and Power Burn, and the problem of buffer underrun was soon resolved.

There are three formats for data writing: disc at once, track at once, and packet writing. Disc at once writes all the data to the disc without any gaps and then closes the disc. Closing the disc makes it so that no more data can be written to the disc. Track at once writes the data to the disc but leaves the disc open so that more data can be added to it later. Packet writing leaves the disc open and allows for data to be deleted or modified on the disc. Deleting data, however, does not free up space because the data still exists on the disc but is inaccessible.

Overburning is a process of burning data to a disc past the normal limits. Overburning can add data to the disc at the risk of making the disc unreadable by some or all players. Overburning can also damage the CD, DVD, or BD writer, so it should be avoided.

Compact Disc

The compact disc (CD) was the first format to see widespread use for data storage. A CD is 4.72 inches in diameter and made of aluminum and plastic. The aluminum contains the data as a series of pits organized into tracks on the disc. The plastic covers the bottom of the disc and protects the aluminum. A label is placed on the top of the disc, and the data is read from the bottom.

A laser with a beam size of 780nm shines on the disc to read it. The beam will either strongly reflect back or refract, which indicates whether the laser passed over a pit or land (areas without pits). A data table is stored at the beginning of the disc so that data can be located efficiently. A standard CD holds 74 minutes of audio or 682MB of data. Newer discs can hold 80 minutes of audio or 700MB of data; 734–842MB can be stored on discs when overburning is used, but these discs may not be compatible with all players, and overburning could ruin the CD burner.

The life span of burned CDs can vary greatly depending on the dye used in creating the CD-R. Cheaper dyes such as Cyanine may last only a few years, while gold can last around 100 years. As you can expect, few CDs are made with gold, and many use a combination of azo, phthalocyanine, or cyanine, which may give them a life span of 10 to 40 years. Factory-pressed CDs, however, can last more than 100 years.

CD-ROM data transfer speeds are rated in multiples of a single speed, which is 153,600 bps. For example, 2x reads at 307,200 bps. The remaining speeds are listed in Table 4-7 along with access time and rotations per minute (RPM). The access time, similar to HDD access time, is the average amount of time it takes to begin reading data; lower access times are preferred.

CD burning takes place at different speeds similar to the way data is accessed on a device. Table 4-8 lists the speeds, their transfer rate, and the time to write an entire CD.

Multiplier	Bits per Second (bps)	Kilobytes per Second (KBps)	Access Time (ms)	Rotations per Minute (RPM)
1x	153,600	150	400	200
2x	307,200	300	300	400
3x	460,800	450	200	600
4x	614,400	600	150	800
6x	921,600	900	150	1,200
8x	1,228,800	1,200	100	1,600
10x	1,536,000	1,500	100	2,000
12x	1,843,200	1,800	100	2,400
16x	2,457,600	2,400	100	3,200
18x	2,764,800	2,700	100	3,600
24x	3,686,400	3,600	100	4,800
32x	4,915,200	4,800	100	6,400
36x	5,529,600	5,400	100	7,200
40x	6,144,000	6,000	100	8,000
48x	7,372,800	7,200	100	9,600
52x	7,987,200	7,800	100	10,400
100x	15,360,000	15,000	100	20,000

Table 4-7   CD Transfer Speeds

DVD

The digital video disc (DVD) was introduced in 1995 where it soon offered companies and consumers a higher-capacity option for data storage over CD. Single-layer DVDs can hold 4.37GB, and dual-layer DVDs can hold 7.96GB. That's more than six times the capacity of a CD for single layer and eleven times a CD's capacity for dual-layer DVD. DVDs are the same size as a CD, but the data is stored using smaller pits on the disc. A more precise 650nm laser reads the data in much the same way as a CD is read. A burned DVD has a life span of approximately 45 years, a burned DVD rewritable has a life span of 30 years, and a factory-pressed DVD can last for more than 100 years.

Blu-ray Disc

The successor to DVD is the Blu-ray Disc (BD). It was released in 2006 along with a competing product called HD-DVD. While single-layer BD can store 25GB as compared to 30GB with HD-DVD, HD-DVD can have only a single layer. Dual-layer BD can store 50GB, triple-layer BD can store 100GB, and quad-layer BD can store 128GB. This, among other factors, eventually won Blu-ray Disc's dominance over the market. Blu-ray gets its name from the blue color spectrum (405nm) of the laser used in reading and writing to Blu-ray Discs. Prior to BD, red lasers such as the 650nm (DVD) and 780nm (CD and LaserDisc) were used because of their low cost, but these lasers were

Table 4-8	Multiplier	Write Speed (MBps)	Write Time (Minutes)
CD Burning Speeds	1x	0.15	80
	2x	0.3	40
	4x	0.6	20
	8x	1.2	10
	16x	2.4	5
	20x	3.0	4
	24x	3.6	3.4
	32x	4.8	2.5
	40x	6.0	2
	48x	7.2	1.7
	52x	7.8	1.5

limited in how precise they could be. Innovation in crystal manufacturing made the blue laser more cost effective to produce and led to the introduction of BD.

ISO

Images of CDs, DVDs, and BDs can be created in a format known as ISO. The name was derived from the ISO 9660 specification for the CD file system, and it is also the three-letter extension used for the image file. ISOs allow for disc images to be loaded into a virtual optical drive so that software can interface with data on a CD just as it would if the disc were in a drive. Many manufacturers are distributing software as ISO downloads rather than packaging CDs or DVDs with their products. This is especially valuable for virtual servers or virtual storage appliances that may not have a physical optical drive assigned to them. In these cases, an ISO file can be mounted in the virtual device so that it can reference the data on the imaged optical disc.

File Systems

Optical media, just like hard drives, standardize the way data is stored and tracked through the use of a file system. The two main file systems in use for optical media are CDFS and UDF. BDFS is also discussed here, but it was used only briefly for Blu-ray Discs.

The Compact Disc File System (CDFS), specified in ISO 9660, allows access to data stored on a CD in tracks and sectors, each 2,352 bytes long. After error correction and header information, each sector can hold 2,048 bytes. CDFS allows for directory structures to be eight levels deep, including the root directory. For example, this directory would be the maximum allowed on CDFS: \data\accounting\us\alaska\ anchorage\2004\january\. This may require some directory structures to be revised prior to being written to CD. CDFS also supports a maximum of 65,535 directories because of its 16-bit path table.

The Universal Disc Format (UDF), specified in ISO 13346, replaced CDFS, and it is used mainly on DVDs and some BDs. UFS allows for a maximum filename length of 255 bytes and a maximum path name length of 1,023 bytes.

Blu-ray Disc File System (BDFS) maintains a database of data allocations on the Blu-ray Disc that takes up a few megabytes in a section of the disc allocated for system management information. It is efficient for storing video streams, but it was used only for a short time. It was replaced with UDF 2.5 in order to make it easier for computers and other systems that already understood UDF to operate with BD.

Flash Media

Similar to the solid-state disks (SSDs) discussed in Chapter 1, flash media utilize Negated AND (NAND) flash memory to store data. Flash media forms the basis of today's sneakernet, allowing individuals to easily copy data to a portable device. Flash media is also used in many mobile devices such as digital cameras, digital camcorders, MP3 players, phones, and tablets. Flash media is either used as built-in storage or via add-in cards such as Secure Digital (SD), Multimedia Card (MMC), CompactFlash (CF), and others, as shown in Table 4-9. Its popularity stems from the fact that it can be constructed in various small sizes and it uses relatively little power. Most offerings allow for approximately 1 million write cycles, which is ten times that of an SLC SSD drive.

 NOTE *Sneakernet* is an old term that referred to a network where data was transferred when people carried floppy disks from one computer to another. The data was carried by "sneakers," aka their feet.

Flash media is also commonly equipped with a USB interface. Once connected to a computer, these flash drives can be accessed like any other local hard drive, making it easy for users to archive data, add capacity, or share data. The size of USB flash drives continues to increase, and their size remains small enough that they could be attached to a keychain or stored easily in a pocket.

Format	Release Date	Size (Width × Height)	Max Capacity
CompactFlash (CF)	1994	43 × 36mm	512MB
MultimediaCard (MMC)	2003	24 × 18mm	4GB
SecureDigital (SD)	1999	32 × 24mm	4GB
SecureDigital High Capacity (SDHC)	2006	32 × 24mm	256GB+
MicroSD	2005	11 × 15	4GB
MicroSDHC	2007	11 × 15	64GB+
Memory Stick	1998	50 × 21	128MB
Memory Stick Pro	2003	50 × 21	4GB
Memory Stick Pro Duo	2002	31 × 20	32GB
xD	2005	20 × 25	2GB

Table 4-9 Flash-Based Add-in Cards

Chapter Summary

This chapter covered storage hardware beginning with optical and copper cables. Optical cables transmit data using light that is directed through a glass core surrounded by a protective cladding. Optical cables are well suited for long-distance applications, high-bandwidth connections, and communications through areas with interference. Optical cables are more expensive than copper, and the hardware used to interface with them is also more expensive. There are two types of optical cables: single-mode fiber (SMF) and multimode fiber (MMF). Single-mode fiber can span greater distances using a small precision core and a laser, whereas MMF uses an LED and a larger core but can transmit more data over shorter distances.

Optical cables connect to other networking devices by using connectors such as the standard connector (SC), local connector (LC), and straight tip (ST). SC and LC have dual connectors bound together for sending and receiving, and their ends are roughly square-shaped. LC is the smaller of the two, allowing for higher density in switching.

Care must be taken to not bend or place stress on optical cables to avoid connection loss or cable damage. Cables should be installed in runways through data centers or pipes in the ground to protect them.

Copper cables use electromagnetic waves to transmit information. Copper is cheaper than optical cable, but it cannot span long distances and is limited in data rate. Copper cables are not as fragile as optical cables, but they must still be cared for. Twisted-pair cabling is most vulnerable to damage through stretching.

- Twisted-pair cabling is the most common copper cable used in computer networking. Twisted-pair cables are defined by category (Cat); they are ranked from 1 to 6, with 6a being the newest.

- Serial cables are used mainly to connect to management consoles on storage networking and computer networking hardware such as fiber switches, routers, and Ethernet switches.

- Twinax cable can support up to 10 Gbps speeds, and it is often used to connect storage devices to a switch as an alternative to fiber connections.

Cables carry data from one place to another, but they cannot act alone. Devices are required to store and transmit data at intermediate points and to send and receive data at end points. End points need to be equipped with a host bus adapter, network interface card, or converged network adapter to interface with cables.

NICs are mostly used with Ethernet networks, including some iSCSI implementations, while HBAs are used for most other connections such as FC or iSCSI.

The CNA can support multiple protocols and is mainly used in FCoE implementations.

Repeaters and amplifiers can be used to simply rebroadcast the signal and extend the range of the cable run, and switches, directors, and routers not only repeat the signal, but also send the signal to other cable segments that ultimately lead to the destination.

This chapter's last section provided information on removable storage, including tapes, optical discs, and flash drives.

- Tapes are a low-cost method of writing sequential data and are mainly used for backups.
- Optical discs are a low-cost way of archiving and distributing information. Data is written to optical discs through a process called burning where a laser burns pits into the disc.
- Flash media takes the form of small cards that can be placed in devices such as phones or cameras or built into these devices.

Chapter Review Questions

1. Which technology would aid in reducing the processing load on a host system?
   A. Amplifier
   B. GBIC
   C. TOE
   D. SFP

2. You notice that a tape backup is quite noisy. As you investigate, you find that the tape repeatedly stops and rewinds during backup operations. What is the cause of this?
   A. Random reads from tape
   B. Backhitching
   C. LTO version incompatibility
   D. Multistreaming

3. A co-worker tells you that you don't need Cat6a because Cat6 supports 10GigE. What is the limitation of using Cat6 instead of Cat6a?
   A. Cat6 must be shielded to protect against EMI.
   B. Cat6 supports only 10GigE using 10GBASE-RF.
   C. Cat6 cannot coexist with Cat5/Cat5e cables.
   D. 10GigE over Cat6 is limited to only 55 meters.

4. Your company is installing a fiber link between its headquarters and an office 15 miles away. You plan to do SAN replication over the fiber link. Which cable would you use for the link between sites?
   A. 9/125
   B. 50/125
   C. 62/125
   D. 100/125

5. A junior team member has been assigned the task of patching Ethernet cable for a new 10 Gbps iSCSI network to a 10GigE switch, but he is unsure about how to wire the cable. What should you tell him? Each cable will be no longer than 12 feet.

   A. Use Cat5 and wire it with EIA/TIA 568A on both ends.

   B. Use Cat5 and wire it with EIA/TIA 568A on one end and 568B on the other end.

   C. Use Cat6 and wire it with EIA/TIA 568A on both ends.

   D. Use Cat6 and wire it with EIA/TIA 568A on one end and 568B on the other end.

6. A storage server writes out approximately 900MB of new encryption keys each month that need to be archived. Data integrity is important, so users should not be able to modify the data once it has been archived. Which solution would be best in this situation?

   A. Burn the keys to a CD-R each month.

   B. Create a job that automatically writes the keys to a backup tape each month.

   C. Burn the keys to a DVD-R each month.

   D. Create a script that replicates the keys to a network share that users have read-only access to.

7. You have purchased a new fiber switch, and you would like to connect several servers and a storage device to it. You purchased fiber cables with LC connectors, and the servers and storage devices are all equipped with fiber HBAs with LC connectors. What other hardware is required for the network to function?

   A. CNA

   B. GBIC

   C. Fiber management software

   D. SFP

8. The server administration team has configured a new database server that must attach to the storage area network. They have purchased it with a fiber HBA that is equipped with dual LC fiber ports. You have a box of fiber cables. One cable is green with two large square ends. Another is orange with two smaller square ends, and the third is round with a bayonet plug. Which one should you use to connect the HBA to the network?

   A. The cable with the large square connector.

   B. The cable with the small square connector.

   C. The cable with the round connector.

   D. The cable is not present in the box.

Chapter Review Answers

1. **C** is correct. The TCP Offload Engine (TOE) offloads the TCP/IP protocol processing to the network controller, alleviating the computer processor from having to perform this work.
   A, **B**, and **D** are incorrect. An amplifier rebroadcasts a signal. Both the GBIC and SFP are transceivers that interface between a network device and a cable.

2. **B** is correct. Backhitching, also called shoe shining, is a condition where the device sending data to the tape does not send data fast enough, so the tape has to repeatedly stop and rewind to put itself back into position to write the next chunk of data in sequence.
   A, **C**, and **D** are incorrect. **A** is incorrect because backup operations are serial and do not result in random reads or writes. Also, a backup operation is a series of writes, not reads. **C** is incorrect because if the LTO version was incompatible, the backup would not run to the media at all. **D** is incorrect because multistreaming would result in better performance but would still be serial operation and not result in stops or rewinds.

3. **D** is correct. Cat6 can transmit at 10 Gbps, but it is limited to 55 meters when doing so. Cat6a can go 100 meters while transmitting at 10 Gbps.
   A, **B**, and **C** are incorrect. **A** is incorrect because Cat6 does not require additional shielding to perform at 10 Gbps. The twisted pairs in the cable are used to protect against internal interference, and interference results in loss of connectivity, not reduced speed. **B** is incorrect because Cat6 can be used with any supported 10GBASE standard to achieve speeds of 10 Gbps. **C** is incorrect because Cat6 and Cat5 can coexist on the same network, and even the same switch, but each cable is limited to their own maximum speed.

4. **A** is correct. First the question asks which cable is needed to run a distance of 15 miles. Of the two main types of optical cables, SMF can span thousands of kilometers, and MMF can reach only a maximum of 2 kilometers, so you will need to use an SMF cable. The answers provided are cable types given using the core/cladding description. The first number is the size of the core in microns, and the second number is the size of the cladding. If the core is less than 10, it is SMF, and if it is between 50 and 100, it is MMF. Option **A**, 9/125, is an SMF cable, so **A** is the answer.
   B, **C**, and **D** are incorrect. **B**, **C**, and **D** are all between 50 and 100, so they are MMF cables and can only reach a maximum of 2 kilometers, so they will not meet the requirements.

5. **C** is correct. Cat6 will provide the required 10 Gbps speed, and the same EIA/TIA specification must be used on both ends to connect to the switch.
   A, **B**, and **D** are incorrect. The iSCSI network will run at 10 Gbps, so the team member will need to use Cat6 or Cat6a. This eliminates options **A** and **B**. Of the two remaining choices, one uses a different specification for each end, and the other uses same. Normal cables use the same specification for both ends.

Only crossover cables use a combination of 568A and 568B, so **C** is the correct answer.

6. **C** is correct. The files must not be changed, so the option should be read-only, and a DVD would be required since a DVD can store more than 4GB of data. **A**, **B**, and **D** are incorrect. The files must not be changed, so the option should be read-only. The read-only share in option **D** would not work because local users on the server could have access to modify the data. Option **B** writes the data to tape, but this could be erased or modified. Options **A** and **C** burn to optical media. Once the media has been written to, it cannot be altered. However, a CD does not have enough space to store 900MB, so a DVD would be required since a DVD can store more than 4GB of data.

7. **D** is correct. A transceiver is necessary to accept the light signal and convert it to an electrical impulse the switch can understand. Fiber switches uses SFPs, and an SFP is required for each port that will have a fiber connection. Fiber switches ship without SFPs so that customers can purchase the appropriate SFP for their network. In this case, an SFP with an LC connector would be needed.
A, **B**, and **C** are incorrect. A CNA is used for FCIP networks and would not be used in this situation. A GBIC is not used with fiber HBAs, so it is incorrect, and fiber management software is not a hardware solution.

8. **B** is correct. The HBA has LC ports and so you must use the LC connector. LC connectors are small with two square ends.
A, **C**, and **D** are incorrect. **A** is incorrect because a cable with two large square ends describes the SC connector, and **C** is incorrect because round bayonet plugs are found on ST connectors. **D** is incorrect because the correct cable is in the box; it is the LC connector.

Virtualization

In this chapter, you will learn how to

- Describe storage virtualization
- Utilize tape virtualization in a practical business setting
- Explain how host virtualization makes it easier to work with storage
- Describe how virtualization is implemented within an array
- Differentiate between virtualization methods used on networks

Chapters 1 through 4 provided a comprehensive overview of storage technologies and principles. Chapter 5 begins the practical exploration of managing storage resources by using storage virtualization. Storage virtualization is the logical abstraction of a physical resource that uses hardware, software, and other technologies to pool or aggregate disparate storage resources such as disks, tapes, logical volumes, or arrays. As part of this process, physical storage is seen as a centralized virtual resource that can be referenced, used, and managed in differing forms allowing for increased scalability and data access. Storage virtualization provides a robust platform for data archiving, backup, and disaster recovery, along with a means for dynamic or on-demand utilization and optimization of storage resources.

What does that mean for storage professionals? Data, and the information derived from it, can be an organization's greatest asset but also its greatest challenge. Legal requirements for data retention periods, the need for data to be accessible whenever and wherever users happen to be, and the requirement for securing data all make managing the sheer volume of data captured, stored, and made available by a company a task often rivaling the operation of its primary lines of business. Successful data management is predicated on striking a balance between a complex mix of architectures, policies, procedures, and technology.

In a perfect world, all these policies/procedures, architectures, and technologies would be compatible, offering a high degree of interoperability and seamless integration throughout the storage fabric. In reality, a company's data and the technology it deploys is typically mixed and needs to interact with other entities that, in turn, deploy differing standards for managing, accessing, and storing data. Data resource management becomes even more complex given that these data and resources may be geographically dispersed across a region, nation, or geopolitical borders. Storage virtualization offers the potential for providing access without users having to understand the underlying complexities of the technology. Storage virtualization also makes it easier to perform migration and management of storage resources in this fast-paced, volatile environment.

In addition to virtualization's ease of management, virtualization enables businesses to better utilize their existing storage technology. Underutilization of storage, data protection, and its availability remain critical issues in the successful management of information systems. Storage virtualization offers an enterprise the real-time capability to dynamically manage and optimize storage resources and data regardless of the complexity, location, or mix of technologies.

Types of Storage Virtualization

Given the many competing vendor-based views of what constitutes storage virtualization, the Storage Networking Industry Association (SNIA) shared storage model provides a generally accepted way of defining and understanding storage virtualization. SNIA defines *storage virtualization* as follows:

- The act of abstracting, hiding, or isolating the internal functions of a storage subsystem or service from applications, host computers, or general network resources for the purposes of enabling application and network-independent management of storage or data

- The application of virtualization to storage services or devices for the purposes of aggregating functions or devices, hiding complexity, or adding new capabilities to lower-level storage resources

The Shared Storage Model (SSM), shown in Figure 5-1, was created in 2001 as a four-layer model similar to the Open System Integration (OSI) Model, where the lowest layer defines the physical aspects of storage virtualization and the highest layer forms the application layer. The SNIA SSM is also similar to the OSI Model in that it has not been implemented by a vendor. Rather, it is useful as a tool for understanding how shared storage works. It also provides a vendor-neutral way to discuss storage system functionality by using the same vocabulary.

At the top of the SNIA SSM is the applications layer, layer 4. This is the reason for the storage system in the first place, and it rests at the top of the model because it is the product of the layers underneath it.

Layer 3 is the file/record layer. This layer consists of the database and file systems that support the application. This layer is responsible for organizing the information required by the application, and it directly interfaces with the application. For example, an application may query a database for information stored in tables, or an application could request a file from a file system. This file system may be local to the device, or it could reside on a network attached storage (NAS) server.

Layer 2 is the block aggregation layer, responsible for connecting to storage. It has three subelements: device, network, and host. *Device* refers to a direct attached storage (DAS) device that contains the storage accessed by the layer. *Network* includes storage

Figure 5-1
SNIA Shared
Storage Model

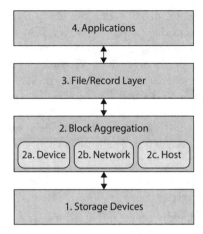

area network (SAN) storage resources, and *host* refers to storage located inside the host machine or server.

Layer 1 is the storage devices layer, which handles striping, mirroring, parity, and read and write operations. The data provided from layer 2 needs to be stored onto media, such as disk or tape, as bits and bytes that are grouped and referenced into blocks.

SNIA has also developed a model for storage virtualization. The SNIA Storage Virtualization Taxonomy identifies five types of storage virtualization. They are briefly introduced here and covered more extensively in subsequent sections of this chapter: tape, disk, block, file system, and file/record.

The first type is tape virtualization. Tape virtualization takes the form of virtual tapes (VTs), virtual tape libraries (VTLs), and tape library virtualization (TLV).

Second are disks. Disks use virtualization to map logical addresses to physical addresses. Cylinder, head, and sector (CHS) is a method for accessing data on a physical disk. The head information describes which platter and side the data resides on, while the cylinder information locates the track on that platter. Lastly, the sector addresses the area within that track so that the head can be positioned to read or write data to that location. CHS physical data is allocated by disk firmware to virtual locations on the medium through the use of logical block addressing (LBA). LBA is a way of referencing a location on a disk without a device having knowledge of the physical disk geometry.

Whereas a controller identifies data based on CHS, logical volumes virtually map blocks using LBA. LBA provides a system with the number of blocks contained on the drive, while the system keeps track of the data contained on each block. It requests the data by block number, and the drive then maps the block to a CHS and retrieves the data.

Next comes block virtualization. Block virtualization is an abstraction of physical storage to logical partitions independent of storage structure, allowing several physical disks to be accessed through a single virtual/logical interface. This results in greater flexibility in storage management in how and where data is stored.

Fourth, file or record virtualization is used to dynamically allocate infrequently used files or records to secondary storage while caching more actively used files on primary storage. When implemented, file-based virtualization presents storage to a device such as a remote share using protocols such as Network File System (NFS) or Common Internet File System (CIFS), whereas block storage is presented to a device as local storage using protocols such as Fiber Channel Protocol (FCP) or Internet Small Computer System Interface (iSCSI).

Lastly, file system virtualization allows a file system to share remote or network attached logical partitions where the location is transparent to the applications, reading and writing to and from the storage.

Tape Virtualization

Because of the onslaught of vendor products and competing taxonomies, getting to the heart of what constitutes tape virtualization may seem frustrating. The abundant availability and deployment of high-performance, high-capacity tape media and drives seem to position one storage technology against the other. Tape media remains a mainstay of computing. While prices have steadily declined against the increased capacity and performance of tape, it still remains a serial technology. The staying power of tape can be seen in its portability, therefore making it the perfect media for data archiving, migration, backup, and rapid disaster recovery. Tape virtualization uses a combination of disk drives and tape media to augment three different tape virtualization techniques:

- **Virtual tape**   This is an interface that emulates the way a physical tape would operate, but data is stored on another medium such as a disk.
- **Virtual tape library**   Disks are used as replacements for tape libraries. They emulate a collection of tapes that can be automatically loaded and inventoried.
- **Virtual tape server**   Intelligent devices and software coordinate storage onto virtual resources.

Virtual Tape

Storage virtualization using the virtual tape method provides a dynamic platform for archiving, backup, and disaster recovery. All of these functions can be performed as background operations, concurrently or in parallel, thus minimizing tape failures and media errors since the data is stored on disk instead. Disks do not suffer from the limitations tapes have of needing to access data sequentially. In this way, VT provides a means of offsetting the serial nature of accessing data or files from tape storage. Disks are used as caches or temporary holding areas for concatenated data sets, fostering rapid data transfers and access to target tape media. The data comprising virtual tapes can be consolidated through deduplication so that identical data is stored only once. Physical tapes may have unused space at the end of a tape once a job runs, but VTs only consume the space that is required by the backup job. For example, 100GB of data is written daily to an LTO3 tape with an uncompressed capacity of 400GB, and then the tape is changed for another; 300GB of the available space is wasted daily. However, utilizing VT, 100GB is written to a virtual LTO3 tape, but only 100GB is consumed on the storage. This results in better utilization of storage media.

The following steps outline the general process for creating VTs. The first step is to identify the media that will be used for creating the VTs. This could include disks, Redundant Array of Independent Disks (RAID) sets, or tapes. The speed of the media chosen will determine how quickly backups to VT can complete and how quickly they can be restored, while the capacity of the media will determine how many backups to VT can be taken before some backups must be overwritten. Avoid selecting media from a single source because if that single source, such as a single RAID array, is lost, all VTs will be lost as well.

Next, a storage pool is created using the resources identified in the previous step. The storage pool aggregates the storage available to the disks, tapes, or RAID sets within it so that it can be allocated as VT storage. Storage pools can be expanded with additional media later as needs change. To optimize the use of target tape media, it is necessary to determine the optimum size and density of the given tape media. These blocks or integrated file streams (IFSs) are placed in pools of storage. This method allows the size of the IFS to be determined dynamically or remain fixed.

Once a storage pool is created, VTs must be created from the storage pool. This is followed by the creation of an image catalog. An image catalog is created indicating the location of data within virtual volumes created on the disk. Lastly, assign the VTs to backup software that will write data to them as if they were physical tapes.

Virtual Tape Library

Specialized servers, devices, and software are used to create virtual tape libraries that reside on disk. The chief benefit of this scheme lies in its ability to emulate various tape formats and media while maximizing utilization of resources. Unlike tape, random data can be transferred to and accessed from disk technology much faster and then transferred to secondary tape storage if necessary. Figure 5-2 shows a VTL solution. Alternately, these disk-based virtual libraries can be used as an independent, stand-alone option. As an enterprise-level virtualization option, VTLs are typically implemented on RAID and other disk array platforms.

 EXAM TIP   A VTL solution could be as simple as a server with backup software that supports VTL. This would then write to local storage but treat it as tape from a recovery standpoint.

Virtual Tape Server

As with other forms of tape virtualization, virtual tape servers integrate disk and tape functionality to provide low-cost, high-performance storage and data management. Multiple files are stored on the virtual volume using volume stacking. A stacked volume can consist of a single or multiple logical volumes on a virtual tape server, as

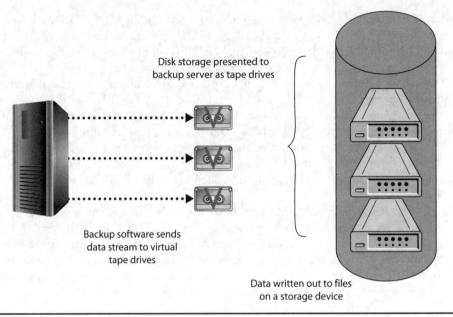

Disk storage presented to
backup server as tape drives

Backup software sends
data stream to virtual
tape drives

Data written out to files
on a storage device

Figure 5-2   Sample VTL solution

depicted in Figure 5-3. The virtual tape server library serves as the index indicating where files or data are stored on logical volumes. VTS technology allows for greater utilization of storage resources with deduplication. The data on VTS servers can be consolidated through deduplication so that identical data is stored only once. Multiple daily, weekly, or monthly backups of the same data store will result in many duplicate files, which would need to be written individually to tape, but can be written only once to a VTS device using deduplication. Once data has been stored on a VTS, it can then be archived to another site or eventually transferred to tape, if necessary, to provide additional backup redundancy.

Network Data Management Protocol

Network Data Management Protocol (NDMP) is a protocol that allows devices to communicate with backup hardware such as tape devices directly without going through backup servers. This is more direct and can result in lower network bandwidth utilization, shorter backup times, and less hardware to maintain and support in the environment. Without NDMP, backups may need to be staged on another device before they are backed up, or restores may need to be performed on another volume before being copied to the production volume. With NDMP, devices such as NAS can issue backup or restore requests directly to the network attached backup device.

Figure 5-3
Virtual tape
server

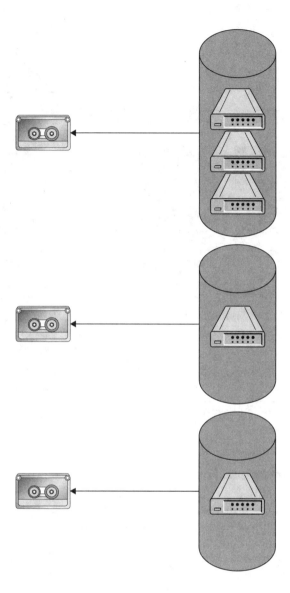

Disk Virtualization

Regardless of design or capacity, disk virtualization uses the firmware within a given drive to translate the physical locations or addresses of data on the disk's CHS to LBA. Disk virtualization addresses the use of heterogeneous disk technologies often intermixed in an enterprise's storage fabric. Disk virtualization provides an additional benefit of data protection and integrity through its ability to bypass defective blocks on the disk by mapping them to healthy logical block locations. Figure 5-4 shows the mapping of LBA to CHS.

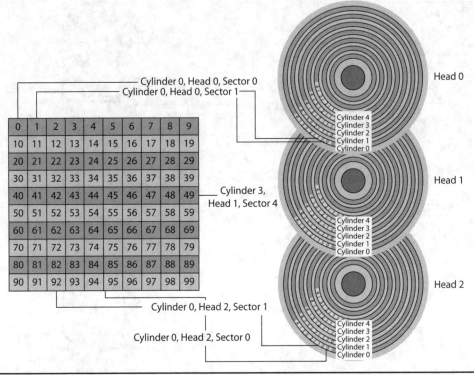

Figure 5-4 LBA-to-CHS mapping

Block Virtualization

Block virtualization allows for logical volumes (LVs) to be created from storage that may consist of multiple drives and multiple RAID arrays. However, systems accessing block storage do not need to understand where and how access is provided in order to utilize it.

In this context, block virtualization facilitates nondisruptive data archiving, migration, backup, and recovery. The topic of block virtualization is best understood in terms of its relationship to storage area networks and network attached storage. Distributed storage assets are abstracted to provide a single logical portal for storage management and optimization. Block virtualization provides a translation layer in the SAN, between the hosts and the storage arrays. Multiple distributed physical disks can be mapped to a single logical volume or interface with block virtualization.

Addressing

Block virtualization works by addressing a single block of data using a unique identifier called a *logical unit number* (LUN). The LUNs for an entire drive are then mapped to virtual storage using an LBA. The LUN is capable of mapping single or multiple physical

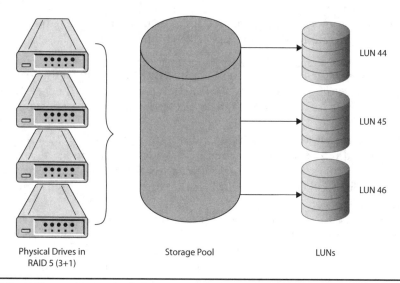

Physical Drives in   Storage Pool   LUNs
RAID 5 (3+1)

Figure 5-5   LUN mapping to physical space

disks within a SAN environment. Storage assets (a logical volume created from one or more physical disks in a RAID set or array) are identified using LUNs and presented as a single logical storage component.

LBA represents an enhancement over traditional CHS addressing and was first introduced with the advent of SCSI disks. As a 28-bit scheme, LBA is capable of addressing disks in excess of 528MB by mapping CHS addresses on a disk or secondary storage. Storage locations are created and accessed via a linear sector address scheme beginning with zero, or LBA 0. Figure 5-5 shows how a LUN maps to physical space.

 EXAM TIP   In SANs or RAID arrays, LUNs of physical disks are mapped via LBA to storage for an entire device.

File Virtualization

File virtualization in a SAN environment overcomes the limitations of data and location dependencies where files are associated with specific servers. Network shares residing on different servers increase fragmentation and underutilization of storage capacity because each server is logically and physically independent. As a consequence, file access and migration can be disruptive because storage resources may have to be taken offline during reconfiguration. Quality of service (QoS) and service level agreements are compromised because applications and hosts will require path reconfiguration. However, file virtualization allows for a single namespace to be used for shared resources while the resources may be distributed to many servers behind the scenes.

 EXAM TIP File virtualization namespaces can be redundantly created so that there is not a single point of failure by hosting them on multiple devices. The namespace mount point can be accessed from any server hosting it.

In short, file virtualization provides a nondisruptive alternative for data access, migration, backup, and recovery. File virtualization provides location independence through the use of logical pools, which use logical rather than physical paths between storage resources, allowing for files to be stored where they can best be protected against loss and aggregated to save space.

Through the use of global namespaces, logical file paths are mapped to physical path names. The goal of a global namespace is to enable a single view of the NAS file system. In this way, transparent access to NAS resources is provided. Entire file systems can be seamlessly read from their former location and written to the new one. File virtualization can be implemented using stand-alone devices or integrated into the NAS or storage system itself.

File System Virtualization

Multiple file systems are aggregated into a single logical system. Users have access to data and storage resources from underlying transparent file systems. The following are types of file systems currently in use:

- **SAN file system** Enables sharing of the same copies of files stored on common storage media among multiple servers of different platforms.

- **Local disk file system** Enables the storage and retrieval of files on local storage. Files are stored in a hierarchical (tree) structure where file location and paths within the structure and naming conventions are specified by the local policies and the file system. A root directory is assigned to the top of each logical drive, and then files and folders can be placed underneath.

- **Distributed file system (DFS)** Provides the ability to logically group shares on multiple servers and to transparently link shares into a single, hierarchical namespace. Shared resources on a network are organized in a tree structure, as depicted in Figure 5-6.

Resources can be in multiple sites; in some cases, resources are replicated to multiple locations, and the data is presented to users based on its availability and locality to the user, with the server closest to the user serving the data rather than traffic traversing slow links, as shown with the profiles share in Figure 5-7.

- **Clustered file system (CFS)** A distributed file system that runs concurrently on multiple NAS nodes. Clustering provides transparent access to all files on

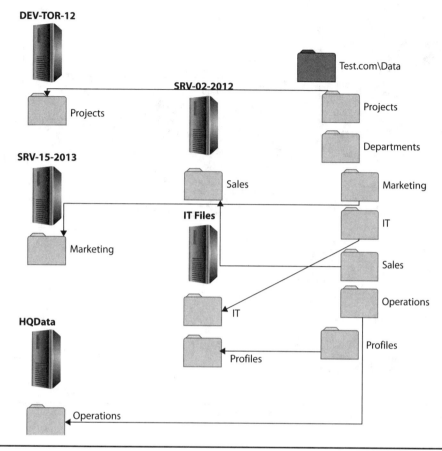

Figure 5-6   Distributed file system

all homogeneous clustered nodes, regardless of the physical location of the file. The number and location of the nodes are transparent. System nodes must be similarly configured and from the same vendor.

File/Record

With file or record virtualization, files and directories are presented as a composite object with a single integrated file interface, but consisting of storage from one or more devices that are either locally attached or on the storage network. Location independence is achieved, allowing users, applications, and devices to access and manipulate files irrespective of where they are stored as if they were stored locally.

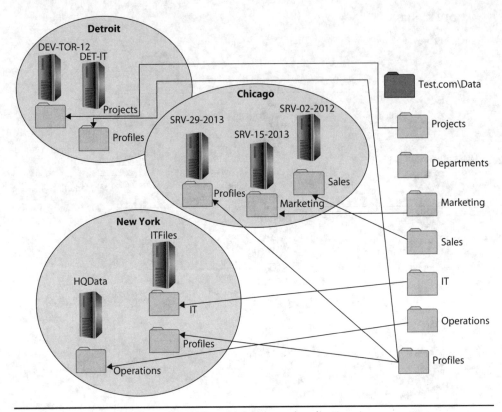

Figure 5-7 Distributed file system with multiple sites and replication

Host Virtualization

In server or host-based virtualization, LUNs from physical disks are aggregated into a larger primary LUN, which is seen as a single device by applications and users. This is accomplished through the use of logical volume managers (LVMs) integrated as part of stand-alone appliances or servers or as part of a privileged kernel of the host operating system. Since virtualization is done at the device or server level, existing paths and mechanisms for control are maintained. Data is dynamically routed, or multipathed, between shared storage. This form of virtualization is typically used with DAS, but can span multiple storage subsystems that are connected within a SAN.

LVM

LVMs create logical partitions capable of spanning single or multiple physical devices. Physical volumes (PVs) are then created within these partitions and are aggregated in volume groups (VGs). LUNs effectively provide logical volume management functionality such as mirroring, partition resizing, disk allocation, and striping. VGs are divided into logical groups (LGs) with designated mount points. Figure 5-8 illustrates the LVM concepts defined next.

- **Extents**　These are the basic building blocks of data and storage used to prevent disk fragmentation through the use of a marker that is placed to indicate the last write of 64-bit blocks (8 pages) of contiguous space that occurred for a file.
- **Physical volume**　This is composed of extents.
- **Logical volume**　This is the equivalent of a disk partition in non-LVM environments; it is seen as a centralized block device.
- **Physical extent**　Each physical volume is divided into contiguous blocks of data. In a VG, PEs are identical in size to LEs in the VG.
- **Logical extent**　Each logical volume is divided into equal-sized blocks of data.
- **Volume group**　This is a large group of storage from which LVs can be created. PVs are aggregated into a singular unit.

LVM creation is achieved in the following steps:

1. Identify physical media to be deployed.

2. Create VG from PV.

3. Create LVs from the VG.

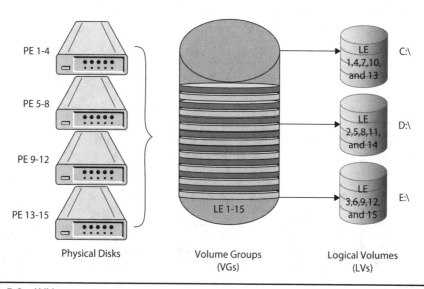

Figure 5-8　LVM concepts

Virtual Provisioning

Virtual provisioning allows a logical unit to appear larger than its actual physical capacity. Dynamic storage allocation is derived from a pool of shared physical storage. In this context, virtual provisioning allows for the downstream addition of other storage devices while the thin pool is active. Thin provisioning is creating a logical volume that can grow as needed. To provision virtual storage, first allocate one or more RAID groups with sufficient capacity for the data you want to store. Next, create a pool, giving it a name, and then assign LUNs from the RAID groups you identified to the storage pool. Finally, allocate storage to hosts, specifying thin provisioning and using the storage pool.

 EXAM TIP When thin LUNs are deleted, the capacity is reallocated to the shared pool either automatically or through a reclamation process.

Implementing Host Virtualization

Several strategies exist to map logical extents into physical extents, including linear mapping, striped mapping, and snapshot. Each of these is described next and shown in Figure 5-9.

- **Linear mapping**   This is the contiguous designation of a range of PEs to an area on an LV. For example, LEs 1–99 are mapped to PV1, and LEs 100–347 are mapped to PV2.

- **Striped mapping**   LEs are interleaved across a number of PVs. In Figure 5-9, the odd LEs are on PV1, and the even LEs are on PV2.

- **Snapshot**   This is an exact copy of an LG at a given point in time. Snapshots will be discussed in more detail in Chapter 7.

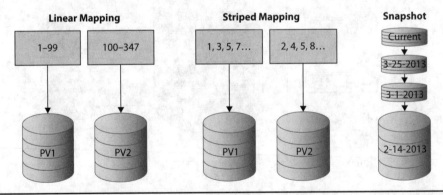

Figure 5-9   Mapping logical extents to physical extents

Array-Based Virtualization

Array-based virtualization, sometimes called storage-based or subsystem virtualization, uses a primary or master array to manage all input/output (I/O) for other arrays in the SAN. The intelligence for virtualization is embedded in some general-purpose servers as network appliances specially architected for the task. Both DAS and SAN storage can be accommodated.

One DAS can virtualize other directly attached DAS, as shown in Figure 5-10; a storage array can virtualize a DAS attached to it, as shown in Figure 5-11; or a storage array can virtualize another storage array, as depicted in Figure 5-12.

Figure 5-10
DAS virtualized by a DAS

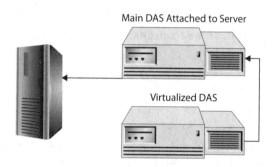

Figure 5-11
DAS virtualized by a storage array

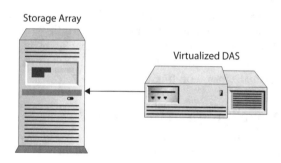

Figure 5-12
Storage array virtualized by another storage array

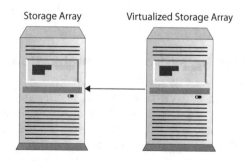

A primary storage controller manages metadata and pooling. Additional storage may be directly attached, adding greater functionality to the storage fabric. Since there are no host dependencies, array-based virtualization is ideal for heterogeneous operating systems, applications, or devices.

Array and block-based virtualization are often combined to take advantage of the robust performance of RAID and LVM versatility. Host-based LVMs can work in conjunction with several RAID LUNs to create virtual volumes that span multiple disk arrays. Load balancing, alternate routing, striping, and mirroring are a few of the functions supported by this block-array virtualization combination.

There are five types of block-array virtualization engines:

- Heterogeneous arrays (controller based) include physical volumes in the array and on external volumes on external arrays.

- Homogeneous arrays (controller based) include physical volumes just in the array with the controller.

- Heterogeneous external virtualization appliances maintain the maps for multiple heterogeneous arrays in the appliance.

- Heterogeneous external virtualization appliances maintain the maps for multiple heterogeneous arrays in the appliance and in the LAN switch.

- Server-based virtualization offers a solution for operating systems and applications that support differing file systems.

The rationale for combining array and block-based virtualization lies in the robust performance of RAID technology and the flexibility of host LVMs. LVMs can work with RAID LUNs to create virtual volumes that span multiple arrays. Load balancing, alternate routing, mirroring, and striping are other functions supported by the array–host–based virtualization combination.

Virtual Provisioning of the Array

To provision an array for virtualization, the array you want to virtualize must be connected to the controllers of the array that is virtualizing it. Each vendor will have its own specification for how to set up the pairing of the two arrays. Once this is complete, one array will provide the front-end I/O for the arrays that are virtualized through it. One or more arrays can be virtualized in this fashion.

Implementing Array-Based Virtualization

When implementing array-based virtualization, it is important to know whether the product you want to virtualize is supported by the vendor. Each array vendor that supports array virtualization keeps a list of the models of arrays that can be virtualized. You will also need to make sure your master array has the front-and back-end capacity to handle the I/O that will be going through it. Virtualizing other arrays is similar to adding more storage shelves to the array in terms of the resources required to interface between the storage.

Network Virtualization

Optimization of network resources is the primary goal of network storage virtualization. The complexity of underlying network resources—servers, nodes, paths, and applications—are abstracted into a consolidated virtual focal point for storage management. The physical infrastructure, services, and provisioning are dynamically orchestrated to provide enterprise-wide network storage management and optimization.

Through the use of virtual aggregation and provisioning, multiple virtual storage networks can be combined to form a larger logical resource or segregated into smaller, special-purpose virtual storage domains. Network virtualization is designed to provide network optimization, including better data migration and integrity, increased throughput and performance, agility, scalability, and data integrity. All network servers and services are treated as a singular pool of resources, which may be used regardless of its location or composition of physical components.

 EXAM TIP Network virtualization is especially suited for networks experiencing rapid expansion or frequent spikes in latent demand.

Concepts

The following concepts are provided to facilitate a deeper understanding of network storage virtualization:

- **Abstraction** This is the underlying complexity of a physical network; its processes and resources are rendered transparent by creating a logical representation.

- **Aggregation** Using in-band or out-of-band techniques, physical network resources are logically grouped into a single virtual resource.

- **Dynamic multipathing (DMP)** This offers cross-platform I/O optimization of heterogeneous storage and network resources.

- **Isolation** Isolating logical partitions provides a mechanism for maintaining storage integrity and performance optimization. Security breaches, bottlenecks, or suboptimal nodes can be bypassed or segregated so that the overall continuity and functioning of the network is not compromised.

- **Partitioning** Logical partitions can be created and dynamically configured to meet system or user requirements. Servers, protocols, and network infrastructure can be combined to meet changing business requirements.

Methods

There are two methods for implementing network storage virtualization: in-band and out-of-band. In-band network storage virtualization is implemented in the data path. Both data and flow control share the same path, as shown in Figure 5-13. Network appliances or devices provide flow control or I/O translation throughout the storage

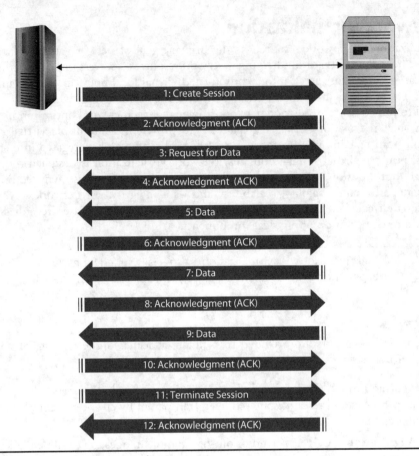

Figure 5-13   In-band storage virtualization

network; in-band provisioning introduces overhead that can contribute to latency and less-than-optimal network performance within a SAN as I/O requests are intercepted and mapped to physical storage locations.

Out-of-band network storage virtualization, illustrated in Figure 5-14, separates data and flow control onto separate channels. Controllers handle flow control processes, such as I/O routing and other control functions, allowing the maximum utilization of available bandwidth and storage. By separating the control functions from the paths where data travels, the latency characteristic of in-band network storage virtualization is avoided.

Aside from issues related to overhead and latency, in-band and out-of-band network virtualization share the same general benefits, including the following:

- Optimization of SAN utilization and performance
- Storage management is off-loaded from the host
- Interoperability and multivendor support
- A consolidated virtual platform for network storage management

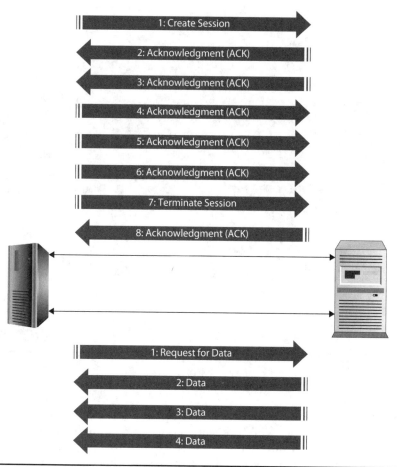

Figure 5-14 Out-of-band storage virtualization

VSAN

A virtual storage area network (VSAN) is a logical partition within a SAN where zoning is used to segment connected devices and resources of a physical network into isolated virtual storage area networks. Communications are restricted to the virtual domains created by zoning. Zoning allows each VSAN to maintain its own services and name server, and it reduces the impact fabric changes have on devices and equipment since fabric changes need to be made only to devices within the same VSAN. Consequently, zone names can be reused as long as they reside within a different VSAN on the same SAN. Figure 5-15 shows three VSANs. One of the VSANs is spread across two regions with another VSAN in between. Data, however, flows between the VSAN transparently to the devices with the VSAN.

EXAM TIP Without a VSAN, zone names would need to be unique across the entire SAN.

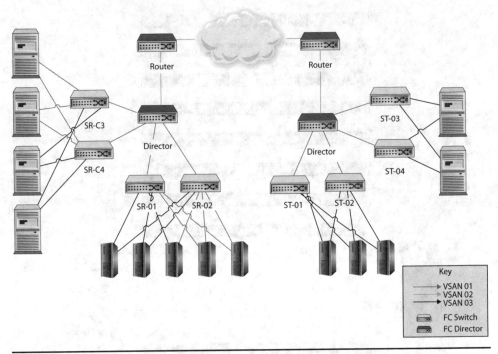

Figure 5-15 VSANs

- **Logical switch** Logical switches can comprise a whole or part of a physical switch in segments of a VSAN. In concept, it is similar to Ethernet VLANs (discussed later in this section) where each port on a switch can be assigned to a logical switch. Communication between logical switches occurs through an extended ISL (XISL) if the communication passes through one or more physical switches that have multiple logical switches on them. Otherwise, logical switches are connected through standard ISLs.

- **Logical fabric** This is another name for a VSAN.

LSAN

A logical storage area network (LSAN) spans multiple physical fabrics. Fibre Channel routers (FCRs) are used to allow specific devices from these autonomous virtual fabrics to communicate while maintaining independence from associated physical fabrics. The paths between the LSAN may be within the local fabric or may span a single or multiple FCRs. Backbone (BB) fabrics may be combined with these FCRs to form what is referred to as meta-SANs. Meta-SANs consist of all logically partitioned storage, fabrics, heterogeneous routers, devices, and other LSANs.

Routers are connected to the fabric through ports on FCRs or bridges. In this way, multiswitch fabrics are created. The Fibre Channel port types were discussed in Chapter 3, but these plus additional ports are used on FCRs and bridges. The following is a list of Fibre Channel port names, including those from Chapter 3:

- A bridge port (B-port) connects an FC switch to a bridge.

- A diagnostic port (D-port) is used to troubleshoot problems with connectivity between switches.

- An expansion port (E-port) is used to connect two switches together to form an ISL.

- An external port (EX-port) is only used on FC routers to connect to FC switches. FC switches use an E-port to connect to the router's EX-port.

- Fabric ports (F-ports) are ports on a switch that are used to connect to end devices. The end devices use N-ports to connect to the switch's F-port.

- A fabric loop port (FL-port) is used in the Fibre Channel arbitrated loop (FC-AL) topology and it connects to end devices in much the same way as an F-port would in the FC-SW topology.

- Generic ports (G-ports) allow more flexibility in an FC switch because they can operate as an F-port or an E-port depending on what is plugged into them. G-ports are used in the FC-SW topology.

- Node ports (N-ports) are ports used by a node in the FC-SW topology. N-ports connect to F-ports on the FC switch.

- A node loop port (NL-port) is a port used by a node in the FC-AL topology. NL-ports connect to FL-ports on the FC-AL switch.

- A trunking E-port (TE-port) is used to connect to other FC switches. It differs from an E-port in that VSAN information can be sent over the port. For example, if two switches are connected with TE-ports and three VSANs span the two switches, information for each of the VSANs can traverse the TE-port. To each VSAN, the port appears to be an E-port, and each VSAN will not be able to see the traffic for other VSANs.

- Universal ports (U-ports) allow more flexibility in an FC switch because they can operate as an FL-port or an NL-port depending on what is plugged into them. U-ports are used in the FC-AL topology.

- A VE-port is an E-port that is used in FCIP.

- A VEX-port is an EX-port used in FCIP.

VLAN

Virtual local area networks are based on the Institute of Electrical and Electronic Engineers (IEEE) 802.1q standard. A VLAN is a logical grouping of ports on a switch that forms a single broadcast domain. Media Access Control (MAC) addresses are divided into logical groups where only members of the virtual group are able to exchange data or communicate. Frames are tagged with the address of the group to which they belong. When a frame is sent to other ports, the hardware copies the frame only if it is configured with the VLAN number within the frame.

VLANS can be implemented as either a group of physical ports (layer 1), a group of MAC addresses (layer 2), or an IP subnet (layer 3).

- **Layer 1 VLAN**   The layer 1 VLAN is a group of physical ports, referred to as *port switching*. It requires a router to be used to access the originating server. When users are relocated, they are assigned a new subnet and IP address.

- **Layer 2 VLAN**   The layer 2 VLAN is a group of MAC addresses. It supports user mobility because LANs are defined by a list of MAC addresses. The protocol manages all MAC address changes, making it possible for clients and servers to always be on the same backbone, regardless of location.

- **Layer 3 VLAN**   The layer 3 VLAN is an IP subnet or virtual subnet. The MAC protocol (type and subnet fields) is used to specify VLAN membership in this form of VLAN. Multiprotocol nodes can span multiple VLANs, and packets are tagged with a VLAN in addition to an IP address so that they can be delivered to the appropriate VLAN.

NPIV

N-ports and their associated N-port IDs, covered in Chapter 3, are used by end devices to connect and identify themselves on an FC fabric. N-port ID virtualization (NPIV) allows multiple N-port IDs to reside on one physical N-port. NPIV is commonly used on hypervisors, which are servers that host multiple virtual machines. NPIV allows each virtual machine on a hypervisor to have its own N-port ID that can be associated with logical units on the SAN. Hypervisors commonly have redundant ports, so NPIV would be used to provide each virtual machine with an N-port ID from each redundant physical port so that each would have a redundant connection to storage.

NPIV allows a single HBA, or target port, on a storage array to register multiple World Wide Port Names (WWPNs) and N-port identification numbers. This allows each virtual server to present a different World Wide Name to the SAN, allowing each virtual server to see only its own storage.

NPIV requires both the switch and HBA to be NPIV capable. N-port initialization when using NPIV would start with the N-port sending a fabric discovery (FDISC) request to the login server (address FFFFFE) to obtain an additional address. Next, it sends a port logon request called a PLOGI to the name server (address FFFFFC) to register this additional address with the name server, followed by an SCR to the fabric controller (address FFFFFD) to register for state change notifications. This process is then repeated for all N-port IDs on the physical N-port.

Provisioning the Logical Fabric

Logical fabrics are provisioned by assigning a fabric ID to the VSAN. Physical FC switches, or logical switches within physical FC switches, differentiate traffic and send it to ports based on the fabric ID they belong to. Traffic must be routed to communicate between VSANs. This can be achieved with a switch, router, or director that is virtual fabric capable.

Chapter Summary

Storage virtualization in its many incarnations was the focus of this chapter. Several general and industry-supported definitions of storage virtualization were provided as an entry point to the maze of differing perspectives that has come to characterize storage virtualization. The flow of the chapter's discussion was organized into three broad threads:

- The rationale and drivers for storage virtualization
- What is being virtualized
- The level or layer being virtualized

The rationale and primary drivers for storage virtualization are the need to deploy transparent, interoperable, enterprise-class storage virtualization. Data integration and data migration concepts were discussed as the primary challenges to this end. As previously noted, the proliferation of proprietary, heterogeneous storage virtualization schema, products, taxonomies, and implementations make it difficult to frame a coherent picture of just what constitutes storage virtualization.

Two broad but generally accepted definitions of storage virtualization from SNIA were presented, along with the SNIA Shared Storage Model and the SNIA Storage Virtualization Taxonomy, offering a simple but comprehensive lens through which storage virtualization can be viewed.

The focus of the chapter then shifted to "what" is being virtualized. Several different forms of storage virtualization were presented. They include tape virtualization, disk virtualization, block virtualization, and file/record virtualization.

Tape virtualization is performed by emulating tape resources so that backup software interfaces with the virtual tape, just as it would with a physical tape. Multiple VTs can be presented as a virtual tape library, which may use a storage array as the destination for the data, but the backup software treats it as if it were writing to tape. A server that provides VT services is known as a virtual tape server.

In disk virtualization, physical data is allocated by disk firmware to virtual locations on the medium through the use of logical block addresses. The storage system does not need to understand the internal disk mechanics of exactly where the data is stored on the physical disk to read and write data from the drive. This frees up the system from having to manage this type of activity and makes it easier to write software or operating systems that utilize storage.

Block virtualization is an abstraction of physical storage to logical partitions, independent of storage structure, allowing several physical disks to be accessed through a single virtual/logical interface. Block storage is presented to a node, such as a server or workstation, as local storage, and the system can interface with it as it would with disks that were located internally, but the data exists on a storage array. Typically, protocols such as Fibre Channel Protocol or Internet Small Computer System Interface are used to provide block storage to nodes.

File system virtualization allows a file system to share remote or network attached logical partitions. These are often represented as shares on a network using protocols such as Common Internet File System or Network File System.

File or record virtualization is used to dynamically allocate infrequently used files or records to secondary storage while caching more actively used files on primary, high-speed storage.

Storage virtualization can be implemented on hosts, arrays, or networks. When virtualization is used with hosts, logical units from physical disks are aggregated into a larger primary LU, which is seen as a single device by applications and users. Array-based virtualization, sometimes called storage-based or subsystem virtualization, uses a primary or master array to manage all I/O for other storage arrays in the storage area network or ones that are directly attached to it.

Network virtualization hides the complexity of underlying network resources, such as servers, nodes, paths, and applications, from the software and systems that use them. These virtualized systems are abstracted into a consolidated virtual focal point for storage management, and it can be accomplished in-band or out-of-band. In-band network storage virtualization is implemented using the same network as the data path, which can create contention and slow down operations. Out-of-band network storage virtualization separates data and flow control onto separate channels, avoiding the contention faced with in-band network virtualization.

Technologies such as VSAN, LSAN, VLAN, and NPIV are used to provide network storage virtualization.

A virtual storage area network is a logical partition within a SAN where zoning is used to segment connected devices and resources into isolated VSANs. VSAN communication is restricted to other devices in the VSAN.

A logical storage area network spans multiple physical fabrics. Fibre Channel routers are used to allow specific devices from these autonomous virtual fabrics to communicate while maintaining independence from associated physical fabrics.

A virtual local area network is a logical grouping of ports on a switch that form a single broadcast domain. Media Access Control addresses are divided into logical groups where only members of the virtual group are able to exchange data or communicate.

N-port ID virtualization allows a single host bus adapter or target port on a storage array to register multiple World Wide Port Names and N-port identification numbers.

Chapter Review Questions

1. Which of the following would be utilized to emulate tape resource backup software?

   A. VM

   B. VTL

   C. IM

   D. QoS

2. In which of the following situations would file virtualization be advantageous?

    A. Replicating data to another storage array

    B. Accessing resources virtualized from a DAS attached to a storage array

    C. Reading or writing data from or to a network share

    D. Creating a storage pool on a storage array

3. Which of the following types of file systems is used to allow centralized logical access to a set of files that are distributed among many shares in different locations?

    A. DFS

    B. CFS

    C. SAN file system

    D. Local file system

4. Which of these is not an element of LVM?

    A. Volume group

    B. Logical extent

    C. Physical volume

    D. Volume management point

5. How does out-of-band storage virtualization differ from in-band storage virtualization?

    A. Out-of-band storage virtualization uses the same path for flow control and data, whereas in-band provides a separate path for data and flow control.

    B. In-band storage virtualization uses the same path for flow control and data, whereas out-of-band provides a separate path for data and flow control.

    C. In-band storage virtualization provides better utilization of bandwidth than out-of-band storage virtualization.

    D. Out-of-band storage virtualization requires less hardware than in-band storage virtualization.

6. Which of the following is not a reason to use a VSAN?

    A. To reuse zone names on different VSANs within the same physical SAN

    B. To create a logical security boundary between VSANs

    C. To reduce the impact fabric changes have on the SAN

    D. To reduce implementation and management effort

7. Which technology is used to allow multiple World Wide Port Names (WWPNs) to be assigned to the same host bus adapter (HBA)?

   A. VSAN

   B. NPIV

   C. HBA SCR

   D. LSAN

8. Which of the following is not a type of block-array virtualization?

   A. Heterogeneous array

   B. Homogeneous array

   C. Local-based virtualization

   D. Server-based virtualization

9. You have a server with a single-port HBA that hosts five virtual machines. These machines must be able to have direct access to logical volumes presented on the storage array, and security must be controlled through WWN zoning. Which technology should you implement to meet these requirements?

   A. LSAN

   B. NPIV

   C. VLAN

   D. VSAN

Chapter Review Answers

1. **B** is correct. A virtual tape library (VTL) looks like a real tape library to software, but the storage location may be something other than tape, such as local or remote disks.
   A, **C**, and **D** are incorrect. **A** is incorrect because a VM is a computer that operates on hardware that is emulated by another machine. It would not emulate tape resources. **C** is incorrect because instant messaging is used to chat with others, not emulate tape resources. **D** is incorrect because Quality of Service is used to prioritize traffic, not emulate tapes.

2. **C** is correct. Reading or writing data from or to a network share uses file virtualization.
   A, **B**, and **D** are incorrect. **A** is incorrect because storage array replication uses block virtualization. **B** is incorrect because a DAS would present storage to a storage array as blocks. **D** is incorrect because a storage pool is a collection of logical units that are used to create storage resources.

3. A is correct. A distributed file system (DFS) maps file shares from many different locations under a single namespace that can be organized into a hierarchy to make it easy for users to find data.

B, C, and **D** are incorrect. **B** is incorrect because a Clustered File System requires that the systems in the cluster have similar hardware. **C** is incorrect because there is no such thing as a SAN file system. **D** is incorrect because a local file system only manages data for the local machine, not for distributed resources.

4. D is correct. A volume management point is not an element of LVM.

A, B, and **C** are incorrect. A volume group, logical extent, and physical volume are all elements of an LVM. Extents are the basic building blocks of data and storage used to prevent disk fragmentation through the use of a marker that is placed to indicate the last write of 64-bit blocks (8 pages) of contiguous space that occurred for a file. A physical volume (PV) is composed of extents. A logical volume (LV) is the equivalent of a disk partition in non-LVM environments, shown as a centralized block device. A physical extent (PE) is a piece of a physical volume organized into contiguous blocks of data. A logical extent (LE) is an equal-sized block of data that comprises a logical volume. Lastly, a volume group (VG) represents the highest level of LVM abstraction. PVs and LVs are aggregated into a singular unit.

5. B is correct. Out-of-band storage virtualization uses a different path for flow control than the one used for data, whereas in-band uses the same path for flow control and data. Out-of-band virtualization thus provides better utilization of bandwidth.

A, C, and **D** are incorrect. **C** is incorrect because it is out-of-band rather than in-band that does this. **D** is incorrect because more hardware is needed rather than less hardware. **A** is incorrect because out-of-band storage virtualization uses different paths for flow control and data.

6. D is correct. VSANs will require additional effort to implement and manage.

A, B, and **C** are incorrect. VSANs offer advantages including the ability to reuse zone names, create logical security boundaries, and reduce the impact of fabric changes on the SAN.

7. B is correct. N-port ID virtualization (NPIV) allows a single host bus adapter (HBA), or target port, on a storage array to register multiple World Wide Port Names (WWPNs) and N-port identification numbers.

A, C, and **D** are incorrect. **A** is incorrect because a VSAN segments a SAN into multiple logically separated SANs. **C** is incorrect because a SCR is used to notify the fabric of changes in state. **D** is incorrect because a LSAN is a SAN that spans multiple fabrics.

8. **C** is correct. Local-based virtualization is not a type of block-array virtualization. **A**, **B**, and **D** are incorrect. Block-array virtualization includes the following: a heterogeneous array (controller based) includes physical volumes in the array and on external volumes on external arrays, a homogeneous array (controller based) includes physical volumes just in the array with the controller, heterogeneous external virtualization appliances maintain the maps for multiple heterogeneous arrays in the appliance, and heterogeneous external virtualization appliances maintain the maps for multiple heterogeneous arrays in the appliance and in the LAN switch. Server-based virtualization offers a solution for operating systems and applications that support differing file systems.

9. **B** is correct. NPIV allows a single port to have multiple N-port IDs and WWNs. **A**, **C**, and **D** are incorrect. **A** is incorrect because an LSAN is a SAN that spans multiple physical fabrics. It will not aid in providing WWNs to each of the virtual machines in this scenario. **C** is incorrect because VLANs are used to segment network traffic, and **D** is incorrect because a VSAN is used to segment a storage network.

Storage Management

In this chapter, you will learn how to

- Provision storage for use
- Manage storage devices using common management protocols
- Select an effective administration method for the task
- Use configuration management techniques to approve, control, and track changes
- Configure monitoring, alerting, and reporting for storage
- Implement a software-defined storage solution

The previous chapters discussed the technical, physical, and theoretical elements of storage. This chapter builds upon that foundation of how hardware, protocols, and other network resources work together and explores the allocation, optimization, and management of storage resources. One of the first steps in this process is to allocate storage resources where needed in the enterprise. The allocation or partitioning of storage resources is referred to as *provisioning*.

Why is provisioning important? Provisioning determines dynamically and in real time where critical system resources are needed. Priorities that will guide the selection of method or technique for provisioning may be based on a few of the following factors:

- Importance or priority of the process, routine, or task
- Importance or priority of data
- The identification of what critical storage and network resources are required to satisfy and maintain system policies and service-level standards

Storage Provisioning

Storage provisioning is the process of assigning disk space to users while optimizing storage resources. Techniques for provisioning storage are LUN, thick, and thin provisioning.

- **LUN provisioning** A logical unit number (LUN) is created and assigned to each enterprise application.

- **Thick provisioning**   The space required is determined when creating the virtual disk based on anticipated storage requirements.

- **Thin provisioning**   The primary goal is to optimally allocate storage on the basis of demand (multiple users) and actual size required.

Provisioning usually begins with the creation of storage known as a *logical unit* (LU) and referred to by a LUN. Storage can be allocated to a device through thin or thick provisioning. Thin provisioning allows the host to believe that it has the maximum amount of space available while the storage system allocates only what is actually used, whereas thick provisioning allocates the entire amount to the storage device. Thin provisioning represents a more optimal means of allocating storage resources than thick provisioning when trying to conserve the amount of space allocated. For example, say a storage administrator configures a LUN with a size of 10GB that can grow to 100GB. This LUN will appear to the operating system as a LUN of 100GB, but the LUN will consume only 10GB of space on the storage array. As more data is added to the LUN, the space consumed on the storage array will increase accordingly, so when 30GB of the 100GB is used, the LUN will take up 30GB of space on the storage array but still appear to the operating system as a 100GB LUN.

With thick provisioning in the same situation, the administrator would need to allocate 100GB of space for the LUN and then map it to the host. The LUN would not grow, and as more space is consumed by the operating system, the storage provisioned on the storage array would not change. In thick provisioning storage, resources are allocated in a fixed manner, oftentimes resulting in less-than-optimal system utilization, but sometimes performance is better with thick provisioning because the system does not need to allocate additional space from the array each time more space is consumed by the host. This space can be allocated in contiguous locations on the storage array, thus avoiding the fragmentation that can occur when thin LUNs are expanded.

Storage arrays may need to reclaim space after it has been allocated to a thin-provisioned LUN if data within the LUN is deleted. Storage arrays may utilize an automatic method for reclaiming space occurring on a scheduled basis, or they may require that space reclamation be performed manually by the storage administrator.

LUN Provisioning

The process of provisioning storage for use begins with the creation of a RAID group from multiple physical disks. (RAID groups were discussed in Chapter 1.) RAID groups allow for the availability and use of a larger amount of storage as compared to a single disk. RAID groups can then be combined to form larger storage pools from which storage can be provisioned. Storage pools can be partitioned into smaller chunks to be allocated to machines. The partitioned chunks created by partitioning a storage pool are called *logical units*, and each logical unit is referenced with a number called a *logical unit number*.

 EXAM TIP   LUNs can be given any number supported by the storage array, but they must be unique within the storage array. The same number can be used on different storage arrays, but it cannot be reused within a storage array.

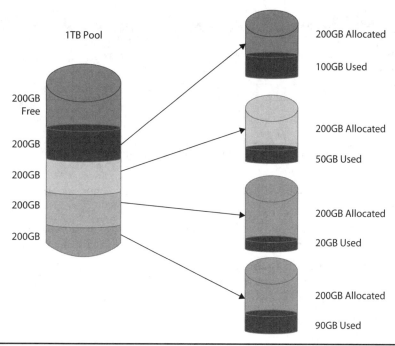

1TB Pool

200GB Free

200GB

200GB

200GB

200GB

200GB Allocated

100GB Used

200GB Allocated

50GB Used

200GB Allocated

20GB Used

200GB Allocated

90GB Used

Figure 6-1 Thick-provisioned LUs

Thick Provisioning

Thick provisioning creates LUs that are a fixed or static size. Thick LUs take up the same amount of space on the storage array as is represented to the host operating system, as shown in Figure 6-1. For example, if a 100GB LU is thick provisioned for a server, the server will see it as a 100GB drive, and it will consume 100GB of space on the storage array.

For example, here is the procedure for creating a thick-provisioned LUN on a Hitachi AMS 200 storage array:

1. Click the array and then click the Change Operation Mode button.

2. Type in the password and click OK.

3. Double-click the array unit.

4. Click the Logical Status tab.

5. Expand RAID Groups on the left.

6. If you click RAID Groups, each RAID group will be shown with its free capacity, as shown in Figure 6-2.

7. Right-click the RAID group from which you want to create an LU and select Create New Logical Unit.

RAID Group	RAID Level	Total Capacity	Free Capacity	Type
00	RAID5(3D+1P)	199.2GB	79.2GB	FC
01	RAID6(5D+2P)	2290.7GB	315.7GB	AT
02	RAID1+0(4D+4D)	1832.8GB	577.6GB	AT
03	RAID1+0(3D+3D)	2060.5GB	0.0MB	AT
04	RAID1+0(4D+4D)	2747.3GB	647.3GB	AT
05	RAID1+0(3D+3D)	400.3GB	192.0MB	FC
06	RAID1(1D+1D)	133.4GB	18.0GB	FC
07	RAID1+0(5D+5D)	3434.2GB	1334.2GB	AT
09	RAID1+0(2D+2D)	1373.6GB	0.0MB	AT

Figure 6-2   Storage array management console showing RAID groups

8. The next screen, displayed in Figure 6-3, allows you to choose options for the new LUN.

9. Use the SAN RAID groups and LUN allocation documentation to find the next available LU and type that LUN into the blank called Logical Unit No.

10. The controllers should alternate, so choose either controller 0 or 1 depending on the other LUs that are in that RAID group. The RAID groups should be balanced in terms of gigabytes allocated between controllers.

11. Choose the size.

12. Click OK.

13. Click OK again.

Thin Provisioning

Thin provisioning allows for the flexible creation of LUs. The LU appears to the host system as the maximum size it can grow to, but it consumes only the amount of space the host uses on the storage system, as shown in Figure 6-4. The term *thin provisioning* creates

Figure 6-3
LUN creation

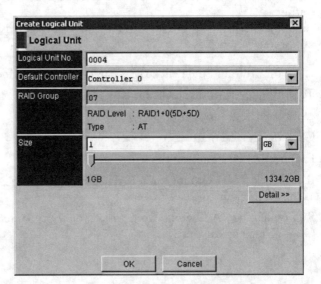

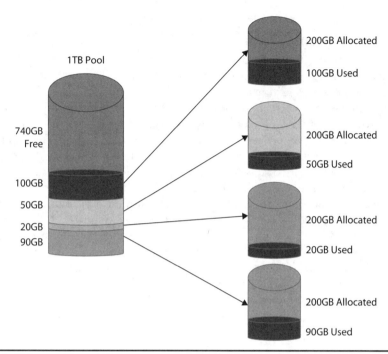

Figure 6-4 Thin-provisioned LUs

LUs of variable size, as contrasted with thick provisioning, where LUs are created with a fixed-size. Thin provisioning, in contrast to thick provisioning, allows for the dynamic creation of LUs, but must be closely monitored to prevent "resource hogging," or overutilization, of critical storage resources. It should be noted that the dynamic growing does put load on the system. With thick provisioning, there is load on the system during the creation process, but because thick provisioning uses a static size, there is no additional load later. Both thin and thick LUs appear the same to the host operating system to which they are assigned.

Both thick and thin provisioning offer two means of allocating storage space. In one instance, storage is allocated in static, fixed-sized blocks and in the other on a dynamic basis. While each scheme is different in terms of how it allocates storage resources, both require a method for reallocating resources back into the pool of available storage. Thin reclamation is a process where space that was previously consumed by a thin-provisioned disk and then left unused can be returned to the overall storage pool. Thin reclamation can be configured to operate when the free space on an LU reaches a specified percentage or a specified amount of free space exceeds 10GB on an LU. Some systems allow for scheduled reclamation, while others can reclaim space immediately following its availability in the LU.

Suppose a 300GB LUN number 105 is created and users store 212GB of data on it for a project. When the project concludes, 100GB of data is archived to tape and removed

> ## Thin-Provisioning Woes
>
> A storage administrator learns that he can save space by provisioning only what is currently needed using thin provisioning. This allows the storage administrator to put off purchasing additional storage for his storage array. He has 2TB left on the array, and he creates twelve 400GB LUs using thin provisioning and creates several virtual machines on a highly available hypervisor cluster using the LUs as their drives. Several months later, he receives a call saying that the 12 machines he set up are all not responding. When he investigates, he finds that all the machines are paused and he cannot access them. The event collection system shows out-of-disk-space errors for all machines. This causes him to check the storage array to find that all the space on the array has been consumed by the thin-provisioned LUs. He migrates two of the LUs to another storage system and then resumes the virtual machines, knowing that he will have to propose purchasing additional storage immediately. Monitoring the size of thin-provisioned LUs in the situation described here would have alerted this storage administrator to the need for additional storage before the problem occurred. Such monitoring solutions are discussed later in this chapter.

from the server. This 100GB is unused now on LUN 105, but it must be reclaimed by the storage system in order for it to be allocated to another LU. The process of thin reclamation does just that. If a thin reclamation limit was set to 10GB with a schedule running every night, the night after the 100GB was deleted, the storage array would return 90GB to the pool to be used by whichever LU may need it next. If the setting was 10 percent instead, then the storage array would return 70GB to the pool, leaving 30GB (10 percent of 300GB) as unused space on LUN 105.

Best Practices for Disk Provisioning

Repeatedly growing an LU can also lead to fragmentation across the storage pool since the new space allocated to an LU may not be in a continuous location on the RAID group. It could even be on a different RAID group in the pool. For this reason, it is best to try to estimate the near-term needs of an LU and to allocate its minimum size according to the expected near-term needs to avoid excessive growth. Growth sizes can also be determined. It may be best for some LUs to increase by larger amounts than others based on their usage. This can be configured as a storage array default or on a per-LU basis. Reclamation thresholds may also need to be increased if an LU regularly consumes space and then frees it up again so that the free space is not immediately returned to the pool. It is sometimes best to re-create thin-provisioned LUs that have been increased several times. The newly created LU will have space allocated from the same area of disk, and this can remove fragmentation problems from the LU.

As with any critical network resource, the provisioning of storage must include practical as well as technical considerations. Storage optimization must include tweaking system performance by assigning storage to hosts and servers, identification and optimization of paths between these host and servers, and zoning and masking. Collaboration and communication are two key elements in successfully provisioning resources for a given enterprise. Collaborative identification of critical data locations, potential provisioning bottlenecks, and enterprise-wide provisioning standards will result in the development of comprehensive storage allocation and management policies that foster security, optimization, and availability of storage resources.

Oversubscription

While thin provisioning is a more robust and dynamic method for allocating storage in a given environment, it can result in situations where demand exceeds available capacity, or oversubscription. Oversubscription allows multiple devices to be connected to the same switch port. Devices share the bandwidth of a single port, and it can be effective when multiple slower connections, such as 1 Gbps fiber links, connect to a single 8 Gbps fiber link. However, if multiple devices are connected to a single port and they have a higher demand for bandwidth than is available, contention will arise, and response times could be impacted. For this reason, it is important to determine the needs and capabilities of nodes before oversubscribing them to a link. High-bandwidth nodes should be on their own port, whereas low-bandwidth ports, or ports that utilize bandwidth only during certain times, can be grouped onto the same port.

Management Protocols

Storage and data management are inextricably bound. As the life source of an enterprise, data is the one of the most valuable assets it possesses. Any circumstance that delays the availability of and access to this critical resource will have serious and potentially unrecoverable consequences. Successful storage management ensures that data is stored and accessible to the enterprise when it is needed. Storage management maintains information about where, in what form, and how data is stored throughout the system. It allows for monitoring, which is invaluable for ongoing system optimization, capacity planning, and troubleshooting.

Data-hungry applications and transactions are a source of ever-increasing demand. Many enterprises react to this demand by buying additional network and storage resources. While the price of network infrastructure and storage have declined exponentially, both still represent potentially sizable capital expenditures for an organization. A well-devised storage management plan can leverage these investments by providing a proactive road map to meeting an organization's data storage needs. The following sections provide an overview of several storage management techniques and trends.

SNMP

Simple Network Management Protocol (SNMP) is one of the earliest management protocols that can be used to manage routers, switches, and other devices such as storage devices. As its simplest operations, SNMP defines four operations: Get, GetNext, Set, and Trap. Get retrieves one or more management information base (MIB) values, GetNext sequentially retrieves data from an MIB table, Set is used to update the MIB value, and Traps are used to flag unusual network and storage conditions.

EXAM TIP SNMP information can be helpful in troubleshooting problems such as unavailable systems, logical volumes, or shares.

SNMP is a method for devices to share information with a management station through UDP ports 161 and 162. SNMP-managed devices allow management systems to query them for information. Figure 6-5 shows a management console for Dell OpenManage that uses SNMP to gather information from servers. Management systems are configured with MIBs for the devices they will interact with. These MIBs define which variables can be queried on a device. This is what makes SNMP so versatile since manufacturers can create MIBs for their devices that can then be installed onto management stations.

SNMP version 1 devices share data with management servers that are in the same family, denoted by a community name configured on the device. This name is somewhat similar to a workgroup name. There is no authentication required to be part of the family like there would be in a domain environment, so this offers little security. Many common off-the-shelf systems management applications and open-source tools offer SNMP management, and the protocol is stable and mature.

SNMP was enhanced in version 2, and SNMPv2 offers performance and security enhancements over SNMPv1. SNMPv2 can achieve greater performance by requesting data in bulk from devices rather than issuing many separate requests. SNMPv2 can operate in one of two modes depending on the security desired and the level of interoperability required. SNMPv2 community mode authenticates devices based solely on the community string they present, whereas SNMPv2 is user based.

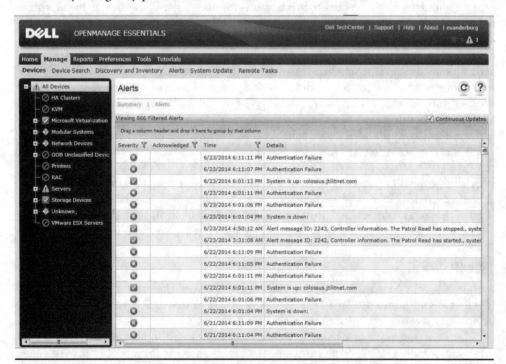

Figure 6-5 SNMP information shown in a Dell OpenManage system

SNMP interoperability between versions 1 and 2 can be achieved through a proxy that converts data between the protocols or through a system that supports both protocols at once. This is a process known as *bilingual network management.*

The latest version of SNMP is version 3, which offers even greater security than version 2. SNMPv3 supports encrypted channels and mutual authentication of both managed devices and management systems. SNMPv3 also offers additional data integrity checks to better protect against corruption or modification of data in transit.

WBEM

While SNMP is commonplace in organizations for monitoring network storage, the increasing demands and complexity of modern networks and the storage assets they connect sometimes require more robust and dynamic methods of managing them. A storage management consortium called the Storage Management Initiative (SMI) sponsored the Common Information Model (CIM), an object-oriented approach to organizing information where objects have attributes and each is created, or "instantiated," from a class that describes the format of the object. Objects can inherit properties from parent objects and pass down properties to child objects below them. This allows for high customization without unnecessary duplication of effort or an increase in complexity. Figure 6-6 shows a sample WBEM tool for a storage array.

Web-Based Enterprise Management (WBEM) was created by the Distributed Management Task Force (DMTF) as a framework to be utilized by a collection of technologies to remotely control servers or other equipment and to configure, audit,

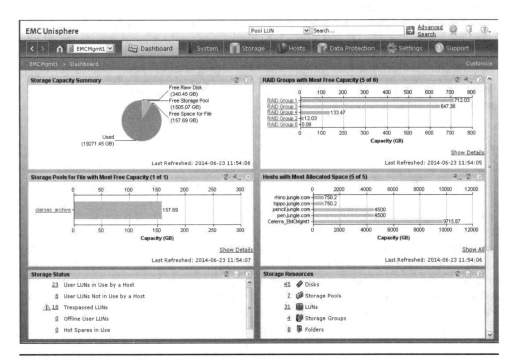

Figure 6-6 WBEM tool for a storage array

update, and monitor devices. WBEM is used to provide a common platform for defining standards for the heterogeneous technologies, services, and applications that comprise most enterprise-wide networks. The standards of WBEM provide a web-based approach for exchanging CIM data across different technologies and platforms. Extensible Markup Language (XML) can be used to encode CIM data, and this is then transmitted between WBEM servers and clients using Hypertext Transfer Protocol (HTTP).

The design of WBEM allows it to be extensible. This means that new applications, devices, and even operating systems can be specified in the future. There are many applications for WBEM, including grid computing, utility computing, and web services.

SMI-S

The Storage Management Initiative-Specification (SMI-S) is a protocol used for sharing management information on storage devices. It is a good alternative to SNMP for managing devices such as storage arrays, switches, tape drives, HBAs, CNAs, and directors. It is a client-server model where the client is the management station requesting information and the server is the device offering the information. The latest version of SMI-S is version 1.5, published in 2011. SMI-S includes specifications for WBEM that allow the protocol to take advantage of CIM, web-based management and monitoring, and XML encoding, among other things.

In-Band vs. Out-of-Band Management

In-band management in a storage network means that data as well as management and monitoring information travel over the same path. In-band management is generally easier to implement because it has a connection to all the devices in band already and, when bundled with a storage system, typically does not require additional or special software to be installed in order for it to function. In-band management provides caching and advanced functions within a storage network. In-band management systems, however, are limited to only managing devices that are in the fabric that they are on.

Out-of-band management involves the use of a path for device management and monitoring that is separate from the data path. Out-of-band management allows the system administrator to monitor and manage servers as well as other network equipment through remote control from outside the environment and to pool management and monitoring resources in a central location for distributed data centers and SANs.

In addition to the benefits listed previously, both forms of error correction/flow control have subtle differences. While in-band management is cheaper than its counterpart out-of-band management, it does not allow access to Basic Input/Output System (BIOS) settings or the re-installation of the operating system. Hence, in-band management is not suitable for solving boot issues. Out-of-band management supports remote management activities such as remotely shutting down; restarting or power cycling hardware; and redirecting keyboard, video, and mouse (KVM).

Storage Administration

Given the complexity of most modern enterprises and their associated networks, storage administration has become an equally daunting task. Capacity planning, configuration management, system utilization, and performance optimization, along with a robust problem identification and resolution strategy, are the key responsibilities of effective administration. Storage administration must be based on proactive practices and is often-times done with a variety of tools and procedures. The following sections provide a brief overview of the most common tools and techniques that can be deployed as part of a comprehensive storage management policy. Administration tools fall into two categories: graphical and command line.

GUI

A graphical user interface (GUI) is a method of interacting with a system whereby programs and operations are represented by small pictures known as icons and menus and where navigation and possible user selections are displayed on the screen as pictures or text that the user can select by clicking with a mouse, pressing keys on the keyboard, or touching the screen. GUIs are relatively easy to learn because users do not need to memorize commands or conform to strict command syntax.

Some forms of GUI administration include management applications and web-based administration tools using HTTP or HTTPS.

Management Applications

Some storage systems can be managed by applications that are installed on a server. The software typically runs on top of one or more mainstream operating systems such as Microsoft Windows, Linux, or Solaris and can be managed in band or out of band.

HTTP/S

Hypertext Transfer Protocol Secure (HTTP/S or HTTPS) is a communication protocol for secure communication over a computer network. First coined in 1991 by Ted Nelson, HTTP/S is implemented by layering the Hypertext Transfer Protocol (HTTP) over the Secure Sockets Layer (SSL)/Transport Layer Security (TLS) protocol, resulting in the addition of the security capabilities of SSL/TLS into that of HTTP communications.

HTTPS works by encrypting and decrypting user page requests as well as the pages that are returned by the web server. The use of HTTPS helps prevent eavesdropping and man-in-the-middle attacks. Netscape is the developer of HTTPS. Both HTTPS and SSL support the use of X.509 digital certificates from servers so that a user can authenticate a sender, if necessary. HTTPS uses port 443 instead of port 80 unless otherwise specified.

CLI

A command-line interface (CLI) is a way of interacting with a computer program where a user or client sends instructions or "commands" to a program using text-based commands. CLI is also known as command-line user interface (CLUI), console user interface (CUI), and character user interface.

CLI was the primary way of interacting with most computer systems before GUI systems were invented, and it was a big improvement over the system that proceeded it, punch cards. The interface is a program that accepts text inputs as instructions and then converts this into the appropriate operating system functions that the equipment, server, or storage device can execute.

CLIs in operating systems are distinct programs that are supplied with the OS. The program that implements text interfaces is called a *command-line interpreter* (also known as *command processor* or *shell*). Examples of command-line interpreters include some of the following:

- PuTTY for SSH access
- Hyperterminal for Telnet access
- Shells for Unix (csh, ksh, sh, bash, tcsh, and so on)
- Command prompt for Windows (CMD.EXE)
- DOS (COMMAND.COM)
- Command shell for Apple
- PowerShell for Windows Vista/7/8 and Server editions

Because of their complexity and the dominance of GUIs, command-line interfaces are rarely used by casual computer users. However, CLIs provide a deeper level of system control and are preferred by advanced computer users as an easy way to issue routine or batch commands and perform complex logical operations, such as the use of looping and conditional programming to an operating system. CLIs allow administrators to write a series of commands that can be executed whenever desired or even on a schedule. CLIs allow for more complex instructions and operations because a series of commands to multiple computers can be executed simultaneously or in sequence rather than having to perform a standard set of tasks manually on many individual servers, computers, or devices.

Some forms of CLI administration include local administration of the device through the serial interface or remote administration via Telnet or SSH.

Serial

The serial port has been used for decades to manage network devices. The serial port is for local administration—when the administrator has physical access to the device. Serial cables have nine connectors, and they are used to connect two devices together. Once a connection has been established, a program such as Hyperterminal on Windows can be used to initiate a connection to the device that is at the other end of the serial cable. Serial ports have a logical communication (COM) port that they are associated with. To create a connection, you must choose the speed, data bits, parity, stop bits, and flow control.

The speed is the rate at which data can be transferred over the cable, measured in bits per second (bps). Common speeds include 1,200, 2,400, 4,800, 9,600, 19,200, 38,400, 57,600, and 115,200 bps. The data bit setting configures how many bits will be framed by a start signal and a stop signal. Most communication frames are 8 bits because this correlates to a single ASCII character, but you may encounter 5, 6, 7, or 9 as well. Parity can be set to either even, odd, or off. When parity is set to on, an extra bit is added to each data bit set to make the number of 1s in the bit set either odd or even. If the receiver finds a bit set that is odd when the parity is set to even, it knows that the data was corrupted in transit. This method is still prone to error because corruption in the data could still result in the parity calculation to prove correct, so other mechanisms for error detection are usually required on top of parity calculations. The last setting is the stop bits. This setting determines how many bits will be used to show that a character stream has ended. This is usually set to 1. Serial communication does allow for flow control if this is specified in the configuration. Flow control allows for a device to pause and resume communication.

Serial communication, specified in Reference Standard 232 (RS-232), operates asynchronously, meaning that there is no signal or time spacing used to keep the communication in sync. There are a number of serial ports, but the most common one is shaped roughly like the letter *D* and has nine ports. This type of serial port can be referred to as DB-9. As the name suggests, serial ports send data serially, one bit at a time. Each set of bits is framed with a start signal and a stop signal. The number of bits that must be framed is specified when configuring a serial port. One of the key limitations of serial cables is their maximum distance of 50 feet. However, there are network-based serial port modules that can be used to connect to serial sessions over an IP address. These devices operate much like Keyboard Video Monitor (KVM) devices, and they encapsulate the information received on a serial port over an IP network and send information received on the IP network to the device connected to the serial port.

Telnet

Telnet is a protocol used to provide a command-line terminal that allows communication and control of another device known as a *virtual terminal*. As an early network access protocol, Telnet was used to connect various remote hosts, computers, or devices in a network using TCP as the transport protocol. Telnet operates over TCP port 23 by default.

 EXAM TIP Telnet exchanges information in plain text, meaning it is not encrypted. Other devices on the network may be able to intercept this traffic and view the username and password used to connect to the device, along with any information that is shared between the user and the device over Telnet.

Telnet is easy to use and configure, and there are many client applications that support Telnet, including the Terminal application built into Microsoft Windows. Telnet, however, does not include many security features and does not encrypt data; thus, it is not suitable for use over an unsecured channel such as the Internet. When connecting to a remote device using Telnet, a virtual private network (VPN) should be used to provide authentication and encryption between the local and remote networks.

SSH

Secure Shell (SSH) is a Unix-based command interface and protocol for getting access to a remote computer or device in a secure manner. Figure 6-7 shows an SSH logon session using PuTTY. SSH is a protocol that is widely used by network administrators to

```
nasroot@D200000731: /proc                                    _ □ ×
login as: nasroot
Sent username "nasroot"
Trying public key authentication.
Passphrase for key
Linux D200000731 2.6.12.5-SI0611K001 #1 SMP Thu Jun 26 10:48:02 JST 2008 x86_64
GNU/Linux

The programs included with the Debian GNU/Linux system are free software;
the exact distribution terms for each program are described in the
individual files in /usr/share/doc/*/copyright.

Debian GNU/Linux comes with ABSOLUTELY NO WARRANTY, to the extent
permitted by applicable law.
```

Figure 6-7 SSH session using PuTTY

control web and other types of servers remotely. SSH is also used for remote command-line login, remote command execution, secure data communication, and other secure network services between two networked computers. SSH does this through a secure channel over an insecure network and a server and a client (both of which need to be running SSH server and SSH clients, respectively).

SSH is composed of a suite of three utilities: slogin, ssh, and scp. All of these are secure versions of the earlier Unix utilities rlogin, rsh, and rcp. SSH commands are encrypted and are secure in lots of ways. Both ends of the client-server application use a digital certificate to get authentication. The passwords are also encrypted for added protection.

SSH makes use of the Rivest, Shamir, Adleman (RSA) public key cryptography for both connection and authentication. Blowfish, Data Encryption Standard (DES), and International Data Encryption Algorithm (IDEA) are among the list of encryption algorithms. The default among these is IDEA.

EXAM TIP Many systems that support Telnet also support SSH. If an exam question asks how to best connect to a system and both Telnet and SSH are listed, SSH is most likely the answer.

The latest version of SSH is SSH2, which is a proposed set of standards from the Internet Engineering Task Force (IETF). SSH2 is more efficient and more secure than SSH, but it is not compatible with SSH version 1. The enhanced security of SSH2 comes from its use of message authentication codes (MACs), additional integrity checking, and a more secure method of key exchange.

The following example procedure generates an SSH key to be used with PuTTY:

1. Download and run the puttygen program to create a key.

2. Select the version of SSH you will use (SSH-1, SSH-2, or SSH-3).

3. Click Generate.

4. Move your mouse around under the public key label until the bar completes. The screen will look like Figure 6-8.

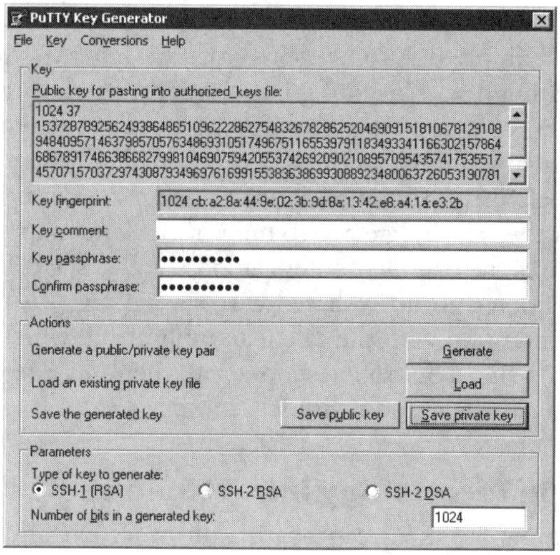

Figure 6-8
PuTTY key
generation

Configuration Management

Storage systems are integrated into the applications and services that support an organization. For example, a storage system may use a directory system such as Microsoft's Active Directory for authentication, or it may publish iSCSI targets to an iSCSI name server such as iSNS. (See Chapter 8 for more information on iSNS.) At the same time, applications such as database management systems (DBMSs), hypervisors, and e-mail systems may obtain their data from the storage system. Many people might need to make changes to these services, which could have an impact on other associated services. For example, a change to a system that appears to be unrelated, such as Active Directory, might cause servers to be unable to authenticate to the iSNS server to obtain iSCSI targets, leading to the applications that reside on those servers to fail when they cannot access their storage. As systems increase in complexity, the need for configuration management grows.

Configuration management is a set of processes that govern how changes are made to systems starting when the system is implemented and ending when the system is retired. Configuration management processes include how those changes are requested, approved, documented, tracked, and audited. Configuration management reduces losses from downtime and rework by requiring that configuration changes go through an approval process. Approvals require a degree of documentation in order to explain what the change is and the purpose for the change. This gives the organization the opportunity to analyze the risks of the change prior to making it. Other stakeholders may need to review the change to see how it would impact associated processes or whether the change might impact future interoperability with ongoing development efforts. By the time a change is made to the system, the organization is well informed on the impact it will have.

Configuration management systems are essential in audits because they give the organization the ability to generate reports listing all the changes to relevant systems. Auditors can review a single system rather than consulting multiple people, time sheets, or other documentation.

Configuration management is also useful in troubleshooting. It is true that components may fail simply due to age, but software typically does not break without some change happening first. The configuration management system is often the first resource troubleshooters reference when dealing with a new issue. For example, a user may report that a calendar function occasionally fails to load. The logs show timeout errors for the calendar application. The troubleshooter checks the configuration management system and finds that the last change was to move the calendar application to a different storage group. This gives the troubleshooter a good place to start. The troubleshooter then finds that the new storage group is shared with several high-I/O applications. These applications are in contention with the calendar application, which is causing application timeouts on the web site. The troubleshooter can then put a request in to move the calendar application to a storage group with less contention.

Information Technology Infrastructure Library

Configuration management can be difficult to understand in the abstract. Fortunately, the Information Technology Infrastructure Library (ITIL) has come to the rescue by establishing a set of best practices for effectively implementing IT services, including configuration management. ITIL calls itself a best practice, rather than a set of standards like the ISO/IEC 20000 service management standard or the Control Objectives for Information and Related Technologies (COBIT) standard. Whereas standards establish a minimum acceptable level, a best practice establishes an optimal level, and this is where ITIL sees its guidelines falling.

The ITIL best practices cover several key areas of IT service management (ITSM), including service strategy, design, transition, and operation. The service transition section includes practical guidance on change management, service asset and configuration management, and release and deployment management.

In order to stay competitive, businesses need to adapt swiftly to a rapidly changing marketplace. A strategy needs to be in place to manage each aspect of service development. ITIL seeks to optimize every facet of project management. One of the most important parts is change management.

The goal of the ITIL service transition section is to provide businesses with the ability to adapt swiftly to new requirements that may change frequently. ITIL describes the process of managing a product from concept to end-of-life. This includes managing changes to the system and the configuration.

To improve management decision making, reliable and secure data must be accessible throughout the product lifecycle. Any change to the system must be handled carefully so that it does not bring about unforeseen costs. Staff must have a clear sense of the value their services provide. The service providers must have suitable information on who is using their service and any difficulties faced by customers so that the service may provide a solution to the issue. The process starts with identifying and planning the collection of relevant data and information. The individual team members may share their knowledge with others, so each individual's competency may change throughout the project lifecycle. The requirements for the system need to be clearly defined in order to provide an effective and efficient system. There is also a need for ongoing improvement to the process to support decision making.

With an increasing rate of change in technology, a business must have a strategy that adapts to a rapidly changing environment. Change may come as a result of a business seeking to reduce cost, improve its services, or resolve errors. These changes will mitigate risk and minimize the severity of any service disruptions. Changes to the system can cause disruption, so any changes need to be done without causing errors. Failure to correctly implement changes on the first attempt may cause negative consequences to the business.

A business needs the ability to deploy a service into production and make effective use of it in order to deliver value to the consumer. In order to create the best experience, the business needs to make changes throughout the development process.

The purpose is to make comprehensive plans for packages for the building, installing, testing, and deploying the service. A business must also make an effort to create a system that minimizes unpredicted impacts. After all of this, there must be a way to manage the expectations of the customer for the planning and deployment of future releases. This will have the effect of optimizing cost while minimizing risk. The overall goal is to improve consistency across the organization for change, service teams, suppliers, and customers.

The following approaches can be taken when deploying changes to a service:

- **Big bang**   The first is the big bang approach, where the service is deployed to all user areas in one operation. This approach is often used if consistency across the organization is important when an application change is introduced.

- **Phased**   The second deployment option is a phased approach, where the service is deployed to only part of the user base initially and then slowly rolled out to more users by following a roadmap plan.

- **Push**   The third option is the push approach, where a service is deployed from a central location and pushed out to all the users.

- **Pull**   The pull method is similar to push, but instead of the central station pushing out the service to the clients, the clients can request for the service to be deployed to them from the central server.

The service transition is used for aligning the new service with any organizational requirements and operations. This will make sure that the organization has the ability to adapt quickly to new business requirements and that the success rate of any changes made to the system is optimized. This will provide the organization with confidence during the change, as well as provide a competitive edge to help with the flexibility of the organization.

Storage Monitoring, Alerting, and Reporting

Monitoring, alerting, and reporting are integral parts of a comprehensive storage management plan. These capabilities foster rapid prototyping; fast moves, adds, and changes; efficient fault-tolerant upgrades; and a proactive resource for capacity planning, performance analysis and optimization, problem identification and management, and system availability, reliability, and security.

Storage monitoring is a major function within storage management. It monitors the pulse and health of a storage network and all associated resources. Monitoring is an expensive proposition. Real-time monitoring is crucial but costly. Hence, care must be taken to prioritize which storage resources and data assets are essential to business health and continuity in the event of their loss. Snapshots may be taken over a period of time to offset the cost of monitoring those resources deemed less critical.

Alerting is the mechanism by which the system administrator or, in some cases, automated routines and policies are made aware of changing conditions in the network, device, and storage. Thresholds are typically established to delimit upper and lower operating parameters across a range of metrics. The true benefits of storage monitoring and alerting are captured in a series of reports. These reports detail the trends in system/ storage utilization, performance, and faults. On the high end, analysis of this data can form the input to a system that "self-heals," or automatically adjusts to maintain system optimization and integrity. In more practical use, these reports allow for the proactive administration of complex system and storage resources.

Settings Thresholds

In storage management, thresholds are used to monitor the storage usage of a database. Administrators can set warning and alarm thresholds in storage management tools, which then compare the set values against real-time readings from the system. If the storage state exceeds the safe levels—or thresholds—that were set for it, an alert flag will be shown beside the object whose value has increased beyond its safety level.

 EXAM TIP Metrics that exceed the alarm threshold should be addressed immediately. For example, an alarm threshold might be a temperature above 90 degrees in a server room.

Every object is created with a default threshold. The children of this object will inherit the same value. However, these values can be overridden when an administrator decides to set a specific value for certain objects—or all of them, for that matter. Once a new value has been set for any object, the children of that object will inherit the set value.

Normally, there are three threshold values or boundaries or zones. These are normal, warning, and alarm. Normal is when an object doesn't show any signs of problems at all or is at its set or default value. A warning happens when an object has reached beyond its set or default value but isn't a cause for immediate concern or hasn't progressed into a threat. An alarm is when action needs to be taken to address the problem because the object has exceeded the set or default values and has progressed into a state where it can threaten the entire system.

Trending

A *trend* is a pattern of gradual change in a condition, output, or process, or an average or general tendency of a series of data points to move in a certain direction over time, represented by a line or curve on a graph. This definition is applied to many facets, especially in forecasting. For example, a business can conduct a survey on what would be the products that consumers will demand in the future based on shopping data.

This same concept can also be applied in storage management. An administrator, through the use of a storage management tool, can compare growth trends for a storage resource between two points in time. Be it the number of files, overall file size, or available free space, a storage management tool gives an administrator all the information needed to better manage storage devices.

The trending information that an administrator gets from a storage management tool will help the administrator determine the growth rate on a volume, calculate capacity, and budget for more storage. By doing this, an organization can better plan for the use of its resources and purchase additional ones before they are needed. As mentioned throughout, data is important to a company, and having sufficient storage to put that data in is crucial. And with the help of storage trending, a business can easily determine when it needs to add more based on data compared over different time periods.

The use of real-time network/system maps or applications that supply access to aggregate data via GUIs, graphs, charts, and other interactive multimedia methods has greatly aided the analysis of data from monitoring and alerts and supplied invaluable tools for forecasting and capacity planning based on observed trends.

Forecasting and Capacity Planning

Storage capacity planning refers to the practice of assessing or making a forecast with regard to future storage requirements. The aim of capacity planning is to strike a balance between providing high levels of system, storage, and data reliability and availability at reasonable operating costs. The goal is to ensure that an enterprise is proactive rather than reactive in addressing capacity planning through forecasting.

In the past, many network as well as storage resources were poorly allocated or in some cases grossly underutilized. Forecasting and capacity planning have taken the guesswork out of meeting an enterprise's growing storage needs. With effective capacity planning, data storage administrators can maximize capital expenditures by procuring only the storage and supporting infrastructure that is currently needed while predicting future growth with a high degree of accuracy. Overall cash flow and fiscal management are optimized.

The following ten questions can serve as a starting point for forecasting and capacity planning. This list is in no way comprehensive, but it can demonstrate the direction and mind-set found in the process.

- How much storage is in use out of what has been allocated?
- How much bandwidth is required between sites, switches, and VLANs?

- How much bandwidth is available for WANs, trunks/ISLs, front-end and back-end ports, and routing ports?
- What is the current read-to-write cache allocation for storage arrays?
- What is the relationship between storage I/O and network traffic?
- What is the recovery time objective (RTO) and recovery point objective (RPO)? (See Chapter 7.)
- How much data must be backed up, replicated, or archived? What is the schedule?
- Where is storage located?
- Where are the users of storage located?
- How will systems, applications, and users interface with the storage system?

Storage administrators can determine how storage is being allocated with the use of storage capacity planning tools that analyze storage systems and then generate a report based on the data available and storage performance. These analysis and reporting tools are disparate and often proprietary. Proprietary forecasting and reporting tools can make it difficult for storage administrators to get an end-to-end look at the overall health of storage resources and report on future capacity and performance needs, but they still save time in collecting and interpreting data. The establishment of baselines helps to elevate the disparity between various data collection and analysis tools.

Recording a Baseline

A *baseline* is defined as statistical information on performance over a period of time. Establishing a baseline is the starting point before comparisons can be made. For example, in business, sales from the first quarter can be compared to those from the second quarter to determine whether the business earned a profit. This same concept is applicable in storage management to determine whether system performance is as expected or within tolerance.

When dealing with storage devices, it helps to know the capabilities and limitations. Understanding this will serve as a reliable and accurate baseline for comparison. Establishing storage baselines will allow the administrator to identify and use values that aid in defining normal performance conditions from abnormal ones. Establishing and monitoring these baselines for various elements of performance and utilization allow the administrator to differentiate between normal and abnormal system conditions.

A baseline is created by capturing data on normal operations over a period of time, so it should be created when a system has reached a point of stability and then should be updated when significant planned changes are made and/or on a periodic basis. The period of time during which you collect data is discretionary, but if your organization does not have a standard, one week is a good starting point. This period typically provides enough time to average usage changes that may occur during the week and to take into account expected periods of low and high utilization. If you don't have a baseline now, consider creating one right away.

NOTE The goal of the baseline is to understand normal traffic. Do not collect a baseline during times when you know that traffic will be outside of the norm, such as the end of the fiscal year on an accounting system.

The baseline should include data on both peak and average performance. The peak statistics show the utilization when it is at its highest level, and the average statistics show the sum of a set of performance statistics taken at regular intervals divided by the number of intervals in the set. Some elements of a baseline include peak and average performance statistics for the following:

- Error rates
- Input and output per second
- Requests
- Queue sizes
- Concurrent users

The average statistics are your normal values, but the peak statistics will help in filtering out the false-positive events that differ from the baseline. For example, consider a situation where average NIC utilization is 10 percent with a standard deviation of 40 percent for the link-aggregated connection to a NAS. Peak utilization, occurring at 8 a.m. and 4:30 p.m., is 35 percent, with a standard deviation of +/– 10 percent. Given this information, anomalous behavior would be NIC utilization that is less than 5.99 percent or greater than 14 percent, except for 8 a.m. and 4:30 p.m., when anomalous behavior would be NIC utilization below 31.4 percent or higher than 38.5 percent.

It is also helpful to map out the average load on data sets within the storage system or systems. A single storage system may host data for a variety of shares and purposes. Some of the data may be accessed continually, and other data may be accessed rarely. Understanding which data is accessed the most will help in planning for expansion or in prioritizing troubleshooting or recovery efforts so that the most critical data is made available first.

You can acquire storage performance metrics using SAN vendor-based tools, third-party storage management programs, or built-in operating system utilities.

Setting Alerts

In the event that storage thresholds or baseline conditions are not met or are exceeded, some form of alerting is needed. In this regard, the type and frequency of monitoring and reporting become critical. The complex task of alerting is shared by humans, applications, and devices. Many applications and devices are able to monitor themselves and send alerts if operating policies are not met. Intelligence in the network has reached a staggering degree of sophistication as broken or ailing paths, devices, storage, and other resources are automatically taken offline or even bypassed in order to maintain system

Displaying Performance Data in Windows with Performance Monitor

Microsoft Windows systems have a built-in tool called Performance Monitor that can be helpful in obtaining performance statistics from the local machine. While this may not be central to the storage device, NICs or HBAs are part of the host and contain useful metrics for the baseline. On a Windows machine, select the Start button and go to Run. Type **perfmon** and press ENTER. This will open Performance Monitor, as shown here:

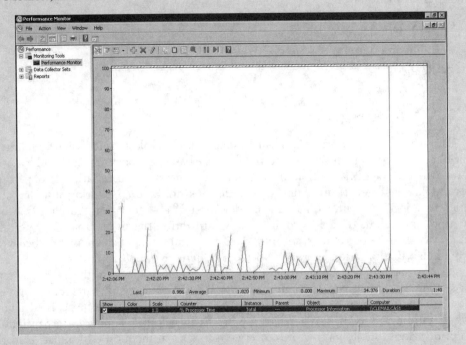

The % Processor Time counter is monitored by default, but you can click the red X to remove it. Click the green plus sign to add more counters. Each counter will be given a line color as it is displayed on the graph.

functioning and integrity. Nonetheless, human vigilance and interaction are always required. Figure 6-9 shows the alerts section for an EMC storage array within a WBEM management tool.

Once an alert has been sent, the storage administrator can take a number of predetermined contingencies and actions. As previously stated, a large amount of resolving or correcting system conditions has been automated with solutions "pushed" to the administrator. By analyzing the type, source, and other critical information related to

Severity	Created	Message	Event Code
Critical	Apr 24, 2014 6:01:53 PM	Enclosure 0 management switch A I2C A bus error.	0x1260830203
Critical	Apr 24, 2014 6:01:53 PM	Enclosure 0 fault occurred.	0x1260830218
Critical	Mar 12, 2014 8:03:01 AM	dskMon[2581]: FS /dev/mapper/emc_vg_lun_5-emc_lv_nas_var_emcsupport mounted on /nbsn...	0x1260180018
Critical	Mar 12, 2014 7:03:02 AM	dskMon[18291]: FS /dev/mapper/emc_vg_lun_5-emc_lv_nas_var_emcsupport mounted on /nbs...	0x1260180018
Critical	Mar 12, 2014 6:03:01 AM	dskMon[1247]: FS /dev/mapper/emc_vg_lun_5-emc_lv_nas_var_emcsupport mounted on /nbsn...	0x1260180018
Critical	Mar 12, 2014 5:03:01 AM	dskMon[16857]: FS /dev/mapper/emc_vg_lun_5-emc_lv_nas_var_emcsupport mounted on /nbs...	0x1260180018
Critical	Mar 12, 2014 4:03:01 AM	dskMon[32022]: FS /dev/mapper/emc_vg_lun_5-emc_lv_nas_var_emcsupport mounted on /nbs...	0x1260180018
Critical	Mar 12, 2014 3:03:01 AM	dskMon[14884]: FS /dev/mapper/emc_vg_lun_5-emc_lv_nas_var_emcsupport mounted on /nbs...	0x1260180018
Critical	Mar 12, 2014 2:03:01 AM	dskMon[30136]: FS /dev/mapper/emc_vg_lun_5-emc_lv_nas_var_emcsupport mounted on /nbs...	0x1260180018
Critical	Mar 12, 2014 1:03:02 AM	dskMon[13081]: FS /dev/mapper/emc_vg_lun_5-emc_lv_nas_var_emcsupport mounted on /nbs...	0x1260180018
Critical	Mar 12, 2014 12:03:01 AM	dskMon[26795]: FS /dev/mapper/emc_vg_lun_5-emc_lv_nas_var_emcsupport mounted on /nbs...	0x1260180018
Critical	Mar 11, 2014 11:03:01 PM	dskMon[9947]: FS /dev/mapper/emc_vg_lun_5-emc_lv_nas_var_emcsupport mounted on /nbsn...	0x1260180018
Critical	Mar 11, 2014 10:03:01 PM	dskMon[25579]: FS /dev/mapper/emc_vg_lun_5-emc_lv_nas_var_emcsupport mounted on /nbs...	0x1260180018
Critical	Mar 11, 2014 9:03:02 PM	dskMon[8448]: FS /dev/mapper/emc_vg_lun_5-emc_lv_nas_var_emcsupport mounted on /nbsn...	0x1260180018
Critical	Mar 11, 2014 8:03:01 PM	dskMon[24065]: FS /dev/mapper/emc_vg_lun_5-emc_lv_nas_var_emcsupport mounted on /nbs...	0x1260180018
Critical	Mar 11, 2014 7:03:01 PM	dskMon[6851]: FS /dev/mapper/emc_vg_lun_5-emc_lv_nas_var_emcsupport mounted on /nbsn...	0x1260180018
Critical	Mar 11, 2014 6:03:01 PM	dskMon[22692]: FS /dev/mapper/emc_vg_lun_5-emc_lv_nas_var_emcsupport mounted on /nbs...	0x1260180018
Critical	Mar 11, 2014 5:03:02 PM	dskMon[5114]: FS /dev/mapper/emc_vg_lun_5-emc_lv_nas_var_emcsupport mounted on /nbsn...	0x1260180018
Critical	Mar 11, 2014 4:03:01 PM	dskMon[20829]: FS /dev/mapper/emc_vg_lun_5-emc_lv_nas_var_emcsupport mounted on /nbs...	0x1260180018

Figure 6-9   Alerts for a storage array in a WBEM management tool

the alert, the administrator may identify trends or patterns of behavior in the system. Used properly, this information allows the administrator to proactively devise strategies to minimize the impact of these issues across time, thus ensuring system health and financial stability.

Auditing Log Files

Log files are another important aspect in the monitoring of storage devices. A log file gives the administrator a complete picture of what went wrong. Some legacy or inexpensive storage devices are not capable of indicating the source and nature of a fault that has occurred. Log files provide details that assist in system monitoring and reporting. Logs provide data about desired system conditions as well as abnormal conditions, which allows the administrator to validate or change those areas of the storage administration plan as needed. While more tedious than other monitoring techniques because of the size and the sheer number, log files are invaluable for longitudinal trend analysis.

NOTE   Be sure to record the machine time for devices when collecting or analyzing log files. If the machines being compared have different times, you will need to adjust the timestamps in the log files to compensate so that you can accurately track activity.

Backup Logs

Backup errors can often be found within the logs maintained by the operating system. The first place to look is in the application log because application-specific errors will be found there. You may also want to check the system log for system violations that may have been caused by a backup operation. This is typically a step performed when gathering additional information on an event found in the application log or in log files maintained by the backup application.

In addition to the operating system logs, backup applications often have their own logs. These logs are the most specific and will provide the most relevant information in troubleshooting backup problems. Some log files are in ASCII format and can be read with any text editor, such as Notepad or WordPad, while others are in binary format and must be opened with an application from the backup vendor or viewed within the backup software. Table 6-1 shows examples of several log files from major backup vendors, including where they are located, their naming conventions, and whether they are stored in ASCII or binary format.

Alerting Methods

An administrator can set different types of alerts in order to be notified if something goes wrong with a storage device, such as a hardware failure, or a high-priority or critical-event log entry is detected. Alerts can be sent when a critical error occurs or when a server or system metric has exceeded its threshold value. For example, alerts could be sent out when a hard drive fails, and then the administrator could check the particular disk that issued the alert, replacing it if necessary.

Backup Application	Default directory	File Naming Convention	ASCII or Binary
Veritas Backup Exec	%ProgramFiles%\Symantec \Backup Exec	[Servername]_[Date]_ [Time] .sdbz	Binary
Veeam Backup & Replication	C:\ProgramData\Application Data\Veeam\Backup	Job.Name of your Job.Type of your Job.log	Binary
IBM Tivoli Storage Manager	%UserData%\tivoli\tsm \ui/Liberty/usr/servers/ guiServer/logs	Tsm_opscntr.log	ASCII
Arcserve UDP	%ProgramFiles%\CA \ARCserve Unified Data Protection\Engine\Logs	[Server]-Backup_[Role]	ASCII
Unitrends Enterprise Backup	%ProgramFiles%\Unitrends \Hyper-V Service	[ServerName]-[Appliance]– [Target]-[Application]	ASCII
Dell EMC Data Protection Suite	User customizable	[MM/DD/YYYY]_ HH:MM	Binary

Table 6-1   Backup Application Logs

Some alerting methods include the following:

- **E-mail**   E-mail is one of the most commonly used methods for alerting. E-mail uses Simple Mail Transport Protocol (SMTP) to deliver e-mail from the alerting server to the mailboxes of those you want to alert, such as storage administrators or other IT staff.

- **SNMP**   Another alert method of choice is through the Simple Network Management Protocol. Through SNMP traps, a management application can receive alert information so that it can be displayed in a network operations center or reviewed on a periodic basis by IT personnel. Management applications may also send alerts via other methods when an SNMP trap is received for specific items.

- **Short Message Service (SMS)**   SMS is used for sending text messages to phones, software that emulates a phone, or SMS software. Many employees carry their cell phone with them, and this is an effective way to reach them wherever they may be.

- **Phone or modem**   Some systems can dial a number and leave a prerecorded message on a phone or cell phone. Others may use a modem to send notifications. Storage devices may be configured with a modem or a network connection to a remote site managed by a vendor so that they can "call home." This way, the vendor knows of the problem and can dispatch support personnel or troubleshoot the issue remotely.

Figure 6-10 shows an alert configuration screen for an EMC storage array. ACLUPD alerts with a critical severity will be sent to the e-mail address sample@sample.com, and ADMIN events with a critical severity will be sent using SNMP to an event collector residing on a server with the IP address 192.168.5.30. This event collector is configured to receive alerts tagged with the community string "EMC-alerts."

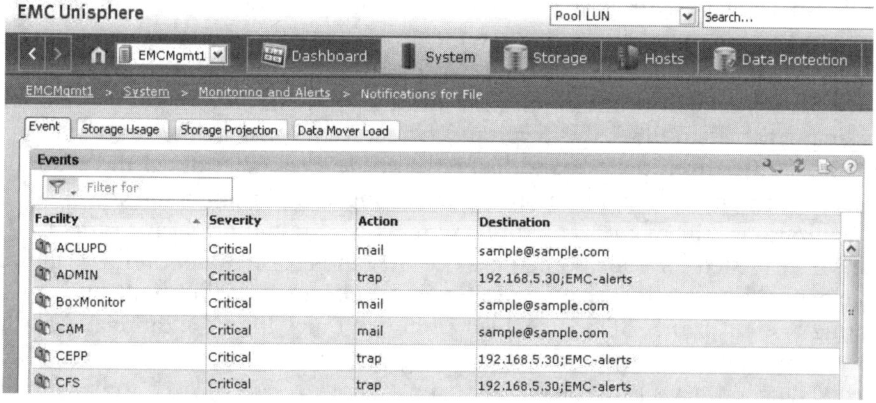

Figure 6-10   Configuring alerts

Software-Defined Storage

Software-defined storage (SDS) combines storage virtualization management with a service management framework to automate common storage tasks such as provisioning and migration dynamically in response to changing application needs. SDS allows applications to monitor their own consumption of the resources and allows applications to tap into unused resources of other systems, when needed and within limits.

Virtualization allowed companies to better utilize the system they had in place, to balance applications that had different I/O usage patterns so that they could all utilize the same resources without contention. However, changes to the virtual infrastructure are still made manually without SDS. SDS allows these changes to be managed automatically, which allows the virtual infrastructure to be customized on demand to the needs of the application. This is an important distinction because manual changes typically cannot be made quickly enough to handle changes in demand. This leads to provisioning a resource buffer to handle requests that cannot be handled on the fly. However, this buffer is really wasted resources because it is only designed for the peak times when a person would otherwise be needed to adjust resources.

SDS automates storage operational actions to allow for software to specify its needs. SDS applications use Storage Management Initiative Specification (SMI-S) or other similar frameworks to determine which resources are available for use. SMI-S is used to create a dashboard of systems management information, which could comprise a Web-Based Enterprise Management (WBEM) system. The resources queried using SMI-S can then be requested and utilized through application programming interfaces (APIs). APIs provide a way for one application to send instructions as well as send and receive data with another application. This is all without the bottleneck of an IT resource making the change.

Storage provisioning, for example, can be implemented from the storage array all the way to the host. Not only can a logical unit number (LUN) be created on the storage array and allocated to a host on the fabric, it can also be mounted on the host, assigned a drive letter, if required, and made available to the application for use. This is the level of integration that SDS offers, and it is powerful indeed.

SDS can also be used to optimize workloads for the hardware that is best suited for them. For example, an application may want to perform a very write-intensive operation, but it is currently configured to utilize a RAID 6 array logical volume with a heavy write penalty. SDS would allow the application to utilize a RAID 10 logical volume for the processing rather than the RAID 6 volume. Under traditional architectures, the application would suffer from performance issues until DevOps determined the cause of the issues, at which point the application might no longer need those resources.

Organizations still rely on enterprise systems that reside on legacy systems. These systems have existed for years, sometimes decades, and are often not on the roadmap for replacement. Newer technologies typically have SDS functionality built into the array operating system so that SDS is enabled from day one without additional software or hardware. However, this is not the case for legacy systems that existed before SDS was created. The good news is that legacy systems do not necessarily need to be completely replaced in an SDS framework. However, they may require a software layer to be added onto them to interface with the rest of the SDS system. This interface may take the form of a storage gateway, virtual controller, or a proxy storage controller.

SDS can improve both operational performance and security. Applications often control access to the data contained within them, and they understand the data that they manage. Those systems external to the application only see the application files. However, the application sees the individual pieces of data within those files and can determine optimal placement according to the operational and security needs of the data. For example, operationally, the application may choose to place files that are accessed frequently by a large number of users onto high-speed flash-based media, while files that are infrequently accessed are placed onto SAS or nearline SAS (SATA) based RAID. At the same time, highly sensitive, frequently accessed documents might be placed onto the flash media contained locally in the organization's private cloud while less sensitive frequently accessed documents are placed into flash media on the public cloud. These are decisions that would be time consuming and difficult to implement manually, but can be implemented with software-defined storage through process automation and policies. For those workflow that are automated, consider following the processes outlined in the ITIL service management framework, discussed earlier in this chapter. These processes have been well thought out and have undergone significant scrutiny by the industry community.

SDS Caveats

SDS does have some caveats. It is complex to set up, and care should be taken in choosing which processes to automate. I worked with a company that spent quite a bit of time automating processes, but many of those processes were only used a few times. The company easily spent 50 hours automating the workflows and creating triggers and rules for a single process, but the process they scripted only took about 30 minutes to complete. It was not a process performed often and, even then, it was not extremely time sensitive, so manual effort wouldn't have been a limiting factor. This type of process did not need to be automated. The company should have spent their time automating more common LUN provisioning and migration activities.

Also, virtualization is essential to SDS, but it is important to not architect too many layers of virtualization in an SDS solution. Some virtualization layers may add latency to storage I/O or critical management functions, which could inhibit performance of the entire application. Generally, it is better to create a design that minimizes virtualization layers. This can also aid in reducing SDS complexity.

A high degree of abstraction between different layers can make it more difficult to isolate problems, especially in a highly changing organization. It is important to maintain equally intelligent monitoring and management systems to keep track of what is going on and to track changes in order to isolate performance issues if they come up. This is also why it is incredibly important to test out workflows in a test environment before placing them in production.

Chapter Summary

This chapter marked a transition from the technical, physical, and theoretical aspects of storage and began the discussion of managing storage and the data it holds as invaluable resources.

- Logical units (LUs) are assigned to a host by associating their logical unit number (LUN) with that host.
- There are two methods for provisioning LUs—thick or thin.
  - Thick LUs are static in size, meaning they consume the same amount of storage on the storage array as is presented to the host.
  - Thin LUs are provisioned with only the actual amount of space that is consumed by the host, but a maximum size is presented to the host.

The second part of the chapter focused on management systems and protocols. To monitor critical events such as free space, management protocols were created. Management protocols allow for information on systems, including critical events and performance, to be gathered and configuration changes to be made.

- The notification of such events is known as alerting.
- Alerts can be set up based on criteria such as the presence of an event and the crossing of a threshold.
- Alerts can be logged or sent directly to administrators.
- Storage devices and network devices often retain logs containing such information that can be reviewed.
- The default log settings may not be appropriate for all circumstances, and some administrators may want to enable logging on other items.
- Logs may be overwritten over time, so they must be archived if administrators want to view them in the future.
- Backup logs are important in ensuring that data is effectively backed up so that it is available when needed in an emergency.
- Management protocols are as follows:
  - SNMP gathers system information from devices and other network components and stores it in a repository.
    - SNMP gathers information from network devices over UDP ports 161 and 162.
    - SNMP interprets the data based on a management information base.
  - The Storage Management Initiative-Specification (SMI-S) operates in a client-server model with clients requesting information from storage resources.
  - Web-Based Enterprise Management (WBEM) is a collection of such technologies that is used to configure, audit, update, and monitor devices.

- In-band management in a storage network means that both data and management move over the same path, whereas out-of-band management uses a separate path for data and management.

- Some management utilities use graphical interfaces such as WBEM systems through the use of Hypertext Transfer Protocol (HTTP) or other HTTP-based management consoles. Other control functions are performed using a command-line interface.

- A serial cable is used to make direct connections from a computer to a device such as a network switch or storage device.

- Telnet and Secure Shell are methods of accessing a computer or device remotely.

  - Telnet does not include many security features and thus is not suitable for use over an unsecured channel such as the Internet.

  - SSH uses an encrypted secure channel to connect a server or device and a client.

- Key concepts of configuration management are as follows:

  - Configuration management is a set of processes that govern how changes are made to systems over the course of the system's lifetime.

  - Core configuration management processes include change requests, change approval, change documentation, change tracking, and auditing.

  - The Information Technology Infrastructure Library (ITIL) is a set of IT service management (ITSM) best practices that include best practices on configuration management under ITIL's service transition section.

- Storage monitoring is summarized as follows:

  - A threshold is an established target value that administrators desire systems to remain above or below. For example, one threshold could be temperature.

  - Baselines are metrics that define normal performance. A baseline is gathered so that future metrics can be compared against it to identify anomalous behavior.

  - Trending is a pattern of change over time that can be used to predict utilization or a need of systems in the future.

  - Forecasting allows for the analysis of trends identified as part of the ongoing process of monitoring and alerting.

- Key points of software-defined storage (SDS) are as follows:

  - SDS combines storage virtualization management with a service management framework that is used to automate common storage tasks.

  - SDS often automates storage provisioning and migration and it can do so dynamically in response to changing application needs.

  - SDS can customize application storage based on application requirements.

  - SDS allows applications to monitor their own resource consumption using management frameworks such as SMI-S.

Chapter Review Questions

1. Which of the following are possible provisioning methods?

   A. Thin and thick

   B. Lazy and thin

   C. Think and thin

   D. Thick and lazy

2. You are making a business case for implementing thin provisioning on your storage arrays. Which reason would you give your manager to explain why thin provisioning should be used?

   A. It replicates data to another storage array.

   B. Resources are minimized until needed.

   C. Space on the array can easily be consumed.

   D. Monitoring of the space available is simplified.

3. Which of the following is a best practice when using thin provisioning?

   A. Nothing. Thin-provisioned software will automatically manage everything.

   B. Run Disk Cleanup weekly.

   C. Set Disk Defragment and Optimize to run daily.

   D. Monitor the disk space used and trends in data capacity.

4. What is the advantage of SNMPv3 over SNMPv2?

   A. Supports encrypted channels and mutual authentication

   B. Performance and security enhancements over v2

   C. Can share data with management servers that are in the same family

   D. Can connect multiple devices to the same port

5. How does Web-Based Enterprise Management (WBEM) help the administrator manage devices?

   A. WBEM has a limited set of management standards that function flawlessly.

   B. WBEM has no expansion to allow future enhancements.

   C. WBEM is a standard that allows both the Common Information Model and Extensible Markup Language (XML) to allow future enhancements.

   D. WBEM is a protocol used for sharing data on storage devices.

6. How does out-of-band storage management differ from in-band storage management?

   A. Only certified operations are allowed in in-band storage management.

   B. Out-of-band installations are less complex.

    C. Out-of-band requires a dedicated management channel.

    D. Out-of-band requires a complex network IP addressing scheme.

7. Where did the OpenEBEM, OpenPegasus, and WBEMsource feature sets originate?

    A. Originally proposed by Apple in the 1970s

    B. DOS and Linux

    C. CIM

    D. PowerShell

8. What is considered the biggest benefit to the CLI?

    A. It is more intuitive.

    B. Commands can be scheduled or sequenced rather than as individual processes.

    C. The graphic user interface is easier to use.

    D. Commands are easier to remember than a long series of steps in the operating system.

9. You have been tasked with documenting the controls in use on your storage network. How should you describe the use of log files?

    A. Log files provide details that assist in system monitoring and reporting.

    B. Log files are used to preserve data integrity.

    C. Log files ensure that third parties meet availability SLAs.

    D. Log files are used only by hardware vendors to troubleshoot hardware issues.

10. Which of the following storage administration methods is not encrypted?

    A. SSH

    B. Telnet

    C. VPN

    D. IPSec

11. Which of the following describes oversubscription?

    A. Oversubscription is when multiple devices receive the same data on the network.

    B. Oversubscription should be avoided whenever possible.

    C. Oversubscription allows multiple devices to be connected to the same switch port.

    D. Oversubscription is an error state when devices consume too much bandwidth.

12. Which tasks are part of configuration management?

    A. Request, approval, documentation, tracking, and auditing

    B. Planning, acceptance, enactment, training, and appraisal

    C. Identification, preparation, analysis, validation, and reporting

    D. Initiation, examination, authorization, implementation, and conclusion

Chapter Review Answers

1. **A** is correct. Thin provisioning allows the host to believe that it has the maximum amount of space available while the storage system allocates only what is actually used, whereas thick provisioning allocates the entire amount to the storage device. Thin provisioning represents a more optimal means of allocating storage resources than thick provisioning.

   B, **C**, and **D** are incorrect. Thick and thin are both methods of provisioning, while lazy and think are not. Choices **B**, **C**, and **D** use the terms lazy or think.

2. **B** is correct. A thin-provisioned drive will increase in size as needed.

   A, **C**, and **D** are incorrect. **A** is incorrect because thin provisioning is not used for replication. **C** and **D** are incorrect because they are disadvantages of thin provisioning.

3. **D** is correct. Monitoring of data storage usage and data usage trends is absolutely necessary to prevent drive space overusage.

   A, **B**, and **C** are incorrect. **A** is incorrect because applications running on thin-provisioned LUNs do not know that they are thin provisioned. **B** and **C** are incorrect. While Disk Cleanup and Defragmentation can be helpful for regular drive maintenance, they do not benefit thin-provisioned disks better than thick-provisioned disks.

4. **B** is correct. SNMP version 3 offers many of the same features as version 2, but it provides better performance and security.

   A, **C**, and **D** are incorrect. **A** and **C** are incorrect because these features are available in both SNMP versions. **D** is incorrect because SNMP does not handle physical connections.

5. **C** is correct. WBEM is a standard that allows both the Common Information Model and Extensible Markup Language (XML) to have future enhancements. WBEM is web based, and XML is a data formatting standard used in both web-based systems and data storage.

   A, **B**, and **D** are incorrect. **A** is incorrect because WBEM does not function flawlessly. **B** is incorrect because WBEM offers many options for future expansion by providing a framework that systems can continue to use even as other technologies and processes change. Lastly, **D** is incorrect because WBEN shares data with management stations and users of management stations, not between storage devices.

6. **C** is correct. Out-of-band requires a dedicated management channel, while in-band uses the same channel for data and management.

   A, **B**, and **D** are incorrect. **A** is incorrect because certification is not required for in-band storage management. **B** is also incorrect because out-of-band installations are more complex, rather than less complex, than in-band solutions. Lastly, **D** is incorrect because out-of-band storage management utilizes the same IP addressing scheme as any other service on an IP network.

7. **C** is correct. These feature sets were born out of CIM.
   A, **B**, and **D** are incorrect. OpenEBEM, OpenPegasus and WBEMsource did not originate with Apple, DOS, Linux, or PowerShell.

8. **B** is correct. Commands can be scheduled or sequenced rather than as individual processes.
   A, **C**, and **D** are incorrect. **A** is incorrect because CLI is often less intuitive since users must know and remember commands and their structure. **C** is incorrect because a CLI does not have a graphical user interface. **D** is also incorrect since a graphical user interface provides visual cues for users to remember a process, and users can fumble around until they find the right option, whereas CLI commands must be entered perfectly in order to execute.

9. **A** is correct. Log files provide details that assist in system monitoring and reporting. An administrator should look to log files when errors are reported because log files contain information on what actions the system performed, what errors were encountered, and the time each action took place.
   B, **C**, and **D** are incorrect. **B** is incorrect because log files do not provide data integrity. **C** is incorrect because log files have no enforcement ability over SLAs. Lastly, **D** is incorrect because log files can be used by anyone who understands them, not only hardware vendors.

10. **B** is correct. Telnet is not encrypted.
    A, **C**, and **D** are incorrect. SSH, VPNs, and IPSec can all be encrypted.

11. **C** is correct. Oversubscription allows multiple devices to be connected to the same switch port. This can save on the number of ports and cables required to network components together.
    A, **B**, and **D** are incorrect. **A** is incorrect because although these devices may be connected to the same port, they do not receive the same data. **B** is incorrect because oversubscription can be valuable in lowering the cost of system implementation. **D** is incorrect because oversubscription is not an error state.

12. **A** is correct. The configuration management steps include request, approval, documentation, tracking, and auditing. A request is made to make a change, and then that request is reviewed and approved. The change is documented and tracked so that it can later be audited to verify that the changes and the results of those changes met expectations and resulted in no harm to the system or other systems.
    B, **C**, and **D** are incorrect. None of these provides the correct configuration management steps.

Business Continuity

In this chapter, you will learn how to
- Identify business continuity objectives
- Determine ideal backup frequency
- Configure backups and validate backup reliability
- Select appropriate backup locations

The ease with which the modern enterprise accesses, transfers, and manipulates data and information has become so transparent that it is often taken for granted. As we stand at the ATM or other cash kiosk and swipe our cards, we fidget impatiently while gigabytes of data speed their way around the world across a complex hybridization of wired and wireless paths to authenticate, check databases, and dispense the requested funds. We would not tolerate the unavailability of such systems. Banking and finance are the obvious industries we think of when we consider business continuity, but of similar importance are those systems that support health, government, utility, transportation operations, and the data in your organization.

The continuity of operations is critical to both government and business settings. The inability to access a system or its data assets can have an adverse and significant effect on a company's profitability or on the ability of a government to provide even the most basic services. In an era where trillions of dollars in transactions and records move around the world in milliseconds, system outages can be crippling. Natural disasters, human error, cyberterrorism, and system failure are just a few of the catastrophic events that can bring operations to a grinding halt if business continuity planning/implementation have not been performed.

Causes for system outages can be broadly classified in the following manner:

- **Human error**   Unintentional mistakes made by humans
- **Intentional**   Malicious actions with the intent to compromise system functioning and data integrity
- **Natural**   Outages or system malfunctions attributable to natural phenomena such floods, earthquakes, storms, and so on
- **System**   Failures or events attributable to hardware, software, or other system infrastructure; normal "wear and tear" or failure

Business continuity planning (BCP), alternately referred to as business continuity resiliency planning (BCRP), is a detailed plan of contingencies and policies that are used to identify critical systems and data assets, how these systems and assets are backed up, and how they would be recovered. More importantly, BCP provides proactive policies and procedures to ensure the continued availability and reliability of these resources in the event of an incident or disaster. System or network recovery is closely related to BCP. In fact, network recovery plans form the foundation for restoring operations following an incident.

In the past, BCP was done by technical experts in isolation of strategic planning from operations or financial planning. Isolated planning cycles resulted in increased exposure to system failure, an inability to respond rapidly to system and competitive demand, and missed strategic targets. Companies addressed this by aligning system management strategies with strategic planning, resulting in reduced system vulnerability to incidents or catastrophes and better utilization in system investments. The result of this collaboration formed the basis of modern BCP.

International standards such the Open Systems Interconnection Model (OSI) and those promulgated by the International Standards Organization (ISO) inextricably linked our lives, enterprise, and economies. For example, a change in the Mumbai stock exchange ripples quickly through the Nikkei, Hang Seng, and other global stock exchanges. While this has been a boon to interoperability and continues to provide new opportunities for trade, diplomacy, and cooperation, it has also made us aware of many negative unintended challenges and vulnerabilities of such interconnected systems.

Hacking, identity theft, and cyberterrorism have become new weapons in modern warfare. While many point to the physical devastation of September 11, 2001, in the United States or other overt acts of terrorism around the world, the manipulation of data and information technology used to plan and execute these events was equally damaging and continues in ever-increasing frequency. Technology has moved beyond being a tool for planning these acts of terrorism to targeting a country's information resources, a community's water or electrical supply, or an individual's personal assets.

Business Continuity Objectives

The primary objectives of business continuity planning are to provide a proactive strategy to prevent or limit the impact of system failures and to rapidly restore operations when these events occur. Business continuity plans work in conjunction with robust network design and policies and procedures to proactively protect against the loss while minimizing the time needed to bypass the compromised resources or bring the system fully online. Without a solid business continuity strategy, an enterprise exposes itself to lost profitability, time, and credibility among its business partners and customers. The cost of recovery when planning is not performed can far exceed the cost of planning properly and building in safeguards and other mechanisms prior to an outage.

Integrity

Data integrity is the assurance that data remains unchanged after operations on the data, such as copying, modifying, or creating, are completed. Maintaining accurate records of system components, transactions, the location of data, and other critical information is a fundamental requirement of robust business operations and a major goal of BCP. This information allows for the prompt restoration of the most recent and consistent state with minimal loss of data. By maintaining accurate records of resources and any changes made to them, complex computing and mathematical formulas can be used to determine whether data remains unchanged between operations.

Availability

Availability is a key metric of system health and is often a key part of service level agreements. Availability refers to the amount of time the system and data are accessible or online for use. Robust system design coupled with agile BCP provide for problem management. Problem management is a fault-tolerant mechanism that protects the integrity of the network when a failure event occurs. Problem management includes problem detection, isolation, identification, and resolution. The affected part of the network is pinpointed, isolated, and bypassed. Secondary and backup paths, storage, and other resources may be used to reroute data and transactions. Chapter 9 covers how to perform storage replication to another device or site.

One component of availability is the ability for a failed system to automatically restart.

State-of-the-art network intelligence and applications provide a high degree of availability and reliability in providing network resiliency. When a main component of a system becomes defective, the affected system can be isolated and its traffic rerouted to other networked resources.

The next component of availability is hardware fault tolerance. System design and configuration, along with a sound backup and recovery plan, work collectively to minimize loss of service when a hardware fault occurs. As a general rule, a high degree of fault tolerance is possible. Redundant components, paths, and other resources maximize fault tolerance in a given network. Maintaining a high degree of fault tolerance can be an expensive proposition. Chapter 9 covers a variety of areas where redundancy can be used to protect against a single component failure such as multipathing, redundant power supplies, clustering, and cache redundancy. System backups should be scheduled and executed in a nondisruptive manner. Given the sophistication and complexity of modern networks, developing a solid backup and recovery policy may be complicated. Many network resources span multiple time zones, regions, or countries. Hence, the development of this plan should be done collaboratively in order to ensure all of the required resources—people, technology, and so on—are available.

Reliability

While a network or storage may be available, reliability refers to the consistency of performance associated with hardware, software, and infrastructure. Data integrity is also another key metric of reliability. These factors may impact throughput, processing time, updates to databases, and other factors related to a company's operations.

Data Value and Risk

The transparency of the complex web of applications, technologies, and data that support modern enterprise has led to a sort of "utility" mentality. By this we mean that we've become so accustomed to accessing vast amounts of data or processing millions of transactions per second that we expect systems to be available and perform as flawlessly as electricity. It is not until we lose access to these resources or the ability to complete these transactions that we become aware of how dependent we are on them. Unlike other commodities such as oil or grain, data is not tangible. Traditional formulas or means of determining the value of or cost-benefit analyses for tangible assets don't apply to data.

Capital investment in networks or systems account for a major portion of an enterprise's operating expenses. Technological obsolescence, innovation, and demand are formidable considerations and contribute to escalating investment costs. Determining the value of the data stored and carried by these systems can be a bit elusive. The aforementioned "utility" mentality has caused many companies to become complacent. Many lack or have inadequate BCPs. It is not until a serious fault or breech occurs that many begin an earnest assessment of the value of their data.

Data valuation and threat assessment are arduous but necessary exercises. Investing the time and resources to do both will inform network design, inform BCP policies, and reduce business impacts when failures occur. For example, it may not be necessary to have redundant paths, servers, storage, and databases at all locations throughout the network. Less critical data or resources will not need to be redundant, allowing those assets deemed critical to be adequately protected. A balanced approach to BCP emerges where system costs and fault tolerance are optimized.

 EXAM TIP A potential incident such as data loss or application unavailability can be referred to as a threat. Risk is determined by multiplying the impact of the threat by the likely occurrence of the threat being realized. For example, if the risk of malware infection impacts the business by a loss of one hour of productivity on average and this is expected to happen once a month, then the cost per year is 12 hours of lost productivity. If the organization values this hour of productivity at $200, then the risk per year is estimated to be $2,400.

Data, and the system that supports it, is one of the most valuable assets an enterprise possesses. Data valuation and threat assessment largely depend on the following:

- Data or the application's value to the organization
- Loss due to the unavailability of the data or application (revenue, time, productivity, brand image, and so on)
- Value the data would have if stolen or accessed without authorization

Accurate data valuation and threat assessment will influence the types and amount of safeguards a company deploys. While elusive, it is not impossible to calculate threat. For example, if the loss of company e-mail for 24 hours would cost the organization $500,000 in lost revenue and the likelihood of this occurring with the current controls in place is 5 percent, the risk this represents is $25,000. The organization can then use this information to determine whether additional controls such as faster restore processes, redundant sites, or other business continuity options would be financially feasible.

Increased awareness of global threat and aggression has led many countries to develop disaster recovery plans and standards specifically designed to prevent and recover from these events. Consequently, international standards for BCP have emerged. For example, in 2004 the United Kingdom began its promulgation of BCP standards as part of the Civil Contingencies Act, which addresses system security, recovery, and protection. As such, the foundations of good BCP include the following:

- **Risk assessment**   The risk assessment analyzes the factors that could impact the integrity, confidentiality, or availability of business systems, along with their likelihood and expected damages, to determine a risk that is typically represented as high, medium, or low or given a cost in dollars.

- **Business impact analysis (BIA)**   The BIA is an estimate of how much it will cost the organization to have systems unavailable because of an incident or disaster. The BIA uses impact scenarios to define likely or possible incidents and the impact or cost it would have on the organization.

- **Recovery requirements**   The recovery time objective (RTO) and recovery point objective (RPO) define how long it will take to restore data and how much data would be lost. These are both described in more detail next.

Whether designed by governments or companies, network management, network disaster recovery, and business operations plans are integrated and used to draft a BCP, which is expressed in optimized system design. Once implemented, this plan must be communicated to all responsible parties in the organization, monitored, and rigorously tested in order to ensure it is capable of responding to the enterprise's ever-changing landscape.

Recovery Point Objective

The recovery point objective is one of the considerations used to guide business continuity planning. The RPO is basically a measure of the maximum amount of data the organization can tolerate losing. In other words, RPO is the age of the files that must be recovered from backup storage for normal operations to resume in the event that the system, computer, or network fails because of communication, program, or hardware reasons. RPO is a time measurement, specified in seconds, minutes, hours, or days. For example, an RPO of two hours would mean that backups must be able to restore data no older than two hours from the point of failure. The RPO specifies how often backups must be made. RPO often helps administrators decide what optimal disaster recover technology and method to use for specific cases. For instance, when the RPO is one hour, backups can be conducted at least once per hour.

EXAM TIP The defined RPO for a given computer, network, or system dictates the minimum frequency with which backup files must be made for that system.

Recovery Time Objective

Another important aspect in business continuity planning is the recovery time objective. RTO is the maximum tolerable time span that an application, system, computer, or network can be down after some sort of mechanical failure or disaster occurs. RTO is a time measurement, specified in seconds, minutes, hours, or days, and it is used to gauge the extent to which interruption disrupts normal operations as well as the revenue lost per unit of time as a result of data loss. In most cases, these factors depend on the affected application or equipment.

RTO dictates how quickly operations must be restored, so if the RTO is five minutes, backups cannot be stored only on offsite tapes because they could not possibly be restored in five minutes. This would require something like a storage device on the network (nearline storage) with the data on it for recovery.

EXAM TIP Nearline storage is a backup that is located on another storage device on the network.

Mean Time Between Failures

The mean time between failures (MTBF) measures hardware reliability as the average number of hours between expected failures of a component in the system. Storage administrators can use the MTBF as a way to determine what level of support should be purchased or to determine how much effort will be required to repair or return a piece of equipment to service during its expected period of usefulness.

Mean Time to Failure

Mean time to failure (MTTF) is another measurement of hardware reliability as the average number of hours between expected failures. It differs from MTBF in that MTTF is used for equipment that must be replaced rather than repaired. This is important for understanding which parts to have on hand in case they need to be swapped out following a failure. As an example, a hard disk drive (HDD) could have an MTTF of 250,000 hours. Some administrators may want to swap out components preventively before they fail so the MTTF can be used to determine approximately when that will be. This is especially important in situations where a component is not redundant.

Backup Frequency

Data must be backed up on a regular basis. Determining the optimal interval or schedule for system or partial backups should not be calculated by "guesswork" or as a result of haphazard estimation. Once the optimal backup schedule and strategy have been determined, it is important that this be communicated to all appropriate partners and be well documented in associated policies and procedures. Periodic drills and reviews should be conducted to ensure those responsible for maintaining the system are familiar with the actual contingencies, their implementation, and documentation. The resultant schedule should be based on RPO and take into account the potential impact this schedule would have on business operations and other production activities. The amount, distribution, and frequency of use of data will determine the interval and types of backup schemes to employ. Furthermore, the availability of personnel and timing are also critical success factors.

Rotation Schemes

Storage administrators often use various backup rotation schemes to minimize the number of media used for the task. This typically involves the reuse of storage media. These schemes determine how and when removable storage options are utilized and the duration. Industry standards and practices have emerged that seek to balance data restoration and retention needs with the rising cost of storage media and the time required to change tapes and manage tape media such as GFS, first-in first-out, or Tower of Hanoi.

One of the most commonly used rotation schemes is the grandfather-father-son (GFS) backup scheme. GFS uses daily (represented by the "son"), weekly (represented as "father"), and monthly (represented as "grandfather") sets. Typically, daily backup sets are rotated on a day-to-day basis, weekly backup sets are rotated every week, and monthly backup rotations are done on a monthly basis. Each set may be composed of a single tape or a set of tapes, though this may depend on the amount of data to be stored. Organizations would retain twelve tapes, one for each month; five tapes for each potential week in a month; and five or seven tapes for the daily backups depending on whether the daily backups are performed every day or just on workdays. In total, 22 to 24 tapes are required for this rotation scheme. Variants of GFS also exist, such as GFS with a two-week rolling rotation instead of just five or seven days and the addition of yearly tapes. Some organizations do only three monthly tapes along with four quarterly tapes instead of 12 monthly tapes. These are all variants of GFS.

 EXAM TIP GFS and variants of GFS are the most common rotation schemes.

Another possible scheme to perform for backup and recovery operations is the first-in first-out (FIFO) scheme, which saves modified files onto the "oldest" media in a set. By "oldest" here, it refers to the media that contains the data that was archived earliest in the group. For example, if daily backups are performed with 14 tapes, one each day, the resulting backup depth would be equivalent to 14 days. However, with each day, the oldest media would be inserted as backups are performed. The organization can go back to any day within the last 14 days, but any that was removed over 14 days ago would not be recoverable. If tape 1 is used on the first of the month, on the 15th of the month, tape 1 would be overwritten and used again. On the 16th, tape 2 would be overwritten and used again.

A more complex rotation scheme is the Tower of Hanoi, a scheme that is based on the mathematics of the Tower of Hanoi puzzle. A recursive method is often used to optimize the backup cycle. More simply put, with one tape, the tape is reused daily, as shown in Figure 7-1.

With two tapes, tapes A and B are alternated. With three tapes, the cycle would begin and end with A before going to C and then repeat. Each time a tape is added to the mix, the previous set is replicated with the next tape placed in the middle. The A tape would be used most often, with C being used the least. Figure 7-2 shows what the rotation would look like with five tapes.

Continuous Data Protection

As the required RPO becomes smaller and smaller, backing up information manually may not suffice. In such cases, a more sophisticated and consistent method may be a more logical choice for the organization. Anything less can put the business in a risky position where it may not only miss the RPO and lose data but also suffer a significant profit deficit. In this case, a continuous backup may be the solution to the

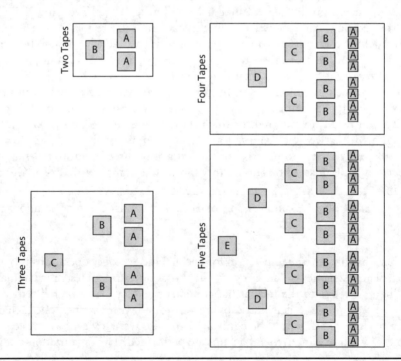

Figure 7-1 Tower of Hanoi tape rotation based on number of tapes

Week 1						
Monday	Tuesday	Wednesday	Thursday	Friday	Saturday	Sunday
A	B	A	C	A	B	A
Day 1	Day 2	Day 3	Day 4	Day 5	Day 6	Day 7

Week 2						
Monday	Tuesday	Wednesday	Thursday	Friday	Saturday	Sunday
D	A	B	A	C	A	B
Day 8	Day 9	Day 10	Day 11	Day 12	Day 13	Day 14

Week 3						
Monday	Tuesday	Wednesday	Thursday	Friday	Saturday	Sunday
A	E	A	B	A	C	A
Day 15	Day 16	Day 1	Day 2	Day 3	Day 4	Day 5

Week 4						
Monday	Tuesday	Wednesday	Thursday	Friday	Saturday	Sunday
B	A	D	A	B	A	C
Day 6	Day 7	Day 8	Day 9	Day 10	Day 11	Day 12

Week 5		
Monday	Tuesday	Wednesday
A	B	A
Day 13	Day 14	Day 15

Figure 7-2 Tower of Hanoi tape rotation for five tapes shown over five weeks

organization's data woes. Also called *continuous data protection* (CDP), this storage system ensures that all the data in an enterprise will be backed up whenever any form of changes is made. Typically, CDP makes an electronic journal containing storage snapshots wherein a storage snapshot is taken for every instance that a modification is done on a backup data. Not only will CDP preserve a record of every transaction made within an enterprise in real time, it can also retrieve the most recent clean copy of an affected file with relative ease.

Contention of Media

Contention happens when more than one device is trying to use the same resource. The device hosting the resource must decide how to allocate it. One scheme provides exclusive access to one user, while another user must wait until that user is finished before using the resource. In another scheme, contention results in both parties using a portion of the available resource. In the first case, one user receives the expected performance, while another user cannot access the file at all until it is available again. In the second scenario, both users have access to the resource, but they both receive less than the expected performance. As you can see, contention results in a series of trade-offs that should be avoided or minimized. So, what resources are typically being vied for in a system? Processor time, memory, storage space, files, and network bandwidth are just a few examples of resources that could be contended for.

Impact on Production

The timing of backup operations can have a negative impact on the performance of a system. Performing backup operations during prime or peak hours of operation can result in increased response time, slower transaction processing, and bottlenecks in terms of storage, transmission paths, and other critical system resources. Backups performed on the same infrastructure as active production or transaction could potentially vie for the same paths, storage, and databases needed by active users. Consequently, capacity planning and performance evaluation of system operations should factor in the elements related to BCP in general and backup schemes specifically. In some instances, it is desirable to create an ad hoc (on demand) or separate network to conduct system backup and recovery tasks. While this is an expensive option, calculations related to the value of transactions or the potential impacts of outages and loss might make it a financially feasible alternative.

Backup Reliability

Once a company has developed a feasible backup and recovery strategy, the next step is to determine which mix of technologies is best suited to the task. The cost, individual characteristics, and availability are used to determine which storage media best matches the scheme's stated goals, including those of reliability. Reliability is a key factor in storage management. Reliability means that the results of a transaction or process are dependable. Given the fundamental importance of data to an enterprise, storage management should not be treated as a secondary function.

Storage capacity, backup and recovery speed, robustness, and maintenance are also important factors in deciding which technology to adopt for backup reliability. For example, tape backups may be a cost-effective and flexible solution for storing backups; however, the sheer volume of physical tapes that needs to be stored, organized, and managed may not be feasible as the volume of their needs increases.

- **Tapes** Tapes are an efficient method for writing sequential data to a removable media and are especially well suited for backups and archiving. Tape media is relatively inexpensive compared to nearline and online storage technologies such as hard drives. Figure 7-3 shows a set of LTO3 tapes.

Figure 7-3

LTO3 tapes

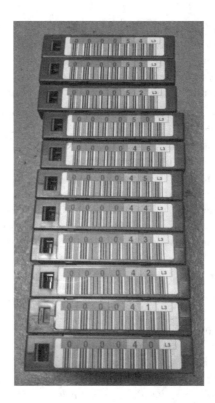

Tape drives read and write data sequentially. When reading data in the middle of a tape, the drive will fast-forward the tape to the desired location and then read the data. This is efficient for data that is located in adjacent areas but inefficient for data scattered throughout the tape.

- **CD-ROMs**   Inexpensive and popular, CDs are widely used for data backups. Copying information onto such media is relatively straightforward, but CDs are inefficient when data must be updated or when data sizes exceed the relatively limited size of a CD at 700MB or a DVD at 4.37GB. However, Blu-ray Discs offer storage up to 128GB, and as their price decreases, they prove to be a data backup alternative for more companies.

- **External hard drives**   While this medium is typically cheaper in comparison to tape drive systems, external drives are not redundant. In the event the external drive fails, all of the data could be potentially lost. External hard drives are best suited for small business or those requiring a low-cost backup and recovery platform. External hard drives can be swapped easily using USB or IEEE 1394 FireWire connections.

- **SAN array (nearline)** Nearline storage is a backup that is located on another storage device on the network. Nearline storage provides a quick recovery time objective, but it requires disks and a server or storage array to be up and running. Nearline storage often uses slower-speed disks such as SATA rather than SAS or FC disks that might be used on production equipment.

- **Online backup services** For the purposes of convenience, companies can choose to back up their data on the cloud. This option can often make sense for companies when data growth rates are high and the cost and time to set up new equipment would impact business productivity. It can also make sense for small data sets where the cost to procure, operate, and maintain backup equipment is too significant for the relatively small amount of data that needs to be protected. However, there are many additional variables that will need to be considered when using cloud backups, including security concerns, data ownership, and bandwidth limitations.

Backup and Restore Methods

The basic principle in making backups is to create copies of specific data so those copies can be used for restoring information the moment a software/hardware failure occurs. Through such a measure, an individual or organization can have a fail-safe when the inevitable data loss happens, something that may be caused by any of the following: theft, deletion, virus infection, corruption, and so on. Each type of backup and recovery method varies in terms of cost, maintenance of data stored, media selection, and most importantly, the scope and amount of what is captured and retained.

To perform such a vital task, you have the option to do so manually, copying data to a different location/media storage individually, but this is hardly ideal. Most companies utilize some form of backup and recovery software. The type of backup used may actually determine how data is copied to the storage media and often sets the stage for a "data repository model," which refers to how a backup is saved and organized. Please note that backup software is often licensed based on the number of machines being backed up and their roles, so a database server might consume a license for a server and for a database application, while a file server would utilize only a server license.

Full

The full backup is the starting point for all other backup types, and it often contains all data in the folders and files that have been selected for the purposes of storage. The good thing about full backups is that frequently opting for this method may result in faster albeit simpler restoration processes later. In most cases, restore jobs using other backup types take longer to complete if many different backup jobs must be combined to perform the restore. The next two options, differential and incremental, both take place following a full backup.

Files have a property called the *archive bit* that notifies software and operating systems of its need to be backed up. The archive bit is set to on when a file changes, and it is reset when certain backup operations are performed. The full backup resets the archive bit on all backed-up files.

Differential

The differential backup contains all files that have been changed since the last full backup. As a consequence, it requires only a full backup and a differential backup to restore data. Nevertheless, the size of this backup can grow larger than a baseline full backup, especially when such a backup procedure is done too many times. The differential backup does not change the archive bit, so each differential backup simply backs up all files that have the archive bit set.

- **Pros**   The time for accomplishing a differential restore is faster than its incremental counterparts.
- **Cons**   Backup times are longer than incremental backups.

Incremental

The incremental backup backs up all the files that have been modified since the last full or incremental backup. Because of such limited scope, this gives incremental backups the advantage of taking the least amount of time to complete, and incremental backups consume the least amount of storage space on backup media. The only thing that makes this option less than ideal is that restore operations often result in lengthy jobs because each incremental backup has to be processed in sequence. Incremental backups back up all files that have the archive bit set and then reset the archive bit. Figure 7-4 shows a weekly full backup followed by incremental or differential backups throughout the week.

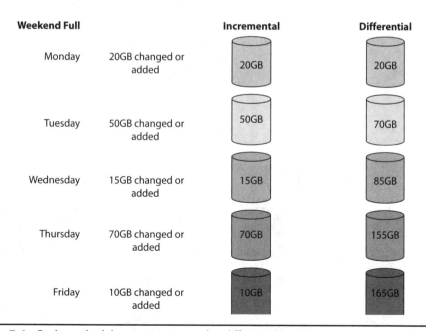

Figure 7-4   Backup schedule using incremental or differential backups

As you can see, the incremental backups are smaller each day because they back up only the data that was changed that day, but the differential backups grow larger each day since they back up all the data that was changed since the last full backup. However, Figure 7-5 shows what backup sets would be required if the server crashes on Thursday. In the incremental solution, the full backup would need to be restored followed by the Monday, Tuesday, and Wednesday incremental backups. In the differential solution, the full backup and then the Wednesday differential would need to be restored.

- **Pros** An incremental backup backs up data faster than the other types and does so while requiring less network drive space, disk, or tape storage space. Plus, you get to keep several versions of one file on various backup sets.

- **Cons** You need to have all incremental backups in hand when performing a restore. Also, it requires a longer time to restore specific documents since you need to check more than one backup set to find the latest version of the file being retrieved.

 EXAM TIP The full backup is performed first, and then incremental or differential backups can be taken.

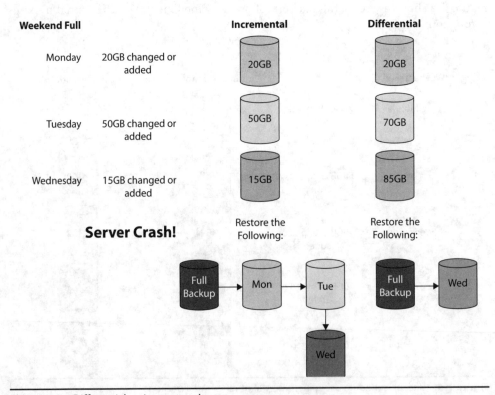

Figure 7-5 Differential vs. incremental restore process

Progressive

Taking incremental backup one step further is the progressive backup, which backs up only the files that have changed. This results in less data needing to be backed up as long as the original full backup is available since data sets can be restored by referencing the full backup and then any changes to the files. For this type, no additional full backups may be necessary after the initial full backup since the server's database keeps track of whether certain files need to be backed up.

Backup Implementation Methods

Backup implementation methods can include LAN-free, serverless, and server-based backups. LAN-free backups offer a way to back up data without impacting devices and services on the local area network. Serverless is primarily an extension of LAN-free, but instead of using a device or appliance to move data, it uses a device or storage that is directly connected using a Fibre Channel (FC) or Small Computer System Interface (SCSI). Lastly, server-based backups utilize a server to control the backup operations. In some cases, the backup server may retain the backup data or this data may be archived to other media.

LAN-Free Backup

Local area network (LAN)–free backup is a process of backing up a server's data to a central storage device without the use of the local area network. Instead, the data is moved over a storage area network (SAN) or using a tape device that is directly attached to the storage subsystem. This is the simplest architecture used with LAN-free, and some of the backup storage used includes tapes or other locally attached storage media. Although there is no backup process that is completely LAN-free because the server still communicates with the backup client, the term is used to illustrate how the bulk of the data is being transferred without the use of the LAN.

The purpose for doing so is to lessen the load on the LAN and reduce the time to complete the backup process. LAN-free is also an alternative to using a simple data copy to storage attached to the network. Apart from reduced backup and recovery times, LAN-free also ensures that there's less disruption on the systems and other applications being run at the same time. A LAN-free backup can be done either with a backup server or using a storage facility such as a virtual tape library.

Serverless Backup

Usually when a backup is done through a server, time and functions are limited because of the backup window. This makes serverless backup a faster alternative. It is a storage area network solution that leads to lower hardware cost, scalability, improved time effectiveness, and fault tolerance. Because the process doesn't depend on the resources and bandwidth of a network, the task can be completed faster. It also enables disk-to-tape or disk-to-disk backup.

The process begins with a server specifying what should be backed up, and then the metadata for the files in the backup set is captured. Once this is done, the server's role is finished, and the device can communicate with the backup device without involving the server unless a change is made to the backup selection list or schedule.

So, what's the difference between serverless and LAN-free backup? Serverless is primarily an extension of LAN-free, but instead of using a device or appliance to move data, it uses a device or storage that is directly connected using a Fibre Channel or SCSI. It can also be implemented through disk imaging using intelligent agents. These agents will then take a snapshot copy of pointers to the data. Serverless backup in a SAN, on the other hand, uses a data mover, which is embedded into the backup storage itself. What this does is manage the backup process.

 EXAM TIP Prior to installing a serverless backup option, make sure that agents or configuration settings specified in the backup solution documentation have been implemented on servers and storage devices.

When it comes to restoring data from a serverless backup, it can be done in two ways: image and session. The former overwrites the drive completely, while the latter restores individual files and directories in file mode. For a successful restoration, a restore job must not be canceled.

Server-Based Backup

Because plenty of information is stored on a server, it must be backed up regularly, typically utilizing backup software or functions built into the operating system such as Windows Backup or file copy scripts.

In a traditional server-based backup, the operation begins when the backup application reads the data from the source to the system memory and then does the formatting needed. The data is then sent to media storage devices where it will be stored. This would require the use of the central processing unit (CPU), various I/O channels, and the system memory. Because the performance of a server is affected while the process is ongoing, server-based backup is not very popular with system administrators. They would have to carry out the task when the application load is less or use other backup methods such as a SAN backup or a high-performance serverless backup.

Backup Reliability Methods

Backup reliability is the level of assurance that backup processes will be able to restore data effectively. The first component of this is ensuring that data integrity is intact, meaning that data has not been altered or corrupted in the process of backing it up or restoring it. One method used to verify integrity is checksums. Next, application verification can be used to provide backup reliability.

Data Integrity

Data integrity refers to how data is maintained accurately and consistently over its entire lifecycle. It plays a vital aspect in the design, implementation, and use of a system used to store, process, or retrieve data. It is the opposite of data corruption, where data is lost during any process. Many aspects can affect data integrity that may differ under a certain context. Generally, though, it can be determined based on the following:

- **Human error**   Errors people made while the data is entered
- **Intentional actions**   Intentional harm to the integrity of data by attackers or malcontent employees
- **Transmission error**   Errors that occur during the movement or transfer of data from one node to another or over the network
- **Bugs**   The presence of software bugs or viruses
- **Hardware malfunction**   The failure of one or more hardware components
- **Natural disaster**   Occurrence events such as fires or floods

Data integrity also ensures that the files saved remain the same from the time the backup is recorded up to the time it's retrieved. Any intended or unintended changes to the data made during storage, process, and retrieval can also affect integrity.

So, how is data integrity ensured? Physical controls such as controlling access to the area where the servers are kept by allowing only authorized users to get in and out of the area is the first step to ensuring data integrity from human error and intentional actions. This should be combined with specific authorization levels for all users. Other integrity concerns such as transmission errors, bugs, hardware malfunctions, and natural disasters are approached with documented system administration procedures, disaster-recovery plans, and incident response plans. Systems also employ integrity-checking features such as checksums and application verification, discussed next.

Checksums

A checksum, or hash sum, is a small block of digital data that is designed to detect errors that may have occurred during storage and transmission. The checksum function or algorithm is what yields the checksum. When designed properly, it can detect many data errors and verify the overall integrity.

Checksums compute a mathematical number that is unique to the data. This number is created through the use of a standard mathematical formula called an *algorithm*. Algorithms are designed so that they accurately produce a unique value for a data set. As you can imagine, if two different data sets produced the same value, we could not rely on their integrity because modified or corrupt data could result in the same hash as unmodified data.

This checksum is sent with the data, and the same computation is performed later to verify that the data has not changed. If the checksum generated later does not match the original checksum, something has changed, and the file will be flagged as inconsistent or corrupt.

Among the checksum algorithms, parity byte or parity word is the simplest because it uses the so-called longitudinal parity check. What it does is break the data into words, assigned with a fixed number of bits, and then computes the data. Whatever the result is will then be appended as an extra word. Upon receipt of the message, the XOR of all its words will then be computed to determine whether it yields n zeroes. If not, then an error has occurred during the transmission. Other checksum algorithms include modular sum and position-dependent checksums. Popular algorithms used for this purpose include Message Digest 5 (MD5) and Secure Hash Algorithm (SHA).

Some of the checksum tools available include CHK Checksum Utility, MD5 and SHA Checksum Utility, Advanced Has Calculator, Bitser, MD5 File Hasher for Windows, Jacksum, RHash, j digest, and Parchive. There's also the straightforward checksum, which is a hashing application used for Windows, and cksum, which is a Unix command.

Application Verification

Backup applications can perform verification on data as part of the backup process. Once a job completes, the backup software will compare the source and destination files to ensure they are the same. This provides more assurance to backup operators and storage administrators that backup jobs are complete and accurate. The verification process does add time to the backup job, though, and it may not be feasible in situations where backup windows are tight.

Backup Locations

Data is the lifeblood of every organization, and it is extremely important that it be available when needed. Once backups have been performed, they must be stored. Careful consideration must be given to protecting these critical copies of a company's data so that they are not corrupted, lost, or stolen. Storage facilities and locations are just as important as the data itself. Both will have an impact on the integrity of these backups, the time it takes to perform restore functions, and their protection from unintentional and intentional corruption.

The choice of backup solutions when it comes to being in a network is also varied. Data can be backed up on discs, through a local server, or through a remote hosting service. The choice of backup location will ultimately depend on the need because as much as data needs to be backed up, it also needs to be protected. Not every file that a certain employee possesses should be seen by all. Confidentiality—even within one organization—is a concern that should be of utmost importance at all times.

Disk-to-Disk

Disk-to-disk (D2D) backups take data from a disk such as a file share and back it up to another disk such as the storage within or attached to a backup server. D2D involves the copying of data from one disk—in particular, a hard disk—to another hard disk or another storage medium of the disk variety. D2D is often used to quickly take data from production servers to an interim storage location that might be later backed up to tape (see "Disk-to-Disk-to-Tape," later in this chapter). This reduces the impact on production servers and decreases recovery time.

In a D2D system, the disk where the original files are to be copied from is called the *primary disk*. The disk where the data will be transferred to is usually referenced as the *secondary disk* or *backup disk*.

D2D is almost always confused with virtual tape, which is different. D2D differs from virtual tape in that it allows multiple backup and recovery operations to access the disk at the same time using a true file system.

The primary advantage of a D2D system is that D2D systems do not have to seek the entire tape to find a specific piece of data. They can proceed directly to the data on the disk much faster, saving time and reducing the RTO.

D2D is also closely related to remote backup services. They are similar in a sense that they both store data on disks. But in the case of remote backup services, the data is held at a remote location, and the services are provided by managed backup providers.

Disk-to-Tape

The term *disk-to-tape* (D2T) is used to refer to a type of data storage backup where information is copied from a disk to a magnetic tape.

In a D2T system, the disk is usually a hard disk, while the tape is a magnetic tape. This kind of system is widely used in enterprises that require vital information to be stored in a safe location in case of disaster recovery so that data recovery can be performed.

Since hard disk storage units are prone to mechanical failure, backups need to be made at regular intervals to prevent catastrophic data loss. This kind of tragic loss of information is the last thing that organizations of any kind and size want to experience. Having data backed up also ensures that a system can be restored to its original state based on the information stored in the backed-up data.

Disk drives have a certain limit when it comes to the amount of data they can store. This is where tape storage units come in to provide the much-needed additional storage capacity.

Magnetic tape units also don't cost that much, making them a cost-effective solution for backing up data. Another advantage that they have is the capacity to hold large data volumes, making them a suitable backup solution for hard disk units.

A D2T system can work live, meaning as a continuous backup mechanism or an incremental backup solution, where data is added at different intervals regularly.

VTL

A virtual tape library (VTL), discussed in Chapter 5, is an archival backup solution that functions like tape-to-backup software but can be stored in whatever manner is most efficient for the organization such as on disks. This type of technology merging allows for the creation of an optimized backup and recovery solution.

VTL is a disk-based storage unit that appears to back up software as tape. Data is transferred onto disk drives just like it would be on a tape library, but in this case, the transfer is a lot faster. A VTL system is usually composed of a virtual tape appliance or server, as well as software that simulates the traditional tape devices and formats.

The benefits of using a VTL backup solution include storage consolidation and quicker data restore processes. The process of both backup and recovery operations are increased when a VTL solution is used.

Disk-to-Disk-to-Tape

The term *disk-to-disk-to-tape* (D2D2T) is used to describe a backup solution where data is initially transferred to a disk-based backup system and then copied again to a tape storage when it is most optimal for the organization.

Both disk-based backup systems and tape-based backup systems have advantages and disadvantages. For a lot of computer applications, it is really important to have backed-up data available immediately when the primary source of information becomes inaccessible. When a situation like this happens, it would be unacceptable to transfer data from a tape because it would take a really long time. Using tape in a D2D2T also allows much older data to be moved to an offsite location for disaster recovery protection.

Tape is economical for long-term storage, making it a really cost-effective solution when it comes to backing up data that needs to be kept for a long time. Tape is also portable, which makes it a good candidate for offsite storage. However, a D2D2T system offers long-term storage along with fast disk-to-disk recovery time. A D2D2T system allows a storage administrator to easily automate backups on a daily basis on disks so that it would be easier to implement quick restores. The data can then be moved to tape when the storage administrator has more time to spare.

Vaulting and E-vaulting

Vaulting is the term used to describe the process of sending data to an offsite location. This is done so that the information remains protected from several problems, which include hardware failures, theft, and others. Data is usually transported off the main location using media such as magnetic tape or optical storage.

When backups of data are sent offsite, this ensures that systems and servers can be reloaded with the latest data in case of a disaster, an accidental error, or a system crash. Having a backup sent out of the main location also ensures that a copy of important information exists outside of the main location.

Vaulting is helpful for companies that back up information—be it classified or unclassified—on a regular basis and desire quick access to the data but the option to recover if the site is lost. Some organizations choose an offsite location of their own to store their backed-up information. However, others acquire the services of third parties that specialize in such services.

Commercial vaults where backed-up data is stored is classified into three categories:

- **Underground vaults**   These are often old war bunkers or mines that have been repurposed for data storage.
- **Free-standing dedicated vaults**   These are facilities built as a data storage facility as their primary purpose.
- **Insulated chambers**   These are most often implemented within existing record center buildings or offices for data storage.

There is also another kind of vaulting, but instead of using physical storage, it transfers data electronically, and this is called *electronic vaulting* or *e-vaulting*. With this kind of process, data is sent electronically through a remote backup service. It offers the same benefit as vaulting because it is still an effective solution that can be used in a disaster recovery plan.

At its core, e-vaulting refers to the process of creating a backup or replicating important data. The copying process can be done onsite, but the copied data is ultimately transferred offsite. The concept of e-vaulting isn't entirely new because a lot of companies have been sending backup tapes and duplicating data onto remote disk arrays and virtual tape libraries for a number of years.

Ultimately, the goal of e-vaulting is about protecting data that matters to an organization. The reason for transferring this information out of the main location is to ensure that a copy exists in case of a disaster. Some organizations also do not use e-vaulting for every document they have, only the most vital ones.

Offsite Tape Storage

Offsite tape storage is the storing of backed-up data in a facility that is different from the main location. An organization has two options when it comes to this type of storage solution: It can use its own facilities that are located in a separate place from the main office, or it can acquire the services of a company that specializes in offsite tape storage.

Whether choosing a company-owned storage facility or trusting the backed-up data to a third party, one thing remains constant: Storing data far from the main location is essential for protecting the data. Having data stored offsite is also a good addition to any disaster recovery plan.

There are benefits and disadvantages to choosing an organization-owned storage facility as well as a storage center owned by a third party. With a facility owned by the company, there is always the problem of running out of room. As data increases, so does the need to back it up, especially if it is vital to the organization. Eventually, all of the backed-up information stored in different mediums will take up space, leaving no room for more in the coming years. A benefit of having a company-owned storage center is that the data is maintained within the hands of the company. It is not passed to anyone outside of the organization and is safe in that regard.

When it comes to acquiring services from a third party, the provisioning of a space for company data is the responsibility of the offsite tape storage provider. However, there is an issue when it comes to the safety of the information contained within the storage mediums. The chance of a criminal event happening in a storage facility is not entirely impossible, which makes company data vulnerable in this regard. This is why data encryption plays a huge role when it comes to handing off backed-up information to a third party. The last thing an organization wants is for someone to have free access to confidential information about them or their clients.

Offsite Storage for Disaster Recovery

Disaster recovery (DR) refers to the process, policies, and procedures that a company has in place for the recovery of valuable assets that are very vital to an organization in case of a serious incident that impacts business operations such as a natural disaster.

Disasters are classified into two broad categories. The first is natural disasters, such as earthquakes, floods, hurricanes, or tornadoes. These types of disasters are beyond the control of humans, but having procedures in place that avoid damaging losses to an organization definitely pays off. The second category of disasters are the ones caused by humans, and these include material spills that are hazardous, failure of infrastructure, and bioterrorism—just to name a few. Just like a natural disaster, it helps to have a plan that ensures the survival of a company despite unfortunate events. This is an area where offsite storage helps an organization.

When a disaster makes a facility unavailable, the organization must have a way to continue business. This usually takes the form of an offsite location that can assume the duties of the original facility. Either data from the primary facility is replicated to another facility or processes are put in place to be able to restore data to the other facility quickly.

With offsite storage, crucial data is stored away from the main location of an organization. This way, in case a disaster happens, be it caused by fire, flood, or man, an organization can still ensure its survival and continue business transactions because all the vital information needed to do that was backed up and stored in a different facility.

The benefits of offsite storage include the following:

- **Reduced overhead costs**   While it may seem practical to store backups within the office, the space dedicated to keep rarely accessed data may often be best used for actual business functions. By sending its records to low-priced facilities that are solely dedicated to corporate storage, the enterprise maximizes its workspace and keeps its data secured.

- **Rapid response system**   By storing essential business data offsite, a company can avert the impact of a major crisis as soon as copies of backup data get delivered to the affected office. In the event that some kind of natural calamity would devastate the company's premises, an offsite backup partner can pull out the necessary data so the organization can get back to doing business as usual.

- **Reduced risks of disclosure**   Having private customer records disclosed to unauthorized individuals can likely shake a consumer's confidence in a brand, which is a concern that every entrepreneur should look into. Instead of putting such data within the company's file room where it's susceptible to malicious intent, it may be best to transport such data to a secure offsite location.

- **Increased availability of in-house IT personnel**   In a day's work, the office's IT department has several tasks to take care of, and babysitting data is just one of them. It may be part of their job description to do so, but their effort in collecting critical data and fixing backup systems may be better spent with working on more business-critical tasks.

Offsite Storage for Business Continuity

Offsite storage for business continuity is similar to that for DR, but it can be used for events of a much smaller scale. Offsite backups may be used if the data on the production storage is accidentally deleted. The offsite copy can be used to restore the data. It differs from offsite storage for DR because the primary facility is still available.

Array-Based Backups

Array-based backups are a form of remote replication that replicates an entire storage array or specified portions of the array at once, and this can certainly make the entire replication process more manageable. The downside to this option is that the tools available for this method are usually vendor specific, requiring the same vendor's products at both locations and sometimes in between to facilitate the replication. This reduces the options businesses have when they decide to invest in such equipment.

Array-based backups utilize technologies such as snapshots, consistency groups, and clones to synchronize data.

Snapshot

Besides the traditional and broad models of replication, organizations can also implement continuous data protection (CDP), and the tools for this method resemble journaling products. They copy each change made to data across the WAN instead of copying individual data, and this often makes it easy to roll back to any single point in time.

For this process, snapshots of data may be pursued. Often, an individual snapshot of a data set is taken at set intervals and then directly sent to a secondary site. But while this method copies the entire data set, it may be quite bandwidth intensive.

At its most basic, a snapshot is like a detailed table of contents but is treated as a complete data backup by a computer. Every snapshot streamlines access to stored data and is certainly one of those backup options that can speed up data recovery procedures.

There are two main types of storage snapshot, and they are split-mirror and copy-on-write. In most cases, there are available tools that can generate either type automatically.

- **Split-mirror**   Split-mirror creates a snapshot of an entire volume when it is executed manually or on a schedule.

- **Copy-on-write**   Copy-on-write creates a snapshot of changes to stored data every time updates on existing data are made or new information is introduced.

Consistency Group

Consistency groups are used for maintaining data integrity and uniformity across multiple volumes or even sites, usually comprising an entire system such as the application, middleware, and back end. The consistency group ensures that a set of writes is performed on each member of the group. Items in a consistency group retain the same data, and writes that occur to one member of the group will not be fully committed until they have been implemented across all members of the consistency group. This ensures that no matter which resource in the consistency group is accessed, the data remains the same.

Clone

A clone is an exact copy of a volume. This kind of backup copy contains all the files in the source volume, and clones have the same content as the original source. A clone is sometimes used as a backup of the startup or boot drive in a computer so that other machines can be created from it, but other uses include creating copies for disaster recovery or testing and development installations, as can be seen in each of the following scenarios:

- **Restore earlier OS after failed upgrades**   Sometimes upgrades made on a computer's operating system go terribly wrong, rendering the entire system dysfunctional. This may be caused either by a lack of hardware support or by an unexpected software incompatibility. With a system clone, an organization can quickly return to the last functional configuration and make the upgrade failure seem like it never happened at all.

- **Restore a "cleaner" system**   Invisible background applications, malware, registry problems, and junkware—all these can clog up a boot drive to a point when the unit lags significantly. To get back to a faster computing experience, some organizations turn to a cloned boot drive system that has been formatted periodically. This makes cloning a server to environments that operate with multiple computers yet share identical configurations. This makes it easy to reset computers back to a point in time where the system functioned properly and is effective when many computers use the same configuration.

- **Restore a unit after a crash**   When a crash of a startup drive happens, a business can have a clone of a boot drive as its savior since it is an essential data recovery tool for such cases. For systems that don't have clones, it can take hours, days, or even weeks before the entire hardware is backed up. Similarly, configuring, reloading, and updating systems stored on optical discs can require an equal amount of time.

- **Increase drive capacity via upgrades**   When drive capacity of a computer is becoming a growing concern for a business or user, cloning can help in upgrading the internal drive in a cheap yet fast way. This may often be the case for laptop computer users whose need for bigger hard drives grows as time goes by.

- **Create a development or test environment**   Clones can be used to create a duplicate environment for testing or writing new software or trying system changes without impacting the production environment.

When cloning a data-only drive, information is often copied in chunks instead of being copied as an entire drive. Cloning is typically accomplished with vendor tools that operate on the storage array to create the clone to another logical unit. With such a program, an organization can transfer invisible files or data that users don't normally have access permission for since the storage array works with the data on a block level rather than a file level.

Chapter Summary

The information in this chapter will assist storage administrators in performing BCP that is best suited for their respective organization. This chapter provided an overview of business continuity, its relationship to network disaster recovery, and the elements of crafting and implementing a sound backup and recovery strategy.

- The recovery point objective is the interval or maximum amount of time the data or system may be lost during an outage.

- The recovery time objective determines the maximum amount of time an enterprise can tolerate an outage.

- Contention may be addressed at the local policy level, which specifies priorities and additional system resources such as infrastructure, servers, and so on.

Various media were discussed in terms of their reliability. Tape is a relatively inexpensive medium for backups in limited amounts of data or small systems. CD-ROM remains a popular, cost-effective choice but offers no redundancy. External hard drives offer more capacity than the two mentioned previously but offer no redundancy. A SAN array requires additional servers and storage on another part of the network. It provides a higher degree of reliability and restoration of system functions.

Next, the various types of backup were explained, each with their relative strengths and weaknesses. Full backs up all data. Differential backs up changes since the last full backup. Incremental backs up all of the files that have changed since the previous full or incremental backup. Progressive incorporates two techniques; it maintains a copy of all files that have changed and then backs up the file or data. Cloud backups can be used on a pay basis for companies where required space is located on storage resources in the "cloud" or at a third-party storage provider.

Several methods for implementing backups were covered. LAN-free is backing up to central storage without using the LAN. Serverless is an extension of LAN-free and provides access to direct connected storage. Server-based is when servers are used for backing up and restoring data.

Data integrity, or the ways in which data accuracy and reliability are maintained, were addressed. It combines both technical and practical aspects in achieving this goal.

- **Checksums**   A checksum or hash sum is a small block of digital data that is designed to detect errors that may have occurred during storage and transmission.

- **Application verification**   This is the ability of backup applications to perform data verification.

- **Backup locations**   These are onsite or offsite alternatives for storing backups.

- **Disk-to-disk**   D2D backups store files to disk rather than other media.

- **Disk-to-tape**   D2T backup files are copied from disk to tape.

- **VTL**   This combines the flexibility of tape and hard drives as a means of storing backups.

- **Disk-to-disk-to-tape**   With D2D2T, data is first copied to disk-based backup storage and then later copied to a tape storage system when optimal for the organization.

- **Vaulting and e-vaulting**   This is a form of offsite storage for backups where specialized vaults—underground, cloud/virtual, protected onsite locations, or freestanding—are used to store backups.

- **Offsite tape storage**   A third-party vendor or storage provider may be used to store backups.

    - **Disaster recovery**   Refers to the comprehensive plan that forms the basis of solid BCP. It contains the policies and procedure to be followed in the event of a failure or other data or system-compromising event.

    - **Business continuity**   Refers to the ability to restore and maintain total or partial system operations in the event of a failure.

- **Array-based storage**   Using this method, an entire storage array is replicated.

- **Snapshot**   Copies of data are taken at predetermined thresholds or intervals.

    - **Split-mirror**   A complete copy is made of the volume.

    - **Copy-on-write**   Copies are made each time the data changes.

- **Consistency group**   Consistency groups are used to maintain consistency and reliability of data across multiple volumes.

- **Clone**   This maintains the structure of an exact copy of all data.

Chapter Review Questions

1. Which of the following is not a direct reason why system outages occur?

    A. Human error

    B. Lack of physical security controls

    C. System hardware failure

    D. Natural disaster

2. An important metric of determining the goal of returning the systems to an operational state is:

    A. Return to service metric

    B. Uptime metric

    C. Recovery time objective

    D. Service level metric

3. Which rotation scheme consists of a daily, weekly, and monthly backup set?

    A. Routine backup

    B. Tower of Hanoi

    C. FIFO

    D. GFS

4. What is the difference between vaulting and e-vaulting?

    A. E-vaulting archives only electronic data, while vaulting is used for both electronic data and paper documents.

    B. Vaulting uses a physically secure location such as a bunker, but e-vaulting is not concerned with where the data is located.

    C. E-vaulting sends data offsite electronically, but vaulting sends data offsite through means of physical media.

    D. Vaulting is used for paper files, and e-vaulting is used for electronic files.

5. Which backup type results in the smallest size and shortest backup duration?

    A. Incremental backup

    B. Differential backup

    C. Transactional backup

    D. Full backup

6. Which backup type requires the fewest number of tapes to restore data to a point in time?

    A. Incremental backup

    B. Differential backup

    C. Transactional backup

    D. Progressive backup

7. Which of the following is the primary advantage of LAN-free backups?

    A. Lower cost

    B. Less impact on the production network

    C. More flexibility

    D. Higher scalability

Chapter Review Answers

1. **B** is correct. Lack of physical security controls does not directly result in a system outage.
   A, C, and **D** are incorrect. **A,** human error, could directly result in an outage if someone unplugs a power or data cable accidentally. A system hardware failure, **C,** could result in a system outage if redundant components or systems are not in place, and **D,** natural disasters, could take out an entire facility, directly resulting in system outages.

2. **C** is correct. The recovery time objective (RTO) specifies how long it should take to recover the data.
   A, B, and **D** are incorrect. **A** sounds like it would be correct, but it is not an industry term. **B** is related to how available a site is, and it could express how much downtime occurred over a period, but not what was required per incident. **D,** the service level metric, is almost the same as the uptime metric, providing an uptime or downtime percentage rather than a time.

3. **D** is correct. Grandfather, father, son (GFS) uses a daily, weekly, and monthly backup set. The grandfather is the monthly, the father is the weekly, and the son is the daily.

   A, **B**, and **C** are incorrect. **A** is incorrect because a routine backup is not specific enough. Routine backups could be quite comprehensive, or they could be simply once a month. **B** is incorrect because the Tower of Hanoi backup method does not operate on a weekly or monthly basis. It is binary in origin, and the rotation is based on the number of tapes in the set and when the first day in the set begins. **C** is incorrect because first-in first-out (FIFO) does not specify whether daily, weekly, and monthly tapes will be created, just that the ones that are overwritten will be the oldest tapes in the bunch.

4. **C** is correct. E-vaulting sends data offsite electronically, but vaulting sends data offsite through means of physical media.

   A, **B**, and **D** are incorrect. **A** is incorrect because neither vaulting nor e-vaulting is used with paper documents. **B** is incorrect because the level of physical security of the data is not a differing criteria between vaulting and e-vaulting. **D** is incorrect because both vaulting and e-vaulting deal with electronic data.

5. **A** is correct. An incremental backup contains only the files that have changed since the last incremental backup, so it is the smallest. Since it is backing up less data, it is also the fastest. For the exam, remember that incremental backups take the shortest time to back up but are longer to restore. Differential backups take longer to back up but are faster than incremental backups to restore.

   B, **C**, and **D** are incorrect. **B** is incorrect because differential backups contain all data that has changed since the last full backup and they are larger than incremental backups. They also take longer to back up but they are faster to restore. **C** is incorrect because a transactional backup is not covered in this text. **D** is incorrect because the full backup takes the longest to perform and to restore.

6. **B** is correct. The differential backup contains the files that have changed since the last full backup. Restoring from a differential always requires only two tapes: the full backup and the differential.

   A, **C**, and **D** are incorrect. **A** is incorrect because a restore operation using incremental backups would require the full backup and all incremental backups taken between the full and the current date. **C** is incorrect because transactional backups are not discussed in this text. **D** is incorrect because progressive backups would require access to each tape where changes occurred.

7. **B** is correct. LAN-free backups have less impact on the production network because data is written to locally attached resources rather than network resources.

   A, **C**, and **D** are incorrect. **A** is incorrect because LAN-free backups cost more due to the increase in equipment. **C** is incorrect because more flexibility is not as crucial as the lower impact LAN-free backups offer on the production network. **D** is incorrect because LAN-free backups do not scale any better than other options.

Security

In this chapter, you will learn how to
- Control access to storage resources
- Explain how encryption is used to protect the confidentiality of data
- Manage the visibility of storage used on the network or fabric

Chapter 7 discussed how the widespread availability of networks, infrastructure, and applications has lulled us as consumers into a false sense of security. In fact, these systems are double-edged swords. On one hand, they are marvelous innovations that simplify our lives by allowing us to complete complex transactions from a variety of devices. On the other, they are potentially dangerous portals for cybercrime. Many trust their most personal transactions—prescriptions, medical appointments, banking, dating, and so on—to the vacuous cloud, never once considering the potential harm unauthorized access to these resources poses.

Network providers, designers, and managers are faced with an equally daunting task of providing an environment for safe and secure transaction processing. Modern networks are characterized as a complex hybridization of digital, analog, wired, and wireless multiplatform/protocol technologies. The adoption of global standards and policies has been the primary catalyst for the high degree of global interoperability we enjoy. Yet it is these very factors that contribute to and are likely predictors that any network and its attached resources are potential targets for breach.

While the news and other information resources provide daily accounts of hacking, identity theft, and cyberterrorism, some of the most common vulnerabilities exist at a basic level. For example, most banks and other applications such as home security systems require a PIN based on a standard number of digits; most ATM PINs are four digits. A random number generator or freeware designed specifically for the task can easily decode the PIN, allowing for unauthorized access.

Complexity is perhaps the major challenge we face in providing security for physical assets, storage, data, infrastructure, and other system resources of a given network. For example, when a birthday approaches and you decide to look for a gift online, the choices are staggering! Free shipping, comparative shopping apps, and competitive pricing all mean you can select a deal from anywhere around the world and have it delivered to your doorstep in a matter of days. Behind the "point, click, buy" phenomenon are systems that gather data from around the world—product information, pricing, availability, shipping options, and so on. Once an item has been selected, it may be provisioned or sourced from a different provider than the site from which it was ordered. "Pick and pack" information is sent to highly automated warehouse operations and passed onto other entities in the supply chain.

The ordered item is then taken off the available or in-stock list, automatically updating the innumerable sites that have offered it for sale. When a threshold has been reached for the amount of the item that needs to be on hand, another application seeks providers, compares prices, and generates an order for more. A great deal of this is automated and has put buying power back into the hands of the consumer. This short narrative does not begin to describe all of the steps and interconnected events the purchase triggered. What it illustrates is the potential for risk and vulnerability.

Many separate systems are interconnected. Each interface—terminal, kiosk, device or portal, database, node, storage, infrastructure, or application—is a potential point of entry into the system. What is even more problematic is the varying degree of network management and security that characterizes these networks. Since networks evolve, they are composed of both legacy and new innovations that also vary in terms of their associated vulnerability for unauthorized access. Each domain within the network may have differing security policies and protection systems in place.

Mobility and cloud networks have allowed us to share information and data seamlessly across a variety of devices. Both have added yet another layer of complexity to the task of controlling who has access to these resources. Tasks such as intrusion detection, data loss prevention, and network access control can be tricky when the access points—tablets, cell phones, laptops, and automobile navigation and info systems—are in motion. This chapter will examine in both practical and technical terms the elements and challenges related to providing network security.

Access Control

Access control is the selective restriction of access to physical or logical entry points and any attached storage or associated resources. Accessing network attached storage (NAS) may be done by directly logging onto the NAS, by using transaction processing, or by using an application that queries the NAS. In this regard, determining whether the requesting party (human or machine) has the right or permission to access a resource is the most fundamental step in providing security for storage. Access control is based on authentication and authorization.

Authentication

Authentication is the mechanism used to establish that the user, application, or device is who or what it claims it is. Access to a resource begins by presenting credentials to an authenticator to determine who you are. Physical authenticators will send the information to a control panel, which is a highly reliable processor. The control panel then compares the information it received to the information in its access control list. When the information matches, the system can grant or prevent access based on the information it contained in its database.

EXAM TIP The term *physical* describes direct access to a site, system, or piece of equipment such that it can be touched, seen, or otherwise interacted with.

Users can be authenticated based on one or more of the following factors:

- **Something you are**   Fingerprint, iris scan, handwriting analysis
- **Something you know**   Password, passphrase, PIN
- **Something you have**   Access card, badge, key

Users can interact with a system directly with physical access, or they can interact remotely. Authentication types differ based on this type of access, and the security controls used for physical (sometimes called *local*) and remote access differ.

Physical Authentication

Physical access is a term used in computer security that refers to the extent to which information assets or the sites that house them can be physically interacted with, such as touched, walked through, or seen. Physical access control is used to determine who has permission to access the resource, the time or interval such resources may be accessed, and which locations may be used.

Physical access controls have become more complex, beginning with simple locks and keys, guards, and hidden stashes. These controls have been enhanced and augmented through electromechanical, electromagnetic, and optical access control mechanisms. Today, even more sophisticated electronic or computer-based access to physical resources is provided by biometrics, such as fingerprint, voice, retinal identification, radio frequency identification (RFID), and other high-tech scanning techniques. These are combined with cameras that have footage that can be archived to alternate sites and encrypted, as well as thermal, laser, and other sensors to detect entry into a facility.

Authentication methods for physical access include checking a badge, employee ID, or state-issued ID or using an authenticator such as a key card reader, PIN code pad, or a biometric scanner.

Remote Authentication

When users connect to a device remotely, such as connecting from a computer at home to a network server or connecting a workstation in the office to a NAS in the server room, they send credentials electronically to prove that they are who they say they are. These credentials usually include a username and password, but could also include digital certificates, a number generated from a token, or a PIN code.

Authorization

The next phase of access control is authorization. Once a system has determined who you are, it needs to determine what access you should have, if any. The fact that you are who you say you are means nothing if that person is not authorized to access the information or system. *Authorization* determines the scope, span, and extent of rights or privileges the requesting entity is entitled to. This is handled through permissions.

There are different kinds of authorization, called *permissions*, that can be granted. This access can be limited to a file, folder, or logical volume. An administrator, or someone with the special permission to grant access to other users, sets all the necessary access rights that others receive. The type of access that will be assigned will vary depending on need and the sensitivity of the data or application.

- **Full control**   This allows the user the maximum amount of control; read, write, and delete are the basic type of access at this level. More complex tasks allowed at this level may include the ability to rename and change the attributes of a file. Full control also grants the ability to assign or revoke privileges to or from others.

- **Read-write**   The user's access is limited in comparison to full control, granting the ability to read, change, or edit (write) a resource or change how and where the resource is stored.

- **Read-only**   This allows a logical volume (LV), file, or folder to be accessed and viewed but not modified.

- **Deny**   This is used to prevent access to the storage resource. For example, one department in an organization may ban a separate department from accessing a certain folder in a drive because of the sensitive nature of the files contained within them. Deny permissions override other permissions.

Permission can be used to provide a range of access choices to a file or database, individual, or group. For example, a group is working on a project where they need both read and write access to certain files. An administrator will give each member of the group the ability to modify files in the system. However, another group may also need access to those files, but in this case, they only need to see the changes made and don't need to modify anything. Ultimately, the system administrator determines the extent of permissions that are granted to users.

On a Unix-like system, permissions are managed in three distinct classes. These classes are known as user, group, and others. A user owns files and directories. It is the owner who determines the owner class of a file or directory. A group is assigned files and directories, which define its group class. The owner of the file may be part of the group. The other class refers to the permissions given to users who are not the owner or member of the group.

Access Control List

An *access control list* (ACL) is a list of permissions that are attached to an object or file. An ACL specifies which users or system processes are allowed to interact with objects, as well as specifying allowable operations for such objects. ACLs are organized like a table with entries as rows. Entries in an ACL specify an action, a subject, and an operation. For example, if a file has an ACL that contains "grant Blake, delete," this means that Blake has been given permission to delete the file. In the same scenario, "deny Aisha read" means that Aisha cannot read the file. In an ACL-based security model, when a subject requests an operation to be performed on an object, the operating system checks the ACL for an applicable entry first to decide whether the operation requested is authorized.

The following list includes a few of the types of systems that use ACLs:

- **File system ACLs**   This is a data structure that contains entries specifying the individual or group rights to a specific object, including programs, processes, or files. Every object that is accessible is assigned an identifier to its ACL. The privileges or permissions given determine whether a user can read from, write to, or execute an object. In some implementations, an ACL controls the permission rights of a group to a certain object.

- **Access control entries (ACEs)**   ACLs are like a table with each row containing a user principal, typically represented by a unique identifier and its assigned permissions. These records, rows, or entries are called *access control entries*.

- **Networking ACLs**   Some proprietary computer hardware has an ACL whose rules are applied to port numbers or IP addresses that are available on a host or other layer 3 device, each with a list of hosts or networks that are permitted to use the service.

- **SQL implementations**   Structured Query Language (SQL) and relational database systems have ACLs with Data Control Language (DCL) statements ported into them to control access to databases, tables, views, and stored procedures. SQL uses GRANT to provide access to an entity, while REVOKE is used to deny access.

File Permissions

File permissions are the permissions assigned at the file system level. A file system has permissions associated with each file and folder, but the permission type can differ between file system types. Not all file systems support permissions. For example, FAT and FAT32 do not support file permissions, so everyone can access the files on the system once they are logged onto the computer. Some example file permissions are

- **Read permission**   Allows a given user the right to read a file. When this permission is set for a directory, a user is granted the ability to read the names of files in the directory, but cannot perform any actions on the directory.

- **Write permission**   Allows the user the ability to modify a file. When this is set for a directory, a user has the ability to modify entries in it, which means that users can create, delete, and rename files in a directory.

- **Execute permission**   Grants the user the ability to execute a file or program that accesses the file. This kind of permission can be set for executable programs such as shell scripts so that the operating system can run them.

Share Permissions

Shared access means that a computer resource is made available from one host to other hosts on a computer network. Programs that can be shared include computer programs, data, storage devices, and printers. Sharing through a network is made possible by inter-process communication over a network.

A shared resource is a device or piece of information on a computer that can be accessed remotely from another computer. Typically, this is done through a local area network or an enterprise intranet. A shared resource is also called a *shared disk* or *mounted disk*. Depending on the object being shared, it is also referred to as a *shared drive volume*, *shared folder, shared file, shared document, shared printer,* or *shared scanner*. Permissions are also assigned to shares. The share permissions determine who on the network can interact with the files. When a user is logged on locally to a machine, the only permissions that apply are the file permissions, but when a user accesses a file on a share, both the share and file permissions are applied, and the most restrictive permission wins. In many cases, administrators will control access to files using file permissions so that security is consistent whether a user is local or remote to the data. In this case, share permissions are often assigned as full control to everyone. This does not mean everyone has full control of the files because access is still determined by the sum of both permission sets. For example, the marketing share has full control assigned to everyone in the group. The file permissions on the marketing folder grant the sales group read-only access.

Bob is a member of the sales group, and he can access the marketing share from his computer, but he cannot change or delete files from the share even though he has full control share permissions because the more restrictive read-only file permissions have priority. This can work the opposite way as well. If full control was granted at the file level but read-only was granted at the share level, users would still only have read-only access when accessing the files over the network share.

Share permissions are important when a file system does not support a particular set of file permissions such as the File Allocation Table (FAT) file system. In this case, since there are no file permissions, the share permissions are the only ones that are evaluated when users request access. There may be instances when a NAS appliance provides administrators with only share permissions but file permissions are managed by the appliance, usually with full control assigned to files created in shared folders. Share permissions alone are used to determine file access and prevent administrators from modifying system data and other protected areas.

The sharing of resources over a network is made possible through protocols such as the Network File System Protocol (NFS) and the Common Internet File System (CIFS), described in Chapter 2. The features of these protocols are provided next as each relates to their security features:

- **NFS3** NFS is a protocol used for sharing files over a network. It is used on Unix and Linux systems and carries little overhead. The first NFS version was specified by Sun Microsystems in 1984 and was used only within the company. Version 2 of the protocol saw widespread use as a file system protocol. The protocol was designed to have little overhead characterized by its stateless design and User Datagram Protocol (UDP) transport mechanism. NFS3 references entities in the ACE as users@domain.

- **NFS4**   NFS version 4 runs only on top of Transmission Control Protocol (TCP). In NFS version 4, finer-grained access control is allowed than in NFS version 3.

- **CIFS**   CIFS operates as an application-layer network protocol that is mainly used for providing shared access to files on Microsoft Windows networks. CIFS shares associate users and groups to the CIFS ACL by using a security identifier (SID) in the ACE as compared to NFS's use of user@domain. This is a string of alphanumeric characters that uniquely identifies the user or group in the namespace, such as a domain or a local machine, depending on the scope of the account.

CIFS makes use of the client-server networking model. A client program makes a request of a server program (which is usually in another computer) for access to a file or to pass a message to a program that runs in the server computer. The server takes the requested action and returns a response. CIFS uses sessions, which allows for connections to be restored automatically in the case of a connection failure.

Some NAS systems may define their own permissions that roughly emulate the permissions mentioned previously. For example, Figure 8-1 shows the share permissions assignment screen for a Hitachi NAS product. Here, View permission is equivalent to read, Modify is equivalent to read-write, and Admin is equivalent to full control.

Permissions Best Practices

The following are some practical approaches to follow in establishing permissions:

- *Apply permissions to groups instead of individual users.* Assign permissions to individual users, set up permissions for a group, and then assign users to that group. This strategy adds flexibility in adding or modifying permissions. A user can be added to one or more groups to gain access to permissions on many different servers. Applying permissions to folders can be inefficient because a folder may contain a large number of files. Assigning permissions to an individual or group as previously described is a more efficient means of updating or managing permissions.

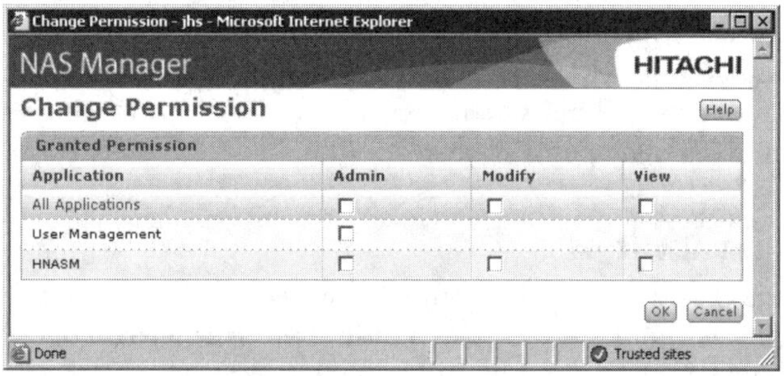

Figure 8-1
NAS permission
configuration

For example, suppose there was a NAS share that had more than 100 million files in it. An administrator needed to make a change to the permissions and add another group. After 30 minutes, the administrator became concerned about the time it was taking to accomplish the task. The size of the NAS share was the culprit. In fact, the operation took 28 hours. While this is an anomaly because most environments will not have 100 million files, enterprises expect permission management to be done in real time with negligible time required. The following bullets discuss some of the basic rules of thumb in providing baseline access control through permissions:

- *Give users least privilege.* The term *least privilege* refers to the minimum permissions that will allow a user to perform their tasks. If a user needs to access files but will never need to change them, that user should be assigned read-only access. Granting ubiquitous rights or privileges to users minimizes the task of managing permissions. However, full access can result in accidental or intentional compromise of data and files.

- *Classify and organize data.* Place data with similar security requirements in the same folder or share. Do not mix highly confidential data that only a few people need access to with data that many people have access to because this will mean that the larger group of people will need to have access to the share to do their work, but they will also have access to the highly confidential data. It pays to organize the data up front so that a consistent and easy-to-understand and manage permission set can be put in place.

- *Use deny permissions sparingly.* Deny permissions always override allow permissions, so if a user is denied read but they are allowed full access, they will not have access to the files because the read deny takes precedence over the allow permission. Failure to properly document deny permissions can be problematic. For example, Bob is a manager of the marketing department. Marketing users have access to a share called corporate_docs, which contains a folder called marketing and a folder called finance. The marketing group is assigned full control to the corporate_docs share, and deny full control has been applied to the finance folder underneath. Another group called managers has full control on the finance folder. Bob is a member of the marketing and managers group, but he is unable to access the finance folder because the deny permissions associated with the marketing group override the permissions granted by the management group. It is better to separate resources so that permissions are simply not applied for a user or group. This way, if access is needed later, it can be granted without first removing deny permissions.

Interoperability

Interoperability refers to the ability of systems and devices to exchange and interpret shared data without the need for additional assistance. For two systems to be called interoperable, both of them should be able to exchange data and then present that data in a manner that can be understood by a user. Over the years, interoperability has become an element of increasing importance for information technology products. This is because the concept of "the network is the computer" is becoming a reality. It is for this reason that the term is widely used in product marketing descriptions. Compatibility is an integral component of interoperability. A product is considered compatible with a standard but interoperable with other products that meet the same standard.

There are two approaches for products to achieve interoperability with other products. The first is to implement systems that have complied with published interface standards. If both systems comply with the same standard, they should have a level of interoperability, but you may need to make configuration changes as documented in their manuals to get some features to work between platforms. One good example of this approach to interoperability is the set of standards that were developed for the World Wide Web (WWW). These standards include protocols such as Transmission Control Protocol/Internet Protocol (TCP/IP), Hypertext Transfer Protocol (HTTP), and Hypertext Markup Language (HTML).

The second approach is to use a broker of services that can convert the interface of one product into the interface of another product when needed. These often come packaged as a gateway appliance that sits between two systems to translate. Specifications such as the Common Object Request Broker (CORBA) and Object Request Broker (ORB) are used in some such systems.

Encryption

Encryption is based on the science of cryptography, which has been used for a long time to keep information protected. Before the dawn of the digital age, the biggest users of cryptography were governments for military purposes. In fact, the practice of encrypting information extends back to antiquity when Spartan generals sent and received encrypted messages through the scytale rod that would be wound around a message to decipher it and to the substitution of letters used by the Romans in the Caesar cipher.

These days, cryptography relies primarily on computers because a human-based code can be cracked by computers, which can try all possibly combinations of numbers quickly. Ciphers—specific codes that involve substitutions or transpositions of letters and numbers—are better known these days as *algorithms*. Substitutions place a specific character or characters in place of another character or block of characters, and transpositions switch the order of characters or blocks of characters. These algorithms serve as guides for encryption and provide a way to create a message and give a certain range of possible combinations. A *key* is what is used to decipher the encrypted data by explaining how the algorithm was implemented. Many people can use a master combination lock; however, each is different in that they assign a combination to the lock. This combination is the key, and it determines how the lock is implemented to provide security.

Encryption works by scrambling data so that it appears as gibberish to those who are unauthorized to view it. It is the process of taking all the data that one system or device is sending to another and encoding it into a form that only the other device or system can decode.

Computer encryption systems belong to the following categories:

- **Symmetric-key encryption**   Two systems or devices using this kind of encryption should have the same key. Symmetric encryption is much faster to implement than asymmetric encryption. An example of where symmetric encryption is used is with wireless networking in your home—you specify the password (key) on the router, and that same key must be used on each wireless client.

- **Asymmetric encryption**   Asymmetric-key encryption or public-key encryption uses two different keys at once, a combination of both a private key and a public key. The private key is kept secret on the device or user, while the public key is made available to others who want to communicate in a secure manner with the device. Messages encoded with the public key can be decrypted only by the associated private key, which is retained only by the authorized recipient. Asymmetric encryption also provides a way to verify that data was sent by a party. If data can be decrypted with a user's public key, then it must have been encrypted with the user's private key, and this can confirm that the message originated from the owner of the private key.

- **Using file encryption**   File encryption is typically used for data at rest. However, it can be applicable to data in motion when the data is encrypted first before being sent.

Encryption Keys

Encryption is a security form that converts information, images, programs, and other data into an unreadable cipher by applying a set of complex algorithms to the original material. These algorithms are the ones responsible for transferring the data into streams or blocks of random alphanumeric characters. Unencrypted text is called *plain text*, and encrypted text is called *cipher text*. An *encryption key* is a piece of information that makes the encryption or decryption process unique. For example, a door can be locked or unlocked, and many doors can use the same model of lock. Each lock is unique because it has only one key that can lock or unlock it. Similarly, two communication sessions can use the same software and encryption algorithms, but one session would not be able to read the data from another session because they use different keys.

Most encryption algorithms alone cannot function without a key except in certain cases when the developer of an algorithm specifically designs it without a key. The combination of an algorithm and a unique key allows it to vary the mathematical process used to encrypt data so that the two copies of the same plain text encrypted with the same algorithm but different keys will result in very different cipher text.

Lots of encryption schemes are available; however, some are more vulnerable to attack or exploitation than others. There are simple algorithms that can easily be decoded because of the widespread availability of powerful computers and decryption tools. For this reason, it is important to utilize up-to-date encryption algorithms.

A symmetric type of encryption uses a single password to serve as both encryptor and decryptor. With the encryption key, a user can mount the drive and work in an unencrypted state and then switch over and return the drive to a cipher when a job is complete. Algorithms provide a secure means of protecting data. One of the weaknesses of a symmetric encryption program is that a single key should be shared, which presents opportunities for it to be leaked or stolen. This is why the constant changing of the key is required to improve security.

Asymmetric encryption schemes use very highly secure algorithms that have different ways of encrypting and decrypting information. The software makes use of two keys, which are known as the *key pair*. One is the public key, which can be shared freely and given to anyone. It can be used to encrypt data that can be read only by the one holding the private key, and it can also decrypt message digests encrypted with a private key, which is commonly done to verify that a message was sent by an individual. The term *nonrepudiation* is often used to describe this action where the private key is used to encrypt. Since the sender is validated by their use of their private key, they cannot deny or "repudiate" that they sent the message.

Whereas the public key is made available to anyone, the private key is not shared. The private key is the one needed to decrypt messages that have been encrypted with the associated public key or to encrypt message digests to verify the identity of the sender. Widespread use of asymmetric encryption software allows for encrypted web sessions such as banking or shopping over HTTPS.

Systems are often implemented using asymmetric encryption to set up a session where symmetric keys are then exchanged. These keys are changed periodically. This allows for the connection to be secure since the key material was exchanged in an encrypted channel, but the overhead of using asymmetric encryption the entire time is avoided, and the keys used are changed often to avoid the potential of keys being deciphered and used during the communication stream.

When securing data, it is important to understand the state the data is in. Data can be either at rest or in motion. At-rest data is present on a storage device but not being accessed. Data in motion is data that is being transmitted across a medium such as network or computer system so that it can be worked with. Data is secured quite differently depending on whether it is at rest or in motion.

Data at Rest

Data at rest is a term that refers to all data that is in computer storage. This excludes data that is traversing a network or is temporarily residing in computer memory that needs to be read or updated. Data at rest can be archival or reference files that are rarely or never changed. Data at rest can also refer to data that is subject to regular but not constant change.

Examples of data at rest include some of the following:

- Files on the hard drive of a laptop
- Files that are stored on external backup media
- Files that are located on a storage area network (SAN) LUN
- Files that are on the servers of an offsite backup service provider

Protecting data at rest is a major concern for all types of organizations, including in the private sector, in the public sector, and in education. Many types of data are subject to regulatory oversight or mandates. Hence, encryption is used to protect data at rest by preventing unauthorized access. Some methods used to encrypt data at rest include disk encryption, file encryption, and tape encryption.

Disk Encryption

Disk encryption refers to the technology that is used to protect information on a logical volume (LV) by converting it into code that is unreadable and cannot be easily deciphered by those who are unauthorized to access or view it. Disk encryption makes use of disk encryption software or hardware to encrypt each bit of data that is present on a disk or disk volume so that unauthorized access is prevented on data storage.

Full disk encryption (FDE) is a term that is used to signify that everything on a disk is encrypted, and this includes programs that can encrypt bootable operating system partitions. This type of encryption is at the hardware level. It works by automatically converting data on a hard drive into a form that is not easy to understand by those who don't have access to data. An advantage of FDE is that it doesn't require special attention on the part of a user once they initially unlock a system or device.

In FDE, volumes containing the data are automatically encrypted once the system is shut down and decrypted when the user logs into the system. One of the disadvantages of FDE is that the process of encrypting/decrypting slows down data access at certain times, especially when virtual memory is being heavily accessed. Also, if a system is left unattended and not locked or the machine is not shut down, an unauthorized individual can access the data unencrypted.

Windows systems can utilize the built-in FDE system known as BitLocker. Even though BitLocker services are available for Windows 7 and newer editions, Windows 7 Home and Professional users cannot use the functionality. BitLocker encryption is available in 128-bit or 256-bit mode. The difference between these modes is in the amount of data that is uniquely used to generate cipher-text blocks. The larger the blocks, the harder it is to detect patterns in the encryption and to break encryption keys.

BitLocker secures files irrespective of the users associated with it, which means that all the users with administrative credentials can turn on/off this feature. BitLocker uses a special microchip, called Trusted Platform Module (TPM), which is hardwired to the motherboard of machines that require all advanced encryption features. Moreover, only administrators have the right to turn on/off BitLocker advanced encryption features. BitLocker keys prevent the operating system itself from booting from a different computer.

An enhancement to BitLocker is BitLocker to Go, which can be used to encrypt files and folders in removable hard drives such as USB drives, thumb drives, and so on. The major factor that you need to consider is BitLocker cannot be enforced while the operating system is running. Since BitLocker can be used only for avoiding offline attacks, you need to rely on standard operating system security techniques to protect your computer while it is running. The major attacks on your system during its running time may be from malicious users trying to access the machine either locally or using a remote connection. Either way, your operating system should be configured with strict user access permissions and a password policy by which such attacks can be mitigated. As another example of FDE, FileVault 2 encrypts the entire OS X startup volume. Users who are authorized have their information loaded on a separate nonencrypted boot volume. In systems that use a master boot record (MBR), a part of the disk remains nonencrypted. There are some hardware-based full-disk encryption systems that encrypt an entire boot disk, including the MBR. While Windows uses BitLocker and EFS encryption technologies, Apple Mac OS uses FileVault. FileVault can be used in encrypting the entire drive for privacy. FileVault version 1 requires Mac OS 10.3 Panther, Mac OS 10.4 Tiger, Mac OS 10.5 Leopard, or Mac OS 10.6 Snow Leopard. FileVault 1 encrypted a user's home directory, but it did not encrypt the entire drive. Users create a password that is used to decrypt the files. If this password is lost, a recovery key may be used as well to decrypt the files.

FileVault 2 expands the functionality of FileVault by using the Advanced Encryption Standard (AES) 256-bit keys. It can also be used to encrypt the entire drive. FileVault 2 uses significantly more CPU than FileVault, and decryption can be performed with a password or recovery key similar to FileVault. FileVault 2 requires Mac OS 10.7 Lion, Mac OS 10.8 Mountain Lion, or Mac OS 10.9 Mavericks to be installed in the system.

Enabling or disabling FileVault is an easy task because you simply need to navigate to the System Preferences page and click Security And Privacy. Click the FileVault tab on the Security and Privacy page to enable/disable the services. There may be situations when multiple user accounts are available in a system. In such cases, administrators need to decide which users are allowed to unlock the encrypted drive. Only those users who are given permission to unlock the drive can access the system. Thus, users who do not have permission to unlock cannot log in to the system. Only after authorized users unlock the drive will other users be able to use the system.

Once the users are assigned permissions for unlocking the drive, a recovery key is displayed, which comes in handy when users forget the password for unlocking the drive. The recovery key can be used in such situations to unlock the drive and set a new password. It is advisable that the recovery key be stored externally in secure places rather than storing the key in the system itself because when the system is locked, the recovery key will also be encrypted and cannot be accessed when you forget the password. The recovery key can also be stored with Apple in the cloud. You will be given an option for storing the recovery key with Apple once it is displayed. If you prefer to store the key with Apple, you will need to answer three secret questions. The answers you provide for the questions will be used for encrypting the recovery key that is sent to Apple. The only way by which you can retrieve the key from Apple is by answering the questions.

FDE is useful for laptops and other small computing devices that are prone to getting lost or stolen. On a corporate level, a storage administrator needs to enforce a strong password policy and provide an encryption key backup process in the event that an employee forgets their password or unexpectedly leaves the company if only one key is used to encrypt the entire hard drive. Many systems allow for a user key and a recovery or administrative key to be created to decrypt the data. This way, data can be recovered if an employee leaves, falls ill, forgets the password, or dies.

File Encryption

File encryption refers to the technology that is used to protect information on a file or folder basis. Similar to disk encryption, it works by converting it into code that is unreadable and cannot be easily deciphered by those who are unauthorized to access or view it.

Encrypting File System (EFS) is relatively simpler than BitLocker, but it can be used to encrypt individual files on the user level. Only a check box needs to be selected in order to turn on encryption. The check box is available in the file and folder properties. Users can also assign the ability to decrypt a file for various other users. The files are ready to use once they are opened. When the check box is unselected, the file becomes decrypted, and any user can access them. There is an alternative for such Windows users where files can be decrypted using the Cipher.exe command at the command prompt. An encrypted file can also be modified and copied to the local system. The EFS certificates can also be exported and stored as backup files in case the decryption key is lost.

EFS uses individual accounts and permissions while encrypting files. Users can encrypt only those files that belong to them. EFS does not require any additional hardware to work, and it is compatible with most machines. EFS does not require administrative permissions to enable or disable encryption on files and folders. Individual users can encrypt their files if needed, but only their files. EFS security keys are stored in the operating system unless EFS is used in domain mode where some key material is stored on the network and some on the local machine, requiring both to decrypt files.

Tape Encryption

Tape-based encryption offers a lot of advantages for storage administrators. Encrypting data on the tape uses hardware on the drive itself, which means that encryption is fast. With a really fast encryption, the backup server is not congested, and the backup process won't be slowed down. Administrators can also send encrypted files offsite using tape encryption with the knowledge that the content in the tape is secure and helps them meet regulatory obligations.

Tape-based encryption is also able to achieve a measure of standardization and interoperability in the form of Linear Tape-Open (LTO-4). This is because organizations can upgrade their LTO-3 tape systems to LTO-4 while also maintaining backward compatibility with existing LTO-3 tape cartridges. This is discussed in more detail in Chapter 4.

Data in Motion

Data in motion refers to information that is being transmitted over a network or in transit. For example, when sending an e-mail, that e-mail is considered data in motion from the moment it is sent until it is received. Other than sending mail, the following are also considered data in motion:

- Data being backed up from a laptop or personal computer onto a central server
- Uploading and downloading files to file-hosting sites

- Data sent and received through the process of logging onto services
- Copying files over the network
- Sending e-mail
- HTML files sent when browsing the Internet

Alteration and interception are the biggest threats to data in motion. Important data such as usernames and passwords are typical examples of those that should not be transmitted over a network without the protection of encryption because they could be intercepted by someone else and used in malicious ways. When unprotected data is intercepted, it can be used by others to impersonate or gain access to sensitive information. Encryption of a network session using a VPN (discussed later in this section) is important for data that traverses less secure zones because it helps ensure a higher security level for data in motion. Data in motion is vulnerable to attackers who may be in between the sender and the receiver because those who want to attack do not need to be near the computer where the data is stored in order to gain access to it. Even private networks are susceptible to this through malware that could be resident on a network machine. Attackers just need to be somewhere "along the path" to tap into the data. VPNs are important in protecting data along the path of communications so that those in between the communication cannot decipher the protected communication.

There are two ways to use encryption in protecting data in motion:

- **Using an encrypted connection** Files sent over an encrypted connection such as an encrypted tunnel will be automatically encrypted while in transit. Even files that were encrypted prior to being sent will get encrypted again while being sent. Examples of encrypted connections include Internet Protocol Security (IPSec) and virtual private networks (VPNs), both discussed later in this chapter, and Secure Shell (SSH) and Secure Sockets Layer (SSL), discussed in Chapter 6.

- **Using file encryption** File encryption is typically used for data at rest. However, it can be applicable to data in motion when data is encrypted first before being sent.

Network Encryption

Network encryption is also known as network-layer or network-level encryption. The network and transport layers of the Open Systems Interconnection (OSI) reference model are the ones responsible for connectivity and routing between two end points. Network encryption is a network security process that applies crypto services at the network layer (layer 3) or transport layer (layer 4), which is above the data link layer (layer 2) but below the application layer (layer 7). With the use of existing network services and application software, network encryption is invisible to the end user and operates independently of any other encryption process being used. Data is encrypted only during transit. Data exists as plain text on the originating device or system and receiving hosts.

Network encryption is implemented through IPsec, which is a set of open Internet Engineering Task Force (IETF) standards that, when used in conjunction, creates a framework for private communication over IP networks. End users and applications do not need to be altered in any form because IPSec works through the network architecture by encrypting the payload or data section of IP packets. IPSec-encrypted packets do not encrypt the header of the packet containing the source and destination address, so they are easily routed through any IP network.

IPSec

IPSec is a protocol suite for securing Internet Protocol (IP) communications by authenticating and encrypting each IP packet of a communication session. There are a number of protocols being used by IPSec for establishing mutual authentication between agents at the beginning of the session and negotiating cryptographic keys to be used during the session. These include Authentication Header (AH), which protects against replay attacks and ensures sender identity and data integrity; Encapsulating Security Payload (ESP), which provides confidentiality and integrity for data packets; and Security Association (SA), which provides the framework for how AH and ESP exchange keys and interact with other layers of the communication.

IPSec can be used in protecting data flows between a pair of hosts, between a pair of security gateways, or between a security gateway and a host. IPSec is an end-to-end security scheme that operates in the Internet layer of the Internet Protocol suite. Other Internet security systems that are in widespread use, including Transport Layer Security (TLS) and Secure Shell (SSH), operate in the upper layers of the Transmission Control Protocol/Internet Protocol (TCP/IP) model. IPSec protects any application traffic across an IP network. Applications do not have to be designed specifically to use IPSec.

IPSec can operate in transport mode or tunnel mode. In transport mode, the packet is encrypted, but the packet cannot be used with Network Address Translation (NAT) because the intermediary devices cannot read the packet information. In tunnel mode, the packet is encrypted and then encapsulated into another packet that has source and destination information in it. This packet can be read and can be easily routed across an internetwork, including across NAT.

VPN

A VPN is an encrypted session between two devices such as two routers or firewalls or between a VPN server and a VPN client such as a remote laptop. Devices connecting through the VPN appear to be on the same network, and they will send data to each other using local network addresses. The VPN encapsulates this data within encrypted packets that are delivered through the intermediary networks and then decrypted at the other end and dropped onto the network unencrypted so that they can be delivered to their destination, as shown in Figure 8-2.

Popular VPN protocols include Secure Socket Tunneling Protocol (SSTP), Point to Point Tunneling Protocol (PPTP), and Layer 2 Tunneling Protocol (L2TP) using IPSec.

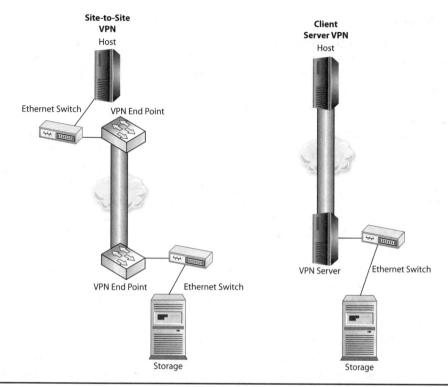

Figure 8-2   Virtual private network

Host Encryption

Encrypting data at the host level provides similar benefits and trade-offs to application-based encryption. There are opportunities to classify data at the host level on a less granular basis. When encryption is performed at the host level, data can be of variable record length. Just like an application-based approach, the encryption solution can add information to the encryption payload to allow for the inclusion of a digital signature or cryptographic authentication. By having this, a "man-in-the-middle" is prevented from substituting bad packets for the good encrypted packets.

Backed-up data can be secured using host-based encryption. One of the cons of host-based encryption schemes is that they are harder to manage if there is a lot of data to encrypt without a centrally managed system.

Storage Visibility

One way of controlling access to storage resources is limiting their visibility on the storage network. Some methods of limiting this visibility include LUN security, zoning, iSCSI security, and storage segmentation.

LUN Security

A logical unit number (LUN) is a unique identifier that references a logical volume by a protocol that is associated with a SCSI, iSCSI, Fibre Channel (FC), or similar interface. LUNs are central to the management of block storage arrays that are shared over a storage area network.

LUN Masking

LUN masking is an authorization process that makes a LUN available to some hosts, as well as unavailable to others. Many storage controllers support LUN masking. When LUN masking is implemented at the storage control level, the controller enforces access policies on the device. As a result, having LUN masking implemented at the storage control level is more secure. When it is implemented in this level, LUN masking protects data integrity since multiple nonclustered servers accessing the same disk do not corrupt the data. Without LUN masking, corruption would occur when two systems access the same LUN simultaneously.

 EXAM TIP LUN masking is implemented on the storage device such as a storage array, and it limits which WWNs can see the LUN.

For example, Windows servers attached to a storage area network can, on certain occasions, corrupt non-Windows (Unix, Linux, and NetWare) volumes on the storage area network by attempting to write Windows volume labels to them. When LUN masking is implemented at the storage control level, the attempt to write volume labels is prevented. This is made possible because the other LUNs are hidden from the Windows server, and it does not realize that the other LUNs exist. LUN masking is a constraint added to LUN zoning to make sure that only the devices that are authorized to access a specific server can access the corresponding port. It subdivides access to a given port, which is why several LUNs are accessed through one port; the server masks can be set to limit each of the server's access to the right LUNs.

LUN Sharing

A LUN can be shared between two or more servers. This is accomplished through clustering or time sharing. Clustering is used when one or more computers are configured to take over the operations of another computer. The disks that are used in these operations must be available to the cluster members in the case of a failure, but only one member will access the disk at a point in time. Time sharing allows a device to access a LUN and then release it for use by another device. This is often used for backing up data. A copy of data can be created to another LUN, which is then allocated to the backup device temporarily.

An important question to be asked about LUN sharing is whether a LUN can be used (read-write) by two or more servers along with an application at the same time and still be able to maintain data integrity. The answer is yes if some form of volume or file synchronization software is used such as a clustered volume manager, a clustered file system, a network file system using NFS or CIFS, or a clustered application. Without the use of some form of software on the servers or a NAS device, there is no way to coordinate access to change data blocks and maintain data integrity.

Host Based

Host-based LUN masking implements the control at the end points or hosts. The visibility of LUNs is restricted at the host bus adapter (HBA). The security benefits of LUN masking implemented at the HBA level are limited since it is possible to forge source identification information such as World Wide Name (WWN), media access control (MAC), or Internet Protocol (IP) addresses in a process known as *spoofing*.

Storage Based

Storage-based LUN masking implemented on the storage device will enforce security when access is requested to storage resources on the controller. This is generally seen as more secure since changes in access require access to the storage device. Figure 8-3 shows the configuration screen for assigning LUNs to a host group called 001:Bear.

Load Balancing

Load balancing is a method used in computer networking to distribute workloads across multiple computing resources such as computers, a computer cluster, network links, central processing units, or disk drives. The aim of load balancing is to optimize the use of resources, maximize throughput, minimize response time, and avoid the overload of any one of the available resources. Making use of multiple components with load balancing instead of a single component can increase its reliability through redundancy. Load balancing is also usually provided by a dedicated software or hardware such as a multilayer switch or a Domain Name System server process.

Load balancing can also be used to ensure the continuation of a service after the failure of one or more of its components. The components are monitored continually, and when they begin to become unresponsive, the load balancer is informed, and it no longer sends

Figure 8-3

Storage-based LUN masking

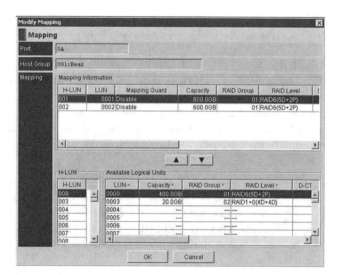

traffic to the component. When a component becomes active or comes back online, the load balancer starts to route traffic to it again. For this to work, there should be at least one component that is in excess of the capacity of the server.

When servers are load balanced, LUN masking and sharing must be implemented identically on both servers, and the storage controller must know that this is a clustered resource. This is often a setting when creating the LUN share.

Zoning

In a SAN, zoning is used to specify access to certain devices on the network. In essence, zoning allows an administrator to control who can see what in a SAN. A *zone* is a logical grouping of ports that can communicate with each other. A *zone alias* is a collection of zone members. The zone alias can be added to one or more zones.

The use of zoning minimizes the risk of data corruption by limiting access to authorized devices. Zoning also helps prevent the unauthorized modification of logical volumes by preventing other nodes from seeing the LUN or mounting it. Although it provides certain benefits, zoning can complicate the scaling process if the number of users and servers in a SAN increases in a significant manner in a short period because storage administrators will need to create zones for each device and storage array pair.

Port Zoning

Zoning can be applied to the switch port where the HBA of the device is connected using port zoning. Port zoning restricts the traffic flow based on the specific switch that a device is connected to. When a device is moved, that device will lose access to the LUNs that have been assigned to it in the port zone. If a different device is the one connected to a particular port, it will be able to gain access to the LUNs that the previous host had access to.

Zone Set

Zone set refers to zones that belong to a single storage area network. A zone set can be activated or deactivated as a single entity across all switches in the fabric. A zone set can contain one or more zones, and a zone can be a member of more than one zone set.

WWN Zoning

World Wide Name (WWN) zoning is another kind of zoning that restricts access through the device's WWN. A WWN, introduced in Chapter 3, is an 8-byte (64-bit) or 16-byte (128-bit) unique identifier on a Fibre Channel network. Devices may display the WWN in a variety of formats. The WWN is typically represented by 16 or 32 hexadecimal characters similar to Ethernet MAC addresses. WWN zoning is also referred to as *name zoning*.

 EXAM TIP The WWN is on the host, and the port the host is connected to can be moved, and access is still preserved. By connecting a new device to a port that was previously used by a WWN zone device, it will not allow access to the resources that the previous device occupied.

Just to review from Chapter 3 before I use these terms again, a *World Wide Node Name* (WWNN) is a WWN that is assigned to an FC device such as a switch or director during manufacturing. WWNNs are encoded into the hardware and cannot be changed. A *World Wide Port Name* (WWPN) is a WWN that is used to uniquely identify ports on an FC network. These ports are generated by software on the device and are based on the WWNN.

There are two kinds of zoning: hard zoning and soft zoning. With hard zoning, every device is assigned to a particular zone and the assigned places do not change. In soft zoning, device assignments can be changed by the storage administrator, as well as accommodate variations in the demands on different servers in the network.

Hard Zoning

Hard zoning restricts the communication that runs across a fabric. Only specifically allowed devices are allowed to communicate with each other. All other connections are refused. Hard zoning requires an efficient hardware implementation in the fabric switches but is much more secure the soft zoning.

Soft Zoning

Soft zoning restricts only the fabric name service. It is "security by obscurity" because devices lack only the information on where resources are, but they could connect to those resources if they guessed the information. Soft zoning shows only an allowed subset of devices. When a server looks at the content of the fabric, it will see only the devices that have been made visible to it. However, it can still attempt to contact any device on the network by address. Soft zoning is much easier to implement, but it is not as secure as hard zoning.

Zoning Best Practices

There are several best practices when it comes to zoning, which include the following:

- Always implement zoning even if LUN masking is used.
- Make use of WWPN identification for zoning for both security and operational consistency.
- All zones should make use of frame-based hardware enforcement, and the best way to do this is to use WWPN identification exclusively for all zoning configurations.
- Zoning aliases and names should be only as long as they need to be. This allows for maximum scaling, especially with really large fabrics.
- Use single initiator zoning with separate zones for tape and disk traffic when an HBA is carrying both kinds of traffic.

iSCSI Security

Internet Small Computer System Interface (iSCSI) is a storage protocol that operates over IP and Ethernet networks. iSCSI uses Challenge Handshake Authentication

Protocol (CHAP) for authentication, but this protocol is vulnerable to dictionary attacks so it should not be relied upon in the field. This is also an optional setting, and it is not enabled by default.

The iSCSI iQN is a node name given to iSCSI initiators. The iQN is formatted with "iqn" first and then the date when the naming authority began owning the domain and the reverse domain name of the naming authority. For example, the iQN for a device called NYMail in the Tropics.com domain for a naming authority that took effect in May 2012 would look like this:

```
Iqn.2012-05.com.tropics.nymail
```

iSCSI traffic is sent without encryption, so the data and the source and destination, iQN, and authentication information are sent in the clear. Nodes on the same network can retrieve this information and potentially retrieve data not intended for them. At a minimum, iSCSI traffic should be segmented onto its own VLAN away from normal Ethernet traffic. Also, consider using IPSec to encrypt iSCSI data between initiators and targets.

iSCSI and iSNS Security

Internet Storage Name Service (iSNS) is a protocol that allows for initiators to discover iSCSI targets. iSNS can retain target information for iSCSI attached devices in iSNS databases. iSNS databases can reside on iSCSI switches or on software-based iSNS databases such as those bundled in Linux, Solaris, and Microsoft Windows servers. iSNS databases can be distributed among many iSCSI switches to allow for larger scalability. iSNS servers on targets register their resources and state changes with SNS databases, which initiators, running iSNS clients, can query to find available targets.

iSCSI security when using iSNS for discovery is provided through simple trust. This makes it vulnerable to spoofing. A device can change its iQN to match another device in order to access that device's LUNs, or a rogue iSNS server could be set up to issue incorrect data to targets and initiators, allowing for unauthorized connections.

iSCSI VLANs

It is common to use a virtual local area network to separate iSCSI traffic on Ethernet switches from computer network traffic. VLANs are created by assigning a VLAN ID to each Ethernet switch that will contain ports in the VLAN. Each port is then associated with the VLAN ID. These ports will not be able to communicate with ports that have a different VLAN ID unless a router is used to route between the VLANs. iSCSI traffic can be isolated from the rest of the network with VLANs; this protects iSCSI traffic from being observed by other hosts on the network, and it isolates the iSCSI network cards from broadcast traffic originating from the computer network. Ports used to connect Ethernet switches need to be configured as trunk ports in order to send VLAN traffic to another Ethernet switch. These trunk ports tag the traffic with a VLAN ID so that the receiving Ethernet switch will know which VLAN to place the traffic on when it arrives.

Discovery Domains

Discovery domains (DDs) are similar to zones in that they determine which parties can communicate with each other. Members of a DD set can query initiators and targets of other members through iSNS. DDs contain targets and initiators that are allowed to connect to one another. Initiators can belong to many DDs so that they can connect to multiple resources. Initiators and targets do not belong to any zones by default, so new initiators are prevented from connecting to resources, and newly provisioned targets are prevented from being accessed until they are placed into a zone. DDs need to be config-ured manually by storage administrators to enable communication between targets and initiators. iSCSI targets and initiators belong to a default DD unless otherwise specified. This means that all devices will be able to view each other unless DDs are configured.

 EXAM TIP   As a reminder, initiators are iSCSI devices that connect to resources, and targets are the resources initiators connect to.

DD are created with an ID and a symbolic name. Here is an example of how DDs might be configured. Database1 needs to connect to three drives that exist on a storage array called DBStorage. A DD could be created called DBStorage-Database1 with both devices in the domain. This would allow Database1 to talk to DBStorage. If another server called Database 2 wants to talk to DBStorage, a second DD could be created called DBStorage-Database2 with DBStorage and Database2 in the domain. In this way, Data-base2 and Database1 can map resources on DBStorage, but they cannot map resources on each other through iSNS. Avoid creating a single DD with all targets and initiators in it. This may seem like a simple way to allow connections to devices, but it removes the ability to restrict target access for initiators, and it will increase the amount of administra-tive traffic on the iSCSI network, which can lead to longer logon times and diminished iSCSI performance.

Storage Segmentation

SAN segmentation involves separating different fabrics logically. While multiple Fibre Channel fabrics can be connected, they are logically isolated in a way that shows their own autonomy and namespaces. Having this kind of scenario also allows the administra-tor to not have to worry about the management of traffic that is crossing different fabrics. In other words, SAN segmentation is similar to how a LAN is segmented.

Storage systems can use virtualization concepts as a tool to enable better functionality and more advanced features within storage systems, as well as across them. Storage sys-tems make use of special hardware and software along with disk drives in order to provide fast and reliable storage for computing and data processing. Storage systems are complex and can be thought of as a computer with a special purpose designed to provide storage capacity, as well as advanced data protection features. Disk drives are just one element within a storage system, together with hardware and special-purpose embedded software within the system.

Storage systems are able to provide either block-accessed storage or file-accessed storage. Block access is delivered through protocols such as Fibre Channel, iSCSI, and SAS, and storage is represented as a logical volume. The NFS and CIFS protocols are used to provide file access, and storage is represented as a share on the network. In a storage system, two kinds of virtualization can be deployed:

- **Block virtualization**   The abstraction—meaning, separation—of logical storage (partition) from physical storage so that it can be accessed without regard to physical storage or heterogeneous structure. This kind of separation gives the administrators of a storage system a great amount of flexibility in how they should manage it for end users.

- **File virtualization**   Addresses the NAS challenges by eliminating the dependencies between the data that is accessed at the file level and the physical location of the files. This provides opportunities for optimizing the use of the storage and also allows nondisruptive file migrations to be performed.

Chapter Summary

This chapter provided both practical and technical elements related to providing a safe and secure environment for data and associated resources. The ubiquity of storage networks, their complexity, and their high degree of interoperability have inextricably linked the economies of countries around the globe. These same characteristics can be problematic because they may also make these critical resources vulnerable to unauthorized access. System access was discussed within the context of how devices authenticate or prove they are who they say they are, how devices are authorized, and how systems interoperate.

Authentication relies upon credentials that an entity presents to an authenticator to be validated. These credentials can include one or a combination of factors such as something you are (fingerprint), something you know (password), or something you have (key).

Authorization determines whether the authenticated user has the right or permission to access this resource and what level of access they have. Levels of access include

- **Full control**   Allows the user the maximum amount of control—read, write, and delete are the basic type of access at this level. More complex tasks allowed at this level may include the ability to rename, change the attributes of, or change access levels for others.

- **Read-write**   The user's access is limited in comparison to full control, granting the ability to read, change, or edit (write), or change how and where the resource is stored.

- **Read-only**   Allows an LV, file, or folder to be accessed and viewed but not modified.

- **Deny**   Is used to prevent access to the storage resource. For example, one department in an organization may ban a separate department from accessing a certain folder in a drive because of the sensitive nature of the files contained within it.

An access control list is a list of permissions that are attached to an object or file. An ACL specifies which users or system processes are allowed to interact with objects, as well as specifying allowable operations for such objects.

Permissions can be assigned at two levels, file or share. File permissions are enforced through the file system, and they apply whether the user is local to the machine or remote. Share permissions are enforced through the network-sharing protocol such as CIFS or NFS. These permissions apply only to users who access the data remotely over the share. The more restrictive of the two permissions is the one that applies, so a user who has full control share permission but only read file permission will be able to only read files.

It is important for systems to be able to communicate with one another and to enforce the security settings throughout the communication stream. This can be difficult when components from many vendors are utilized together, but standards make this process a bit easier. Consider using components that comply with the same standard in order to make interoperability easier. If this is not possible, consider using a broker, either hardware or software, that will translate between two incompatible systems.

Encryption is a popular way of securing data. Encryption uses a mathematical formula called an algorithm to perform substitutions and transpositions on data. Substitutions place a specific character or characters in place of another character or block of characters, and transpositions switch the order of characters or blocks of characters. The cipher text is made unique by use of a key that determines how the algorithm will be applied to the data. Asymmetric algorithms use a private key to encrypt the data, which can be decrypted only by the associated public key, whereas symmetric algorithms utilize the same key for encryption and decryption.

Data can be encrypted when it is at rest or in motion. Data at rest refers to all data that is in computer storage. Data in motion refers to information that is being transmitted over a network or in transit. Alteration and interception are the biggest threats to data in motion. Usernames and passwords are typical examples of important data that should not be transmitted over a network without the protection of encryption because the data could be intercepted by someone else and used in malicious ways. When unprotected data is intercepted, it can be used by others to impersonate or gain access to sensitive information.

Full-disk encryption is one option for securing data at rest. This encrypts an entire hard drive so that it cannot be read until an entity is authenticated. The main disadvantage to this is that it treats all data on the drive the same, and once the drive is unlocked, all the data on the drive is available. It is up to the entity (user or service) to log off when not using the disk for it to remain safe. Another form of data at rest is backup tapes. These backup tapes can also be encrypted to protect archival data.

Data in motion over the network can be encrypted using protocols such as IPSec. IPSec can be used in protecting data flows between a pair of hosts, between a pair of security gateways, or between a security gateway and a host. IPSec is an end-to-end security scheme that operates in the Internet layer of the Internet Protocol suite.

Storage must be visible in order to be used. Visibility is also a way of protecting data by making it available to only the hosts that need it. LUN masking and sharing are ways to protect visibility of storage resources. LUN masking is an authorization process that makes a LUN available to some hosts, as well as unavailable to others.

In a storage area network, zoning is used to specify access to certain devices on the network. In essence, zoning allows an administrator to control who can see what in a SAN. A zone is a logical grouping of ports that can communicate with each other. A zone alias is a collection of zone members. It can be added to one or more zones.

Internet Small Computer System Interface uses a similar technology called discovery domains. DDs are similar to zones in that they determine which parties can communicate with each other. Members of a DD set can query initiators and targets of other members through Internet Storage Name Service, a protocol that allows for initiators to discover iSCSI targets.

DDs contain targets and imitators that are allowed to connect to one another. Initiators can belong to many DDs so that they can connect to multiple resources. Initiators and targets do not belong to any zones by default, so new initiators are prevented from connecting to resources, and newly provisioned targets are prevented from being accessed until they are placed into a zone.

iSCSI uses Challenge Handshake Authentication Protocol for authentication, but this protocol is vulnerable to dictionary attacks. The iSCSI iQN is a node name given to iSCSI initiators. The iQN is formatted with "iqn" first and then the date when the naming authority began owning the domain and the reverse domain name of the naming authority. iSCSI traffic is sent without encryption, so the data and the source and destination, iQN, and authentication information are all sent in the clear. Nodes on the same network can retrieve this information and potentially retrieve data not intended for them. For this reason, it is common to use a virtual VLAN to separate iSCSI traffic on Ethernet switches from computer network traffic.

Chapter Review Questions

1. A security audit of your storage network infrastructure results in a recommendation for using multiple authentication methods. You currently use a password for accessing the storage array management console, and your system is not compatible with biometrics. What could you use in addition to the password to satisfy the security requirement?

   A. Something you know

   B. Something you value

   C. Something you are

   D. Something you have

2. A Macintosh user will be traveling to a foreign country, and they are concerned about the data on their hard drive being read if it is stolen. They have heard about full-disk encryption, so they ask you for a recommendation. Which technology should they use?

   A. EFS

   B. BitLocker

   C. FileVault

   D. IPSec

3. A user needs to change the name of a file on a NAS. Which authorization level will provide the least permissions necessary?

  A. Read

  B. Read and write

  C. Full control

  D. Read, deny full control

4. How are access control lists (ACLs) organized?

  A. Hierarchal tree

  B. Relational database

  C. XML

  D. Table

5. Randy is a member of the helpdesk and San Francisco groups. The helpdesk group has full control share permissions on the IT policies share. The helpdesk group also has full control file permissions over all files and folders on the server that hosts the IT policies share. The San Francisco group has deny file permission on the folder above the IT policies share. Randy attempts to access the IT policies share, but it returns an error saying "access denied." What must be done to allow Randy full control access?

  A. Grant Randy full control share and file permissions to the IT policies folder and share.

  B. Add Randy to the administrators group.

  C. Remove Randy from the San Francisco group.

  D. Remove Randy from all groups.

6. Two new users join the company, and Tom, the storage administrator, creates accounts for both on the NAS and assigns them read permission to the DATA share. Cindy notifies Tom that this is not a best practice. How could Tom perform the task differently to adhere to best practices?

  A. Create a group and assign read permission to the DATA share for the group. Add new users who need access to DATA to that group.

  B. Write a script that adds read permission to accounts in a list. When new users are hired, simply add them to the list and run the script.

  C. Grant all users full control over the DATA share so that permissions do not need to be applied to individual users.

  D. Utilize a central authentication mechanism to control permissions for the NAS.

7. Which of the following is an example of data in motion?

  A. Files on a server

  B. Files transferred over FTP

  C. Files archived to tape

  D. Files on a thumb drive in your pocket

8. Asymmetric encryption requires what?

   A. Interfaces to a central authenticator

   B. Homogeneous systems

   C. Virtualization

   D. Public and private keys

9. You have been tasked with implementing LUN masking on your storage network. Where should you enforce LUN masking security?

   A. The server or device where the LUN resides

   B. The device accessing the LUN

   C. The network devices in between source and destination

   D. The iSNS server

10. Which trait of iSCSI is a possible security concern?

   A. iSCSI uses encapsulated packets over unsecure networks.

   B. iSCSI does not authenticate requests for management information.

   C. iSCSI traffic is unencrypted by default.

   D. iSCSI packets are easily corrupted.

Chapter Review Answers

1. **D** is correct. Something you have such as a token device could be used along with the password to authenticate and satisfy the mutual authentication security requirement.
   A, **B**, and **C** are incorrect. **A** is incorrect because you are already using a password, which is something you know. **B** is incorrect because something you value is not a way to authenticate. **C** is incorrect because something you are requires biometrics, which is not supported on the system.

2. **C** is correct. FileVault can be used for full-disk encryption on Macintosh computers.
   A, **B**, and **D** are incorrect. **A** is incorrect because EFS is used for file-based encryption. **B** is incorrect because BitLocker is used with Windows computers. **D** is incorrect because IPSec is used for encrypting data in motion, not data at rest.

3. **B** is correct. Read and write would provide the necessary permissions.
   A, **C**, and **D** are incorrect. **A** would only allow the user to see the file and open it but not change it. **C** would provide more than required, and **D** would not allow any access.

4. **D** is correct. ACLs are organized like a table with entries as rows.
A, **B**, and **C** are incorrect. ACLs are not organized in a hierarchical tree, relational database, or using XML.

5. **C** is correct. Removing Randy from the San Francisco group will remove the deny permission associated with the San Francisco group, allowing him to access the data. Since deny permission overrides allow, this was preventing Randy from accessing the share.
A, **B**, and **D** are incorrect. **A** is incorrect because Randy already has full control by being a member of the helpdesk group, but the deny from his other membership is overriding it. **B** is incorrect because the administrators group would still not override the deny from the San Francisco group. **D** is incorrect because removing Randy from all groups would not allow him to access the share at all.

6. **A** is correct. Create a group and assign read permission to the DATA share for the group. Add new users who need access to DATA to that group. It is a best practice to assign permissions to groups rather than individual users. Group membership can be easily changed rather than making individual permission changes on potentially many different shares or systems.
B, **C**, and **D** are incorrect. **B** is incorrect because the script would only work for the current permission set. If additional permissions are needed in the future, the script would need to be updated and then executed against all the appropriate users again. **C** is incorrect because full control for all users would give many users more access than they need. **D** is incorrect because a central authentication mechanism for the NAS would still only manage the NAS. The same group, however, could be used on many different devices.

7. **B** is correct. Files transferred over FTP would be an example of data in motion because these files are being transferred over the network. They are moving, whereas all the other options are stationary.
A, **C**, and **D** are incorrect. **A** is incorrect because files on a server is an example of data at rest. The files do not move when they reside on the server. **C** is incorrect because files archived to tape stay on the tape. While the tape may be transported somewhere else, the files themselves stay put. **D** is incorrect because the files reside on the thumb drive and do not move on their own from the drive to another location. The drive may be physically transported somewhere else, but the file still exist on the thumb drive.

8. **D** is correct. Public and private keys are required for asymmetric encryption.
A, **B**, and **C** are incorrect. **A** is incorrect because a central authenticator is not necessary. However, a trusted key repository is needed. **B** is incorrect because systems can be heterogeneous as long as the same encryption protocols are supported. **C** is incorrect because virtualization is not required for asymmetric encryption. Asymmetric encryption can operate on both virtualized and non-virtualized systems.

9. **A** is correct. The server or device where the LUN resides would enforce the security.

   B, C, and **D** are incorrect. **B** is incorrect because storage-based LUN masking enforces the mask on the device where the LUN resides. **C** is incorrect because, as the term says, it is storage based so it resides on the storage, not the network. **D** is incorrect because the iSNS server does not enforce security. It simply makes devices aware of targets.

10. **C** is correct. iSCSI traffic is unencrypted by default.

    A, B, and **D** are incorrect. **A** is incorrect because iSCSI does not encapsulate packets. Other protocols such as IPSec can be used to encapsulate packets, and encapsulation increases security, so this would be a good feature if it existed. **B** is incorrect because iSCSI does not have a mechanism for authenticating management requests. **D** is incorrect because iSCSI traffic is no more easily corrupted than other IP traffic.

Design

In this chapter, you will learn how to
- Identify the components of a storage architecture
- Implement redundant storage components for high availability
- Explain the functions and types of storage replication

Storage architecture is the description of a storage system's parts and functions and how they are combined to achieve the storage goal. I have saved this topic until now so that the concepts leading into the architecture could be discussed first, but designing a storage architecture is the first step before implementing a storage system.

Storage Architecture Components

Storage architecture has to do with the way a storage system is designed. The architecture defines how components such as hosts and storage systems will communicate, whether that communication will be over optical or copper cables, and whether the storage provided will be locally attached or via a storage network. The storage architecture must take into account the required space and speed necessary to support the applications that will reside on it. Various principles may guide how the system is designed. Let's compare the construction of a building to the implementation of a network. If you were going to design a building, you would have to ask certain questions first:

- Is this building commercial or residential?
- How many people will live/work in this building?
- What is the budget for this building?

Similarly, when designing a storage solution, you must consider whether the storage will be file based, as in a network attached storage (NAS) solution; block based, as in storage resources mapped as logical units to end machines; or a solution that uses both.

Just like a building would be sized for the number of people, a storage solution needs to be adequate for the number of nodes that will connect to it and the number of users it will serve.

Budget is always a concern, and any solution that will actually be implemented must be within the budget. The budget often determines what is most important to implement.

NOTE   Storage vendors will usually give you the best pricing when purchasing a system. Additional components such as more disk shelves and disk drives usually cost much more later than they do when first purchasing. If possible, obtain quotes for such components when purchasing the initial system and make sure the quotes are valid over the period during which you plan to own the equipment.

Availability is another component that needs to be considered. How much can the organization tolerate an outage of the storage system? Can certain systems tolerate more downtime than others? Availability is increased by minimizing single points of failure through redundancy. Sometimes more than a single point of failure is protected against with redundancy. For example, a critical system may be clustered to protect against the failure of more than one node.

Types of Storage Architecture

When designing a storage solution, you must consider whether the storage will be file based as in a NAS system, block based with storage resources mapped as logical units to end machines, or a solution that uses both. For example, if you, as the storage administrator, are setting up a new database cluster that requires access to shared disks, a block-level architecture would be required because database systems require disks that function like local disks because of the high number of transactions that are performed. A file-level architecture would result in too much overhead for each transaction because of the protocols used to establish and manage communication to a share. However, if you are setting up a series of network shares for Windows and Linux servers and workstations, you would use a file-level architecture with the Network File System (NFS) and Common Internet File System (CIFS) protocols. Many situations require both systems to be implemented. Some storage systems support both block and file architecture, whereas other implementations may require separate systems to manage different types of access.

Imagine the situation mentioned earlier with the clustered database server, but now the requirement is to implement a document management application that will be used 24/7, requiring high availability. A clustered database would be used for the back end of the system, while application servers would point to a series of shared folders for accessing the documents. A hybrid block/file architecture would be well suited here because the files could be hosted on a file server that allowed concurrent access to all the servers in the application farm, but the database servers would need a block-level architecture to support the transactions on the disks.

The choice of architecture will shape some decisions made later. For example, backing up a block-level architecture would be achieved by executing backup jobs through the hosts that access the storage or by utilizing storage functions to make a copy of the logical units presented to hosts. However, a file-level architecture may retrieve data for backups over the network just as other hosts would interact with the network share. Furthermore, backups of a file-level architecture can take place concurrently with user access, with the possibility of the backups impacting performance.

Block-Level Architecture

Systems utilizing a block-level architecture present data to hosts like local storage would appear to them so that they can interact with it in the same way. Block-level disk access is used by disk drivers such as Small Computer System Interface (SCSI). Block-level architectures require few operations to access the disk as compared with file-level architecture implemented in protocols such as File Transfer Protocol (FTP) or Common Internet File System/Server Message Block (SMB). This makes the block-level architecture very efficient. Chapter 5's discussion of block and file virtualization illustrates in more detail how storage systems accomplish this.

Block-level storage architecture is more flexible and versatile when compared with file-level architecture. The basic functionality of block-level storage is as follows: The storage space on the server is distributed in the form of raw volumes, which are then virtually converted to individual hard disks. Once this is done, the file system or virtual machine can use the volumes and mount them to execute applications, host files, or house database systems. Since the block-level architecture presents just a logical volume to a host, the host can utilize whatever file system is best for the host and applications that reside on it.

The block-level architecture provides a translation layer in the storage area network (SAN) between the hosts and the storage arrays. Multiple distributed physical disks can be mapped to a single logical volume or interface with block virtualization. Hosts reference locations in storage by blocks using logical block addressing (LBA). LBA, introduced in Chapter 1, is a way of referencing a location on a disk without a device having knowledge of the physical disk geometry. LBA provides a system with the number of blocks contained on the drive, while the system keeps track of the data contained on each block. It requests the data by block number, and the drive then maps the block to a cylinder, head, and sector (CHS) location on physical disks in the storage array. The data at this location is then retrieved and sent back to the host.

File-Level Architecture

Systems utilizing a file-level architecture present data to hosts as shares on a network. Network shares residing on different servers increase fragmentation and underutilization of storage capacity because each server is logically and physically independent. Systems utilizing a file-level architecture implement protocols such as File Transfer Protocol or Common Internet File System/Server Message Block to share data with other machines.

High Availability

High availability describes a system with little downtime. This is achieved through redundant components and systems, the ability to detect component failures, and the ability to switch between redundant components effectively. When designing a system, it is important to understand how available the system must be. This will determine how much redundancy is needed in the solution.

Redundant components are discussed in the next section, but systems can also be redundant. Redundant systems include clusters and replicated systems. High availability with replicated systems is discussed in the "Replication" section.

Failover

Failover is the transfer of services from one component to another in a redundant system. In failover, the functions of a system component—be it processor, server, network, or database—are assumed by another system's components when the primary component becomes unavailable. Unavailability can be the result of a failure or scheduled downtime. A system capable of failover is used to make systems more fault tolerant. An example of hardware failover is the transfer of power distribution from one power supply to another.

Service Level Agreement

A *service level agreement* (SLA) for a technology service is part of a contract that defines the required availability of the system in terms of a percentage, such as 99 percent uptime. SLA numbers are sometimes referred to by the number of nines in the percentage, referred to also as the class of nines, with Class 1 being one nine. Three nines is 99.9 percent, while five nines is 99.999 percent. Table 9-1 shows how many minutes of downtime are allowed per month and per year for each nine.

SLAs will typically assign fees or credits due to the customer if the SLA percentage is not met. Depending on the agreement, these fees may be a single fee for breach of contract or a set of fees that increase based on the amount of downtime over what is allowed per month or year in the agreement.

Internet access or WAN access is critical for businesses today, and storage administrators should be familiar with the SLAs governing their Internet connections and WAN links so that they know how much downtime to expect and can plan accordingly.

Storage administrators may also be required to meet SLAs for other companies or for internal operations. Storage administrators should be aware of which SLAs govern their systems and track metrics to ensure that they are meeting SLAs. Some methods for meeting SLAs are providing redundant components to systems that require high availability. Also, it is important to implement a change management program. A change management program requires that changes be documented and approved before they are implemented. This ensures that the required amount of consideration is given to changes prior to implementation and that those changes are documented in case something goes wrong. Often, the first question to ask when there is a problem is, what has changed? A change management system can effectively display that information to aid in troubleshooting.

Class of Nine	Availability Percentage	Downtime per Month	Downtime per Year
Class 1	90 percent	72 hours	36.5 days
Class 2	99 percent	7.2 hours	3.65 days
Class 3	99.9 percent	43.8 minutes	8.76 hours
Class 4	99.99 percent	4.32 minutes	52.56 minutes
Class 5	99.999 percent	25.9 seconds	5.26 minutes
Class 6	99.9999 percent	2.59 seconds	31.5 seconds

Table 9-1 Downtime Allotted per Class of Nine

Single Point of Failure

A *single point of failure* is a result of malfunction of a single configuration, network, hardware, or software causing the entire system or process to fail. Consider an environment where there is one server in which more than one application runs. A fault in the server would result in the server crashing, which would result in all the applications running on the server to be stopped. This could potentially result in data loss and corruption of data, and most certainly will result in downtime for the application. The solution to a single point of failure is redundancy. When architecting a solution, consider what would happen if any single component in the system failed. If this component will result in the application being unavailable, consider implementing redundancy to protect against this.

Online Transaction Processing

Online transaction processing (OLTP) refers to a system that provides immediate response and high availability. OLTP systems often require high throughput and consistency between systems. Critical systems such as automated teller machines (ATMs), line-of-business applications such as banking terminals, order kiosks, airline ticketing stations, enterprise resource planning (ERP) applications, and online sales systems are examples of OLTP.

Some components of an OLTP solution include a database, management portals, business intelligence systems, reporting functionality, scheduling, analysis, web services, searching, document management, and workflow.

Some examples of OLTP systems include the following:

- Financial planning
- Product planning
- Manufacturing
- Service delivery
- Marketing and sales
- Inventory management
- Product development
- Shipping and logistics
- Accounts receivable and payable

Cloud Services

Cloud services are remote technology resources made available for organizational use but are managed and maintained by a third party. Cloud services offer flexibility because an organization needs to pay only for the resources it uses, but it can have access to high-quality, high-value resources that the organization may not be able to procure on its own. Cloud services are typically used to provide high availability, and these services come with an SLA to guarantee a minimum level of availability. Cloud servers also offer fast provisioning. Even with an existing storage system, storage administrators must add to it

Figure 9-1
Cloud services

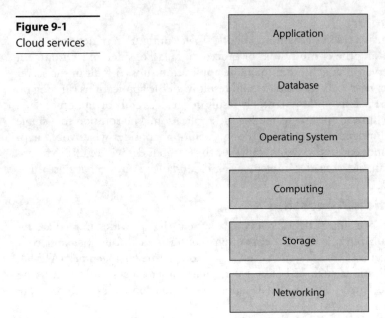

Application

Database

Operating System

Computing

Storage

Networking

by ordering disks and placing them into shelves and possibly ordering shelves too. Some business ventures cannot wait for a product to be ordered. With the cloud, additional resources can be allocated as soon as a contract is initiated. Cloud services are provided on a subscription basis with monthly fees based on how much of the cloud services are utilized.

Cloud services can be classified based on the amount of services provided. If you think of an application as the highest-level service, then you can work backward to understand the elements that support an application. These would be a database, the operating system the database resides on, the computing resources running the operating system, the storage resources holding the data, and the networking resources connecting it all together. This is pictured in Figure 9-1. The application is a tool that is used by end users, such as a program for composing documents, editing pictures, or storing data. Most applications utilize a database to organize the information that they work with. Some systems may not require a database, and in these cases, the database layer does not exist. The operating system is the software that interfaces with the Basic Input/Output System (BIOS) and computing hardware. Computing is a computer, laptop, cell phone, terminal, or other device that allows the user to provide input or display output. Storage is used to retain data such as documents, movies, music, application files, and other data that users work with. Lastly, networking connects computing equipment so that different equipment can communicate.

Software as a Service

Cloud services that provide an entire application to a company are known as Software as a Service (SaaS). SaaS applications can be accessed via a web browser such as web e-mail, instant messaging, and social networking or via a virtual interface where the application appears to run on a local machine but is actually running remotely. Many SaaS solutions require no client software installation other than a web browser, and they can run entirely within a web browser. Other SaaS applications may require virtual client software or other local components to be installed. SaaS can be deployed quickly since little or no local software is required, and they can be updated when the application changes with similar ease.

Some examples of cloud services include Office 365, Google Docs, Google Voice, Salesforce.com, and Dropbox. Some cloud services are free or ad supported, but many are subscription services with regular fees to continue access to the software.

Security is a concern with SaaS since the application and its data are hosted on the cloud provider's servers; another concern is performance, which is constrained by the client's Internet connection. Some users of cloud services may automatically be presented with the latest version of software, requiring users to learn the new software. Some SaaS solutions allow for data exports or for data to be stored locally. For example, Office 365 and Google Docs allow for documents to be saved either in the cloud or to a local machine, whereas Dropbox stores files on each machine that has the Dropbox software installed on it and also in the cloud. This provides users with fast access to files and allows for access even if the SaaS solution is unavailable.

Platform as a Service

Cloud services that provide an operating system and database for the user to install an application on are referred to as Platform as a Service (PaaS). PaaS is pictured in Figure 9-2.

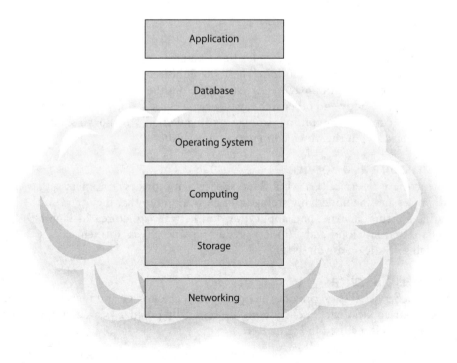

Figure 9-2 Platform as a Service (PaaS)

Figure 9-3
Infrastructure as
a Service (IaaS)

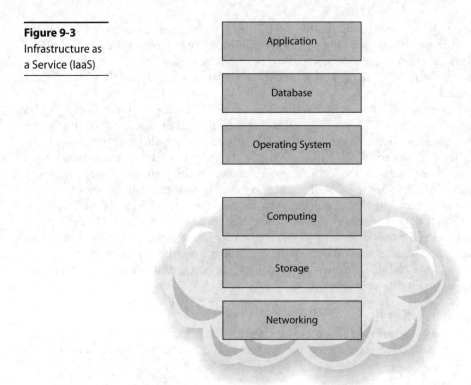

PaaS allows a customer to install an application, but prerequisite applications may or may not be installed on the PaaS solution. These prerequisites such as .NET, Java, PHP, or application-specific libraries may require support from the cloud provider to configure. For example, GoDaddy and other web hosting services are PaaS. They provide the operating system, database, computing, storage, and networking to allow a site to function, but customers can put their own content on the web site.

Infrastructure as a Service

Infrastructure as a Service (IaaS) is a cloud service that provides customers with computing resources and the underlying storage and networking so that they can run their own operating system, database, and applications on it. IaaS is pictured in Figure 9-3. For example, Amazon Cloud and Windows Azure provide servers in their clouds that you can install software on as you see fit.

Storage as a Service

Storage as a Service (StaaS) provides customers with the storage and networking to host data for their applications. Such systems are especially popular as archiving or backup solutions. StaaS is pictured in Figure 9-4.

Figure 9-4
Storage as a
Service (StaaS)

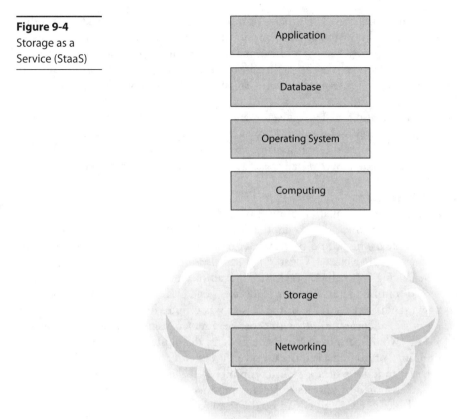

Redundancy

Various storage components are available that would satisfy the requirements of providing high availability and therefore prevent a single point of failure. Most of these storage components are often referred to as *redundant* storage components because they provide more than would be absolutely necessary to provide the service with protection in case a component fails.

Clustering

A *cluster* is a group of two or more systems that operate under a single namespace and addressing scheme to service requests. The goal of clustering is to place fault tolerance on the applications and services that run on the systems. Applications on clustered systems can run on any node in the cluster. Cluster nodes can take over a crashed application from a failed node when failures occur. In the absence of clustering, the application becomes unavailable for users when the server crashes. This condition will prevail until the server is restored to working condition. The process of moving services from one node to another in a clustered system is known as *failover*, and it can occur automatically or manually.

With *automatic failover*, crashed applications can be resumed, or failed over, from the primary node to a secondary node in the cluster. Hence, high-availability clusters are used with critical databases, e-mail systems, mission-critical business applications, and even some file shares.

Administrators can also transfer services to another node in a cluster, freeing up a node when updates are required in a process known as *manual failover*. Automatic failover is triggered by an event, most often a failure of some component in the system. Manual failover is a user-initiated failover usually issued to perform system maintenance.

Failover Clustering

Failover clustering is the combination of multiple redundant nodes or servers to enable the transfer of services from one node to another within the redundant system, known as a *cluster*. One example of this would be a transfer of a service or application hosted on the cluster to another node in a cluster. Clustering is the use of two or more devices together to provide load balancing and failover services. For example, a clustered e-mail server would allow for users to continue accessing their mailboxes, send and receive e-mail, and perform other messaging tasks even if a node in the cluster was offline. Resources such as mailbox stores and services that communicate with other mail servers using Simple Mail Transport Protocol (SMTP) would be moved from one node in the cluster to another if that node failed, with minimal or no impact to the users of the system.

In failover, the functions of a system component—be it processor, server, network, or database—are assumed by another system component when the primary component becomes unavailable. Unavailability can be the result of failed hardware, failed software, or scheduled downtime. A system capable of failover is used to make systems more fault tolerant by having multiple nodes in the cluster that can handle the workload.

Active-Active

Active-active is a phrase used to describe two or more independent processing nodes or systems that operate as a single unit. Both nodes can service requests at the same time, and the load is spread between them. Active-active is also referred to as *dual active*. Each of the nodes in this network has access to the same or identical resources, such as disks, which gives each node the access and usage of a single application. Requests in an active-active system are balanced across available processing capacity. If one of the nodes fails, another node in the active-active cluster will take over all processing. However, performance may suffer while a node in the cluster is in a failed state.

Active-Passive

An *active-passive* network configuration provides a fully redundant instance of a node. The secondary node is brought online only when its primary node fails. This type of configuration usually requires more hardware than active-active clusters, but performance does not suffer when a node fails. More hardware is required because each node in the cluster must be capable of servicing all requests at full performance. Similar to active/active, each of the nodes in the active/passive cluster has access to the same or identical resources, such as disks.

Power Supply

All computer systems run off power of some sort. Without power, these systems cannot continue functioning. Multiple power supplies guard against the failure of a single power supply.

 EXAM TIP A redundant power supply should be configured so that each is equipped with necessary wattage for the device.

Having dual power supplies alone will not protect against all power failures. Ensure that redundancy is put in place along the entire chain from device to power supplier. This would include separate power distribution units (PDUs) for each power supply, and each of these PDUs would go into a separate circuit. If these circuits are protected by an uninterruptable power supply (UPS), one UPS should be allocated to the primary power, called *A power*, and another to the secondary power, called *B power*.

Controller

Dual controller storage arrays are standard in enterprise storage arrays where most components are configured in a redundant fashion. Dual controller units are equipped with two identical controller heads that are each capable of operating the entire storage array. Disk enclosures must have at least one back-end connection to each controller in a dual controller unit, and each front-end path to a host or switch needs to be cabled to both controllers so that if one controller fails, the other controller can connect to all the back-end disks and front-end devices. Dual controller units are a bit more complex in design than single controller units because the controllers must be kept in sync so that one can take over the other's operations in the case of a controller failure.

 EXAM TIP Twice as many cables and ports are required to implement a dual controller unit, and this increases the cost.

Dual controllers can be configured as active/passive or active/active. Active/passive configurations route all input/output (I/O) through a single controller, while the second controller simply stays aware of all I/O. If the active controller fails, the passive controller becomes active and assumes all the duties that were being performed on the failed controller. Active/passive solutions result in consistent performance even when a single controller has failed, but the maximum performance of the unit is equivalent to that of a single controller unit.

Active/active controllers distribute the I/O between both controllers to achieve higher performance. Both controllers stay aware of their counterpart's operations and will assume those operations if the other device fails. Controller failure does result in a loss of performance while the storage array is operating on a single controller. Keeping the two controllers in sync while both are performing work requires more complexity, leading to a higher cost for active/active controllers.

Redundant Paths to Disks

Redundant paths to disks are used to achieve high availability within a storage system or between local devices and remote disks. When one path to a disk or disk shelf becomes unavailable, I/O can be directed to another available path. Redundant paths to disks can exist between the host and a storage system. When using dual-domain and dual-path architectures, redundant pathways are created from servers to storage. The redundant paths created by these configurations are meant to reduce or eliminate single points of failure within the storage network, as shown in Figure 9-5.

The techniques for creating redundant paths to remote disks are discussed in the "Path/Bus" section. This section is concerned with redundant paths internal to storage. Disk shelves in a storage system are connected to storage controllers using an interface such as Fibre Channel (FC) or Serial Attached SCSI (SAS) using the back-end ports on the storage controller(s). Some arrays may be configured with a single path to each disk shelf. This is most common with storage systems that have only a single controller.

Figure 9-5
Dual-domain
and dual-path
redundancy

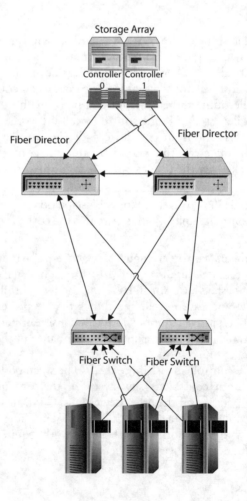

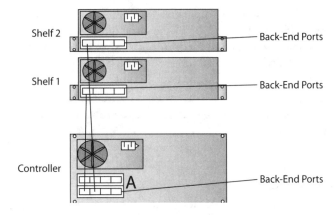

Figure 9-6
Single path

Shelf 2 — Back-End Ports

Shelf 1 — Back-End Ports

Controller — A — Back-End Ports

However, this presents a single point of failure for the system. If that link fails, access to the disks in that shelf will be terminated, which will most likely result in a loss of availability to storage resources contained on those disks, as shown in Figure 9-6.

Given the criticality of the data hosted on many storage systems, often storage systems are configured with redundant pathways to redundant controllers. Each shelf would have two connections, one to the back-end port on controller A and another to the back-end port on controller B, as shown in Figure 9-7.

Hot Spare

Hot spares are disks that remain idle in a storage system until a disk fails. At this point, the hot spare is added into the failed array as a new disk so that rebuilding operations can begin immediately. As discussed in Chapter 1, Redundant Array of Independent Disks (RAID) 1 and RAID 5 can support the loss of a single drive without the loss of data. If, however, a second drive fails before the first failed drive can be replaced, data loss will

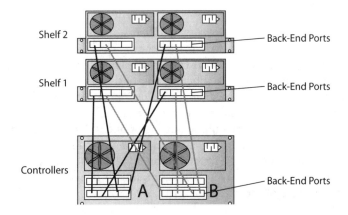

Figure 9-7
Redundant paths

Shelf 2 — Back-End Ports

Shelf 1 — Back-End Ports

Controllers — A — B — Back-End Ports

occur. Hot spares minimize this period of vulnerability by allowing the rebuild to start immediately. Hot spares must be of the same type, so if SATA and SAS disks exist in the array, a hot spare would be needed for both. Also, hot spares must be of equal or greater size than the failed disk, so if an array consists of 1TB and 2TB drives, the hot spare would need to be at least 2TB to cover a failure of either disk size.

 EXAM TIP   Be sure that each drive type is covered by a hot spare.

Multipath I/O

Multipath I/O (MPIO) is a framework that is designed to mitigate the effects of a device such as a host bus adapter (HBA) failure by providing an alternative data path between storage devices and a Windows operating system. MPIO allows up to 32 alternative paths to add redundancy and load balancing for storage environments, and it is built into many common systems today such as Microsoft Windows; storage systems from EMC, IBM, or Hitachi; and Linux, Solaris, BSD, macOS, and VMS. MPIO needs at least two network devices or two ports connected from host to the storage device. MPIO can provide load balancing and link failover services.

Load Balancing

Load balancing is the aggregation of traffic over multiple connections. Load balancing improves performance and resource utilization by dividing the traffic over two or more ports. Load balancing often requires software to be installed on the host or storage device to configure the load-balanced ports, but some systems come with load balancing built into the operating system.

Link Failover

Link failover is the transfer of network services from one network interface card (NIC), HBA, or converged network adapter (CNA) to another. Network functions can be assumed by another network device when the primary component becomes unavailable.

Hot-Swap

Various parts of the storage array are *hot-swappable*, meaning that the component can be removed without powering off the device. This allows for failed components to be replaced without impacting the functionality of the device or service. Such devices include power supplies, interface cards, hard disks, controllers, and fan units. The process for replacing a failed component that is hot-swappable is as simple as removing the failed component and then inserting the new component. Systems that are hot-swappable will detect the loss of the redundant component and run all operations on the other component and then configure the new component when it is added. Some manual configuration may be required when replacing components depending on the device replaced and the manufacturer of the hardware.

Path/Bus

Buses and paths in a network are the transmission path that is used by the signals to transmit data to the devices present in the line. The devices across the line that are addressed by the bus will receive the signals, while others may discard them if the data is not addressed to them since buses are shared mediums. Buses may be of various capacities, and the size of a bus is called its *width*.

A *path* is the connection between one or more devices in a network. Paths can be redundant by configuring multiple cables and interface devices at each point along the network. Redundant paths are known as *multipath*, but nonredundant paths are known as *single path*.

Multipath

Multipath connections have more than one path from source to destination. A multipath server would have two connections to a storage device. These connections would need to go through different systems to prevent a failure of one system along the path from disrupting communications for both paths. This requires at least two switches and two connections at the destination storage device, as depicted in Figure 9-8.

Single Path

Single-path systems have only one path of communication between devices. Single-path systems suffer from a single point of failure because the loss of a single port, cable, or switch will make the device inaccessible.

Figure 9-8
Redundant paths
from server to
storage array

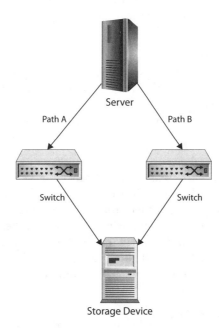

Server

Path A   Path B

Switch   Switch

Storage Device

Switch

Switches can be configured in redundant pairs with more than one switch performing the same function. Switches can also be equipped with redundant components and hot-swappable components to increase their availability. Switch power supplies, Ethernet modules, Small Form-factor Pluggable (SFP), and Gigabit Interface Converters (GBICs) can be redundant and/or hot-swapped on certain switch models. This also applies to other network devices such as routers, firewalls, and directors, as mentioned in Chapter 4.

HBA

Host bus adapters are hardware devices that are essential in storage area networks in providing interconnection between a host or storage device and the storage network. Redundant HBAs provide protection in case one HBA fails. Multipath software will need to be loaded on the host or storage device in order to fail over traffic to another port if a port fails. Some software can also balance the load between both HBAs.

NIC

Network interface cards are important hardware devices that connect computers with their networks. Earlier they were connected with the system using expansion cards, but of late, motherboards come with NICs built on them. NICs provide necessary circuitry and hardware support for connecting the system with the network. It is essential to provide redundancy because one failure in a NIC may present a communication failure over the network. Similarly to HBAs, NICs will need to be combined into a single logical network interface so that automatic failover and/or load balancing can be configured. This is sometimes referred to as *teaming* the NICs.

Link Aggregation

Link aggregation is the use of multiple parallel network connections in order to increase throughput beyond the limit that one link can achieve. Link aggregation is especially useful for increasing bandwidth between switches on a network because these are common congestion points, but it can be used for NICs, HBAs, and CNAs as well.

Array

Redundant arrays can provide fault tolerance for an entire array. Redundant arrays are most often seen in remote replication sites and cold sites. Remote replication sites are those that are located in another office or data center physically separate from the primary location. Software and a communication link between the two sites are used to replicate data between the two arrays to keep the data consistent. If the array at one site fails, the other can pick up the load. Redundant arrays can also be used at the same site to provide local fault tolerance, but this is much less common than remote replication.

Cache Redundancy

Cache battery backup is used to protect against power loss to the cache. The cache battery may be used to store data until power is restored, or it could be used to write the cache data out to a disk called a *vault disk*. In this case, when the storage array is powered on again, the data is written from the vault disk to cache again. This is simpler than flushing the data out to various disks because only one disk or disk set needs to be powered up, and the controller can write the data out sequentially to the disk or disks quickly.

Cache Battery Backup

Cache is high-speed memory that can be used to service I/O requests faster than accessing a disk. Controller head cache is used for storing data that is waiting to be sent over the interface in response to a read request or for storing data that is waiting to be written, or flushed, to the disks in response to a write request. Data may also remain in cache when the controller head considers it likely that the data will be requested for further read or write operations.

As you can see, the data in cache is important to the reliability of the storage system. Storage arrays make use of a battery-backed cache to prevent loss of data in the case of a power failure to the array. A battery-backed cache can keep unwritten data alive in case of power failure so that the data can be written to the disk once power has been restored.

Cache Mirroring

Cache mirroring stores identical pages in independent memory. If one memory location is lost, the other will be used to service requests. Cache is usually mirrored on redundant controllers. A mirrored cache must be kept in a consistent state called *cache coherency*.

A cache-mirroring mechanism is applied to a storage device to make sure that data is protected from loss or damage because of the loss of a controller. Mirroring writes the same data to all controllers in an array so that each is fully aware of operations and is ready to assume the duties of another controller.

Replication

Storage replication is the process in which the stored data is copied from one storage array to another. Replication can occur locally over a SAN or local area network (LAN) or to remote locations over a wide area network (WAN). This will improve the reliability of the system along with providing fault tolerance and easy accessibility. Users in remote locations can also access data that is replicated to a remote location, thus increasing their performance.

Replication allows for information, resources, software, and hardware to be shared so that they are available to more than one system. The significant benefits of replication include improving reliability and fault tolerance of the system and performance for users at replica sites. While *data replication* refers to storing the same data on multiple systems, *computation replication* refers to sharing computing tasks among systems.

 EXAM TIP The SCSP exam is concerned with data replication rather than computation replication. For the exam, remember that answers for replication questions will not include such items as distributed computing or processor replication.

Replication can be classified as active replication or passive replication. Active replication allows for client requests to be serviced by any storage system in the replication. This is especially useful when users are distributed but they require performance similar to a local storage array. Replica storage arrays can be placed at each location, and these replicas service client requests.

Passive replication is used for fault tolerance and business continuity. In passive replication, only one storage system responds to requests unless that system goes offline. If the primary system goes offline, a priority is given to other systems, and the next one in the line picks up the connection.

Replication can be managed directly by the storage array and its replication partner, or it can be managed by a host. Management that occurs on the SAN network is termed *in-band* replication management, and management that occurs outside of the SAN network is *out-of-band* replication management.

Replication is different from the backup scenarios discussed in Chapter 7 in that replicated systems or applications can be immediately utilized, while backups must be restored before they can be utilized.

Point-in-Time Replication

Replication can occur at differing intervals. A *point-in-time* (PIT) replica is one that is identical to the source as of a specific date and time, whereas continuous replication keeps the source and the destination synchronized at specified intervals. PIT replicas may track changes between the PIT replica and the source so that synchronization can take place at a later time, or changes may not be tracked if the PIT replica is being stored for archival purposes, historical querying, or litigation holds.

A common method for tracking changes is to use a bitmap. Bitmaps associate each block on the source volume to a bit within the bitmap. If the bit is set to 0, no changes have been made since the PIT was taken. When changes are made to blocks in the source volume, their corresponding bits in the bitmap are changed from 0 to 1. If the PIT needs to be synced later, a logical OR operation between the PIT and the bitmap will indicate which blocks need to be replicated to make the PIT consistent with the source volume.

The logical OR operation compares two bit strings to produce another equal string of bits. Each bit in both strings is compared. If a 1 exists in either bit, the resulting OR operation for that bit is a 1 as well. If, however, both bits are 0, the OR operation for that bit is a 0. For example, if a logical OR operation is performed on the bit strings 0010 and 0111, the end result would be 0111. The OR operation compares the first bit from both strings and produces a 0 because both are 0. The second bit is a 1 because there is a 1 in the second place of the second bit string. The third bit is also a 1 because there is a 1 in both bit strings. The last is a 1 because there is a 1 in the second bit string.

Continuous Replication

A *continuous* replica is synchronized with the source at regular repeating intervals. Synchronous replication and asynchronous replication are both examples of continuous replication. Synchronous replication will wait for transactions to be committed at both the source and destination sites before proceeding, while asynchronous replication will push updates to the destination site while still processing new transactions. Asynchronous replication tolerates some level of inconsistency between the source and destination to achieve better performance for write operations, but synchronous replication provides the best reliability.

Synchronous

Synchronous replication does not finalize transactions or commit data until it has been written to both source and destination. The major advantage of synchronous replication is that it ensures all the data remains consistent in both sites. On the other hand, this type of replication is quite expensive, and it also slows down the speed of the primary system. The maximum distance covered by this type is 300km because of link latency. Hence, this type of data replication is used in high-end applications that cannot tolerate any data loss.

Synchronous replication will either write data in both primary and secondary data drives or does not save it at all. Any failure in either the remote system or the connection stops the write operation in both the devices immediately. This is the reason for the zero-loss guarantee provided by this type of replication. Both the local and remote systems should provide acknowledgment that they have received the data, and only then does the write complete. This is also the reason for the reduction in the performance of the system because most of the tasks wait for the write operation to complete before performing other operations. Similarly, write operations start only when they receive confirmation that the destination is ready for writing the file.

Asynchronous

In asynchronous replication, the data is written in the primary system first, followed by the secondary system. Acknowledgment of the write is provided to applications or the operating system, and further changes can be made without requiring confirmation that the data has been written to the replica. This is in contrast with synchronous replication because the write operation is considered complete as and when information is written to both devices. Even though asynchronous increases the performance of the system when compared to synchronous replication, the prevention of data loss is not guaranteed because some data could be committed to the source but not yet replicated to the destination replica. Noncommitted data is stored in a buffer until it can be sent to the replica.

It is important to monitor the size of the buffer in asynchronous replication. If bandwidth between replica sets is overutilized, the buffer could grow large, and data could become significantly inconsistent. Business requirements should dictate the maximum tolerance for inconsistency between replicas.

 EXAM TIP Understand how buffer size impacts consistency in asynchronous replication.

NOTE Some enterprises use a combination of synchronous and asynchronous replication. Systems are often deployed using synchronous replication to another array at the same site, and then this array is replicated asynchronously to a remote site. This provides faster recovery and failover if a single array fails at the site than if asynchronous replication were used alone, while still providing recoverability if the entire site fails.

Scope

Replication can be performed with systems being connected both locally and remotely. Local replication is replication that occurs within the same data center or storage array, whereas remote replication is replication that occurs to another site. Some forms of replication can be used for both local and remote, such as logical volume manager (LVM) and continuous data protection (CDP).

LVM replication replicates identical volume groups and can be used for both local and remote replication. LVM requires volumes to be created at the source and destination storage arrays that have the same size. The two volumes must be synchronized initially, either through a backup and restore or by copying the data through the replication link. Once initial synchronization has taken place, a synchronization schedule, either synchronous or asynchronous, can be put in place to keep the data current between both sites. LVM maps each block for the virtual volume group to a physical volume group on the source and destination systems, and writes are issued to both systems as a mirror. The primary advantages of LVM replication are that it is supported on arrays from multiple vendors and that support for LVM replication is built into many systems. However, LVM can utilize a noticeable amount of processor resources and can slow down applications on host systems, if implemented on the host, or storage response time, if implemented on the storage device.

CDP replication can be used for both local and remote replication. In local replication, CDP is primarily used for business continuity because it provides a way to retrieve data from a point in time. CDP replication uses change tracking through a journal volume so that changes can be reapplied or rolled back from a PIT image. Writes to the volume are also sent to the journal volume for tracking. Changes are recorded in the journal along with the time stamp for when they were made to the production volume. The length of time that CDP data can be recovered is limited only by the amount of space available for the journal volume.

Local

Local replication is replication that occurs between devices at the same site. Local replication methods include LVM and CDP, mentioned previously; local replication is reliable because of the presence of many high-bandwidth links on the local network. Local replication is usually less complex because third parties that manage a WAN and the devices that interconnect remote sites are not part of the local replication solution.

Remote

Remote replication is replication that occurs to another site. The primary difference between local and remote replication is that remote replication must take into account additional latency from the link between the source and destination and lower bandwidth than is available on the local network. In addition to LVM and CDP replication, remote replication can occur via log shipping, disk-buffered replication, or storage array remote replication.

Log shipping replicates data by tracking changes in log files on the source machine. These log files are transmitted from the source to the destination replica when the log file is full, and the replica updates its data based on the changes recorded in the log. Replication intervals can be set by configuring the maximum size for the log file. Smaller log files will result in more frequent replication. Log shipping can be used over low-bandwidth links and is supported on many platforms. Log shipping is especially popular for database management systems (DBMSs).

Disk-buffered replication creates a PIT replica of the data and then transmits it to the remote site. Once the transmission completes, the process begins again, so the system is in either a PIT replica state or a transmission state. Both processes may take a significant amount of time depending on the activity load of the replicated system. For example, a large database is stored on an array and replicated to a remote array using disk-buffered replication. The PIT replica takes an average of 15 minutes to create and then 45 minutes to transfer, so replicas are sent approximately once per hour. When the replica is fully applied at the remote site, 45 minutes of updates have taken place on the primary site, so there is a significant difference between the two sites in this example. Disk-buffered replication is well suited to low-bandwidth links where the RPO is specified in hours.

 EXAM TIP   Local replication occurs between devices at the same site, while remote replication occurs between devices at different sites.

Site Redundancy

Site redundancy is the technique by which a complete duplicate of computers and data present in the computers at one main location is replicated at a different business location. Both the main site and the remotely located site are connected all the time so as to provide duplication of data as and when it is created. Hence, the failover takes place quite instantly, thereby ensuring users never experience the failure of the main system. It is important for all businesses to set up site redundancy so as to prevent their businesses from crashing for at least a short amount of time. Another advantage of site redundancy is that software upgrades to the systems can be performed without disturbing any users using the system. It can also help in providing network services to users from various geographic locations. There are certain requirements for the implementation of site redundancy, and it depends on the nature of the business and the data associated with it.

Storage network architecture is one of the important areas of research for people in the world of information technology because more and more data is created every second. It is important to employ effective techniques at all levels of the organization to reap the complete benefits. Hence, it is important to understand all the terms and techniques. All of the mentioned hardware and software practices are being used all over the world. Leading manufacturers bring out new technologies now and then, making it possible for users to work safely and effectively. The only problems for users would be finding suitable products for their business needs. Once the analysis for effective products is done, the organizations can work on implementing the same for their business.

Consistency

Replication consistency is achieved through consistency groups. These groups are used for maintaining data integrity and uniformity across multiple volumes, or even sites, usually comprising an entire system such as the application, middleware, and back end. The consistency group ensures that a set of writes in it retains the same data, and writes that occur to one member of the group will not be fully committed until they have been implemented across all members of the consistency group. This ensures that no matter which resource in the consistency group is accessed, the data remains the same.

Chapter Summary

This chapter discussed how to design and set up a storage system that provides high availability through redundancy and avoids a single point of failure. To design the architecture for a system, you must first understand the requirements of the system. Storage systems may provide block storage, which is storage mapped as logical units to end machines. Storage solutions may also provide file-based storage, which is storage allowing multiple users to access it concurrently over a network share such as CIFS or NFS. Storage systems are not limited to block or file and can consist of a combination of the two.

High availability is a system with little downtime. This is achieved through redundant components and systems, the ability to detect component failures, and the ability to switch between redundant components effectively. High-availability systems avoid a single point of failure, which is any component whose failure would result in the unavailability of the entire system.

Redundancy is achieved by utilizing pairs of equipment or by including redundant components within systems. Some components that are commonly configured redundantly include the power supply, controllers, paths and buses, switches, HBA, NIC, arrays, and cache. Various parts of the storage array are hot-swappable, meaning they can be removed without powering off the device. Disks can use RAID for redundancy and also hot spares, which are drives that remain idle in a storage system until a drive fails.

Redundant components may be configured for load balancing whereby traffic is distributed among the various redundant components. This allows for greater throughput when all components are available. Link aggregation is the use of multiple parallel network connections in order to increase throughput beyond the limit that one link can achieve. Link aggregation is especially useful for increasing bandwidth between switches on a network because these are common congestion points.

Failover is the transfer of services from one component to another in a redundant system. In clusters, this would be a transfer of a service or application to another node in a cluster. With hardware, this could be the transfer of power distribution from one power supply to another.

Redundant paths to disks are used to achieve high availability within a storage system or between local devices and remote disks. When one path to a disk or disk shelf becomes unavailable, I/O can be directed to another available path.

Some storage systems, known as OLTP, provide immediate response and high availability. Some components of an OLTP solution include a database, management portals, business intelligence systems, reporting functionality, scheduling, analysis, web services, searching, document management, and workflow.

Systems may also take advantage of cloud services, allowing certain components of the storage architecture to be offloaded and managed by a third party. Cloud services that provide an entire application to a company are known as Software as a Service (SaaS). Cloud services that provide an operating system and database for the user to install an application on are referred to as Platform as a Service (PaaS). Infrastructure as a Service (IaaS) is a cloud service that provides a customer with computing resources and their underlying storage and networking so that they can run their own operating system, database, and applications on it. Lastly, Storage as a Service (StaaS) provides a customer with the storage and networking to host data for their application.

Replication is used to make copies of data so that a system can remain functioning even if an entire system or site is unavailable. Local replication is replication that occurs within the same data center or storage array, whereas remote replication is replication that occurs to another site. Replication requires consistency between source and target systems. Replication consistency is achieved through consistency groups. The consistency group ensures that a set of writes in it retain the same data, and writes that occur to one member of the group will not be fully committed until they have been implemented across all members of the consistency group.

Replication can occur at differing intervals. A point-in-time replica is one that is identical to the source as of a specific date and time, whereas continuous replication keeps the source and destination synchronized at specified intervals. Continuous replication can be synchronous or asynchronous. Synchronous replication will wait for transactions to be committed at both the source and destination sites before proceeding, while asynchronous replication will push updates to the destination site while still processing new transactions. Asynchronous replication tolerates some level of inconsistency between the source and destination to achieve better performance, but synchronous replication provides the best reliability.

Chapter Review Questions

1. Tom wants to provide additional storage to five database servers. The database servers must see the storage as local disks. Which storage architecture should Tom implement?

   A. Block-level architecture

   B. File-level architecture

   C. Hybrid architecture

   D. Network architecture

2. Mary has an application that requires high availability. She would like to run the application on three servers that will share the load and provide failover in case one server fails. Which technology should she deploy?

   A. Software as a Service

   B. Clustering

   C. Link aggregation

   D. Cache mirroring

3. Howard manages the IT systems for HBD Industries. HBD Industries provides an application to its vendors allowing them to view when inventory needs to be replaced. After several downtime events, HBD's vendors request a contract ensuring a specific level of availability. What should Howard create for the vendors?

   A. Business associate agreement (BAA)

   B. Availability metering

   C. Network schematic

   D. Service level agreement (SLA)

4. A risk assessment informs Joan that there is a single point of failure on the controller in her storage array. Which of the following should Joan implement to resolve the single point of failure?

   A. Add a second controller and redundant cabling to front-end and back-end ports.

   B. Implement online transaction processing.

   C. Add more host bus adapters to the controller.

   D. Configure cache mirroring in the controller.

5. Subramanian is deploying an application that he expects will need regular increases in storage to satisfy customer demand, but he cannot predict what those increases will be. He would like to utilize a cloud-based solution to house his application. Subramanian plans to configure the application, database, and operating systems but would like the hardware, including storage, to be located in the cloud. Which cloud solution would fit Subramanian's needs?

    A. Storage as a Service (StaaS)

    B. Infrastructure as a Service (IaaS)

    C. Platform as a Service (PaaS)

    D. Software as a Service (SaaS)

6. Which of the following describes failover?

    A. Failover is the automatic provisioning of additional storage when a device consumes the currently available storage.

    B. Failover is the transfer of services from one component to another in a redundant system.

    C. Failover is the initiation of a disaster recovery plan to contain a data breach.

    D. Failover is the implementation of redundant hardware in a system that has a single point of failure.

7. At 2 A.M., John is paged because the storage array lost power. He discovers that several users were updating data on the array, but their changes have been lost. He calls his storage vendor and is told about a technology that will retain data that has not been flushed to disk even if power is disconnected from the array, but he cannot remember what the technology was called. Which technology did the storage vendor mention?

    A. Cache mirroring

    B. Cache residency

    C. Cache battery backup

    D. Cache failover

8. You have a development site and a production site. When changes to the development site are approved for production, you want to deploy them using replication. Which replication technology would best suit this situation?

    A. Synchronous replication

    B. Asynchronous replication

    C. Continuous replication

    D. Point-in-time replication

9. You wish to set up multipathing for load balancing on a server in a storage network. How many ports will be required at minimum in the server to set this up?

   A. 1

   B. 2

   C. 4

   D. None; multipathing is set up on the switch instead.

Chapter Review Answers

1. **A** is correct. The block-level architecture presents data to hosts as local storage would appear to them so that they can interact with it in the same way.
   B, C, and **D** are incorrect. **B** is incorrect because a file-level architecture would present the storage as a share instead of a local disk. **C** is incorrect because a hybrid architecture would present the storage as both local disks and shares, but only the former is required. **D** is incorrect because the term "network architecture" does not describe an architecture in particular.

2. **B** is correct. Clustering is the use of two or more devices together to provide load balancing and failover services.
   A, C, and **D** are incorrect. **A** is incorrect because Software as a Service would run the application in the cloud, not in a failover cluster. **C** is incorrect because link aggregation would provide more bandwidth and failover for a single link, but it would not fail over an entire server. **D** is incorrect because cache mirroring is a technology used to provide high availability to storage arrays with more than one controller.

3. **D** is correct. A service level agreement (SLA) for a technology service is part of a contract that defines the required availability of the system in terms of a percentage, such as 99 percent uptime.
   A, B, and **C** are incorrect. **A** is incorrect because a business associate agreement may or may not spell out the required service level. **B** is incorrect because availability metering will not enforce the availability. It will simply track the availability metrics. **C** is incorrect because the network schematic will only show where items are and how they are related.

4. **A** is correct. Add a second controller and redundant cabling to front-end and back-end ports. Dual controller units are equipped with two identical controller heads that are each capable of operating the entire storage array.
   B, C, and **D** are incorrect. **B** is incorrect because OLTP is an enterprise application and supporting systems, but this question only asks about the storage array. **C** is incorrect because more HBAs in a single controller does not address the risk of a controller failure, since all HBAs in that controller would not function if the controller failed. **D** is incorrect because cache mirroring cannot be configured until a second controller is added.

5. B is correct. Infrastructure as a Service (IaaS) is a cloud service that provides a customer with computing resources and their underlying storage and networking so that they can run their own operating system, database, and applications on it.

A, C, and **D** are incorrect. **A** is incorrect because Storage as a Service would not provide the hardware to run the application, operating system, and database. **C** is incorrect because Platform as a Service would not allow Subramanian to install his own operating system. **D** is incorrect because Software as a Service would not allow for the operating system, database, and application to be installed since they would already be provided by the cloud service.

6. B is correct. Failover is the transfer of services from one component to another in a redundant system. In failover, the functions of a system component—be it processor, server, network, or database—are assumed by another system's components when the primary component becomes unavailable.

A, C, and **D** are incorrect. **A** is incorrect because the automatic provisioning of additional storage is thin provisioning. **C** is incorrect because disaster recovery plans are implemented by humans, not through a failover process. **D** is incorrect because failover relies on redundant hardware, but it is not the configuration of hardware that comprises failover.

7. C is correct. The data in cache is important to the reliability of the storage system. Storage arrays make use of a battery-backed cache to prevent loss of data in the case of a power failure to the array. A battery-backed cache can keep unwritten data alive in case of power failure so that the data can be written to the disk once power has been restored.

A, B, and **D** are incorrect. **A** is incorrect. Cache mirroring will keep the same data on both controllers' cache, but a loss in power would mean that the mirrored cache on both controllers would be lost. **B** is incorrect because cache residency keeps data in cache so that it can be retrieved quickly, but this data would be lost if power was lost. **D** is incorrect because failover would change processing to another controller, but it would not work if power was lost to both devices.

8. D is correct. A point-in-time (PIT) replica is one that is identical to the source as of a specific date and time.

A, B, and **C** are incorrect. **A** and **B** are incorrect because both synchronous and asynchronous replication are forms of continuous replication, and they would replicate changes that have not been approved for deployment. **C** is incorrect because continuous replication keeps the source and destination synchronized at specified intervals, which might not match up with the approvals.

9. B is correct. Multipathing requires at least two paths for redundancy. In this case, the redundant links will also be used for load balancing so traffic will be distributed among the two links.

A, C, and **D** are incorrect. **A** is incorrect because one link would not provide the redundancy required for multipathing. At least two links are required for multipathing. **C** is incorrect because the question asks for the minimum required; two ports are the minimum. **D** is incorrect because multipathing requires multiple ports on the server in addition to configuration on the switch fabric.

Environment

In this chapter, you will learn how to
- Select ideal locations for equipment in server rooms or data centers
- Identify power requirements for storage implementations
- Determine storage system HVAC needs
- Explain the pros and cons of different methods of data center fire suppression
- Install or maintain storage equipment without hurting yourself or damaging equipment

Storage systems are housed in a data center or server room. These facilities must be adequately cooled and powered for the equipment to function correctly.

Facilities

Equipment such as storage arrays, networking equipment, and servers are typically stored in a server room or data center. For large installations, an organization may build and maintain its own data center, but smaller installations, especially replication sites, may be housed in a shared data center that is managed by a third party.

The size of the facility or space within the facility will determine how much equipment can be installed. If you are designing a server room from scratch, build one that is bigger than you expect you need if possible because larger areas will allow for better airflow and heat dissipation. Small areas can suffer from rapid increases in heat when equipment is turned on or when environmental systems are enabled or switched over, but larger systems are more capable of sustaining such changes with smaller fluctuations in ambient temperature.

Storage and network equipment is typically stored in data centers or server rooms using racks. The majority of racks found in data centers and server rooms can house equipment 19 inches wide. Racks are divided into units, called *U*, that are each 1.752 inches tall. Racks come in different sizes with capacities ranging from 18U to 50U, but the most common full-height rack has 42U.

Each U has two posts on each side of the front and back where a device can be mounted. Rack-mountable devices are equipped with metal or plastic pieces that stick out from the edge of the device. These pieces are called *ears*, and they can be attached to the posts in a rack using screws. Larger devices may require shelves or rails to hold them in the rack. These shelves or rails attach to the holes in the rack in much the same way ears do. Front- and back-locking doors, as well as covers for the sides and top, can be purchased for racks to increase security. It is important to ensure efficient airflow with rack doors and to organize cables so that doors can close easily without the possibility of pinching cables, especially fiber-optic cables that can be broken easily.

Racks are organized in rows, with each rack in a row facing the same direction, as shown in Figure 10-1. Aisles separate the racks and provide space to maintain, add, or remove equipment. For this reason, aisles must be at least a full rack depth so that equipment can be fully removed from or inserted into a rack.

Racks in data center typically rest upon a raised floor. A raised floor is an artificial floor that is usually made of 24-inch by 24-inch tiles that are supported by a 12-inch to 24-inch tall framing structure. The floor tiles can be removed to access power cables and other components that may reside underneath the floor. Many times, the floor is used as a channel for cold air. Cold air can be directed to the appropriate place in the data center using perforated tiles in some locations, and it can be restricted using a solid tile. Figure 10-1 shows the perforated tiles on the raised floor.

Figure 10-1   Racks in a data center

Figure 10-2
Color-coded
cables

Cable Management

The average computing device will have many cables attached to it. For example, a storage device with dual power supplies will have two power cables. It may have dual connections from each controller to each storage shelf and several front-end connections.

As a rack is filled, the number of cables in the rack can be difficult to manage. It is important to label cables on both ends. Another way to manage cables is to color code them, as shown in Figure 10-2. For example, in each server, blue cables go to the primary NIC and green cables go to a secondary NIC. (These two NICs are teamed with load balancing and failover.) Yellow connections could be for remote access cards, and purple connections for monitoring. Gray cable could be for diagnostics.

It is also important to bundle cables together, routing them along the edges of the rack. This will prevent individual cables from being bumped or snagged when working around the rack, and it will allow for better airflow to and from the equipment in the rack, as shown in Figure 10-3.

Cable management also helps prevent cables from being subjected to electromagnetic interference (EMI) produced by power cables because it is much easier to keep bundles away from one another than a large mesh of power and data cables.

Cables that travel between racks should be routed through ducts that run above the racks. Ducts are usually made of colored plastic and are suspended from the ceiling. They help to remove strain from cables that would occur if the cables were hung directly from the ceiling or draped over racks. They also keep the cables organized and protected from impact.

Figure 10-3 Bundled cables

Cooling

Heating, ventilation, and air conditioning (HVAC) systems control the ambient environment, which includes temperature, humidity, airflow, and air filtering. A data center is a high-density, enclosed space that generates a significant amount of heat. Data centers require dedicated HVAC units with high-quality cooling capabilities to ensure adequate operating temperatures and humidity.

HVAC systems are used to cool data centers or server rooms and to control humidity (discussed next). Improper cooling can potentially damage storage and networking equipment, resulting in more frequent component failures, performance issues because of system throttling, or complete system failure. Controlling the environment in a data center, therefore, is important in maximizing the availability and performance of essential equipment.

Every hardware device has its own environmental requirements, and these include temperature levels that are acceptable for it. These environmental requirements are described in a product specifications document or in a physical planning guide. HVAC systems should be configured so that enough cool air is provided to reduce temperatures to acceptable levels as defined by equipment manufacturers. Most equipment will operate effectively when the temperature is warmer than 50 degrees and lower than 82 degrees Fahrenheit (10–28 degrees Celsius).

The British thermal unit (BTU) is a measurement of heat. One BTU is roughly the amount of heat of a lit match. Each watt of power consumed generates on average about 35BTU, so plan cooling using this formula. For example, when adding 20 new 2U servers in a rack that each consumes 200W of power, this will consume 4,000W and generate approximately 140,000BTU.

 EXAM TIP Try to distribute racks evenly based on power requirements and BTU generated. This will avoid placing too much load on certain circuits or creating zones that are warmer than others.

Much of the equipment purchased today will draw cool air in from the front and expel hot air out the back. However, some equipment may be configured to expel hot air from the front. It is important to install all equipment in a rack such that they pull cool air from the same direction. This creates what are known as hot and cold aisles in the data center. Hot aisles receive hot air from computing equipment and route it to be cooled, while cool aisles provide cool air to reduce the temperature of computing equipment. Equipment should be oriented to pull air from the cool aisle and expel air into the hot aisle. If installing equipment that pulls cool air from the back in a rack filled mostly with equipment that pulls cool air from the front, mount the device front to back so that it pulls cool air from the same direction as the rest of the equipment. If this is not properly addressed, systems will pull in hot air, which will not effectively cool the equipment and will result in more frequent component failures, performance issues because of system throttling, or complete system failure.

Humidity Control

Humidity differences can potentially damage a disk or other storage and networking hardware. Low humidity can create an environment where electrostatic charges can build up, eventually leading to electrostatic discharge (ESD), which could potentially damage components. High humidity can cause condensation. Since water is a conductor, condensation can create electrical shorts in computing equipment or simply damage the equipment directly. Electrical shorts are alternative unintentional pathways for electricity to flow. Condensation can also accumulate in disks, especially when moved from environments with different temperature and humidity levels. Give disks time to acclimate to a new temperature and humidity level before putting them into service.

Temperature and humidity can both be monitored by a variety of tools. For example, Figure 10-4 shows the monitoring screen for a temperature sensor. This sensor has a web interface and e-mail alerting features.

Fire Suppression

With all the electricity and heat produced by computing equipment, fires are a possibility in a server room or data center. They present the potential for loss of equipment and, more importantly, loss of life. A variety of fire suppression systems are available to put out a fire, but they differ based on their cost and effectiveness.

THUM - Server Room THUM

Last Reading taken at: 06/19/2014 02:53:57 PM

Temperature: 69.492 °F
Humidity: 49.49 %
Dew point: 49.78 °F
Heat Index: N/A °F

Temp Alarm High Limit: 78 °F   Temp Alarm Low Limit: 60 °F
RH Alarm High Limit: 200 %   RH Alarm Low Limit: 10 %

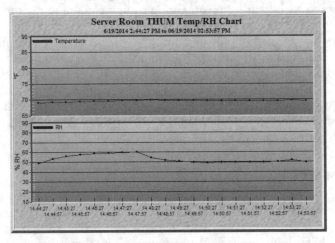

Page generated by a Practical Design Group, LLC - THUM (Temperature Humidity USB Monitor)

Figure 10-4   Web-based temperature monitoring

Fire suppression systems must first detect a fire in order to be effective, and they must be able to do it with a high level of accuracy. The incorrect deployment of fire suppression systems can damage equipment and injure employees or clients, but a system that does not respond to real threats can result in even greater loss. Most fire detection systems will sense for heat and smoke, and the presence of both is required to trigger an alarm.

The next step is to put out the fire using a system such as water sprinklers or gaseous agents.

Water Sprinklers

Water sprinklers are the most common kind of fire suppression system available in businesses, but they are not as popular in server rooms and data centers because of the impact they have on the sensitive equipment housed there. Sprinkler systems can be one of two types, wet pipe and dry pipe. Wet pipe systems contain water all the time, but dry pipes have only air inside to avoid condensation building up on the outside of pipes and potentially dripping onto equipment. Both systems, however, destroy computing equipment when deployed, so they are useful only in preventing loss of life. Sprinkler systems have low installation and maintenance costs and can be activated immediately upon sensing a fire. However, damaged pipes could leak water and damage equipment; their use results in the destruction of computing equipment and damage to facilities.

Gaseous Agent Fire Suppression Systems

Gaseous agents remove components that fire needs to exist such as heat or oxygen, and they do so without damaging computing equipment. However, these agents are harmful to humans, so they cannot be activated immediately upon sensing a fire. Instead, people in the facility should be warned first with alarms and lights, and then the system can be activated once the facility is evacuated.

Gaseous agents that remove heat from fire include FM-200, HFC-125, and HFC-227ea, while carbon dioxide and inergen remove oxygen. Gaseous agents do not damage computing equipment, but they can harm people, and they cost more than sprinklers to implement and maintain. For this reason, it is important to post signs letting people know that gaseous agents are in use for fire suppression, as shown in Figure 10-5.

Halon was a popular gaseous agent used in data centers until it was discovered that its use damaged the ozone layer, so it is no longer used in new data center fire suppression systems. Data centers generally prefer to use gaseous agents rather than water to avoid damaging computing equipment. Of the available gaseous agents, FM-200 is commonly used and is widely available. However, inergen is also popular because it is a clean agent that can suppress fires without harming humans and equipment.

Figure 10-5
Fire suppression
warning sign

Storage Power Requirements

All computer systems run off power of some sort. Without power, these systems cannot continue functioning. Power consumption directly affects operating costs, and these costs continue to rise. Let's define a few terms before continuing too much in the discussion of power. Electricity consists of voltage, current, and resistance. Volts (V) measures voltage, ampere (or amps or A) measures current, and ohms measures resistance. A watt measures electrical power, which is equal to current multiplied by voltage (A × V).

Let's apply these terms to something a little easier to understand. Imagine squeezing Play-Doh out from a tube. In electrical terms, the voltage (volts) would be the amount of pressure applied to the Play-Doh, and the current (amps) would be how fast the Play-Doh moves through the tube. Resistance (ohms) is somewhat more difficult to understand, but it would be related to the size of the tube. The Play-Doh could go through a tube of many different sizes, but it would be much easier to push the Play-Doh through a larger tube than a smaller one. The larger tube offers less resistance. Lastly, imagine you need 1 cubic foot of Play-Doh to create a Play-Doh airplane. That 1 cubic foot would be the power (watts) necessary in this example. Stepping back to the resistance for a second, you could reduce the pressure or current needed by increasing the tube size, which reduces the resistance. The same is true for electrical power.

With the Play-Doh in mind, consider electrical power requirements for computing equipment. Equipment may have a requirement of the amount of power in watts, but it needs to be delivered at a certain speed in amps, which is impacted by the resistance or ohms. Resistance is determined by the size and quality of the conductive material in a medium such as a cable. Cable size is measured in gauges, with smaller gauges representing larger wires. The quality is associated with the conductive material used and its purity.

 EXAM TIP The ratio of voltage to amperage can be changed to provide the same amount of wattage to a device, but devices will have a specific voltage and amperage requirement. If a question on the exam offers a solution of changing voltage or amperage, ensure that you make this change only if the current voltage or amperage is not what has been specified by the device manufacturer.

This section discusses the two types of power, alternating current and direct current, and then how to plan for the required capacity of the devices placed in your server room or data center. Next, this section covers how to divide devices across circuits and the importance and role of grounding and uninterruptable power supplies.

AC

Alternating current (AC) is an electrical current that alternates or changes direction, meaning that the power flows from positive to negative and then switches to flow from negative to positive. The number of times it changes direction is measured in hertz (Hz). In the United States, AC power is distributed at 60 Hz. AC power is created by a power company and is used to provide power to its destination at homes and businesses.

The reason why it is used instead of DC power is that transformers can be used to change the ratio of amps to voltage. Power companies use this to distribute power more efficiently. Power can be sent from the power plant to distribution centers at high voltage over a relatively small wire, and then the voltage can be reduced as it is sent from distribution centers to neighborhoods and again at residences or businesses to 120V or 240V. This is what makes power lines so much more dangerous than the wires in your home.

DC

Direct current (DC) is an electrical current that does not change direction. DC power always flows the same way. DC power is what is used within computer systems, so the AC power provided at the wall must be first converted to DC power before it can be used in a computer system. Power supplies in computer systems take AC power and convert it into DC power at various voltages, including 12V, 5V, and 3V, to power components such as hard disks, optical drives, chipsets, and other components that make up a computer system.

NOTE Batteries already provide DC power, so there is no need to convert power from batteries first.

Grounding

Grounding is the return path for electric current. It is called a *ground* because it eventually terminates in the earth. The ground wire deposits extra electricity into the earth where it can be easily and harmlessly dissipated. Without a ground, extra current would end up crossing into another part of the electrical system where there is least resistance, and this could harm electrical components or people.

EXAM TIP Grounded devices will pass extra current through the ground so that it does not destroy sensitive computing equipment. When working on computing equipment, ensure that you are also grounded using a wrist strap.

Sufficient Capacity

Power requirements can vary depending on how densely populated a rack is. The rack density refers to how many devices are in the rack. High-density racks have many devices in them, while low-density racks may have only a few devices.

Devices in low-density racks may be larger but with only marginally greater power requirements than the equipment in high-density racks. High-density racks from a power perspective are those that consume more than 8 kilowatt (kW) of power. A fully populated rack of servers (one that has every available slot in the rack filled with a server) can consume up to 35kW. The kilowatt rack consumption is determined by adding the wattage of all units in the rack together, so if a rack has 20 servers consuming 500W each, the consumption would be 10,000W, or 10kW.

Storage administrators must ensure that sufficient power capacity is available for the equipment they plan to place in a rack. Some devices will require 20A power, while others will require 30A power. Many racks come equipped only with 20A circuits, so the addition of 30A circuits will require additional power lines to the rack.

EXAM TIP   30A circuits have only one receptacle per circuit such as the L6-30r or L5-30r, so each device that requires a 30A plug will need a circuit. Those that have redundant power will require multiple circuits. When looking at plug and receptacle types, names that end in *p* refer to plugs and *r* refer to receptacles.

Computing devices have a normal operating power level but a peak level as well. Normally, computer systems consume more power as they are starting up. This is because it takes more power to start devices such as hard disks that are still than to keep moving devices in motion. Also, power management and energy-saving services that may throttle down fans and other devices require software to run and are normally unavailable when a system first starts up. For this reason, it is best to stagger the start time of equipment so that too much load is not placed on power circuits.

Circuit load should also be designed such that there is additional unused capacity for handling many devices using peak power. Some building codes may require a certain percentage of power overage, so be aware of these regulations or check with your local governing bodies if unsure before making such decisions.

- **Critical load**   The critical load is the total power required by computing equipment such as servers, routers, computers, and storage devices. It does not include supporting devices like cooling and lighting.

- **Total load**   The total load is the total power consumed including both the critical load and the devices required to support the critical load, including cooling, lights, and support systems.

Power distribution units (PDUs) are often used to connect computing equipment to circuits. PDUs are devices that plug into a circuit and provide multiple power receptacles for equipment to be plugged into. Many PDUs come with surge suppression features, and some come with metering capability, as shown in Figure 10-6. Surge suppression will divert excess power that could potentially damage computing equipment to the ground connection. However, PDUs will have a maximum amount of power they can handle before they cease protecting equipment. Ensure that the PDUs you use have enough capacity for your equipment.

It can often take as much power or more to cool equipment and support the environment as it does to run the equipment, so if you are operating the data center or server room, double the power cost of equipment to factor in the total load rather than just the critical load.

Lastly, the power required for all racks must be supported by the line coming into your office space or data center facility. The line coming into your office or facility will

Figure 10-6
PDU with
metering

be rated for a certain number of amps. A small office may have 300 amps that then are divided among the circuits connected to the breaker box.

Division of Circuits

When utilizing dual power supplies, ensure that each power supply is connected to a different circuit. Typically these circuits will be labeled A and B, so your primary power supply would be connected to the A circuit, and your secondary power supply would be connected to the B circuit.

Uninterruptable Power Supply

Uninterruptable power supplies (UPSs) are used to provide power to computing equipment if the power to the facility or location is lost or interrupted. UPS systems can also condition power, keeping the power at a consistent level to avoid instances where power is too high, known as *spikes*, or too low, known as *lulls*. UPS systems are equipped with batteries and are rated for the amount of voltage amps (VAs) they can support over a length of time.

Select a UPS that can handle the load of your servers for the amount of time it will take to gracefully shut down the servers. UPS devices are rated in VA. To determine the required VA, divide the total wattage consumed by the devices you want to connect to the UPS by 0.6 to adjust for overhead. For example, say you have a storage array, a Fibre Channel switch, and five servers, as listed here:

- **Storage array main unit** 1,000W
- **Storage array disk shelf** 500W
- **Fibre Channel switch** 50W
- **Servers** 200W each

The total wattage is 2,550. You multiply this by 0.6 to get 4,250VA required.

Some environments require servers to remain in operation during a power failure. These sites are typically equipped with a backup generator, so UPS systems will take the load while the generator is started up. The initial startup of a generator can produce spikes or lulls, which should be compensated for by the UPS. In this case, the UPS will need to be able to supply power for the amount of time it takes for the generator to start up and reach full operating capacity.

The last thing to consider about UPS is the power circuit required. To determine the circuit required, divide the VA by the voltage of the circuit to find the amps required. For reference, Table 10-1 shows the circuit limitations.

Circuits larger than 30A need to be hardwired. Hardwiring connects the UPS to a box, which then connects to the circuit breaker. This is shown in Figure 10-7.

The UPS will also need to have receptacles for each of the devices connected to it. If the storage array in the example was running on a 30A L6-30P, the UPS would need to have a 30A L6-30R for it to plug into. I have had the unfortunate experience of working with many clients who have ordered a UPS only to find that the unit ordered does not have the requisite power receptacles for their equipment. The L14-30R and L6-30R look

	Amps	Voltage	Max VA
Table 10-1 Circuit Limitations	15A	120V	1,800VA
	20A	120V	2,400VA
	30A	120V	3,600VA
	30A	208V	6,240VA
	30A	240V	7,200VA
	50A	208V	10,400VA
	50A	240V	12,000VA
	60A	208V	12,480VA
	60A	240V	14,400VA

Figure 10-7
Hardwiring

similar, as shown in Figure 10-8. Honestly, the only way I tell them apart is by reading the label. Each plug and receptacle should be labeled. Plugs will have the label in the plastic in between the connection pins or on the side of the plug and possibly printed on the cable sheathing as well. Receptacles will have the label printed in between two circles that go around the circumference of the receptacle. The L5-20R, L14-30R, and L6-30R are all shown in Figure 10-8.

Figure 10-8 L5-20R (left), L14-30R (center), and L6-30R (right)

Safety

Equipment is valuable, but the people who operate and maintain it are even more valuable. The installation or ongoing maintenance of storage equipment may involve moving or lifting these devices. Care should be taken because serious injury or loss of life can occur. Employers must strictly enforce worker safety protocols. Continual training and drills are essential in maintaining a safe environment. The U.S. Occupational Safety and Health Administration (OSHA) plays an important role in providing guidelines and policies that help minimize the potential of injury or death.

Weight Considerations

The weight of a device is often an overlooked consideration in site preparation. The total weight of all devices in a rack can be anywhere from just the weight of the rack to 2,000 pounds, and the average server weighs 35 to 50 pounds.

Rack Stabilization

As stated earlier, rack stabilization ensures that the rack is secured and will not move. There are some basic practical ways to avoid destabilization of racks and other types of shelving. For example, placing heavier devices on the bottom of a rack will prevent the unit from toppling over. When stabilizing a rack, it is best to bolt them together or have special stabilizing feet attached in order to provide additional stability.

Floor and Rack Loading

Racks should be placed and loaded so that they will not fall on people or break through the floor. As you can imagine, this could easily damage equipment, break cables, hurt personnel, and cause downtime for the systems in the rack. Consider the floor load and rack load when placing and filling racks. Floor load refers to the maximum weight per square foot that a floor can support. Likewise, rack load refers to the maximum allowable weight that a rack can tolerate.

Floor load is not much of an issue in facilities that have concrete floors, but many facilities, especially data centers, have raised flooring.

It is important to know how much weight a floor can carry so it doesn't get loaded with more weight than it can handle. It is a good practice with raised floors to install racks so that they span multiple floor tiles. This spreads the weight across several tiles.

Load racks starting from the bottom to avoid the rack tipping over. Especially heavy racks can be mounted to the floor. Figure 10-9 shows a rack that has a few servers loaded starting from the bottom. This rack is not mounted to the floor, but there are two legs with holes for mounting bolts if necessary.

Proper Lifting Techniques

Understanding the mechanics of lifting can prevent injury. Wearing a brace or support appliance is just part of the safety equation. For example, when lifting a heavy object, it is always better to bend the knees before lifting, rather than bending from the waist to pick it up. Many workers are unaware of the proper techniques for lifting

Figure 10-9   Rack loaded from bottom

or moving heavy objects. Here are some practical tips and techniques to consider in order to prevent injury:

- Hold the object being lifted close to the body when standing or ready to move to reduce the strain on the lower back.

- When lifting a heavy object, decide first where the object will be placed and what it takes to get there. If it is too heavy to lift for one person, assistance should be requested. In some cases and when possible, large heavy boxes should be separated into several smaller, lighter boxes.

- Stand close to the object when lifting it from the floor. Kneel and then rest one knee on the floor. Make sure the object is close to your body. Next, rest the object on your knee and then stand up while maintaining a natural curve in the lower back and using your leg muscles to lift.

- Some might prefer to squat rather than kneel when lifting from the floor. In this case, tilt one edge of the object to get a good grip and then use your leg muscles to lift.

Antistatic Devices

Electrostatic discharge (ESD) is the equalization of electrical charges between two objects. ESD happens when one object with a higher electrical charge comes into contact with one of a lesser charge. The higher-charged object will transfer some electrons to the lower-charged object. You may have felt this when you received a static electricity shock from touching a metal object or a friend. Objects can build up a charge as they move and interact with other objects. Children often get a kick out of building up a charge by scuffing their feet on a carpet and then touching their friends to shock them. This illustrates how the charge is built up and how it is discharged. ESD is felt by people only when it is of a significant enough charge, but ESD can damage computing equipment even when it is not felt.

Thus, it is important to protect computing equipment from ESD due to improper handling and to prevent the buildup of an electrical charge in components. ESD due to improper handling can be avoided by using an antistatic wrist strap, sometimes combined with an antistatic mat. Antistatic wrist straps have a piece of metal that presses against the skin and is connected to a wire that grounds the individual. ESD is passed through the wrist strap so that it does not pass into a computing component. An antistatic mat grounds the components that rest upon it so that both the technician and the device are at the same charge because both are connected to a ground. Antistatic bags can be used to prevent the buildup of charge in electrical components.

Chapter Summary

This chapter provided best practices for power, cooling, fire suppression, and cable management in a server room or data center environment and how to perform installation and maintenance in a safe manner.

Computing equipment is stored in racks that are organized in rows in a server room or data center. These computing devices generate heat that must be cooled, so it is best to arrange devices so that they pull cool air in from the same direction. The measurement of how much heat is generated is the British thermal unit.

Humidity can damage computing systems. Low humidity can lead to electrostatic discharge, while high humidity can lead to condensation causing electrical shorts.

Fires can easily damage computing equipment or harm personnel. The key to preventing such damage is to first detect fires accurately and then utilize a suppression system. Suppression systems include water sprinklers and gaseous systems. Water sprinklers are cheap, but they damage computing systems. Gaseous systems can harm people, but they do not damage computing systems.

Power is critical for computing system operation.

- A watt measures the amount of power required.
- A volt measures the pressure.
- An amp measures the current.
- An ohm measures the resistance.

Alternating current changes direction from positive to negative and then back again, and direct current always flows from positive to negative. Computing systems utilize DC power. Remember the following about power:

- The ratio of amps to voltage can be easily changed in transmission using a transformer.

- AC can be converted to DC with a power converter or power supply.

- Grounding takes excess electricity and sends it to the earth.

Ensure that your rack or data center has sufficient capacity for the devices installed. Certain devices will require different amperage circuits. Circuits must be able to provide power to all devices at peak load. Devices consume more power at startup. Power distribution units are used to split connections from the outlet, and they can provide metering and surge suppression. Redundant power supplies should be connected to different circuits. Uninterruptable power supplies provide power when power from the line is lost. UPS systems also condition power, reducing it when it is high, and supplementing it when it is low, so devices receive consistent power.

Computing devices can be very heavy. Heavy racks should be stabilized so they do not fall. Load racks from the bottom to the top with the heaviest items on the bottom. Lift heavy items with a friend if possible and kneel or squat first before lifting. Protect devices from electrostatic discharge. Wrist straps and mats ground the person and equipment, and antistatic bags prevent the buildup of charge in components.

Chapter Review Questions

1. When running cables between racks, the cables should be:

   A. Run under the floor tiles so that they can be easily accessed and kept cool

   B. Hung directly from the ceiling to reduce the amount of clutter overhead

   C. Run through ducts that are suspended from the ceiling

   D. Wired loosely with the cable hanging to reduce the strain on the cables

2. Which of the following makes it easier to protect data cables from being subjected to electromagnetic interference (EMI) created by power cables?

   A. Letting the cables hang loose

   B. Bundling cables

   C. Color coding

   D. Wiring power and data cables through ducts

3. Of the following, what is the best setup to keep a server room cooled?

   A. An area larger than what is necessary to contain all the racks where equipment is set up to pull cool air from both the front and back of the rack and expel hot air to both the front and back of the rack

   B. An area just large enough to contain all the racks where equipment is set up to pull cool air from the front of the rack and expel hot air to the back of the rack

   C. An area just large enough to contain all the racks where equipment is set up to pull cool air from both the front and back of the rack and expel hot air to both the front and back of the rack

   D. An area larger than what is necessary to contain all the racks where equipment is set up to pull cool air from the front of the rack and expel hot air to the back of the rack

4. An electrical current is sent from the power company to a home or business using alternating current (AC), which is measured in hertz (Hz). What is *hertz* best defined as?

   A. The number of times the current changes direction per second

   B. The ratio of amps to voltage

   C. The power dissipated per second

   D. The resistance in the wire

5. A rack has 20 servers, each consuming 700W. Is this a high- or low-density rack, and why?

   A. This is a low-density rack because it consumes less than 35kW of power.

   B. This is a high-density rack because it consumes more than 10kW of power.

   C. This is a high-density rack because it consumes more than 8kW of power.

   D. This is a low-density rack because it consumes less than 10kW of power.

6. Which of the following best describes an object that provides power to computer equipment just long enough to safely shut down the servers after the regular power goes out?

   A. Power distribution center (PDC)

   B. Automatic transfer system (ATS)

   C. Power distribution unit (PDU)

   D. Uninterruptable power supply (UPS)

7. James and Leo are installing a new server on the racks in the server room at their office. Choose the best installation with regard to safety and temperature.

   A. The racks are loaded placing servers in the uppermost slot first such that cool air is taken in the front and warm air is let out the back. James then moves the racks into position by lifting from the base. The cables coming from the server are then tied up and wired along the edges of the rack.

   B. James and Leo move the racks into position; they then load the servers onto the racks from the lowest available slot to the top of the rack such that cool air is taken in the front and warm air is let out the back. The cables coming from the server are then tied up and wired along the edges of the rack.

   C. James and Leo move the racks into position and then load the servers onto the racks such that air is taken in from both the front and the back and air is let out through both the front and back. The cables coming from the server are then tied up and wired along the edges of the rack.

   D. James and Leo move the racks into position; they then load the servers onto the racks from the lowest available slot to the top of the rack such that cool air is taken in the front and warm air is let out the back. The cables are left untangled and unbound.

Chapter Review Answers

1. **C** is correct. Cables should run through ducts suspended from the ceiling.
   A, **B**, and **D** are incorrect. **A** is incorrect because power is typically distributed through the floor, and power cables can cause electromagnetic interference in data cables. **B** is incorrect because hanging cables directly from the ceiling will put strain on the portions of the cables that hang down. **D** is incorrect because loose cabling will result in a messy bunch of cables that will interfere with airflow, be harder to identify, and possibly come into contact with power cables or other sources of interference.

2. **B** is correct. Bundling cables makes it easier to keep cables away from devices that can produce EMI.
   A, **C**, and **D** are incorrect. **A** is incorrect because loose cables will result in a messy bunch of cables that will interfere with airflow, be harder to identify, and possibly come into contact with power cables or other sources of interference. **C** is incorrect. Color coding will make it easier to identify the cables and their purpose but will not prevent EMI. **D** is incorrect because this would place power and data cables in close proximity.

3. **D** is correct. Larger areas can handle short-term changes in temperature more effectively than small areas, and racks that pull air and expel air from the same direction will not mix hot and cool air in intake areas.

   A, **B**, and **C** are incorrect. **A** and **C** are incorrect because hot air should only be expelled from one side of the rack. **B** is incorrect because more space will allow for greater tolerance in temperature changes.

4. **A** is correct. Hertz is the number of times the current changes direction per second.

   B, **C**, and **D** are incorrect. **B** is incorrect because the ratio of amps to voltage is not defined as a specific term. **C** is incorrect because the power dissipated per second would most likely be measured in the heat produced using a metric such as BTU. **D** is incorrect because resistance is measured by ohms.

5. **C** is correct. High-density racks from a power perspective are those that consume more than 8 kilowatts (kW) of power.

   A, **B**, and **D** are incorrect because high-density racks are those that use more than 8 kW.

6. **D** is correct. Uninterruptable power supplies (UPSs) are used to provide power to computing equipment if the power to the facility or location is lost or interrupted.

   A, **B**, and **C** are incorrect. **A** is incorrect because a PDC does not provide power to equipment when the facility loses power. **B** is incorrect because ATS units are used to switch power between circuits if one circuit fails. **C** is incorrect because power distribution units (PDUs) are used to split connections from the outlet and they can provide metering and surge suppression.

7. **B** is correct. The rack should be loaded from bottom to top to avoid tipping the rack over. Each device should pull cool air from the same direction so that the hot air from one device is not pulled into the intake of another device. Cable management will prevent cable snags, result in better airflow, and help prevent cable failures due to EMI.

   A, **C**, and **D** are incorrect. **A** is incorrect because the servers should be loaded from bottom to top, not top to bottom. **C** is incorrect because air should be taken from only the front or back. **D** is incorrect because the cables are not managed in this solution.

CHAPTER 11

Advanced Topics

In this chapter, you will learn how to
- Determine strategies for data migration
- Select technologies and strategies to meet compliance requirements
- Store more data on the same hardware with deduplication and compression

This chapter introduces more advanced topics in storage management, including data migration, compliance, and deduplication and compression. Storage administrators often are tasked with improving the availability and speed of access to systems. Previous chapters explored making copies of data for business continuity (Chapter 7) and remote replication (Chapter 9), but this chapter looks at migrating data within a storage array to achieve high performance.

Another challenge for storage administrators is compliance with regulatory requirements and litigation holds. Some data, such as financial data, must be retained for a specified amount of time to adhere with regulatory requirements. Similarly, data related to ongoing litigation must be retained in case it is required for trial. Removing data for either of these reasons can result in fines, loss of customer reputation, or loss of a legal case. Therefore, it is important to be able to implement strategies to comply with these regulations and litigation holds on storage arrays and in other places where organizational data is stored.

Lastly, as data grows, storage administrators are looking for ways to store more data using the same hardware. Deduplication and compression technologies offer excellent options for conserving space without sacrificing availability.

Information Lifecycle Management

Data migration is a form of storage management where data of varying formats is transferred between hosts or storage systems. Data migration is a major driver for advanced storage system adoption. Not only is data often stored in heterogeneous technologies and applications, but it may take on a variety of forms and characteristics, all with differing implications for storage, access, availability, and recovery. Data migration can be array, host, or appliance based.

In *array-based data migration*, software on the storage array, built either into the array software or as an add-on feature, is used to manage migration, including setting up migration pairs, scheduling, and synchronization.

In *host-based data migration*, software residing on the device receiving the storage or managing the storage, known as a *host*, is used to manage the movement of data from one location to another.

In *appliance-based data migration*, stand-alone network appliances migrate files and volumes, interfacing with storage systems and providing a separate interface for managing the replication.

Data migration should be undertaken with a great deal of planning and care. Here are just a few considerations when migrating data:

- **Duration of the migration task**   Depending on how much data must be migrated, data migration tasks can take a relatively short or long time. Longer migrations could impact the productivity of users of the system or, in worse cases, the availability of the system or systems that reside on the storage being migrated.

- **Contingency plans should outages or other problems occur**   If data migrations cause a loss in availability, storage administrators should have a plan of action for restoring key systems quickly to meet recovery time objectives (RTOs).

- **Compatibility issues**   Migrating data between heterogeneous systems may require devices in between to manage the replication. This is a common use for migration applications. Devices from different vendors may not support replication standards or may implement standards in such a way that makes replication, or the form of replication desired, difficult or impossible. Storage administrators must be aware of the requirements for replication in such systems and plan for how to handle compatibility issues.

- **Data integrity**   The value of migrated information diminishes rapidly if the information migrated changes in the process. Sometimes metadata (data about data), such as creation date, author, and other information, is changed when information is moved. This can often be accepted as part of the migration process. However, information and the bits and bytes that make up files containing information should not be modified in transit. When information is consistent, its integrity is intact, but if changes occur, integrity is lost.

EXAM TIP   File hashing uses a mathematical formula to generate a value that uniquely represents a file. Hashing is used to verify data integrity. The calculated hash value generated prior to a migration can be compared to the hash value generated using the same hashing algorithm on the data once it has been migrated. If the hash values match, the integrity of the data can be assumed to be intact. However, if the hash differs, the data should be retransmitted and compared again. Popular algorithms used for this purpose include Message Digest 5 (MD5) and Secure Hash Algorithm (SHA).

- **Lost or missing data**   Similar to data integrity is data loss. Loss of data occurs when data on the source that is scheduled for migration is not present on the destination following a data migration. This can occur when a migration process skips files because of corruption, network contention, or other error conditions, and it is often logged in a migration log file that can be reviewed by administrators. Some storage administrators may find it helpful to set up alerts to notify them of files that are skipped in migration schedules.

Value of Data Based on Frequency of Access

Data that is accessed frequently is often viewed as more valuable than data that is accessed infrequently because the loss of availability to such data would have a greater impact on business productivity. Because of this, such data is often given more protection against loss or manipulation, and it is often placed on storage with higher availability, including additional redundancies and faster access speed.

HSM

Hierarchical storage management (HSM) presents files and directories as a composite object with a single integrated file interface. HSM provides a mechanism for the automated movement of files or records from primary storage to more cost-effective, slower, secondary storage without changing the way they are represented to end users of the storage system. The term gets its name from the use of different storage tiers or levels that reside in a hierarchy organized by storage speed. The data is organized by moving it from one storage tier to another. This process of moving files one medium to another storage medium is called *migration*.

Real-time monitoring and network policies are used to determine how data and storage are migrated in HSM. Based on the criteria established in the file system policies, HSM determines where in the tier the hierarchy files should be located. HSM aims at archiving files in a more effective way so that the user is not required to decide when files need to be archived. Users can store all files in the same place, but the HSM determines which files should be placed on fast storage and which should be placed on slower storage or archived to offline or nearline storage.

The most common use of HSM is in distributed systems and not in stand-alone systems. Types of storage devices used in HSM include RAID arrays, storage arrays, disks, flash media, optical drives, and tapes.

The only task that managers need to do is configure the system with thresholds for each tier so that the system can measure file access and make choices as to where each file should be stored. These rules automatically back up files if the defined thresholds are met. And once this configuration is done, all system backup/archiving is done without user interruption.

 EXAM TIP   It is best to take a baseline of the system first to understand what normal activity looks like before configuring HSM rules.

One real-time example of a hierarchical storage management system is streaming video sites. Short video previews, along with the most often accessed videos, may be loaded to high-speed disks. When a user selects a video that is present on a slower disk, the preview is loaded from high-speed disks, while the remainder of the video is loaded from a slower disk at short delay. This improves the performance of the system and reduces the cost of storage because archived data is stored on cheaper disks and high speed is provided with only a few high-speed disks.

Storage Tiers

As discussed previously, HSM is storing information in various hierarchies of devices to reduce the cost of storage. This is achieved by using tiered storage. Different types of data are stored in different storage devices, and storage managers who know the importance of the data and the credibility of the devices decide on this differentiation. Storage tiers are typically found in larger organizations, but as the costs of storage tiers go down, more smaller organizations are taking advantage of storage tiers in managing data.

Various tiers of storage are managed by every organization, and the degree of tiering depends on various factors. In the earlier days, only two-tiered storage was in practice because of a lack of automated tools to manage data. With the advent of technology, multitiered storage is now available for storage managers.

Tier 0 and tier 1 usually hold sensitive information that needs to be retrieved in a short amount of time. All important business files that users will access now and then are stored in tier 0 and tier 1. Other files that are not often needed but would be used anytime are stored in tiers 2 and 3, while old information used only for analysis or not important reasons is stored in tier 4, as shown in Figure 11-1.

 EXAM TIP The tiers are organized with tier 0 at the top containing the data that has the highest availability need.

Figure 11-1
Tiers

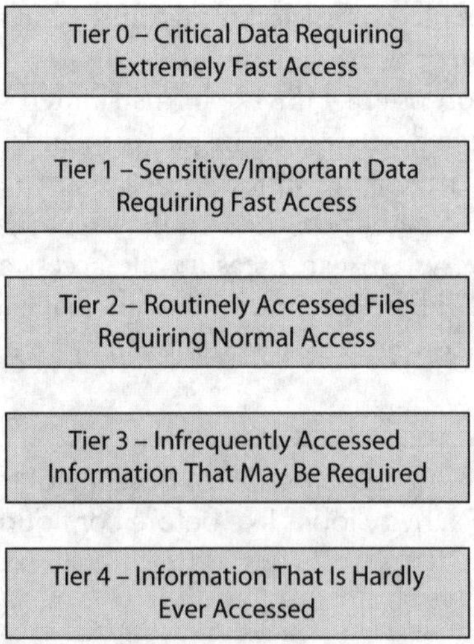

Tier 0 – Critical Data Requiring Extremely Fast Access

Tier 1 – Sensitive/Important Data Requiring Fast Access

Tier 2 – Routinely Accessed Files Requiring Normal Access

Tier 3 – Infrequently Accessed Information That May Be Required

Tier 4 – Information That Is Hardly Ever Accessed

Manual Storage Tiering

Manual storage tiering, or passive storage tiering, refers to the process of collecting performance information on a set of drives and then manually placing the data on different drives based on the performance requirement for the data. The process is labor intensive and does not dynamically adjust as the load on the application increases or decreases over time. Manual storage tiering is passive, where data is placed on one tier based on its importance and the data remains in the same tier all through its lifecycle until being deleted.

 EXAM TIP   Storage administrators can choose what file types should be migrated. For example, a storage administrator may decide that executable files need not be migrated along with many other file types because business rules define a minimum load time for applications.

Automated Storage Tiering

Automated storage tiering (AST) refers to the storage software management feature that dynamically moves information between different disk types, such as Serial Attached SCSI (SAS) to Serial Advanced Technology Attachment (SATA), and between Redundant Array of Independent Disks (RAID) levels, such as RAID 10 consisting of striped mirror sets or RAID 5 consisting of striping with parity. The storage types are organized based on their speed and given a tier number. Active storage automatically moves data to less expensive tiers, thereby freeing higher tiers for relevant data. This is done so that space, performance, and cost requirements are met.

RAID Levels

Remember RAID levels back in Chapter 1? If not, here is a quick refresher. RAID 0 is a stripe set. Data is split between two disks with no fault tolerance. This results in the fastest speed, but a loss of any disk means the loss of all data. RAID 1 is a mirror set consisting of at least two drives, where each drive contains identical information. Either drive in the mirror can be lost without any loss of data. RAID 5 uses striping along with parity information. The parity information can be used to rebuild the data from any single disk in the array if it is lost. RAID 5 has fast performance but not as fast as striping, but it can handle the loss of a disk. Parity rebuilds reduce the performance of the array. RAID 6 is like RAID 5, but with more parity information calculated to prevent data loss even when two disks are lost in the array. RAID 10 requires an even number of disks and a minimum of four disks. The disks are paired off, and a mirror is created for each pair. These mirrors are then striped together. RAID 10 has better performance than RAID 5, and it can support the loss of half the disks before data loss occurs as long as each lost disk is from a different mirror set. RAID 50 is two RAID 5 arrays mirrored. If you need more detail on RAID sets, reread Chapter 1.

AST makes use of policies that are set up by storage administrators. For example, a data storage manager can assign data that is not used frequently to slower, less expensive universal serial bus (USB) SATA storage, as well as allow it to be automatically moved to higher-performing locally attached Small Computer System Interface (SCSI) or solid-state drives (SSDs) when it becomes more active. The converse of this situation also holds true.

Compliance

Regulations specify how certain data such as personally identifiable information (PII), electronic personal health information (ePHI), and financial records must be stored and protected. Once an organization determines which regulations it must comply with, storage and other technology must be implemented to satisfy the requirements of these regulations. Compliance requirements usually contain security and retention specifications. Security was discussed in Chapter 8, but retention is discussed here.

Retention Policy

An organization's retention policy is an important part of storage management because it defines how long information should be stored and maintained in the system until it is ultimately deleted or destroyed. Despite the desire of most organizations to save data, data should have an expected life span that ends with deletion or destruction. With the continual increase of digital information, it is essential for organizations to have a proper retention policy to properly store, organize, and manage organizational data. Otherwise, the organization will be overwhelmed with data, making it harder to search for the data that is needed and more costly to store and manage the data. It can also create additional risks for data breaches or e-discovery because there is more potential data to be lost or collected in a legal case.

The most common retention policy in use now is deleting documents and files after disuse, which means deleting files that are a certain year old and that are not used for certain period of time. This would ensure that frequently used files are not deleted even though they are old and ensure that never used files are deleted even though they are not old.

In planning a retention policy, organizations must consider the value of data over time and the type of data they are storing. Some data may need to be retained for a specified interval in regulations. Such legal requirements define proper retention policies for certain data types such as financial documents, personal information, hazardous chemical, or safety information.

The major benefits of retention policies include reduced costs of managing data, better organization, faster retrieval of important information, and lower cost and burden to produce data relevant to litigation holds.

Retention policies reduce the costs of managing data. Without regular removal, organizational data will grow exponentially and make it costly and difficult to store and maintain, resulting in additional hardware, maintenance, backup, and security for data that may no longer be providing value for the organization.

Retention policies result in better organization and faster retrieval of important information. When unnecessary information is pruned from storage systems, relevant data can more easily be found and retrieved. This is especially true when HSM or other tiering technologies are used because it allows for a greater likelihood that relevant data will reside on faster tiers since unnecessary data that could potentially consume faster tier storage has been removed from the system entirely.

Retention policies result in a lower cost and burden to produce data relevant to litigation holds. Litigation holds operate on data that has not been removed already. When lawsuits require any evidence in the form of electronic information, this should be easily fetched and displayed to the concerned authorities. Having large chunks of data would increase of time and efforts in fetching data from the system. Also, in some cases, the most important files may be deleted, and no further legal action can be carried forward without the availability of data. In such cases, retention policies would serve the organization by defining what documents may be deleted and when they should be deleted. Also, deleting information from the system would sometimes help during legal cases. Some information present in the system may serve as evidence during the trial, which may turn the case against the organization itself. Therefore, retention policies would ensure that unwanted data is not stored in the system anymore and ensure that information that is to be used in a legal case is not deleted.

It is important for system administrators and storage managers to classify data based on the information it contains. For example, a document might be classified as a contract, HR file, or tax document, to name a few. The organization may have policies for each of these data types that would define how long the document should persist in storage and whether the document should be archived at a point in time to secondary storage.

Archiving and Purging

The data present in the organizations is increasing every day, which increases the cost to manage data. Additional storage can be implemented, or data can be archived or purged. Purging is the concept of deleting obsolete data from the database if that the data is not important to the organization. Data is deleted based on age, type, and importance.

When the data is archived, it is moved from primary storage to a secondary storage device such as a tape or an offline disk. The data is stored in backup tables so that the metadata and structure of the original data is still preserved so that it can be reintegrated into the data set if necessary at a later time.

Preservation and Litigation Holds

Litigation holds, sometimes known as *legal holds*, are exceptions to an organization's normal data purging activities. Litigation holds specify that data potentially relevant to ongoing or expected litigation be preserved. The reason for this exception is to prevent organizations from deleting incriminating or damaging files from their storage that could be used against them in court, and organizations and employees who do not comply with litigation holds could face spoliation of evidence charges that can result in fines or jail time. Spoliation is intentionally deleting evidence related to litigation.

> **EXAM TIP** An organization's legal counsel (your attorney) will send a notification to hold data related to certain key terms. Storage administrators must then set aside media that would normally be recycled, overwritten, or destroyed such as backup tapes, e-mail archives, and changes or deletions to files on network shares.

Through a process known as *culling*, files related to the litigation can be copied to a litigation repository so that they preserved for discovery in the litigation. Discovery is the process in a legal case where each party obtains evidence from the opposing party. An organization may have many different litigation holds and could manage multiple repositories to hold such information. There are automated tools that can actively scan data, such as e-mail, instant messages, and data repositories, to copy out data when changes are made or new data is added. For example, the popular e-mail program Microsoft Exchange has litigation hold features built in to track changes made to mailboxes, allow for the export of the mailboxes, and prevent deletion of messages from a mailbox.

The most important consideration for an organization in deleting data is to make sure that no important legal document is deleted from the system. Also, there are legal requirements on how long data should be stored in the system. The documents such as agreements with customers, management policies, structural documents, and so on should be stored somewhere in the system and should be restored as and when needed. Hence, organizations should ensure that such data is stored in the primary database or increase the speed of retrieving such data from archival storage. Litigation hold or preservation order is nothing but the instruction issued to the members of the organization to preserve all records and documents that are of importance to an anticipated lawsuit from being destroyed or modified. The data should be easily accessible even though it is stored in archival storage. To hold data properly for litigation, it is essential to have a sound retention policy in the organization. It is the responsibility of storage managers or system administrators to ensure that such data is properly preserved when a litigation hold is issued.

Advanced Storage Methods

In addition to the storage methods discussed so far, including file and block storage, organizations can use content-addressable storage (CAS) or object-oriented storage (OOS) for specific data needs.

Content-Addressable Storage

Content-addressable storage is a mechanism through which information that does not change often is provided a name that indicates its storage location. Files in CAS are given a retention period that defines how long the files will exist in storage. Once the file is created, it cannot be deleted or changed until its retention period expires. CAS allows for fast access to data because storage systems do not need to query a file table to identify the place on disk where the blocks making up the file exist.

Object-Oriented Storage

Object-oriented storage stores data in the form of objects rather than files or blocks. Every object includes the original data, some amount of metadata, and a unique identifier. This type of storage can be implemented at multiple levels such as device, system, and interface levels.

The retrieval of data in OOS is simple. The operating system reads the unique identifier and the metadata that is stored along with the data and fetches the same from the storage. OOS is not well suited to data that is dynamic, but OOS is highly advantageous when it comes to distributed data such as cloud operations.

Deduplication and Compression

Deduplication and compression are the techniques that can be used to store more data on the same hardware by storing only one copy of a file or portion of a file and replacing all duplicates with pointers. However, this comes with the cost of high complexity in implementing the techniques such that the performance of the system does not drop but storage space is enhanced.

Deduplication is the technique by which storage space can be reduced by eliminating redundant data that is present in the system. The redundant data is replaced with references to original data, which are called *pointers*. For example, on a mail server, deduplication would hold a single copy of messages or attachments in the database. The recipients' mailbox would have a reference pointer to the database copy. When the same message or the same attachment is sent to multiple users, only one copy is stored in the database, and mailboxes all point back to the same file.

Deduplication Levels

Deduplication can be performed by checking for duplicate files, called *file-level deduplication*, or by looking for duplicate blocks that make up files, called *block-level deduplication*.

File-Level Deduplication

File-level deduplication is used with backup and archiving solutions to store only one copy of a file. Duplicate files are identified by creating and comparing a hash of files on the system with new files that are added. If a file with a duplicate hash value is added, a pointer or stub is created that points back to the file already on the disk, and the new file is not copied over. File-level deduplication is also called *single-instance storage* (SIS).

 EXAM TIP When used in backup solutions, once a file has been backed up, it will not be copied again unless it is changed. This dramatically reduces the amount of storage necessary for ongoing backups.

Block-Level Deduplication

Block-level deduplication compares the blocks that make up a file to blocks that already exist on the storage system. Two files may be different, but they may have portions of data that are the same. If identical data is comprised within a block, the system will identify the identical blocks and store only one of them. Block-level deduplication, sometimes called *subfile deduplication*, since it operates at a level beneath the file, can result in greater disk savings than file-level deduplication.

To speed up the process of hashing all the blocks, block-level deduplication stores the unique hash of each block in a database. When new files are created or copied to the storage, the system creates hashes of the blocks making up those files and queries the database to see whether they already exist. Blocks are stored on the system if they are not already in the database, and their hash values are added to the database. If a duplicate is found, a pointer to the original file is created instead.

Inline and Postprocess Deduplication

There are two variations in performing deduplication, and they are inline and postprocess deduplication. *Inline deduplication* is the process by which duplication of data is prevented immediately as the data enters the storage system. When data enters the storage device, the hash calculations analyze for any duplicate data. If duplicates are found, inline deduplication does not store the data, but instead adds a reference to the original data. The advantage of inline deduplication is the prevention of data duplication at the creation of data itself, which eliminates the need for more storage space. However, inline deduplication comes at a cost of lower performance of systems in storing data because of hash calculations and redundancy analysis.

Postprocess deduplication performs a redundancy analysis once the data is stored in the system. Since the system waits for new data to be stored before calculating hash functions and analyzing for redundancy, there is little drop in performance of the system with the use of postprocess deduplication. However, the disadvantage of postprocess deduplication is the need for more storage space in order to store duplicate data until it is analyzed for duplicates.

Source and Target Deduplication

Data deduplication can also be classified based on where the process occurs, either at the place where data is created or at the place where it is stored. Depending on the location of the process, the deduplication process is classified as either source deduplication or target deduplication.

Source deduplication is performed at the source of the data (that is, where the data is originally created), and target deduplication is performed at the place where the data is stored. Most often, source deduplication is performed as the system periodically checks the file systems for duplicate hashes when new data is created. When the hashes of new data created match with the existing hashes, the new data is removed and replaced with the pointer to the original data.

Deduplication Software and Appliances

Many leading storage device manufacturers have come out with strategies and software for performing deduplication. When looking for a deduplication system, consider these requirements. The software and appliances should provide required deduplication functionality without affecting the performance of the system. The software should increase the speed of backups and reduce the amount of bandwidth needed. Also, the software should save both time and money in implementing the features. An organization's requirements will determine which software would be suitable for its business needs.

Performance and Capacity Implications

The deduplication process increases the performance of system reads by a greater percentage than if deduplication is not in use. It also increases the storage capacity of the systems. The files can now be stored in a reduced storage space. Also, the deduplication technique helps in reducing the number of bytes transferred between the source and the destination. This significantly reduces the bandwidth that is required. However, the deduplication process does come with a performance impact to analyze files, so this must also be considered when deploying a solution.

Reduction Ratios for Data Types

Any new technology is considered effective only when the numbers show the benefits. The effectiveness of the deduplication technique discussed previously can be expressed in the form of a reduction ratio that is the ratio of protected data that can be stored to the actual capacity of the system. For example, a 20:1 reduction ratio means that 20 times the amount of data can be stored and protected than the actual data storage capacity of the system. In real time, this means that when there is a 1TB system, deduplication makes it possible to protect up to 20TB data. To calculate the reduction ratio, create a fraction with the total amount of data stored on top and the amount of deduplicated data on the bottom and then reduce the fraction. For example, if 500GB of data is deduped to 125GB, you would create a fraction that looks like this:

500/125

This fraction turns into 4/1 when reduced. You would represent this as 4:1.

Many files that share similar portions of data, such as groups of files based on the same template, multiple versions of files, or backups of the same data, can see the highest reduction ratios, while disparate data sets will see less of a reduction.

Chapter Summary

This chapter provided an overview of more advanced topics in storage management, including data migration, compliance, deduplication, and compression.

Data Migration

- Data migration is the transfer of data consisting of files or even file systems from one system to another. Data migration is implemented in three different locations:
  - Array-based data migration uses software on the storage device to manage the migration.

- Host-based data migration uses software on the device receiving the storage to manage the data migration.
- Appliance-based data migration uses a device that is neither the storage device nor the host that is accessing the storage. The appliance is outside the transfer between devices, but it manages the data migration.
- Companies generally assign a higher value to data that is accessed more frequently because the loss of availability to this data would result in greater cost to the organization. This business logic is used to make decisions on how to best store data, such as with hierarchical storage management. HSM can move files to faster or slower media based on the frequency of access. This helps reduce the costs of storing data and results in higher performance of the data used most often.
- Media is categorized by its speed in tiers. Tier 0 is the fastest media, and lower tiers are progressively slower. Tier 0 might be data that is stored in SSD or cache, while tier 4 may be data archived to tape. The process can be manual or automatic.

Compliance

- Storage administrations must adhere to regulations that specify how certain types of data, such as personal identifiable information, financial information, or health information, must be handled.
- A retention policy defines how long information should be stored and maintained in the system until it is ultimately deleted or destroyed.
- The classification of data helps storage administrators apply the correct business logic and compliance requirements to the data.
- Archiving and purging can reduce the amount of data that is maintained in active storage.
- Litigation may require some data to be preserved past its normal archival or purging period because it may be relevant in an expected or ongoing legal case. This data must be protected against deletion.

Advanced Storage Methods

- Content-addressable storage (CAS) is a mechanism through which information that does not change often is provided a name that indicates its storage location.
- Object-oriented storage (OOS) stores data in the form of objects rather than files or blocks. Every object includes the original data, some amount of metadata, and a unique identifier. This type of storage can be implemented at multiple levels such as the device, system, and interface levels.

Deduplication and Compression

- Deduplication removes identical data from a storage system. Only one copy of duplicate data is stored on the system, and additional copies are only pointers back to the first copy.

- File-level deduplication looks for identical files, while block-level deduplication looks for identical blocks within files.

- Inline deduplication performs the deduplication when it is received by the storage system and before data is written to disk. This option requires the least amount of storage space but can impact performance.

- Postprocess deduplication writes data to disk and then deduplicates it later when resources are available. This process requires additional storage for the data that has not been deduplicated, but it has a lower impact on performance.

- Deduplication can be performed on the storage array, managed by the host, or managed by a separate appliance.

Chapter Review Questions

1. In host-based data migration, what is the host?

   A. The physical device receiving the storage

   B. The software on the device sending information to be stored

   C. The device managing the storage

   D. A network software used to transfer data between devices

2. Longer migrations could cause which of the following? (Choose the best answer.)

   A. A decrease in the productivity of users and a decrease in the availability of the systems that reside on the storage being migrated

   B. An increase in available space on the receiving device

   C. A more effective storage of data and a more thorough analysis of the data being migrated

   D. A decrease in the availability of the systems that reside on the storage that is not being migrated

3. Appliance-based data migration specifically refers to which of the following?

   A. A data migration in which software on the array is used to manage migration, including setting up migration pairs, scheduling, and synchronization

   B. A data migration in which stand-alone network appliances migrate files and volumes, interfacing with storage systems and providing a separate interface for managing the replication

   C. A data migration in which a host is used to manage the movement of data from one location to another

   D. A data migration in which data of varying formats is transferred between hosts or storage systems

4. Tom is organizing a data system and realizes that certain pieces of data are not accessed as regularly. What should Tom use in order to save money and increase productivity?

   A. Remove the infrequently accessed files from the system and transfer all the remaining data to a larger hard drive.

   B. Use personally identifiable information to redistribute itself into a more easily accessible data structure.

   C. Upgrade the entire system to a solid-state drive to speed up access for all data on the system.

   D. Use hierarchical storage management to automatically move files from primary storage to more cost-effective, slower, secondary storage without changing the way they are represented to end users.

5. What is the most common retention policy in use now?

   A. Deleting files that are of a certain age that have not been used recently

   B. Maintaining all files ever used but transferring older files to a secure secondary file system

   C. Deleting files that are of a certain age, regardless of the frequency of their use

   D. Maintaining all files ever used but transferring files that have remained unused for a certain length of time to a secure secondary file system

6. Inline deduplication refers to:

   A. A redundancy analysis performed once the data is stored in the system

   B. The removal of duplicates within a data set before it is entered into the data system

   C. The process by which the duplication of data is prevented immediately as the data enters the storage system

   D. The process that cannot impact performance that prevents identical data from entering a storage system

7. In addition to increasing the performance of the system and increasing the storage capacity of the systems, deduplication:

   A. Creates a hierarchical storage management system

   B. Helps reduce the number of bytes transferred between the source and destination

   C. Removes data with similar, but not identical, information from a system

   D. Ensures that at least two versions of a file are always present on a system

Chapter Review Answers

1. **A** is the correct answer. The device receiving the storage is known as a host. **B**, **C**, and **D** are incorrect. **B** is incorrect because the software sending the information is an application. **C** is incorrect because the device managing the storage could be external to the one providing or receiving the storage. **D** is incorrect because a host is a machine, not software.

2. **A** is the correct answer. Longer migrations could impact the productivity of users of the system or, in worse cases, the availability of the system or systems that reside on the storage being migrated. **B**, **C**, and **D** are incorrect. **B** is incorrect because migrations, long or short, would have the same impact on available disk space. **C** is incorrect because longer migrations are no more effective than shorter ones. **D** is incorrect because the availability of systems being migrated would be impacted first. Other systems may be impacted, but not as greatly as the ones being migrated.

3. **B** is the correct answer. In appliance-based data migration, stand-alone network appliances migrate files and volumes, interfacing with storage systems and providing a separate interface for managing the replication. **A**, **C**, and **D** are incorrect. **A** is incorrect because software on the array that manages the migration is array-based migration. **C** is incorrect because this depicts host-based migration. **D** is incorrect because the answer simply describes migration in general.

4. **D** is the correct answer. Having a cheaper, slower secondary storage for less commonly used items allows the size of the primary storage volume to be smaller, thereby allowing for a decrease in costs for the primary storage. Also, keeping fewer items in the primary storage volume increases the overall speed at which items can be accessed and subsequently increases the end user's ability to be productive. **A**, **B**, and **C** are incorrect. **A** is incorrect because removing the infrequently accessed files would make them unavailable. **B** is incorrect because PII is information that cannot be used to redistribute itself. **C** is incorrect because upgrading the entire system to solid state would be overly expensive.

5. **A** is the correct answer. The most common retention policy in use now is deleting documents and files after disuse, which means deleting files that are a certain age and that are not used for a certain period of time. **B**, **C**, and **D** are incorrect. **B** and **D** are incorrect because maintaining all files ever used results in management costs and risks for data that are unnecessary for the business. **C** is incorrect because frequency of use should be a determination of the data value.

6. **C** is the correct answer. Inline deduplication is the process by which duplication of data is prevented immediately as the data enters the storage system.

   A, **B**, and **D** are incorrect. **A** is incorrect because inline deduplication performs the analysis while the data is stored. **B** is incorrect because inline deduplication does not perform the operation before the data is transferred. Instead, it is performed while it is transferred. **D** is incorrect because performance can be impacted.

7. **B** is the correct answer. The deduplication process increases the performance of the system by a greater percentage and increases the storage capacity of the systems. The deduplication technique also helps reduce the number of bytes transferred between the source and destination.

   A, **C**, and **D** are incorrect. **A** is incorrect because deduplication does not create a hierarchy of any sort. **C** is incorrect because deduplication operates on identical pieces of data, not just similarities. If it operated on similarities, some data would be lost. **D** is incorrect because deduplication stores only one version of a file.

CHAPTER 12

Performance and Troubleshooting

In this chapter, you will learn how to
- Optimize performance
- Explain performance metrics and tools
- Correct network malfunctions
- Resolve host connectivity problems
- Troubleshoot backup issues

One of the chief challenges system or network administrators face is the ongoing task of maintaining optimal performance in a changing environment. The purpose of this chapter is to familiarize you with the various metrics, techniques, and strategies used to optimize performance, as well as the methodologies used to troubleshoot network, host, connectivity, and backup issues.

Optimize Performance

The principles and practices of storage optimization are the same whether it's removable media such as portable hard drives, thumb drives, phone storage, or the large pools or arrays of storage that make up a large geographically dispersed storage area network (SAN). At the most basic level, performance optimization depends on factors such as the characteristics of the medium, including access speeds for read-write operations, its size, amount of used or available space, and type (sequential versus direct), as well as the way information is stored, indexed, or categorized.

Previous chapters introduced you to metrics such as recovery point objective (RPO), recovery time objective (RTO), and quality of service (QoS). All three are often understood within the context of recovery and business continuity when in fact achieving their target or best performance levels are tied, in part, to good storage optimization.

Necessary IOPS

One of the most basic metrics used in measuring storage performance is called *input-output operations per second* (IOPS). IOPS is used to measure how much data can be processed over a period of time, and it can be computed with the following formula:

IOPS = 1 / (average latency + average seek time)

For example, if a Serial Attached SCSI (SAS) drive running at 10,000 rpm has an average latency of 2.5 ms and an average seek time of 4.5 ms, you would take 1 / (.0025 + .0045), which gives you 142.857, or 143 IOPS rounded to the nearest integer.

Table 12-1 provides typical IOPS values for devices. These numbers represent more of what you can expect rather than drive maximums listed on most sites.

A caveat should be noted when determining the true IOPS value of a given medium. Many manufacturers state values that are obtainable only in the most controlled or ideal circumstances. This practice is not unlike mileage per gallon (MPG) capabilities that auto manufacturers list when advertising vehicles. For example, Car X is listed with an MPG rating of 35 miles to the gallon on a highway. The weight of the driver, grade of gas, surface or condition of the road, installed options, and weather are just a few of the strictly controlled factors that few drivers, if any, will see on a consistent basis that will meet the target MPG rating. Similarly, true IPOS values will be impacted by the type of medium, access method, data management scheme, and amount of reserved or protected space needed to operate. Consequently, actual IOPS may be much lower than what is stated by the device's manufacturer.

 EXAM TIP You can measure the IOPS of your systems to gain a baseline and then later compare IOPS values to determine whether performance is the same, has improved, or has deteriorated. IOPS can also be used to determine whether the required performance is provided by a system for an application.

You can obtain IOPS metrics using a variety of tools, but one tool I recommend is IOMeter. It is free and available for both Linux and Windows. Figure 12-1 shows IOMeter's dynamo command running on a local hard disk.

Table 12-1 Typical Drive IOPS Values	Drive	Typical IOPS
	SATA drive at 7,200 rpm	75
	SATA drive at 10,000 rpm	125
	SAS drive at 10,000 rpm	150
	SAS drive at 15,000 rpm	200
	SATA-based solid-state drive (SSD)	5,000
	PCI Express–based SSD	12,000
	Fibre Channel (FC)–based SSD	15,000

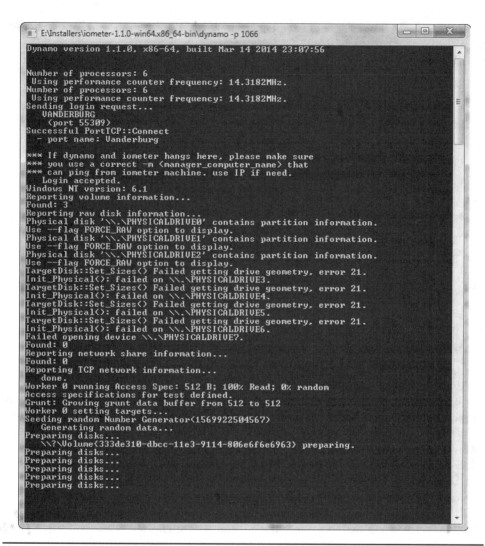

Figure 12-1   IOMeter dynamo command

Random vs. Sequential I/O

Random input/output access is usually used in environments such as databases and other
general-purpose servers. In this access, all disks will be spending equal time servicing the
requests. In simple terms, random access is seeking a random spot instead of retrieving
data one bit after another on the disk. Caching and queuing can help reduce random I/O
by allowing multiple writes to be saved to the cache and then written in a more sequential
manner because the data can be written in a different order than the order it was stored
in cache. The previous section introduced the concept of IOPS for reading and writing.
There are also calculations for sequential and random IOPS.

There are several types of measurements related to IOPS: random read IOPS, random write IOPS, sequential read IOPS, and sequential write IOPS. Interestingly, flash-based media provide the same IOPS for random or sequential I/O, so these differentiations are used only for hard disk drives (HDDs).

- **Random read IOPS**   Refers to the average number of I/O read operations a device can perform per second when the data is scattered randomly around the disk
- **Random write IOPS**   Refers to the average number of I/O write operations a device can perform per second when the data is scattered randomly around the disk
- **Sequential read IOPS**   Refers to the average number of I/O read operations a device can perform per second when the data is located in contiguous locations on the disk
- **Sequential write IOPS**   Refers to the average number of I/O write operations a device can perform per second when the data is located in contiguous locations on the disk

RAID Performance

Storage professionals are often called on to create groups of disks for data storage. Grouping disks together allows for the creation of a larger logical drive, and disks in the group can be used to protect against the failure of one or more disks. Most grouping is performed by creating a Redundant Array of Independent Disks (RAID). RAID performance is contingent upon the type of RAID used, the size of the disks, and the number of disks in the RAID group.

RAID Type and Size

Several RAID specifications—called RAID *levels*—have been made. These levels define how multiple disks can be used together to provide increased storage space, reliability, speed, or some combination of the three. Although not covered here, RAID levels 2–4 were specified but never adopted in the industry; hence, they were never implemented in the field. When a RAID is created, the collection of disks is referred to as a *group*. It is always best to use identical disks when creating a RAID group. However, if different disks are used, the capacity and speed will be limited by the smallest and slowest disk in the group. RAID 0, 1, 5, and 6 are basic RAID groups introduced in the following sections. RAID 10, 0+1, 50, and 51 are nested RAID groups because they are made up of multiple basic RAID groups. Nested RAID groups require more disks than basic RAID groups and are more commonly seen in networked or direct attached storage groups that contain many disks.

RAID 1 is good for protecting against disk failure, but it offers poor performance. It is good for situations where few disks are available but good recoverability is necessary, such as for operating system drives. RAID 5 is good for sequential and random reads and fair for sequential and random writes. It is best used in database management systems (DBMSs) and for file storage. RAID 6 is good for sequential and random reads but poor for sequential and random writes. RAID 10 is good for sequential and random reads and writes. It is best used for online transaction processing (OLTP) and database management system (DBMS) temp drives.

The IOPS calculations introduced earlier can be applied to RAID groups as well as individual drives. Things get a bit more complex when RAID is factored in because the design of the RAID solution will impact whether it is optimized for read or write performance. Remember the calculation for IOPS provided earlier.

IOPS = 1 / (average latency + average seek time)

Read IOPS can be computed simply by multiplying the IOPS for a single drive by the number of drives in the RAID group. However, write IOPS is a bit different. To determine write IOPS for a RAID array, you must factor in the write penalty for different RAID types provided in Table 12-2. The reason RAID 5 has a higher write penalty is that parity must be computed. RAID 6 computes twice as much parity, so it has an even higher write penalty. Write IOPS is computed as follows:

Write IOPS = read IOPS / write penalty

Let's consider some examples. A four-drive RAID 5 using SAS 10k drives would be computed as follows using the IOPS value from Table 12-1:

- 4 drives × 150 IOPS = 600 read IOPS for the RAID group.
- Write IOPS would be 600 / 4 write penalty, or 150 write IOPS.

Now, consider the same four drives but in a RAID 10. Here, the read IOPS would still be 600, but the write IOPS would be 300 (600 IOPS / 2 write penalty).

You can see from these calculations that the type of drives and type of RAID utilized will impact the read or write IOPS available to applications running on logical drives from the RAID group.

Number of Disks

It is sometimes easy to think that more disks, often called *spindles* in this situation, in a RAID group will increase read and write performance, but there is a point where adding more disks can negatively impact write performance because of the number of parity

Table 12-2	RAID Type	Write Penalty
Write Penalties	RAID 1 (Mirror)	2
	RAID 5	4
	RAID 6	6
	RAID 10	2

computations necessary. Rebuild times also increase as more disks are added to the RAID group. Since RAID 10, RAID 1, and RAID 0 do not use parity, parity computations and rebuild times do not apply to them. Rather, it is RAID 5 and RAID 6 where you will need to consider parity and number of drives.

RAID groups that use parity include RAID 5, RAID 6, and the nested RAID groups RAID 50 and RAID 51. In such RAID groups, data is written to a collection of blocks from each disk in the RAID group called a *stripe*. The set of blocks in the stripe for a specific drive is called a *strip*, so a stripe is made up of strips from each drive in the RAID group. One strip in the RAID set is used for parity, while the others are used for data.

 EXAM TIP Strip size or strip depth is the number of blocks in a strip, and stripe size is the number of blocks in the entire stripe. You can compute stripe size by multiplying the strip size by the number of data disks in the RAID group, so a RAID 5 (4+1) with a strip size of 32KB would have a stripe size of 128KB (4 × 32KB).

Parity is a value computed for a bit string by performing an exclusive OR (XOR) operation on two bits. The four possible XOR operations are listed in Table 12-3. When both bits are the same, the XOR is 0, and when they are different, the output is 1. For example, consider a five-disk RAID 5, which can also be referenced as 4+1, with 4 drives for data and 1 for parity. If the bit string in the first stripe is 1010, 0100, 0111, 1000, then you would XOR the first two stripes, 1011 and 0100, to get 1111. You then XOR that with the next strip, so 1111 and 0111 is 1000. Finally, you XOR 1000 with the fourth strip, 1000, producing 0000. 0000 would be written to the fifth strip in the stripe.

The parity bit can be used to replace the data on a lost drive. In the previous example, the first bit string has 1010, 0100, 0111, 1000, and 0000. If disk 3 fails, you do your XOR operations again on the remaining disks to find the value for the missing one, XOR 0000, and the first drive, 1010, is 1010. This with the second drive is 1011 and 0100, equaling 1111. Now you take this and the fourth drive to derive the value for disk 3. 1111 and 1000 is 0111, which was the missing value on disk 3.

Our example computed and used parity to reconstruct the data for the first bit striped to the disks in this RAID 5 set. If you want to store 4MB of data on the RAID group, this data would be striped across four disks, so each disk would get 1MB, which is equivalent to 8 million bits since each byte has 8 bits in it and a megabyte has 1 million bytes in it. This 4MB file results in 8 million parity computations. The time it takes to process those computations and store their results is called the *write penalty*. For RAID 6, two drives are used for parity, so data must be written to both, increasing the write penalty.

Table 12-3	A Value	B Value	XOR of A and B
XOR Table	0	0	0
	0	1	1
	1	0	1
	1	1	0

As the number of disks grows in a RAID group, the number of bits that must be evaluated for a parity computation grows. Rebuilds, likewise, must evaluate more disks to determine which bit to write to the recovered drive. Rebuild times can be significant and can greatly impact the performance of a RAID group. These rebuild times can take several hours to several days depending on the speed of the drives and number of drives in a set.

 EXAM TIP Creating larger and larger RAID 5 groups is not always the answer to increasing performance since larger parity computations and recovery can reduce performance.

Defragmentation

Defragmentation is a common method used to improve the performance of storage. Data and files are spread across disks as they are written, with each bit taking the next available location on the disks. This location is not always contiguous, with the previous bit resulting in more random reads instead of sequential reads as data gets more and more spread around the disk. Ideally, data should be placed on the disk such that the read-write head is positioned above it immediately after the previous bit of data was read from disk. When data is fragmented, the platter must rotate, and the head must be moved to a new location before the next bit of data can be read, which increases latency and access time, ultimately compromising the device's performance. Defragmentation reorganizes the data so that it can be read sequentially to reduce latency and wear and tear on disks because of head and platter activity. For more information on how data is read from a hard drive, access time, and rotational latency, see Chapter 1.

To better understand the value of defragmentation as an optimization tool, think of a file cabinet. When the cabinet is properly organized, all of the folders are alphabetized, and the individual files are alphabetized as well. Suppose each time you retrieved a file within a given folder you replaced that folder at the front or end of the other folders. Over time this practice would result in folders being out of sequence, and files may or may not be in the appropriate folder. Additionally, the file may be in the correct folder but not in alphabetical order. The longer this condition is allowed to persist, the longer it will take you to find the folder and file needed. Defragmentation can be seen as a process where the folders and the files within them are realigned or sorted. Figure 12-2 shows the Windows Disk Defragmenter tool. Red bars show areas of the disk that are fragmented, and blue areas are files that are not fragmented or located on contiguous areas on the disk.

Solid-state storage has a shorter use life when compared to hard drives because of the way it is constructed. Transistors called *floating gates* hold a charge to represent a binary 0 or 1. This value is changed by making the oxide layer surrounding it conductive. However, this can be performed only so many times before it breaks down. Since this change in conductivity happens each time there is a write or erase, the life span of the disk is tracked based on write/erase cycles. The average rating for single-level cell (SLC) SSD and multiple-level cell (MLC) SSD is 100,000 and 10,000 write/erase cycles, respectively.

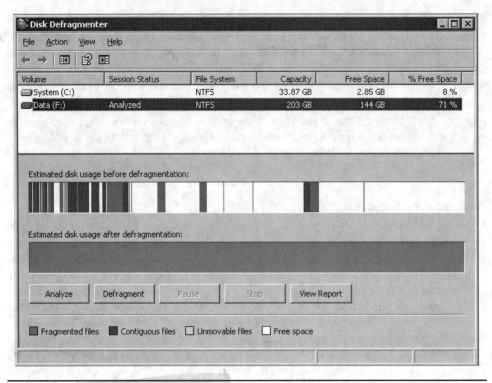

Figure 12-2 Windows Disk Defragmenter

Thus, the performance of SSDs is degraded each time data is accessed or written to it. Defragmenting or defragging SSDs does not result in any appreciable performance in enhancements. Consequently, defragmenting an SSD actually diminishes the life span of the drive by increasing the number of write cycles and results in no benefit.

Impact

Defragging involves the movement and relocation of a lot of data, which can significantly impact the performance of currently running operations and routines. Some defragging applications are dynamic in that they are able to determine the level of drive utilization or activity and adjust its process by slowing down when needed and resuming when it is not competing for I/O cycles. The result is that current processing speeds or performance is not compromised.

As previously mentioned, SSD drives do not benefit from defragging. There is no latency due to seek time because, regardless of where data is located, it takes the same amount of time to write or read data from solid-state technology.

EXAM TIP   Defragging an SSD will shorten the potential life of the device because each write cycle diminishes its performance over time.

Schedules

Most defragmentation operations can be scheduled during times when it will not hinder ongoing business operations and tasks. Additionally, defragmentation schedules can be automated so that storage can be optimized at a specified time and date without user or operator intervention.

Most storage media and defragging utilities are capable of automatic operation without the presence of a user or operator. The process of defragging competes with current I/O execution and may even result in a significant slowdown, so it is common to set up defrag schedules so that these operations do not occur during peak network or system utilization.

Cache

Cache is high-speed memory that can be used to service I/O requests faster than accessing the disk. Cache is referenced and organized by pages. Pages store data as well as a link to the location of the data on disk and a value called a *dirty bit*. The dirty bit is set to on when data is new or changed in cache, and this tells the controller head that the data needs to be flushed to disk.

In a storage environment, recently queried data, along with data that the system expects will be queried next, is stored in read cache, while data that is waiting to be written to the disk is placed in write cache. This allows the disk to function more independently from the interface so that one is not waiting on the other. The interface can load data into cache or read data from cache as it is received, and data can be written to the disk from cache or read into cache when it is optimal.

Read vs. Write Cache

Read and write cache are used to increase the speed at which data is retrieved or stored on an array. Read cache stores data from the disks in an array that the system anticipates will be requested. This speeds up requests for data if the data is resident in cache. Write cache is used to speed up the writing of data to an array, and there are two types of write cache, write-back and write-through cache. These three types of cache are described here:

- **Read ahead** Read-ahead cache retrieves the next few sectors of data following what was requested and places that into cache in anticipation that future requests will reference this data. The read-ahead cache results in the best performance increase with sequential data requests, such as when watching videos, copying large files, or restoring files.

- **Write back** Write-back cache sends an acknowledgment that data has been successfully written to disk once the data has been stored in cache but has not actually made it to disk yet. The data in cache is written to disk when resources are available. Write-back cache results in the best performance because the device is able to accept additional I/O immediately following the write acknowledgment. However, write back is riskier because cache failures or a loss of power to the disk could result in a loss of pending writes that have not been flushed to disk.

- **Write through**   Write-through cache waits to send an acknowledgment until a pending write has been flushed to disk. Although write-through cache is slower than write backup, it is more reliable.

Figure 12-3 shows the cache properties of a controller in an EMC array. Here, the read and write cache are enabled for both controllers, and the write cache is mirrored.

An array that is used primarily for write traffic should have a large write cache to enhance performance, while one that primarily supports read traffic would benefit from a larger read cache. Storage administrators should understand the type of traffic they will receive and customize cache accordingly. Figure 12-4 shows how the read and write cache is allocated on storage array controllers.

De-staging

De-staging, or flushing, is the process of writing data from cache to disk. This process is usually performed when resources are available or when cache reaches an upper watermark, meaning that it is getting too full. De-staging is configured to start when the cache fills to a predetermined percentage or watermark. Figure 12-5 shows the cache de-staging properties of a Dell storage device. It is set to begin de-staging at 80 percent capacity.

Figure 12-3
Storage array
cache properties

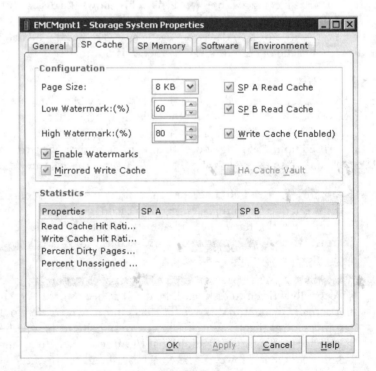

Figure 12-4
Storage array
cache allocation

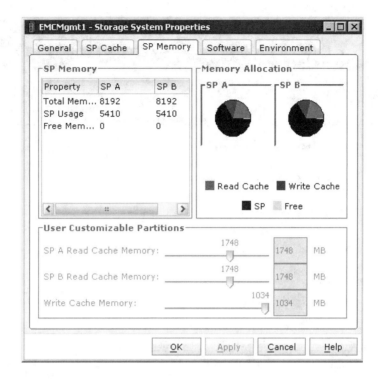

Cache Hit and Miss

When a request is made for data that exists in the cache, it is known as a cache read hit. The storage array immediately services the request by sending the data over its interface without retrieving the data from disk. Cache read hits result in the fastest response time. When requested data does not exist in the cache, it is known as a read miss. It is a failed attempt for data to be retrieved from the cache memory. This results in longer access time because needed data must be fetched from the primary storage on the disk.

You can improve the cache read hit percentage by increasing the size of the read cache or by changing the read-ahead cache from least recently used (LRU) to most recently used (MRU), or vice versa (see Chapter 2 for more on LRU and MRU). As you can see in Figure 12-4, there is only so much cache available, so if you allocate more to read, you are taking it away from the write cache. It is important to evaluate your application needs so that you understand the number of reads and writes you can expect from the system. This will allow you to properly size the read and write cache.

Impact of Replication

Storage replication is the process in which the stored data is copied from one storage array to another. Replication can occur locally over a SAN or local area network (LAN) or to remote locations over a wide area network (WAN). In doing so, the reliability, availability, and overall fault tolerance are greatly enhanced. Replication allows for

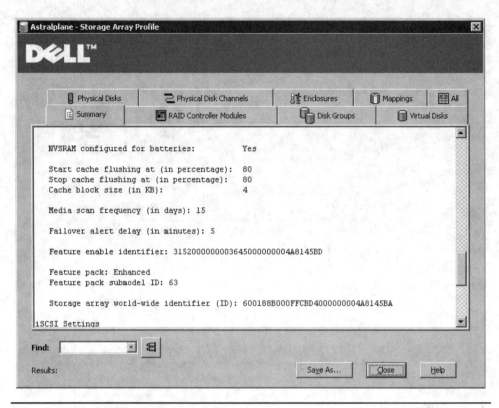

Figure 12-5   Cache de-staging properties

information, resources, software, and hardware to be shared so that they are available to more than one system. The significant benefits of replication include improving reliability and fault tolerance of the system.

Backup operations often use a local replica, called *nearline storage*, and a remote replica. The local replica may contain portions of the backups that are most recent, while more comprehensive backups are kept offsite. Sometimes the nearline and remote backups are identical. The advantage of this method is that restore operations can be completed in much less time than it would take to copy data from a remote backup site. Of course, the main reason for using a remote backup replica in the first place is to provide availability if the initial site goes down. In such cases, the organization would perform operations from the backup site or restore to another site from the remote backup replica.

Point-in-time (PIT) replicas can provide protection against corruption or changes in a system, and they are also used for litigation holds (see Chapter 11). However, this requires the system to keep track of all changes following the PIT replica, which can diminish performance.

Synchronous replication does not finalize transactions or commit data until it has been written to both source and destination. This form of replication is used for both local and remote replication scenarios. The major advantage of synchronous replication is that it ensures all the data remains consistent in both places. On the other hand, this type of replication can slow down the speed of the primary system since the primary system has to wait for acknowledgment from the secondary system before proceeding. If this is causing performance issues, you may need to consider upgrading equipment or switching to an asynchronous replication method.

Some enterprises use a combination of synchronous and asynchronous replication. Systems are often deployed using synchronous replication to another array at the same site, and then this array is replicated asynchronously to a remote site. This provides faster recovery and failover if a single array fails at the site than if asynchronous replication was used alone, while still providing recoverability if the entire site fails. See Chapter 9 for a review of synchronous and asynchronous replication.

The potential impact of several factors should be addressed when considering replication—latency, throughput, concurrency, and synchronization time. The impact these factors will have on a given storage environment is determined by the type of storage network. In a server-to-server or transactional environment, latency and throughput are the primary elements for optimization, while in an environment that uses merge replication, sync time and concurrency are the dominant factors. Overall care should be taken in balancing these factors, regardless of the type of replication deployed.

Latency

Latency is the time it takes to go from source to destination. In other words, it is the travel time, and it can have a significant impact on replication. Electrical impulses and light have a maximum speed. It may seem like light is so fast that latency would not matter, but it can have an impact at greater distances. Light travels at 186,000 miles per second in a vacuum and approximately 100,000 miles per second in fiber-optic cables. Therefore, it would take five milliseconds for light to travel 500 miles, the distance from New York to Cleveland, over fiber-optic cabling. Five milliseconds may not feel like much time for a human, but it can feel like a long time for a computer. Modern processors operate around 3 GHz, which equates to 3 billion cycles per second or 3 million cycles per millisecond, so a processor would go through 15 million cycles while the replica traveled 500 miles. Of course, sending replica data from one place to another is not as simple as dropping it on a wire. Devices forward or route the replica data to its destination along the way, and each of these devices will add latency to the equation.

Throughput

Throughput is a measure of the amount of data that can be processed over a link within a given interval or time period. In replication, the throughput between replica pairs must be sufficient for the data that will be transferred in order to avoid transmission errors, replica failures, or inconsistency between replicas. In some cases, initial replication may need to be performed on a different network or via direct-attached drives if throughput is insufficient. Further changes will then be replicated over the replica link.

Concurrency

Concurrency refers to the number of possible simultaneous replications that can be performed. This can especially be an issue as systems scale. For example, you implement replication between a data store and three remote offices. The offices synchronize with the central data store every five minutes. As the company grows, 15 more offices are added with their own replicas, but they have issues synchronizing because the central store can handle only five connections simultaneously. In such a case, it might make sense to upgrade the replication method to handle more concurrent connections or to create a replication hierarchy where not all sites replicate to the central store, but rather replicate to other hub sites, which then replicate back to the central store.

Synchronization Time

Synchronization time is the time interval it takes for data replication to be complete. Imagine the situation with the distributed system mentioned earlier. This system copies a local replica to each site, and users work from their replica, which is synchronized with the central data store. Imagine this is a product fulfillment system and a user from San Francisco orders a part from the warehouse for a customer and shortly thereafter a user from Boston orders the same part. This could cause a problem when the data is synchronized with the central data store if there is only one part in the warehouse, since both users were working from their local data store. In such cases, it may be necessary to decrease the synchronization time so that data is synchronized more often. It may also necessitate business rules to handle replication conflicts.

Partition Alignment

Partition alignment refers of the starting location of the logical block addressing (LBA) or sector partition. Maintaining partition alignment is essential in maintaining performance. Partitions can become misaligned when the starting location of the partition is not aligned with a stripe unit boundary in the disk partition that is created on the RAID. Data on misaligned partitions ends up being written to multiple stripes on the physical media, requiring additional write steps and additional parity steps. Partition alignment is a problem for SSD drives as well because it results in additional write cycles, decreasing the life span of the SSD.

With the growing use of virtualization, virtual hard disks can also suffer from partition misalignment where a virtual hard disk's sectors are mapped between sectors on the physical media.

If you suspect that your partition is misaligned, compare the I/O requests made with the I/O requests processed. If the processed amount is significantly higher than the requests, you might have a partition alignment problem. You can also look at the offset of the partition using a tool such as sfdisk in Linux. The offset should be divisible by 8 or 16. Here is an example of a partition that is misaligned:

```
sfdisk -uS -l /dev/sda
```

This command executes the sfdisk utility with the -uS and -l switches. The -uS switch reports sectors in blocks, cylinders, and megabytes, while the -l switch lists the partitions of the device. We are performing this command on the /dev/sda partition. Here is the output:

```
Disk /dev/sda: 2088 cylinders, 255 heads, 63 sectors/track
Units = sectors of 512 bytes, counting from 0
Device     Boot    Start    End         #sectors     Id    System
/dev/sda1    *      63       208844      208782       83    Linux
/dev/sda2           208845   16771859    16771732     8e    Linux LVM
```

This command shows that the first partition is misaligned because it is starting at 63. If it started at 64, the partition would be aligned, but this way it is starting one sector too early.

SSDs organize data into blocks and pages instead of tracks and sectors. SSD drives support LBA, so their storage is presented to the system as a series of blocks, and the controller board converts the LBA block address to the corresponding block and page. Partition misalignment must be avoided to minimize unnecessary reads and writes, which will not only result in performance degradation, but also shorten the life of the SSD.

Queue Depth

Queue depth is defined as the total number of pending input and output requests that are present for a volume. When the queue is full, there may be some lag time between the occurrences of server errors being reported by the presenting application. Too many pending I/O requests results in performance degradation. Whenever there is no space for any more requests, the QFULL condition is returned to the system, which means that any new I/O requests cannot be processed. There are several Java or alternative Internet-based sources for monitoring queue depth.

Each LUN will be allocated a section of the queue depth, and the amount of space allocated is dependent on the vendor. For example, some may have a total queue of 8,192 slots but allocate 64 slots for each LUN so the device can support up to 128 LUNs. This is important to know because it is tempting to think that 8,192 slots are available for the queue, but only 64 slots are available per LUN.

Some storage arrays and devices are equipped with Storage I/O Control (SIOC), which dynamically manages the queue depth, allowing for the controller on the storage unit to process commands in a way that is most efficient for it, such as processing data for two I/O requests that are in the same area of the disk. SIOC also throttles devices that try to dominate the queue to the exclusion of other devices, a problem that existed before queues were divided into sections per LUN. However, for the most consistency in performance, queue depths may need to be assigned manually for certain LUNs. For those who do not have SIOC and find queue depth is directly related to performance problems, it may make sense to split the data into multiple LUNs to take advantage of separate queues.

For example, one company had a virtual environment that went back to a single storage array. All their virtual machines ran off two 2TB LUNs that were mapped back to a RAID group on the storage array. They were experiencing performance issues, so we looked at a number of metrics. The queue depth was high for both LUNs. We allocated two new 1TB LUNs and split the machines from one of the 2TB LUNs between these two new LUNs. We then monitored the queue depth and saw a dramatic decrease and increase in performance, so the company allocated two more 1TB LUNs and removed the two original 2TB LUNs.

Storage Device Bandwidth

Storage device bandwidth is defined as the connectivity between the server and the storage device. The goal is to maximize the performance of or movement of data between the servers and storage devices in a given network. In this case, data transfer is enhanced, allowing applications to run at optimal speeds. There are a number of third-party utilities or applications to aid the system administrator in maintaining optimal bandwidth performance. Care must be taken in selecting the tools and strategy for managing storage bandwidth.

A balance must be struck between the increased complexity of applications and the costs of the storage networks they depend upon. This is especially true when multiple storage systems are interconnected. Load balancing is often problematic, as a vast number of geographically dispersed storage resources of different types and ages coexist in a network. Less-than-optimal load balancing will result in overutilization of some storage resources, while others in the network are grossly underutilized. Oftentimes new investments are made in storage to increase overall network performance when in fact better awareness and optimization would have addressed observed network performance issues.

If bandwidth is insufficient, consider adding more network cables and switch links or upgrading cables, NICs, and switches to versions with higher capabilities, such as moving from Gigabit Ethernet to 10 Gigabit Ethernet.

Bus and Loop Bandwidth

Bandwidth is how much data can be transferred during a measured interval such as a second, as in megabits per second. Whether the network is bus or loop, data transfers will utilize bandwidth and storage, and network administrators must be familiar with their application needs to determine whether the network links can provide the required bandwidth.

In previous chapters, we discussed the types of networks, and bus and loop were mentioned as compared to star networks. While bus and loop have predominantly been replaced by star networks, the bus and loop are still common within electrical systems such as circuit boards, and these systems differ from switched systems in the way contention for resources is handled.

A bus is a connection between two points. Typically, controllers or circuits will connect devices and manage the data that flows through the bus. In a parallel bus, traffic flows down multiple lanes in the bus simultaneously, as compared to the serial bus where data flows sequentially. Since a bus connects two points, the connection is dedicated to those points and contention is minimized. However, in the loop, traffic flows in one direction and must pass between multiple nodes in the loop to reach its destination. Each node in the loop receives an equal share of the bandwidth, and performance is predictable and reliable, but there is much overhead as data passes further through the loop than it would in a bus.

Both the bus and the loop are constrained by how much data can be transferred at one time. Storage administrators should be aware of the bandwidth available in system components so that they can understand where systems may be constrained. For example, imagine a storage system that is attached to a network with two 8 Gbps fiber connections. This system is upgraded to twelve 8 Gbps connections to handle additional servers that each issue a significant number of reads and writes (I/O). However, if there are only two 8 Gbps back-end ports for each disk shelf, the system may be constrained by the available back-end bandwidth.

Cable Speeds

Cable speeds can impact performance. Cables are rated for a maximum speed, and they often perform at a rate much lower than their maximum. The applications in use will determine how much bandwidth is necessary. For example, streaming 1080p high-definition video at 24 frames per second might require 25–40 Mbps, and a business application streams a maximum of 10 concurrent videos at a time from storage over the WAN. This would require up to 400 Mbps of WAN bandwidth.

Ensure that the cables in use are adequate for your needs. LAN cables are typically Gigabit Ethernet such as CAT5e, but WAN connections may vary greatly. Table 12-4 compares a variety of WAN connections and their speed.

Disk Throughput vs. Network Bandwidth vs. Cache

One big frustration for storage administrators is the inaccuracy of service requests made by users. The famous "system is slow" is one of my favorites because I have heard it so many times, and it provides almost no direction for the troubleshooter. In cases like these, you will need to investigate each part of the communication stream to determine where the slowness is occurring.

I/O commands start through an application that issues a command to the host bus adapter (HBA). Let's explore a write command. The HBA determines the LUN the I/O

Table 12-4	Name	Type	Speed
WAN Connections and Their Speeds	T1/DS1	Copper	1.544 Mbps
	T3/DS3	Copper	45 Mbps
	E1	Copper	2.048 Mbps
	E3	Copper	34 Mbps
	OC-3	Optical	155 Mbps
	OC-12	Optical	622 Mbps
	OC-48	Optical	2.5 Gbps
	OC-192	Optical	10 Gbps
	Fractional Metro Ethernet	Copper	Up to 1Gbps
	Gigabit Metro Ethernet	Copper	1 Gbps
	10GigE Metro Ethernet	Copper	10 Gbps

write command is destined for and places it into a frame on the storage fabric. The frame travels through the fabric, possibly through one or more switches, and arrives at the storage array controller HBA. The controller receives the command, identifies the RAID group associated with that LUN, mirrors the command to other controllers in the unit, and writes the command to cache. It is up to the storage array to then send the command to the RAID controller, which sends individual commands to each of the disks in the RAID group, computes the parity, and writes the data to each stripe in the RAID group. In most cases, once the command is written to cache, the storage array can send an acknowledgment back through the storage array, over the network, and back to the host, which then sends it to the application. However, if many commands have been received and the disk throughput is not capable of keeping up, the command may have to wait for the cache to be flushed to disk before it can be processed.

As you can see, the process involves a lot of steps, and one or more of those steps could be contributing to the problem. It can be broken down into three states: network bandwidth, cache, and disk. Each of these elements can be measured in IOPS so that you work with the same data point for comparison's sake.

Disk throughput can be measured by evaluating the rotational latency and interface throughput of the disk or storage array. In the case of SSD, rotational latency is not a consideration since SSDs do not have moving parts. Rotational latency is the amount of time it takes to move the platter, the round, flat surface inside an HDD where data is written, to the location of the desired data. Rotational latency is measured in milliseconds (ms). The interface is how the drive connects to the controller in a disk system such as IDE, SATA, and SAS (see Chapter 1 for more details).

Network bandwidth can be measured with different tools such as Cacti, Splunk, or PRTG network monitor, depending on where in the network you are evaluating the bandwidth. Each switch port will display its utilization on a managed switch. Simply connect to the switch's management IP address and select the port you want to see, as shown in Figure 12-6.

A network interface card (NIC) in a computer can also display bandwidth statistics and sent and received packets. This can be useful to determine whether a switch port or NIC is saturated or underperforming. Figure 12-7 shows the statistics of a NIC on a Microsoft Windows client. SNMP and SMI-S–based management tools also offer a way to view statistics from a variety of devices such as switches, storage arrays, and other components.

Lastly, cache can be measured by reviewing the size and utilization of read and write cache along with cache read hits. This information can be obtained from command-line interface (CLI) or management tools provided by your storage vendor.

Embedded Switch Port Speed

In an embedded switch, all functions are performed at the chip level, resulting in increased reliability and overall performance. It is important that the device speed matches that of the cable and port to which it is attached. For example, if a port on the switch is rated or configured for 1 Gbps but the attached cable is rated lower, port errors will occur. These errors will result in the retransmission of the lost data along with the demand being made

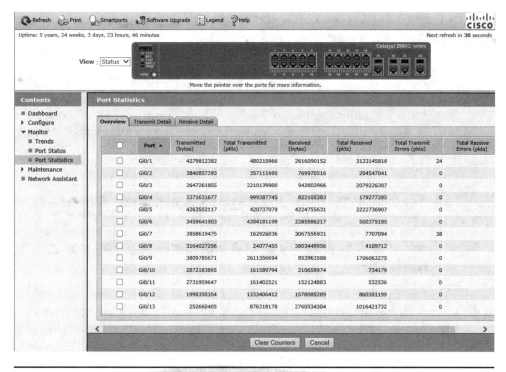

Figure 12-6 Bandwidth metrics from a switch management interface

Figure 12-7
NIC statistics
for Microsoft
Windows client

on the port by current data traffic. The devices, ports, and cables on the other end must also be capable of supporting the same speeds.

Shared vs. Dedicated

It is important to understand the differences between shared and dedicated storage. While shared storage is more economical, its higher-cost alternative, dedicated storage, offers greater reliability, availability, and overall performance. Shared storage is a storage system that is utilized for multiple purposes, resulting in some level of contention for resources. Dedicated storage is used only for a specific system, application, or site.

 NOTE The concept of shared storage is different from network shares. Shared storage refers to systems that are utilized for multiple purposes, while network shares are used to allow concurrent access to files over a file sharing protocol such as Common Internet File System (CIFS) or Network File System (NFS).

Since dedicated storage hosts data for a single application or site, all the space present in the server is allotted to that application or site. With shared storage, sites must contend for storage space and performance because they share the server with other sites. In doing so, storage costs are distributed by many companies. The trade-off is the potential risks associated with the differing policies and applications used by those companies connected to share resources. The sheer volume of traffic by its very nature will result in more errors and potential performance degradation or even outages.

Dedicated storage allows for a higher degree of control of how the storage is configured and used. The risks associated with errors or downtime are minimized because they are fewer in number and are easier to identify and resolve. As always, network administrators must determine where and what applications are best served by shared storage and what applications would justify the increased costs of dedicated storage.

Multipathing for Load Balancing

Load balancing in networking is defined as distributing work among various computer resources, thereby maximizing throughput and minimizing response time. This method also ensures that resources are not overloaded because the workloads are shared among various resources. Multiple components can also be used for load balancing, which would help in increasing the reliability of the system through redundancy.

Options for selecting redundant paths include fixed path, most recently used, and round-robin path. In fixed path, the system always follows the same path for accessing the disk. It goes for an alternative path only when the fixed path is not available. In most recently used, the latest used path is preferred, and when it fails, a backup path is used. In round-robin fashion, multiple paths are used in automatic rotation technique.

Network Device Bandwidth

Network bandwidth refers to the bit rate of data communication resources and is expressed in terms of kilobits per second, megabits per second, gigabits per second, and so on. Bandwidth helps in calculating the net maximum throughput of a communication path. It defines the net bit rate, also called the peak bit rate, of the device. There are a number of readily available online utilities, such as ZenOss, Cacti, Splunk, or PRTG network monitor, to benchmark performance of a network. Figure 12-8 shows a tool called ZenOss displaying each network interface in an environment along with whether the interface is responding to pings and whether SNMP information is being collected on it.

These bandwidth analyzers provide updated values as and when needed and in some instances detect and diagnose network performance issues. The more sophisticated analyzers track and maintain historical trends in addition to those functions just described. User-friendly graphical interfaces can make the task of identifying trends and patterns throughout the network and its attached devices easier. Figure 12-9 shows the PRTG network monitor tool displaying the status of a number of devices along with a latency graph.

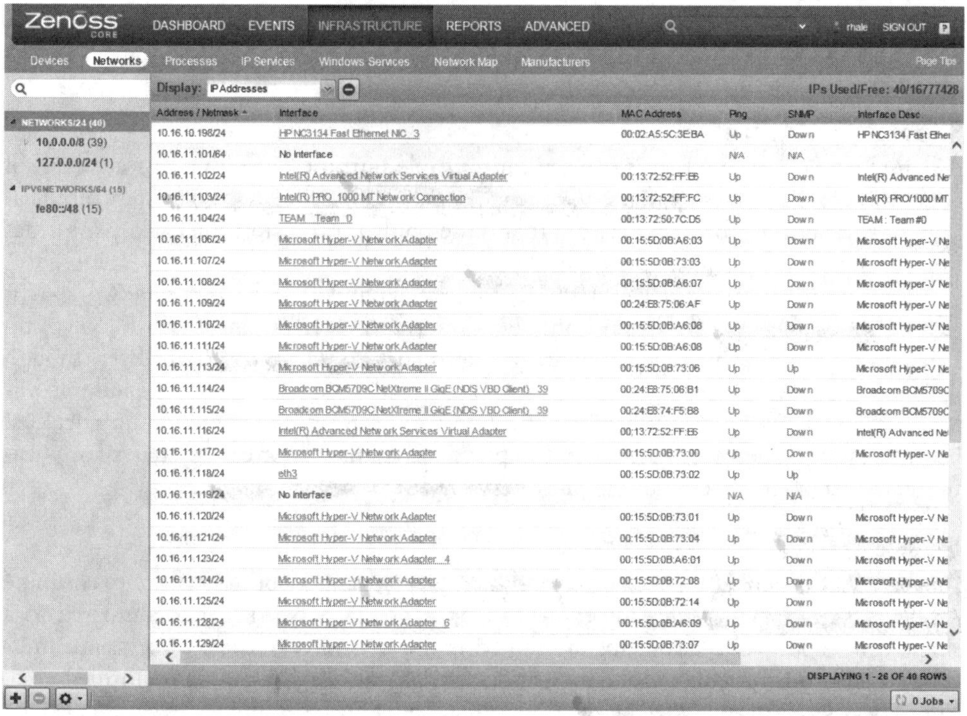

Figure 12-8   ZenOss network adapters view

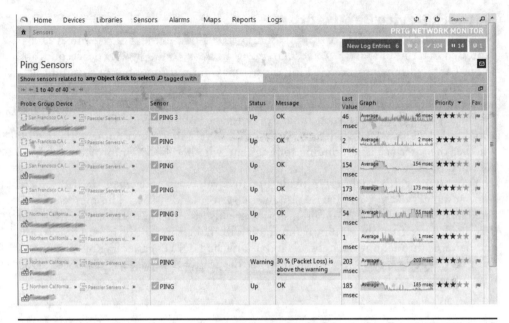

Figure 12-9   PRTG network monitor

Shared vs. Dedicated

A shared network is one that is utilized for multiple purposes, resulting in some level of contention for resources. Dedicated networks are used only for a specific system, application, or site, such as a backup network that is used only for transmitting backup information from production servers to archival servers.

When more than one device requests the service and resources of a network, it is termed *shared bandwidth*. When only one sender and receiver pair is capable of unrestricted communication in a network, it is termed *dedicated bandwidth*. Even though dedicated network communication comes with the advantages of flexibility and reliability in terms of bandwidth utilization, this boost in performance comes at a higher cost because a unique network must be put in place and managed for each system or application rather than all systems and applications utilizing a single network.

Teaming

Teaming is a form of link aggregation and failover used in network interfaces to combine multiple connections, increasing the throughput of the network when compared to a single connection. This also helps in improving the reliability of the network since multiple connections provide redundancy of data. Link aggregation can be performed at all three lower levels of the OSI Model. The primary advantages of link aggregation are that it addresses problems such as bandwidth limitations and lack of resilience.

Class of Service

The Ethernet class of service (CoS) was introduced in Chapter 3. CoS is a way of prioritizing types of traffic at layer 2 using one of eight CoS levels, referenced as CS0 through CS7, with CS0 offering the lowest priority and CS7 the highest. CoS can have a tremendous impact on bandwidth. Overall, this impact should be good because priority will be given to the traffic that is deemed most critical. Users of lower-priority applications, however, may complain of bandwidth problems when a significant quantity of high-priority traffic exists on the network such as Voice over IP (VoIP) or video conferencing.

Adequate Share Capacity

It is important to understand the expected utilization and performance requirements for shares so that they can be provisioned appropriately. Shares with high-performance requirements or high load might need to be on a separate set of disks, whereas multiple low-performance shares or those that are infrequently used could reside on the same set of disks. Growth is also a concern for share placement.

 EXAM TIP While many network attached storage (NAS) devices allow for share expansion, it is still best to place shares in a location where they can grow naturally without the need for administrative intervention.

Performance Metrics and Tools

There are many tools available, both online and as stand-alone third-party applications, to assist network administrators in their task of analyzing the performance of a storage device or network. Most storage vendors make software to manage performance on their devices, such as the Hitachi Tuning Manager, EMC ControlCenter, NetApp SANscreen, IBM Tivoli Storage Productivity Center, Dell EqualLogic SAN Headquarters, HP Storage Essentials, and Brocade Data Center Fabric Manager. However, you should know that these tools are not often bundled with the hardware, so they must be purchased separately. Some third-party tools include Solarwinds Storage Resource Monitor. This tool works for EMC CLARiiON, Dell modular disk, IBM DS3000 through the DS55000, and Sun StorageTek 2000 and 6000 models. There is also a free product called Solarwinds SAN Monitor that offers some storage performance and capacity information.

This is not an easy task since there are many performance metrics that must be considered to calculate the exact values that would result in network or system optimization. Monitoring performance enables organizations to identify issues as and when they occur, thereby preventing major failures and faults. The performance metrics tools for networking should track the response time and availability of networking devices along with uptime and downtime of routers and switches. The tools that are employed for analysis of performance have many built-in dashboards and reports that help support staff.

Before purchasing and installing any tool, it is necessary to thoroughly understand the minimum and recommended system requirements for the application to run efficiently and as expected. A system's random access memory (RAM), available hard disk space, network connectivity, operating system (OS), and central processing unit (CPU) speed will need to be known in order to determine whether the performance analysis tool is compatible with your system. It is never a good idea to barely meet the minimum requirements. These requirements will allow the program to run, but it will not be a very pleasant experience because the program will perform quite slowly for you and other users of the system.

It is best to exceed the recommended specifications when deploying an application. This is partially to help plan for future upgrades. No application is free from patches and updates as new vulnerabilities and bugs are discovered, and you will want to allow for the system to be upgraded and patched without requiring a hardware upgrade first.

Switch

Both iSCSI and FC use a device called a *switch*, and the two devices are both similar and different. FC switches allow for the creation of a Fibre Channel network that is an important part of a storage area network. Fibre Channel devices allow communication among multiple devices. It also restricts unwanted traffic among various network nodes.

Port Statistics

Port statistics can provide valuable data on the performance of switch ports on the storage network. They can also be used to baseline the performance of the network. Statistics can be viewed on the switch management interface, or they can be collected using Simple Network Management Protocol (SNMP) or Storage Management Initiative-Specification (SMI-S) by a storage management tool.

SNMP is a method for devices to share information with a management station through UDP ports 161 and 162. SNMP-managed devices allow management systems to query them for information. Management systems are configured with management information bases (MIBs) for the devices they will interact with. These MIBs define which variables can be queried on a device. Download the MIB for your switch model and load it into your management tool. Next, configure the switches and your management tool with the same community string and point the switches to your management tool as the collection point so that the tool will receive the SNMP messages.

SMI-S is a protocol used for sharing management information on storage devices. It is a good alternative to SNMP for managing devices such as storage arrays, switch tape drives, HBAs, converged network adapters (CNAs), and directors. It is a client-server model where the client is the management station requesting information and the server is the device offering the information. The Manage Engine OpStor tool, shown in Figure 12-10, shows several fabric switches and how many ports are used, operational, and problematic.

Some important port statistics include the frame check sequence, total input drops, total output drops, and runt counters.

- **Input queue**   This is the number of frames currently waiting in the input queue. While a switch may have many ports, it is not actually capable of sending and receiving data on every port simultaneously. When many frames are received

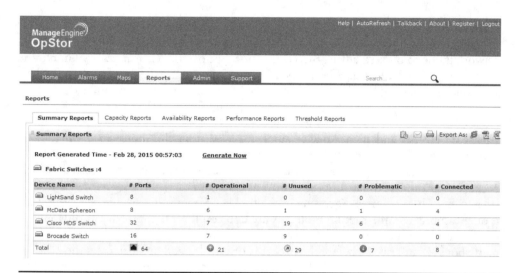

Figure 12-10 Manage Engine OpStor

at the same time, some are put into an input queue and held there until the switch can send them to their destination port. If the queue fills up, the oldest frames are dropped, and new ones are added. Each dropped frame increases the total input drop counter.

- **Output queue** Similar to the input queue, the output queue holds frames that are waiting to be sent down a destination line. Many devices may desire to send data to the same device, but it can receive only so much data at once, so some data must be queued. If the queue fills up, the oldest frames are dropped, and new ones are added. Each dropped frame increases the total output drop counter.

- **Runt counters** Runts are frames that are smaller than 64 bytes, the minimum Ethernet frame size.

- **Frame check sequence (FCS)** FCS is a field in frames that is used to detect errors. FCS accomplishes this through cyclic redundancy checks (CRC) or parity. CRC generates a number using a mathematical formula from the data in the frame. If a different computation is achieved on the receiving end, the frame is considered corrupt. Parity assesses all the bits in the frame and includes a 1 if the bits are odd and a 0 if they are even.

 NOTE Frames operate at OSI layer 2.

Thresholds

Thresholds allow limits to be set for an interface, switch, or globally. These then allow the network traffic to proceed efficiently. These can still be overridden as necessary but only at the switch or interface level. Effective performance can use thresholds to determine when additional links should be added or when traffic prioritization must be put in place.

Hops

Each OSI layer 3 and higher device along the way from the source to destination is known as a *hop*. Layer 3 and higher devices include routers, firewalls, proxies, and layer 3 switches, and they can also be known as *gateways* since they are the point at which packets enter or leave a network segment. The hop count is a component of end-to-end latency. Each hop requires processing of the packet or frame, and that adds a delay. This is one reason why some routing protocols use hop count as their primary or only metric in determining route cost. Each packet is given a time to live (TTL) that defines how many hops it can traverse before the packet is dropped. Each hop decreases the TTL by one before sending the packet to the next hop. The device that drops a packet will send back an Internet Control Message Protocol (ICMP) time exceeded message to the sender notifying them of the dropped packet.

The tracert command can be used to view each of the hops between a source and destination. The command shows the latency for each hop so you can see where problems might lie in the network or internetwork. Figure 12-11 shows the tracert command executed for www.snia.org.

Port Groups

Port groups connect more than one port together under the same configuration, thereby providing a strong base for virtual networks that are connected together. The port

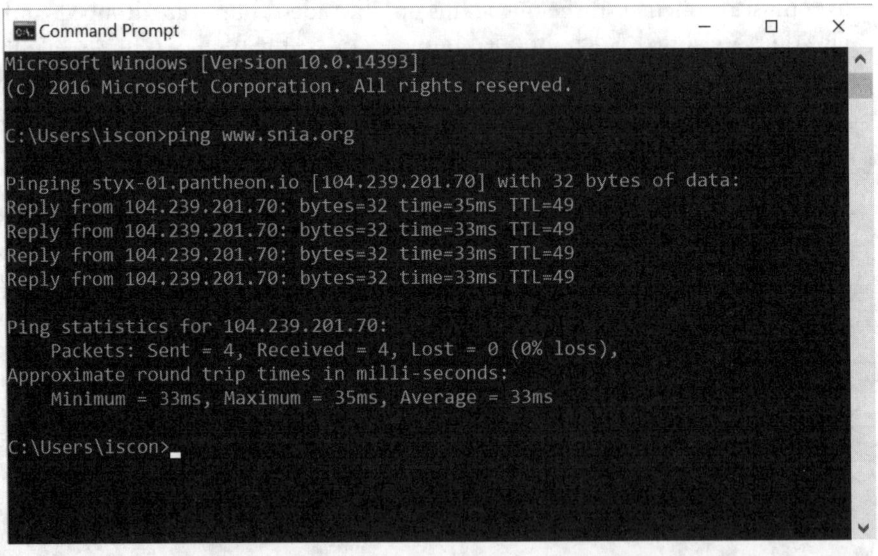

Figure 12-11 Tracert command

groups have a unique network label based on the current host. The port groups that are connected together to the same network are always given with the same network label. Moreover, port groups that are connected with more than one network have more than one network name.

ISL

In an FC switched-fabric (FC-SW) network, storage devices and hosts are connected to one another using switches. Switches are devices with many ports that allow connectivity between devices. FC-SW fabrics scale out by adding switches connected together using interswitch links (ISLs). The ports comprising the ISL need to be FC E-ports (see Chapter 3), a specific port designed for communication between FC switches.

The ISL port statistics maintain information related to Ethernet frames or errors that traverse ISLs. ISL port statistics can be viewed on the switch interface or through management tools that collect SMI-S information from the switch.

ISLs may need to be expanded if traffic data is being dropped and queues are full. Expanding an ISL means adding one or more ports to the ISL, which increases the available bandwidth. Another option is to move connections from a saturated switch to another switch that is less saturated.

Communication crossing the ISL will contend for available bandwidth, so ISLs can be a primary limiting factor in FC SAN performance. You can achieve the best performance by reducing the number of ISLs that need to be crossed.

Bandwidth

Bandwidth is a term that is used for measuring data communication over a network. It is usually expressed in the form of bits per second, and the other forms of expression are kilobits per second, megabits per second, gigabits per second, and so on. Bandwidth also refers to the maximum capacity of a networking channel. This is especially important for WAN connections. Track bandwidth metrics and consider upgrading bandwidth speeds or reducing network traffic if utilization approaches the maximum provided by your Internet service provider (ISP).

Packet capture and protocol analysis tools can also be helpful in diagnosing network or bandwidth issues. Wireshark and Capsa are tools that will collect all the packets that traverse a port. This data can be analyzed to determine what type of data was flowing through the connection, which nodes were part of the communication, and the protocols and ports utilized. Statistics can be computed based on the data such as percentage of data per protocol, most used protocols, most popular nodes, and so forth. These can be helpful in diagnosing issues or in creating benchmarks.

Array

The storage array is a device that functions as a data storage machine with high availability, ease of maintenance, and high reliability. Storage arrays typically come with an interface that allows storage administrators to view performance metrics such as cache hits, CPU load, and throughput. These items are discussed in more detail next.

Cache Hit Rate

When a request is made for data that exists in the cache, it is known as a cache read hit. The storage array can immediately service the request by sending the data over its interface without retrieving the data from disk. Cache read hits result in the fastest response time. Use the cache hit ratio to optimize cache sizes.

CPU Load

The CPU load is a measure of the amount of work the CPU is doing as the computer functions. Tools such as the Windows Activity Monitor or Task Monitor can show processor or CPU utilization as a percentage of capacity on the host, and array tools can show similar statistics for storage arrays. High CPU load could indicate the need for a faster processor or throttling of certain storage services. This can help to identify applications that may need to be throttled or uninstalled to improve processor availability. Figure 12-12 shows performance statistics for an EMC storage array, including

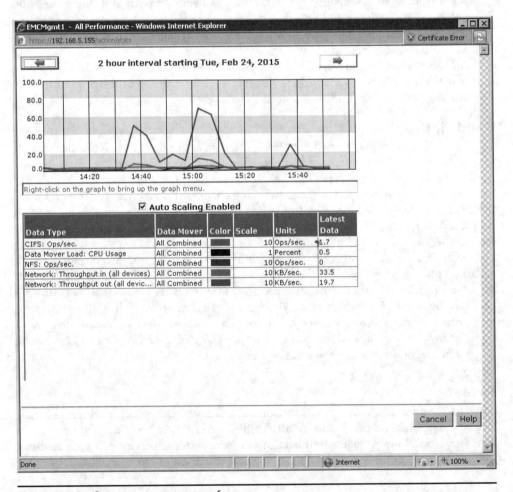

Figure 12-12 Storage management performance

the CPU utilization for the data mover. This screen was obtained through the system management software provided by the storage vendor.

Port Stats

The port stats on the array are similar to those on a switch. The following are some useful statistics:

- **Frame check sequence (FCS)**   FCS is a field in frames that is used to detect errors. FCS accomplishes this through CRC or parity. CRC generates a number using a mathematical formula from the data in the frame. If a different computation is achieved on the receiving end, the frame is considered corrupt. Parity assesses all the bits in the frame and includes a 1 if the bits are odd and a 0 if they are even.

NOTE   Frames operate at OSI layer 2.

- **Output queue**   The output queue holds frames that are waiting to be sent down a destination line. If the queue fills up, the oldest frames are dropped, and new ones are added. Each dropped frame increases the total output drop counter.
- **Runt counters**   Runts are frames that are smaller than 64 bytes, the minimum Ethernet frame size.

Bandwidth

Front-end ports are used for host connectivity. Hosts will directly connect to these ports or, more commonly, connect through a SAN via a switch. The front-end ports need to be configured to work with the transport protocol that is in use on the network, such as Fibre Channel (FC), Internet Small Computer System Interface (iSCSI), or Fibre Channel over Ethernet (FCoE). Back-end ports are used to connect a storage array controller to storage shelves containing disks. Back-end connections will use whichever technology is specified by the array such as FC or SAS.

Thresholds

Thresholds were discussed earlier for switches. Thresholds on storage arrays are often defined for available capacity. The Manage Engine OpStor tool, shown in Figure 12-13, shows several storage arrays, their capacity, how much is used, and how much is available (free).

Throughput

Throughput is the amount of data transferred over a medium in a measurable time interval, and it is usually measured in IOPS, mentioned at the beginning of this chapter.

Front-end ports are used for host connectivity. Hosts will directly connect to these ports or, more commonly, connect through a SAN via a switch. The front-end ports

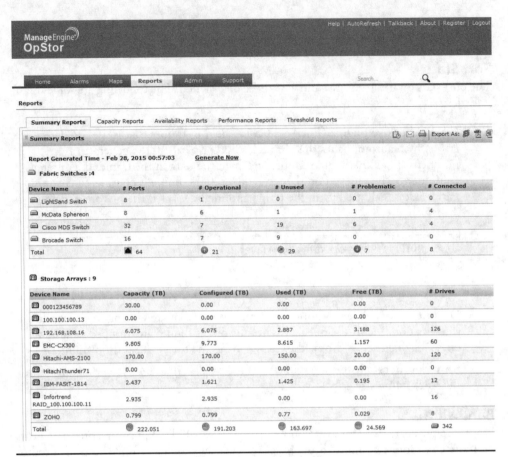

Figure 12-13   Manage Engine OpStor array capacity thresholds

need to be configured to work with the transport protocol that is in use on the network such as Fibre Channel, Internet Small Computer System Interface, or Fibre Channel over Ethernet. Front-end port throughput determines how much data can be transferred to and from the storage array to the devices accessing it. Ensure that the front-end ports can provide enough throughput for both normal and peak loads.

Back-end ports are used by the controller to communicate with disk shelves and other array components such as virtualized arrays. Back-end connections use whichever technology is specified by the array such as FC or SAS. Throughput for back-end ports determines how much data can be transferred from the disks in a storage array to the storage array controller. This is one component for determining how long it will take the array to process requests.

I/O Latency

Latency is the time it takes to go from source to destination. In other words, it is the travel time. Latency is a factor in communications that occur within storage arrays or even storage components, and it is also a factor in network communications. Electrical impulses and light have a maximum speed, so longer distances will result in higher latency. Of course, sending data from one place to another is not as simple as dropping it on a wire. Devices forward or route the data to its destination along the way, and each of these devices will add latency to the equation. Latency measurements are typically described in milliseconds.

Host Tools

The following are some of the popular tools that can come in handy for analyzing the state and performance of the system.

Sysmon

Sysmon is a Microsoft Windows tool developed by Mark Russinovich and Thomas Garnier. The tool is installed as a driver and logs additional activity to the event log about network connections, running processes, and file changes.

1. Download sysmon from http://download.sysinternals.com/files/Sysmon.zip.

2. Extract the sysmon.exe file from the sysmon.zip file to your computer.

3. Open a command prompt and navigate to the directory where you copied sysmon.exe.

4. Install the sysmon service and driver by executing the following command:

```
sysmon -accepteula -i
```

You have now installed the driver and configured the service with default settings, as shown in Figure 12-14. The sysmon service will now log events and place them in the Windows event log. The service will start automatically whenever the system restarts,

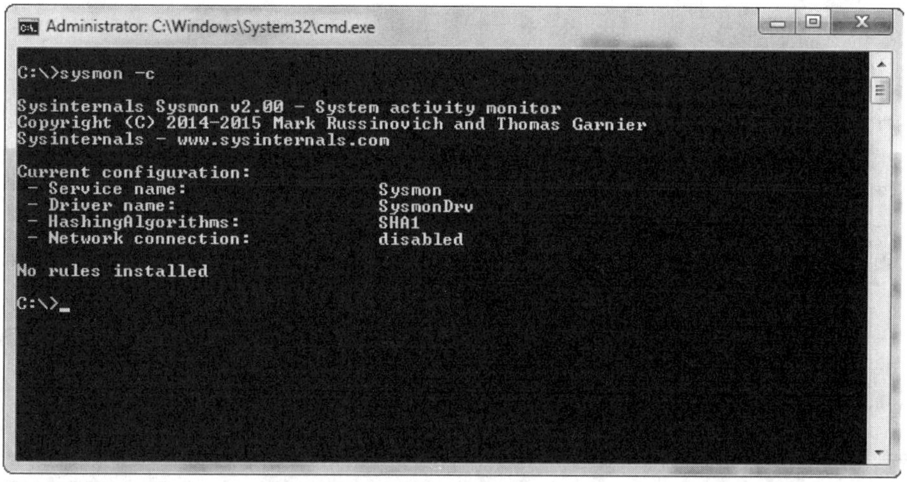

Figure 12-14   Sysmon default settings

so you will not need to execute these steps again unless the service is disabled. To uninstall the driver, execute the following statement:

```
sysmon -u
```

Performance Monitor (perfmon)

Performance Monitor (perfmon) is a Windows tool that gathers performance metrics, called *counters*, and displays them in a graph format. This is how you use the tool:

1. Go to Start | Run and then type **perfmon** and press ENTER.
2. The Performance Monitor tool will load.
3. Click Performance Monitor on the left side of the screen under Monitoring Tools, and a graph will appear. The default counter, Processor Time, is displayed in the graph.
4. Click the green plus sign to add more counters. Figure 12-15 shows the Bytes Sent/sec counter being added for the Broadcom NetXtreme Gigabit Ethernet adapter. Select the counter you want and then click Add. Click OK when done adding counters.

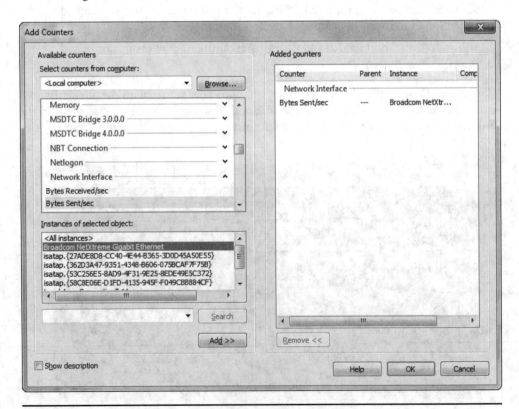

Figure 12-15   Adding counters to Performance Monitor

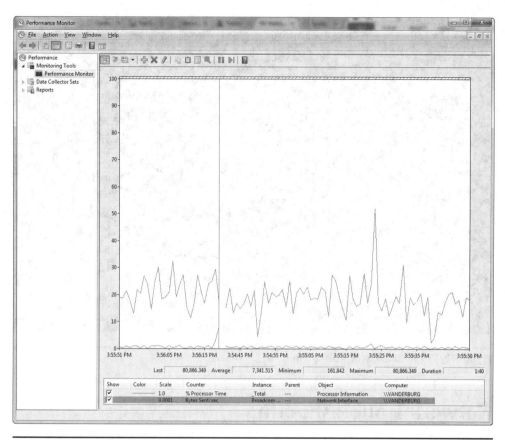

Figure 12-16 Performance Monitor graphs

The counters will appear in the graph. You can hide the Processor Time counter by unchecking the box next to it. Figure 12-16 shows the Performance Monitor graph for Processor Time and the Bytes Sent/sec counter added in step 4.

IOstat

IOstat is a Linux tool that provides users with reports on performance statistics. At the Linux shell or terminal, type **iostat**, and you will be presented with the default counters of CPU usage and disk reads and writes for each logical volume. You can view network statistics by typing **iostat –n**. IOstat can also be scheduled to run at intervals and can log on to files for later review. Figure 12-17 shows the output for IOstat with the default counters.

NOTE If IOstat is not installed, run the following command (depending on the version of Linux you are using):

```
sudo apt-get install sysstat
```

```
eric@Gamma: ~
eric@Gamma:~$ iostat
Linux 3.13.0-45-generic (Gamma)        03/02/2015      _x86_64_      (8 CPU)

avg-cpu:  %user   %nice %system %iowait  %steal   %idle
           4.54    0.31    1.30    0.34    0.00   93.51

Device:             tps    kB_read/s    kB_wrtn/s    kB_read    kB_wrtn
sda                1.35        10.05        23.09    1234079    2834276

eric@Gamma:~$
```

Figure 12-17 IOstat with default counters

Network Troubleshooting

Troubleshooting network problems involves several steps. First the source or location of the problem must be pinpointed. At this stage, all affected resources such as nodes, devices, or paths are identified. Next the nature and extent of the problems must be determined. This may involve a range of resources, such as conducting sophisticated network analyses and reviewing user accounts of the problems. Once the scope and nature of the fault have been determined, in-house knowledge bases that document previous system malfunctions may provide a quick path to resolution. The creation of and maintenance of such knowledge bases have proven invaluable in reducing mean time to repair (MTTR).

Experience has taught network administrators that many system faults are attributable to simple triggers or conditions. The following discussion provides practical advice in approaching level 1 problem resolution.

Changes, both authorized and unauthorized, are often the biggest culprits. Mistakes can be made in changing the configuration, naming conventions, or associations. Users are typically unaware of or outright dishonest as to the changes they've made or the potential for error associated with them. Ask simple questions to get at the root of problems. Did the user change their password? Have they installed any software since the last time they performed the action that currently does not work? Have they enabled or disabled system services, removed files, or changed system settings? If the change sounds like a plausible explanation for the problem, reverse the change and test again.

Simple tests can be another first line of defense in using simple practical means of problem resolution. For example, if a user cannot connect to a NAS, you might begin by pinging the NAS by name. If the NAS pings by name, the device is up and available, the name to IP address mapping provided by DNS or a host file is correct, and the computer you are running the ping command from has a connection to the NAS.

Determine whether a nearby computer attached to the same resource is experiencing the same problems. If both have the same issue, you may try it again from a machine on another virtual LAN (VLAN) or from a host on the same VLAN as the NAS. This could eliminate network segments. If the NAS does not ping, you may check to see whether it is powered on or in a startup error state.

Continue narrowing down the scope until you have a few possible solutions to test. Test each possible solution until you find one that works. If none of the solutions works, reevaluate your scope and assumptions to come up with new possible solutions. Once the solution is found, document it and verify that the problem has been resolved. Review whether changes should be implemented so that this problem can be avoided in the future.

Connectivity Issues

Connectivity issues are problems that inhibit or prevent a device from communicating on a network. Indicators include such things as services failing because they cannot connect to storage resources, users complaining that data is inaccessible or shares are unavailable, errors on failed redundant paths, or excessive errors in communication hardware. Troubleshooting these issues requires the storage administrator to identify the component, such as a cable, Gigabit Interface Converter (GBIC), or HBA, that is causing the problem.

Begin the troubleshooting process by isolating and eliminating options until you are left with the culprit. In the case of a bad connector, you would eliminate options such as the cable, GBIC, or HBA by trying different cables, GBICs, or HBAs. If the problem remains, you can most likely eliminate the component you swapped out.

 NOTE Ensure that you follow your organizational change management and notification procedures before making changes to production hardware, even when troubleshooting an issue.

Failed Cable

If a host cannot connect to the network but other hosts on the same switch can connect, it could be a problem with the cable, switch port, or network interface card. If you determine that the problem is with the cable, try the following steps:

1. Make sure the cable is fully seated in the NIC or HBA port and the switch port. You should see status indicators near the cable on the NIC or HBA to indicate whether it is sending and receiving traffic. If you do not see the indicators, unplug the cable and plug it in again.

2. If this does not work, try replacing the cable with one that you know is good or test the cable with a cable tester to determine whether it is faulty.

Misconfigured Fibre Channel Cable

A misconfigured Fibre Channel cable could cause a loss of connectivity. Open the HBA card properties and check to see what the World Wide Name (WWN) is for the card. Ensure that a zone has been created for the WWN. If so, open Disk Management and rescan the disks to see whether the Fibre Channel disks show up. If multipathing or management software is loaded on the machine, open it and look for card errors. Research errors on the manufacturer's web site or support pages.

Failed GBIC or SFP

A failed GBIC or small form-factor pluggable (SFP) will have many of the same symptoms of a failed cable. The good news is that a GBIC or SFP is quite easy to swap out. If you have trouble with a fiber cable, try changing this first using the following steps:

1. Press the release tab on the fiber cable and gently pull it out of the SFP or GBIC. Place plastic safety caps on the fiber cable ends to protect them from damage.
2. Press the release tab on the SFP or GBIC and pull it out of the switch port.
3. Insert a new SFP or GBIC of the same type in the empty switch port.
4. Remove the plastic safety caps and plug the fiber cable into the SFP or GBIC.
5. If this does not work and this is a new GBIC or SFP installation, verify hardware and software support for this type of GBIC or SFP.

Failed HBA or NIC

If you are unable to establish a connection and replacing the cable does not work, it could be a problem with the HBA or NIC. To replace the card, use the following steps:

1. Shut down the device and unplug the power cable.
2. Unplug the cable or cables attached to the failed HBA or NIC.
3. Attach an antistatic wrist strap to your wrist and secure the grounding click on the wrist strap to a ground.
4. Open the case and remove the screws around the NIC or HBA.
5. Pull upward firmly on the card and place it in an antistatic bag.
6. Insert the replacement card into the slot from which you removed the bad card.
7. Screw in the card and assemble the case again.
8. Plug the cables into the new HBA or NIC.
9. Attach the power cable and power up the device.
10. Configure the NIC with the IP address the previous NIC had. If replacing an HBA, change the WWN on the zone to the new WWN of the replacement HBA.

Intermittent HBA Connectivity

Intermittent HBA connectivity could be due to latency, saturation of a link, or port errors. Log in to the switch the device is connected to and check for port errors. See whether other devices are having the same problem. If so, check the ISLs between source and destination switches to see whether they are saturated or experiencing errors.

VLAN Issues

A VLAN allows storage administrators to configure a network switch into multiple logical network address spaces, which segments traffic and adds flexibility in network design. The downside is that it can be easy to plug a cable into the wrong port and get a different VLAN, so it is important to document the ports that are assigned to VLANs, the VLAN numbers, and their purposes.

Devices on the wrong VLAN may not be able to connect to certain network resources. Use the ping command to test connectivity to other devices. For example, ping 192.168.3.25 would test connectivity to the host with the IP address 192.168.3.25. A router or a layer 3 switch is required to route traffic between VLANs. If VLAN routing has been set up and VLANs cannot talk to one another, check the cables that connect the VLANs to the layer 3 switch or router and verify that the routing configuration is correct.

If the device is using Dynamic Host Configuration Protocol (DHCP) to receive an IP address, see which network the IP address is on. For example, a network could be divided into three VLANs: 192.168.1.1, 192.168.2.1, and 192.168.3.1. If the device is plugged into the wrong VLAN and it is using DHCP, it may receive an IP address for that VLAN, and this will allow you to determine which VLAN it is on. Check documentation for the port it is plugged into and verify that it is configured for the correct VLAN.

The ipconfig command in Windows and the ifconfig command in Linux display the IP address for a device that can be used to determine which VLAN it is on. The output from the ipconfig command, showing the IPv4 and IPv6 addresses, domain name, subnet mask, and default gateway, is displayed here:

```
C:\Windows\system32>ipconfig
Windows IP Configuration
Ethernet adapter Gigabit Ethernet:
   Connection-specific DNS Suffix  . : TEST.com
   Link-local IPv6 Address . . . . . : fe80::311d:7e57:eae:41f1%27
   IPv4 Address. . . . . . . . . . . : 192.168.5.50
   Subnet Mask . . . . . . . . . . . : 255.255.255.0
   Default Gateway . . . . . . . . . : 192.168.5.1
```

Zoning Issues

Zones are a wonderful way to implement security on a SAN, but they do increase complexity, requiring the storage manager to troubleshoot and manage zones. Chapter 8 describes storage zoning, so we will only briefly review the topic here. Please look back to that chapter if you need additional information. Zoning is a way of defining which devices can access storage resources. Port zoning assigns storage resources to ports on switches. Devices that are connected to those ports can view the storage resources. WWN zoning assigns resources to the unique name assigned to a Fibre Channel HBA. With WWN zoning, a device can be moved to a different port and still access the same resources, but if the HBA is changed, the zoning configuration will need to be updated.

Zoning Misconfiguration

Drives that have been assigned will not show up if zoning has been misconfigured. Hosts on a zoned SAN are provided access to drives, represented on a SAN using their logical unit number (LUN), by mapping that LUN to the host's WWN. The first step to diagnose this is to check the WWN of the HBA that is in the device. Next, look at the zoning configuration to see which LUNs are mapped to the WWN. Add or remove LUNs from the zone if the correct LUNs do not appear. If the WWN of the HBA is not in the zone, add it.

You may need to issue a rescan after the zoning configuration has been fixed so that the host will pick up the new LUNs. You can issue this command in Microsoft Windows within the Server Manager console with the following procedure:

1. Open Server Manager by clicking Start; then right-click Computer and select Manage.

2. Expand the storage container and select Disk Management.

3. Right-click Disk Management and select Rescan Disks.

4. (Optional) You may also need to right-click Logical Volumes and place them online once they reappear in Disk Management.

Zoning Errors

Zoning errors can provide valuable insight when troubleshooting a problem. Look for zoning errors in storage array, switch, and HBA error logs because these will provide the most technical information.

Interoperability Issues

There are many components in a storage network that have to operate together. Sometimes the configuration of different devices can come into conflict, reducing performance or losing the connection entirely. One situation that can happen is when a device is connected to a port that is offline. Verify that the port status is set to online on the switch.

Another is duplex mismatch. Check for duplex mismatch by verifying that the duplex setting and speed are set to the same values on the NIC and switch. Duplex mismatch occurs when a switch or NIC is configured for full duplex, while its partner switch or NIC is configured for half duplex. Full-duplex communication allows for data to be sent and received at the same time, while half-duplex communication sends data and then receives data but not both at the same time. Connections can drop, and communication is typically very slow when duplex mismatches occur.

Host Troubleshooting

The following section includes troubleshooting tips for diagnosing host issues. The tips include hardware or software incompatibility, outdated firmware or drivers, incorrect NIC configuration, a bad NIC, storage tiers, improperly connected NIC, incorrect firewall settings, and incorrect cluster or multipath settings.

Hardware or Software Incompatibility

Modern operating systems support a wide range of hardware, but not all hardware is supported by all operating systems. Most operating systems maintain a hardware compatibility list that can be queried to determine whether the device is supported. Another way is to go to the web site for the vendor that produced the hardware component to see whether it has support. Support is usually offered through a piece of software known as a *driver* that allows the operating system to communicate with the hardware. Search for drivers for the operating system in use.

Sometimes drivers can have compatibility errors. If using Microsoft Windows, check Device Manager for errors. If conflicts exist or the network adapter is being detected as an "other device," try using the update driver function to have Windows scan for updated drivers automatically. If this does not work, check the vendor's web site and download the latest driver for your operating system and install it. If this does not work, try uninstalling the driver software and then restart the computer to have Windows redetect and install the device.

Outdated Firmware or Drivers

Modern Linux, Mac, and Windows operating systems will attempt to update drivers automatically with software, but some drivers may not be registered with the operating system vendor and must be updated manually. Check the vendor's web site and download the latest driver for your operating system and install it.

Incorrect NIC Configuration

Incorrect NIC configuration can limit or inhibit network connectivity. The first step in diagnosing an incorrect NIC configuration is to determine what the current configuration is. The ipconfig (Windows) or ifconfig (Linux) command will display the current configuration of your network cards. Figure 12-18 shows the output of the ifconfig command. From a command prompt, examine the results and then compare them to the documented configuration for the device. If documentation does not exist, determine the default gateway, Domain Name System (DNS) server, subnet mask, and an available IP address. Open the NIC configuration and configure these values; then issue a ping to verify connectivity with the default gateway and other network resources.

Bad Connector

Begin the troubleshooting process for a bad connector by isolating and eliminating options until you are left with the culprit. In the case of a bad connector, you would eliminate options such as the NIC cable or port by trying different cables, ports, and NICs. If the problem remains, you can most likely eliminate the component you swapped out. Try the connector with a different component that you know is good. If that system is unreachable, try replacing the connector on the device you are having

```
⊗ ⊖ ⊡   eric@Gamma: ~
eric@Gamma:~$ ifconfig
eth0      Link encap:Ethernet  HWaddr 5c:26:0a:03:56:64
          UP BROADCAST MULTICAST  MTU:1500  Metric:1
          RX packets:0 errors:0 dropped:0 overruns:0 frame:0
          TX packets:0 errors:0 dropped:0 overruns:0 carrier:0
          collisions:0 txqueuelen:1000
          RX bytes:0 (0.0 B)  TX bytes:0 (0.0 B)

lo        Link encap:Local Loopback
          inet addr:127.0.0.1  Mask:255.0.0.0
          inet6 addr: ::1/128 Scope:Host
          UP LOOPBACK RUNNING  MTU:65536  Metric:1
          RX packets:17426 errors:0 dropped:0 overruns:0 frame:0
          TX packets:17426 errors:0 dropped:0 overruns:0 carrier:0
          collisions:0 txqueuelen:0
          RX bytes:1757970 (1.7 MB)  TX bytes:1757970 (1.7 MB)

wlan0     Link encap:Ethernet  HWaddr 00:27:10:06:07:c8
          inet addr:192.168.1.151  Bcast:192.168.1.255  Mask:255.255.255.0
          inet6 addr: fe80::227:10ff:fe06:7c8/64 Scope:Link
          UP BROADCAST RUNNING MULTICAST  MTU:1500  Metric:1
          RX packets:773347 errors:0 dropped:0 overruns:0 frame:0
          TX packets:240531 errors:0 dropped:0 overruns:0 carrier:0
          collisions:0 txqueuelen:1000
          RX bytes:322672941 (322.6 MB)  TX bytes:37319101 (37.3 MB)

eric@Gamma:~$ ▮
```

Figure 12-18   ifconfig

trouble with. If spare components are available, you can try using them in the unreachable system. However, you must first make sure that the component from storage is good before performing this test. Otherwise, you may swap a bad component for another bad component.

EXAM TIP   Please note that you should not swap out components unless you have first confirmed that the machine you intend to swap with can be made unavailable. This may require you to schedule downtime with internal or external stakeholders so that their work is not interrupted, or, if redundancies are in place, you will want to coordinate with information technology workers so that they do not respond to component failure alerts. Your organization may also have a change management system in place to track and approve changes made to systems, in which case you will need to follow change management procedures before swapping components. Communication is the key, and it will save you many headaches down the road.

Bad Cable

Cable failure is more common than you would think. Both optical and twisted-pair cables are sensitive in their own ways. Optical cables are expensive and sensitive pieces of equipment. If a fiber-optic cable is bent too far, the light inside the cable will be reflected and dispersed, resulting in a loss of signal until the bend is corrected. The fiber-optic core can also be damaged if bent too far and will need to be replaced.

Twisted-pair cabling must not be stretched or the twists will elongate and make it more susceptible to crosstalk (XT). Higher categories have more twists per inch and are more sensitive to stretching than lower-category cables. This is why you can tug on a phone cable quite a bit before losing connectivity, whereas a CAT6 cable might begin to lose data after a few good pulls. Also, don't run Ethernet cables near power lines or light fixtures because these generate electromagnetic interference (EMI) that can disrupt communications. If cables must be located near power or lights, consider using shielded tubes or tape to provide extra protection against EMI. The bend radius for twisted-pair cabling must be at least four times the outer diameter of the cable to avoid kinking.

You may also run into problems if a cable is longer than its maximum transmission length. The maximum length of optical fiber depends on the data rate, with higher data rates reducing the maximum transmission length since higher data rates suffer greater from attenuation.

The process for troubleshooting a bad cable is similar to that of troubleshooting a bad connector. Swap the cable out for one that you know is good. This may be one from another system or a spare component in storage.

 EXAM TIP   Document the troubleshooting steps you perform along the way. Some might use pen and paper, a word document, a template provided by your organization, or a change management or knowledge management system. I troubleshot a storage system for a couple days and finally had to call in a friend to help me. He asked me to walk him through the troubleshooting I had performed so far, and I simply sent him my troubleshooting document, which I printed from a change management system, outlining each step and my conclusions. Other colleagues have not been so fortunate, and they learned the hard way that memory is prone to error and that those who fail to document are doomed to repeat their steps.

Bad Port

As you can probably guess by now, you can identify a bad port by connecting the system's cable and connector to a different port. The difference here is that two ports are required to make a connection, so you will have to test both to see whether one or the other is the failed component. If the connection is an ISL, you will need to configure another ISL on a new port on one switch and then move the cable to that port. If the connection still fails, move the cable back to the initial port, remove the configuration you just added, and add a configuration for an ISL on a different port on the second switch in the ISL connection.

If the connection is between a switch and an end device such as a host, array, or tape drive, try connecting to another port on the host, array, or tape drive to see whether the connection works. In some cases, you will not have another port to connect to on the device because all ports may be in use. In this case, your troubleshooting options will depend on how the device is configured. If all the ports are configured as one link, you can swap the cables on the device and use the device management software to view the link status. If the good port goes offline and the one that previously was offline goes online, you have identified the culprit. Ensure that you follow your organizational change management and notification procedures before making changes to production hardware, even when troubleshooting an issue.

You can use the fcping command to issue an FC Extended Link Service (ELS) request to a port or pair of ports by using their WWN. Ports that receive an ELS request will respond, letting the user know that it is active and able to communicate.

Running the fcping command from an FC switch to WWN 21:01:00:E0:8B:A5:26:6A would produce the following output:

```
storageplusswitch:admin> fcping 21:01:00:E0:8B:A5:26:6A
Pinging 21:01:00:E0:8B:A5:26:6A [fd1091] with 12 bytes of data:
received reply from 21:01:00:E0:8B:A5:26:6A: 12 bytes time:1194 usec
received reply from 21:01:00:E0:8B:A5:26:6A: 12 bytes time:997 usec
received reply from 21:01:00:E0:8B:A5:26:6A: 12 bytes time:1222 usec
received reply from 21:01:00:E0:8B:A5:26:6A: 12 bytes time:1035 usec
received reply from 21:01:00:E0:8B:A5:26:6A: 12 bytes time:902 usec
5 frames sent, 5 frames received, 0 frames rejected, 0 frames timeout
Round-trip min/avg/max = 902/1070/1222 usec
```

The first line after the command confirms that you are pinging WWN 21:01:00:E0:8B:A5:26:6A, which has an FC-ID of fd1091. Each ELS reply is then given, along with the time it took to receive a reply. The last line of the output shows the statistics beginning with the shortest (min), average (avg), and longest (max) ELS reply in the set. The output of this command shows that all five out of five pings were sent and ELS replies were received for each of the five, with the shortest response taking 902 microseconds, the average 1070, and the longest 1222.

Bad NIC

If you are unable to establish a connection and replacing the cable does not work, it could be a problem with the NIC. To replace the card, use the following steps:

1. Shut down the device and unplug the power cable.

2. Unplug the cable or cables attached to the failed NIC.

3. Attach an antistatic wrist strap to your wrist and secure the grounding click on the wrist strap to a ground.

4. Open the case and remove the screws around the NIC.

5. Pull upward firmly on the card and place it in an antistatic bag.

6. Insert the replacement card into the slot from which you removed the bad card.

7. Screw in the card and assemble the case again.

8. Plug the cables into the new NIC.

9. Attach the power cable and power up the device.

10. Configure the NIC with the IP address the previous NIC had.

NIC Improperly Connected

The main cause of improperly connected NICs is that they are not fully seated. To verify that the NIC is seated, use the following steps:

1. Shut down the device and unplug the power cable.

2. Unplug the cable or cables attached to the NIC.

3. Attach an antistatic wrist strap to your wrist and secure the grounding click on the wrist strap to a ground.

4. Open the case and push down on the NIC to ensure that it is fully seated. Look at the connection between the card and the device motherboard and ensure that it is flat against the interface port.

5. Tighten the screw down on the NIC card so that it cannot wiggle in the case.

6. Plug the cables into the NIC again.

7. Attach the power cable and power up the device.

Incorrect Firewall Settings

Firewall software is used to block communications over specific logical ports such as port 443 for Secure Sockets Layer (SSL), port 22 for Secure Shell (SSH), port 23 for Telnet, port 389 for Lightweight Directory Access Protocol (LDAP), or 161 for Simple Network Message Protocol (SNMP). Connections may be blocked to and from the device if a firewall rule has not been configured for the connection. If you suspect the firewall may be blocking the connection, temporarily turn the firewall off and see whether the connection resumes. If the connection works, run the following command to see which port the connection is utilizing:

```
netstat -a
```

The netstat command will list many connections, as shown in Figure 12-19, so you will need to know the IP address of the computer connecting to it so that you can identify the line that contains the connection in netstat. Next, turn the firewall back on and create a rule in the firewall for the connection specifying the port identified in netstat.

Incorrect Cluster or Multipath Settings

Cluster settings allow multiple computers to connect to the same resources, but if incorrectly configured, multiple computers could try to modify data at the same time, resulting in conflicts. Clusters usually have a software component that is built into the operating system. Ensure that the clustering component is enabled and that all the nodes appear in the cluster.

```
⊗ ⊖ ▢   eric@Gamma: ~

eric@Gamma:~$ netstat -a
Active Internet connections (servers and established)
Proto Recv-Q Send-Q Local Address            Foreign Address          State
tcp        0      0 *:db-lsp                  *:*                      LISTEN
tcp        0      0 localhost:17600           *:*                      LISTEN
tcp        0      0 Gamma:domain              *:*                      LISTEN
tcp        0      0 localhost:ipp             *:*                      LISTEN
tcp        0      0 192.168.1.151:37691       ord30s21-in-f14.1:https  ESTABLISHED
tcp       28      0 192.168.1.151:33657       productsearch.ubu:https  CLOSE_WAIT
tcp       38      0 192.168.1.151:59634       client-10a.v.drop:https  CLOSE_WAIT
tcp       38      0 192.168.1.151:58033       ec2-174-129-206-1:https   CLOSE_WAIT
tcp       38      0 192.168.1.151:33573       client-8a.v.dropb:https  CLOSE_WAIT
tcp        0      0 192.168.1.151:40128       ord31s22-in-f5.1e:https  ESTABLISHED
tcp       37      0 192.168.1.151:49213       ec2-23-23-217-150:https  ESTABLISHED
tcp       38      0 192.168.1.151:59698       client-10a.v.drop:https  CLOSE_WAIT
tcp       38      0 192.168.1.151:48729       client-10b.v.drop:https  CLOSE_WAIT
tcp       38      0 192.168.1.151:37272       client-9b.v.dropb:https  CLOSE_WAIT
tcp       38      0 192.168.1.151:39576       client-16a.v.drop:https  CLOSE_WAIT
tcp        0      0 192.168.1.151:33788       74.125.69.189:https      ESTABLISHED
tcp       38      0 192.168.1.151:35186       client-9a.v.dropb:https  CLOSE_WAIT
tcp        9      0 192.168.1.151:43032       192.168.1.1:netbios-ssn  CLOSE_WAIT
tcp       38      0 192.168.1.151:54613       client-17a.v.drop:https  CLOSE_WAIT
tcp       38      0 192.168.1.151:49296       d-5b.sjc.dropbox.:https   CLOSE_WAIT
tcp        0      0 192.168.1.151:53871       192.168.1.110:https       ESTABLISHED
tcp       38      0 192.168.1.151:35493       client-15a.v.drop:https  CLOSE_WAIT
tcp       38      0 192.168.1.151:43490       ec2-23-21-220-80.:https   CLOSE_WAIT
tcp       38      0 192.168.1.151:55926       ec2-50-19-218-118:https   CLOSE_WAIT
```

Figure 12-19   netstat -a command

You might also find that only one node can access the LUNs. If this is the case, ensure that the storage device LUN mapping is set for cluster and that the WWNs for each node in the cluster are in the LUN mapping.

Multipathing allows multiple NIC or HBA ports to be used for load balancing and failover. This is accomplished through built-in operating system multipath I/O (MPIO) drivers or via vendor software such as Hitachi Dynamic Link Manager (HDML) or EMC PowerPath. Open the software and verify that all NIC or HBA ports are configured in the multipath and that load balancing and failover are enabled. Also, check for errors in the software and research errors on the vendor's web site if errors are found.

Backup Troubleshooting

Reliable backups are crucial in maintaining adequate system availability and preserving organizational documents and other intellectual property. Backup systems need to be regularly monitored for backup failures, errors, and warnings. Storage or backup operators often create alerts for these events so that they can correct issues as quickly as possible. In some cases, backup alerting may be integrated with other IT service processes such as an issue tracking system, also known as a trouble ticket system or request management system. Such systems have a workflow defined to create a task based on a system event. The task is then assigned to a person or placed in a queue. That person will then need to resolve the error. Some of the most common backup problems are described here. They include space limitations, open files, blocking by virus scanners, and incorrect permissions.

Space Limitations

It is important to properly size backup drives to avoid space errors and to ensure that the required files are archived successfully. Proper planning requires understanding the current size of backups and growth rates, because backups need to be able to handle current demand and short-term or long-term backup growth. Most backup suites will perform compression on the backup files as they are stored, and many will deduplicate the data. Both methods can dramatically reduce the amount of space required to store data, but they can also make it difficult to understand how much space will actually be consumed by initial and successive backup jobs. Some backup vendors offer estimating tools to help with this process. You can also perform your own computations.

Let's say you have 4TB of data to back up, with a 5 percent (200GB) change in data for every incremental backup. Now if you do an incremental backup every day, you require 1,400GB (that is, 200GB × 7). Having a full backup once a week will require the entire 4,000GB of space needed weekly. Thus, you would need 5,400GB (or 5.4TB) of free space for the backups. Over the course of a month, you might have four weekly backups and the incremental in between, which is overwritten each week. That would require 4,000GB each week and one week of incremental backups at 1,400GB. Together that is 17,400GB. As you can see, space requirements increase quickly with multiple backup sets.

If there is a 2:1 compression ratio for the data, you would need 8,700GB (17,400GB / 2) of storage space per month for a compressed backup. If the deduplication ratio is 4:1, you would need 5,350GB (17,400GB / 4). If you both compress and deduplicate the data, assuming the ratios stay the same, it would be half the size due to the 2:1 compression ratio, so you would need 2,625GB.

Running Out of Space on the Destination

If you are running out of space on the destination drive, add more capacity, decrease the backup interval, or change the backup method to utilize fewer full backups. It is also common to find old backup files from jobs that have been changed or removed that are still resident on the backup server. If these files are no longer needed, remove them to clean up space.

Running Out of Space on the Target

Backup software will sometimes create temporary files on the target machine when it is backing up files. However, the backup job may fail if insufficient space is available on the target. Microsoft Volume Shadow Copy Service (VSS), for example, requires around

1GB of free space on each volume being backed up. The Microsoft VSS backup error shown here clearly states the problem:

```
There is not enough disk space to create the volume shadow copy on the storage
location. Make sure that, for all volumes to be backup up, the minimum
required disk space for shadow copy creation is available. This applies to
both the backup storage destination and volumes included in the backup
```

You can troubleshoot out-of-space errors by performing the following steps:

1. If there are backups older than a certain date, archive them on a separate disk, pending deletion if the organization determines they are not needed.
2. Run Windows disk cleanup to get rid of old files.
3. Make sure to empty the Recycle Bin so that the space will be reclaimed by the system.
4. Remove temporary files.
5. Empty web browser cache.
6. Delete unused files in the downloads folder or folders that may have been downloaded by users or applications.
7. Remove or deduplicate redundant files on the computer.

Open Files

Backup systems must make archival copies of files, but sometimes those files are in use by users or applications. For example, a backup of a file server may be scheduled for 1:00 A.M. but some users might still have documents open on their workstations when they go home for the night, so those documents are currently locked for editing. Virus scans could also leave files open and result in an open file error. In addition, application files are often in use by their associated applications and will require interaction between the application and the backup software in order to back up those files while the application is in use.

For example, database applications may load database files into memory and have exclusive control over those files the entire time the database service is running. It is not practical to shut down the database servers to perform a backup because this would result in the unavailability of the application, so the backup software needs to be able to interact with the database application. Rather than just backing up files, application-specific agents can back up databases or portions of data sets within a file. An e-mail backup could be performed on select mailboxes or just on public folders using the backup agents, whereas a simple file backup would not offer this granularity. Similarly, hypervisors (servers that host virtual machines) have agents that allow for virtual machines or files within virtual machines to be backed up.

Backup systems have various methods to archive files that are open, but those systems must be enabled for the resource in order for them to function. Here are some examples of open file errors:

```
Too many open files

Snapshot error encountered

"The process cannot access the file because it is being used by another process"

"Command completed with open file errors"

Failed to open file or Unable to open file
```

You can troubleshoot open file errors with the following steps:

1. Install application-specific backup agents. For example, if you're backing up a database server running Microsoft SQL Server, install the backup agent for Microsoft SQL Server. If you're backing up an e-mail server, install the e-mail agent. The agents are provided by the backup software vendor, and a separate license is typically required for each agent. Configure the backup job to back up elements of that system rather than the files themselves. For database servers, choose databases or even tables within the database. For e-mail servers, choose the mailboxes, calendars, or folders you want to back up. For hypervisors, choose the virtual machines you want.

2. Many open-file backup systems for Windows rely on the Microsoft Volume Shadow Copy Service. Ensure that VSS is running on the target machine.

3. Give the backup agent a user account with sufficient privileges to read the files, or access the application and ensure the account is not denied permission. In some cases, this may require administrative credentials (for example, when backing up critical services such as Microsoft Active Directory or certificate services).

4. Set users to automatically log off late at night for maintenance. Notify the users that this will happen in case they need to run a program overnight.

Virus Scanning

Virus scanners look for malicious or suspicious activity on a machine and block that activity when they find it. Suspicious activity is determined by virus signatures or patterns of behavior. Backup software can sometimes appear suspicious to antivirus scanners because backup software attempts to read many files and change their archive bit. Backup agents may be terminated by the target's antivirus software if it believes the backup agent is acting suspiciously.

Backup jobs that are being blocked by virus scanners often run extremely slow and produce a large number of errors, typically one or more for each file that could not be accessed due to blocking from the virus scanner. If you determine that backup failures are the result of antivirus software on the host, use the following procedure to exclude or whitelist the backup agent in your antivirus software. It is a best practice to deploy exclusions and whitelists using a central administration utility so that changes do not have to be made on machines individually. It is also a best practice to test exclusions on several machines before deploying the changes to all machines. Follow this procedure to exclude the backup service from antivirus scans:

1. Identify the filename and path of the backup agent process.

2. Open the antivirus utility or central administration utility and navigate to the location where applications can be marked safe. Antivirus vendors may use different names for this section. Some names include application exclusions, whitelisted applications, and safe applications.

3. Browse to the path where the backup agent process resides and select the backup agent executable to exclude agent activity from virus scans.

Permissions

Backup software needs to have permission to access the files in a backup set on the target machine. When a backup is made, the program needs to have the ability to read the files and directories that are part of the backup set. Here are some examples of permission errors:

```
Cannot make required directory

Permission to perform this operation was denied.

'Permission denied, user '(username)' on '(client)' does not have 'Backup
local data' privilege'

Initialization functions cannot open one of the Tivoli Storage Manager
logs or a related file: /var/opt/tivoli/tsm/log/dsmerror.log. errno = 13,
Permission denied

Failure for the Data Protection for SQL backup. If scheduled, the return code
on failure will read "1914" in the schedule log.
```

The first error you might run into is a lack of permission for the file or folder that is selected on the target server. Correct this error by granting read access for the target directory to the account the backup agent is running under. You can also receive permission errors if the account the backup agent is using is locked out or disabled. Unlock it if it is locked, or enable it if it is disabled. Enabling or unlocking a local account is performed in computer management on the local machine if running a Windows server. Enabling or unlocking a domain account is performed on a domain controller using the Active Directory Users and Computers snap-in in a Windows environment.

Permission errors can occur if the account is denied access. Verify that the target folder does not have a deny permission set for the account that the backup agent uses. Deny permissions always take precedent over allow permissions, so the agent account could be granted access but still be unable to access the files. Remove the deny if it is in place. Sometimes a deny permission is inherited from a parent directory. Disable inheritance on the directory and then remove the deny. This will remove the deny on the folder and subfolders but preserve the deny for higher-level folders. Similar errors can occur if the account is denied the special permission to log on as a batch job. Make sure that the account is not part of the "deny logon as a batch job" policy in the Windows domain controller security policy or in the local policy of the server. Log on to a Windows domain controller and use the Group Policy Management Console to change this for a domain policy, or use "modify the policy on the local machine" if the computer is not part of a domain.

CAUTION Never run services under a user or administrator's account. Service accounts should be created for services, and their passwords should be set to something extremely long and complex. Service account passwords should not be set to change because this can result in interrupted service. Using a user or administrator's account could result in that account having permissions the user himself does not need, and if that user ever leaves the company, disabling his account would disrupt the services that run using that account.

You might receive permission errors if the password for the backup agent account has expired. It usually best to set a very complex password on the backup account and to change the password manually rather than automatically expiring the password or setting it to a change interval, because if the password is not changed within that interval, the backup agent account will not authenticate. Storage administrators will need to ensure that they change the password on each service that uses the account in order to avoid authentication errors. If a password is not updated on each service, some targets may receive permission errors. Verify that the password used by the service account is correct. Retype the password into the service settings and then restart the service. Another administrator may have changed the password but did not update the service settings for each service that uses the account.

Some errors that appear to be permission errors are actually connectivity errors. First verify that you can ping the target. You can ping the target by name, and this will verify that the backup server can correctly resolve the DNS name to an IP address, and it will also confirm whether the machine is responding. If the machine does not respond, check and make sure that it is connected to the network and that it is running. You might also receive a permission error that is actually a connectivity problem if a local server firewall or hardware firewall in between the target and the backup server is blocking the connection. Attempt to telnet to the target machine from the backup server using the port the backup agent uses. If this connection fails, add a firewall rule to allow that port or service through. The following command verifies connectivity between the backup server and a target with the IP address 192.168.10.220, assuming the agent uses port number 6103:

```
Telnet 192.168.10.220 6103
```

Chapter Summary

The goal of this chapter was to provide you with a solid foundation in the practices and principles associated with maintaining business continuity through network optimization. The metrics used to measure network performance were presented, and we discussed how their interaction impacts the day-to-day operation of an enterprise. The number of operations or instructions a storage device is able to handle was identified as an important factor at layer 1 of the OSI model—the physical layer.

Timing and scheduling were discussed as means of maintaining a balance between network functionality and monitoring. Defragmentation, or defragging as it is more popularly referred to, is a process by which misaligned files and wasted space on a storage medium are optimized. The sheer capacity of modern-day storage devices makes this a time-consuming and complicated process that could potentially impact peak-time traffic by stalling critical system cycles and resources.

The similarities and differences between standard SATA and other hard drives were contrasted and compared to SSD technology. Each type of disk benefits from different forms of optimization and robustness. The design, architecture, and shelf life of various storage media must be taken into consideration because each will present its own unique opportunities and challenges for the network administrator. The latter part of the chapter went into a more technical discussion of the various types of errors and offers practical steps for identifying, isolating, and ultimately resolving them.

The maintenance of documentation or creation of a knowledge base cannot be overemphasized. This is perhaps the most potent tool in a network administrator's arsenal. Many administrators focus on sophisticated tools or procedures, failing to reap the benefits that could be derived from documenting the ways in which problems were resolved. This data not only provides a means for rapid MTTR, but also may aid in identifying and tracking patterns that, when integrated into the overall business continuity planning, help maintain a high level of performance while leveraging network investment.

Reliable backups are crucial in maintaining adequate system availability and preserving data integrity. Backup systems need to be regularly monitored for backup failures, errors, and warnings so that they can be resolved in a timely manner. Storage administrators should be familiar with common issues and resolution steps. Some common backup issues discussed here include running out of space on the target or the destination, open files, virus scanning, and permissions.

Software References

Various tools were mentioned in this chapter. For your convenience, a link is provided for each tool here so that you can download or learn more about them. Some tools can be purchased directly, while others require contacting the vendor.

- **Brocade Data Center Fabric Manager**
  www.brocade.com/downloads/documents/data_sheets/product_data_sheets/DCFM_DS_00.pdf

- **Cacti**
  www.cacti.net

- **Capsa**
  www.colasoft.com/capsa/

- **Dell EqualLogic SAN Headquarters**
  www.dell.com/downloads/global/products/pvaul/en/equallogic-san-headquarters.pdf

- **EMC ControlCenter**
  www.emc.com/data-center-management/controlcenter.htm

- **EMC Powerpath**
  www.emc.com/storage/powerpath/powerpath.htm

- **Hitachi Dynamic Link Manager**
  www.hds.com/products/storage-software/hitachi-dynamic-link-manager-advanced-software.html

- **Hitachi Tuning Manager**
  www.hds.com/products/storage-software/hitachi-tuning-manager.html

- **HP Storage Essentials**
  www8.hp.com/us/en/software-solutions/storage-essentials-resource-management/

- **IBM Tivoli Storage Productivity Center**
  www-03.ibm.com/software/products/en/tivostorprodcent/

- **Manage Engine OpStor**
  www.manageengine.com/products/opstor/

- **Microsoft Volume Shadow Copy Service (VSS)**
  https://msdn.microsoft.com/en-us/library/windows/desktop/aa384649(v=vs.85).aspx

- **NetApp SAN screen**
  www.netapp.com/us/products/management-software/sanscreen/

- **PRTG network monitor**
  www.paessler.com/prtg/

- **Solarwinds Storage Resource Monitor**
  www.solarwinds.com/storage-manager.aspx

- **Solarwinds SAN monitor**
  www.solarwinds.com/products/freetools/san_monitor/

- **Splunk**
  www.splunk.com

- **Wireshark**
  https://www.wireshark.org

- **ZenOss**
  www.zenoss.com

Chapter Review Questions

1. What is IOPS primarily used for?

   A. To determine which connection should be throttled

   B. To determine the performance of a drive or system

   C. To determine the amount of reserved or protected space needed to operate

   D. The reorganization of a database

2. An operation in which data is reorganized so that it can be read sequentially to reduce latency and wear and tear on the disks is called what?

   A. Disk damage reduction (DDR)

   B. Defragmentation

   C. Sequential reorganization

   D. Sequential data systemizing

3. Which of the following best defines a cache read miss?

   A. When the cache crashes

   B. When data from the cache fails to save to the disk

   C. When the data requested does not exist in the cache

   D. When a request for data that exists in the cache fails to initialize

4. Consider a RAID 5 consisting of four drives. If the bit string in the first stripe is 100, 101, 110, then what value would be written to the fourth drive?

   A. 111

   B. 101

   C. 000

   D. 010

5. In an embedded switch, what causes the increase in reliability and overall performance?

   A. The allocation of a certain task to a separate board

   B. Network connectivity

   C. All functions are performed at the chip level

   D. The use of gold embedded in the circuit board to increase conductivity

6. What is the CPU load a measure of?

   A. The amount of work necessary from the CPU to run a single program

   B. The amount of work the CPU is doing as the computer functions

   C. The average load that a CPU can handle under regular conditions

   D. The amount of power necessary to run the CPU

7. After discovering that a host could not connect to the network, Barnabus determined that there was an issue with the cable. What should Barnubus' next step be?

   A. Replacing the cable with one that he knows is good

   B. Testing the cable with a cable tester to determine whether it is faulty

   C. Ensuring that the cable is properly connected to the NIC or HBA port and the switch

   D. Checking for issues with the switch or the NIC

8. Tom is a backup administrator for ABC Tools. He configures a daily full backup of a file server, a NAS share, and a database server that all must remain available 24/7. The backup runs at 2:00 A.M. The next morning Tom checks the backup and finds that the backup failed with the following error on each of the database files: "The process cannot access the file because it is being used by another process." What should Tom do to resolve the error and ensure that the files are backed up?

   A. Modify the backup job to exclude the database files.

   B. Configure a pre-job execution script that stops the database services and a post-job execution script to start the database services.

   C. Install the backup agent for the database software and reconfigure the backup job to back up the databases using the agent.

   D. Connect to the database server as administrator and grant Tom full control of the root directory.

Chapter Review Answers

1. **B** is correct. IOPS is defined as the most basic metric used in measuring storage performance.
   A, **C**, and **D** are incorrect. **A** is incorrect because throttling determinations would be based on resource contention, not IOPS. **C** is incorrect because the amount of reserved or protected space would be determined by the applications running on a volume, not IOPS. **D** is incorrect because reorganization of a database would be based on variables such as query execution time, index lookup time, and other DBMS statistics.

2. **B** is correct. Defragmentation reorganizes the data so that it can be read sequentially to reduce latency and wear and tear on disks due to head and platter activity.
   A, **C**, and **D** are incorrect. **A** is incorrect because disk damage reduction is not an industry term. DDR in technology refers to a type of RAM. **C** is incorrect as well because this is not an industry term. It describes what defragmentation does, but the actual term is defragmentation. **D** is incorrect because it is not an industry term.

3. **C** is correct. A read miss is when data is requested of an array but the data does not reside in cache. In such cases, the data must be read from disk and then stored in cache before it is sent to the user or application.

A, **B**, and **D** are incorrect. When cache crashes, the cache would be inaccessible. In redundant cache situations, such as those with redundant controllers, read and write requests would be serviced by the other controller, but this would not result in a read miss. **B** is also incorrect because saving to disk is a process associated with writing data, not reading data. **D** is incorrect because cache failures, much like cache crashes, trigger a series of events wholly unrelated to cache read misses.

4. **A** is correct. The XOR of the first and second drives is 100, and 101 is 001. This combined with the third is 001 and 110, which is 111. Remember, the XOR is 0 when the bits are the same and 1 when the bits are different.

B, **C**, and **D** are incorrect. If you came up with 101, 000, or 010, please check your math again. The XOR of the remaining values 100, 101, and 110 equals 111.

5. **C** is correct. In an embedded switch, all functions are performed at the chip level, resulting in increased reliability and overall performance.

A, **B**, and **D** are incorrect. **A** is incorrect because allocating a task to a certain separate board could have a variety of effects depending on the task allocated, the ability of the board to perform that task, and the interconnection between the board and the rest of the switch. **B** is incorrect because network connectivity is essential to switch performance, but it does not necessarily increase performance. **D** is incorrect because connectors are built to industry standards and a change to one connector would have no impact unless a change was made to the cable that connects to it and the architecture of the cable.

6. **B** is correct. The CPU load is essentially the total of all things that the CPU is currently supporting. For example, if a man is carrying a pallet of bricks, the current load he is supporting is the amount of weight he is carrying in that moment.

A, **C**, and **D** are incorrect. **A** is incorrect because the CPU load consists of much more than just one application's requirements. **C** is incorrect because average load is different from load. **D** is incorrect because load is not determined by power. The CPU must be provided the power required in its specifications, no more or less.

7. **C** is correct. Before making any changes, Barnabus should ensure that everything is attached correctly.

A, **B**, and **D** are incorrect. **A** is incorrect because replacing the cable takes more time than checking the connection. It is best to try the easiest thing first to save time in troubleshooting. **B** is incorrect because testing the cable with a cable tester will require disconnecting it and testing steps that take longer to perform than checking the connection. **D** is also incorrect because Barnabus determined the problem was with the cable, not the switch or NIC.

8. C is correct. Tom should install the backup agent for the database software on the database server. This will allow the backup software to talk to the database application to back up the databases while they are running, and the backup software will not need to interface with the locked files that are currently preventing the job from completing. Tom then should reconfigure the backup job to use the agent.

A, **B**, and **D** are incorrect. **A** is incorrect because excluding the database files would not back up the database files. **B** is incorrect because stopping the database services with a script would make the databases and the applications dependent upon them unavailable to users. **D** is incorrect because enterprise applications should run under a service account, not an individual user or administrator's account. Also, the files are clearly locked by the database application in this question, and changing the permissions would not correct the locking issue.

APPENDIX

Practice Exam

This practice exam has been written to emulate the types of questions you can expect to see on the SCSP exam. Try to simulate a real testing environment and find a quiet spot where you will not be interrupted. Give yourself 90 minutes to answer all 100 questions.

Once you have answered as many questions as you can in 90 minutes (or are satisfied with your answers if you finish before your 90 minutes are up), go to the "Quick Answer Key" section to score your exam. Review the in-depth answer explanations and references for any answers that were incorrect, and then go to the "Analyzing Your Results" section to review your score.

Questions

1. After configuring storage on a storage array for a host, you find that a technician has moved fiber cables on the fiber switch, causing the assigned LUNs to disappear from the host. What should you do to prevent this from occurring in the future?

   A. Utilize WWN zoning.

   B. Secure the SFPs to the switch with zip ties.

   C. Utilize port zoning.

   D. Restrict access to the SAN zoning to storage administrators only.

2. A host connected to an iSCSI SAN is experiencing high CPU utilization. Which option would resolve the issue with the least effort and cost?

   A. Replace the CPU with a faster one.

   B. Replace the NIC with a NIC with TOE.

   C. Upgrade copper cables to fiber.

   D. Upgrade Cat5e cables to Cat6a.

3. Which of the following would be considered an initiator? (Choose two.)

   A. HBA

   B. iSCSI NIC

   C. Switch port

   D. Storage controller

4. Snapshots are taken every 15 minutes of an e-mail server and then sent to a nearline storage array. The e-mail backups on the nearline storage array are archived to tape at 10 P.M. each day. Restore tests have confirmed that it takes 30 to 45 minutes to restore an e-mail backup from tape and 2 minutes to restore from nearline storage. What is the RPO?

   A. 2 minutes

   B. 15 minutes

   C. 30 minutes

   D. 45 minutes

5. You have been tasked with backing up a storage array to tape. The backup window is only a few hours, and all the data must be completely written to tape during the backup window. Which technology should you use to accomplish the objective?

   A. Disk to disk

   B. Tape autoloader

   C. Disk to disk to tape

   D. Tape library

6. Users complain about slow access to files on a database server. The database server has its database files stored on an iSCSI SAN. You check the logs on the storage array and switches and see no errors. You then issue a packet capture on the network and find a significant amount of FTP traffic during the times when users have complained. What should you do to improve performance without impacting the speed of FTP transfers?

   A. Give iSCSI traffic a higher priority.

   B. Give FTP traffic a lower priority.

   C. Segment the iSCSI traffic on its own VLAN.

   D. Replace NICs with NICs that support TOE.

7. At 2 A.M., your storage vendor calls you to tell you that she is on the way to your data center to replace a failed disk. How did the storage vendor know about the failed disk?

   A. Call Home

   B. Event logs

   C. SSH administrator CLI

   D. SNMP traps

8. You are evaluating the price of a new storage array for your company. The company requires the fastest speed but not high capacity. Which disk technology should you look for in the storage array?

   A. SCSI

   B. SAS

   C. SSD

   D. SATA

9. Business requirements state that two switches located in different data centers must have the same domain ID. They are part of the same SAN. Which technology will allow you to use the same domain ID on both FC switches?

   A. WSAN

   B. VSAN

   C. Domain ID mirroring

   D. Alternate domain IDs

10. A multipathed server connected to a SAN loses access to storage resources after a switch fails. What should you do to correct this?

    A. Cable both HBAs to different switches.

    B. Install updates to the host's multipathing software.

    C. Configure the ports on the switch to be in the same LAG group.

    D. Configure the failover option on the zone.

11. Which component is not configured for high availability in the solution depicted in the illustration?

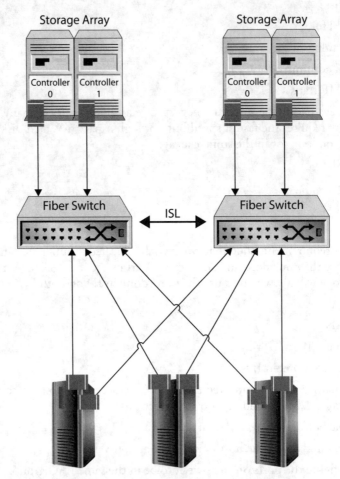

A. Storage array

B. Switches

C. Host

D. ISL

12. Your company would like to move department shares to a central device that will handle access through NFS and CIFS for Windows and Linux machines. Which solution will satisfy the requirements?

A. iSCSI storage array

B. Software as a Service (SaaS)

C. NAS

D. DAS

13. A directory on a file share is running out of space, so the IT director orders several new hard drives. Which of the following options would work to increase the space for the directory when the drives arrive? (Choose all that apply.)

A. Create a RAID set with the drives and a logical volume. Add the volume to the storage pool that the file share resides on and verify that the share is set to autoexpand.

B. Create a RAID set with the drives. Select the volume that is running out of space, choose Extend, and select the unpartitioned space on the new RAID set.

C. Create a RAID set with the drives and a logical volume. Mount the volume in a temporary location and move the files in the directory that is running out of space to the new volume; then unmount and mount the volume in the folder location of the directory that was running out of space.

D. Extend the existing RAID set to include the additional drives.

E. Create a RAID set with the drives and a logical volume. Move the data from the directory that is running out of space to the new logical volume and then share it. Change the name of the old share. Use DFS to create a root share with the name of the old share. Create DFS links to the old and new logical volumes so that the former folder structure is maintained.

14. A storage array is configured with seven 500GB SATA disks, five 300GB SAS 15k disks, and five 400GB SAS 15k disks. At a minimum, how many hot spares will be needed and what type are they?

A. One hot spare consisting of a 500GB SAS 15k disk

B. Two hot spares consisting of a 500GB SATA disk and a 400GB SAS 15k disk

C. Three hot spares consisting of a 500GB SATA disk, a 300GB SAS15k disk, and a 400GB SAS 15k disk

D. One hot spare consisting of a 500GB SSD disk

15. You are setting up a new storage array, and you want to have two RAID groups using RAID 5 and a hot spare. You will need 5TB of available storage, and you have a box of 500GB SAS disks. How many disks would you need?

A. 13

B. 12

C. 11

D. 10

16. Your organization utilizes the following backup schedule: full backups every Saturday at 10 P.M. and incremental backups Sunday through Friday at 10 A.M. and 10 P.M. A large number of files were deleted from the NAS on Wednesday at 5 P.M. Which backups must be restored, and in what order do you restore the files?

   A. Full backup and then the 5 P.M. backup on Wednesday

   B. Full backup and then the 10 A.M. backup on Wednesday

   C. Full backup and then the Sunday 10 A.M., 10 P.M.; Monday 10 A.M., 10 P.M.; Tuesday 10 A.M., 10 P.M.; and Wednesday 10 A.M. backups

   D. The Sunday 10 A.M., 10 P.M.; Monday 10 A.M., 10 P.M.; Tuesday 10 A.M., 10 P.M.; and Wednesday 10 A.M. backups

17. How many disks does a RAID 10 array require at the absolute minimum?

   A. 1

   B. 3

   C. 4

   D. 5

18. Your team has a series of reports that must be shared between members located all around the world. They want to use a cloud-based solution to host the files. What type of solution should you consider?

   A. SaaS

   B. PaaS

   C. CaaS

   D. STaaS

   E. IaaS

The following scenario is used for questions 19, 20, and 21:

Nutty Corporation has a clustered e-mail server consisting of four servers (MailNode01, MailNode02, MailNode03, and MailNode04) that connect to an iSCSI SAN for their storage. There are six LUNs assigned to the four clustered servers. They are labeled 001-Quorum, 002-MSDTC, 003-MailDB01, 004-MailDB02, 005PublicFolder, and 006-MailDBArchive. A full backup is performed on LUNs 003, 004, 005, and 006 each night at 8 P.M. using out-of-band backup software. Snapshots are taken of all LUNs assigned to the cluster twice a day at 2 A.M. and 2 P.M. Your manager has informed you that restore operations should be performed in-band whenever possible. The four servers each have four NICs. Two are link aggregated for load balancing and failover for iSCSI traffic, and two are link aggregated for load balancing and failover for use on the LAN. Two VLANs are configured, with one for iSCSI traffic and another for LAN traffic.

19. At 4 P.M., an integrity check detects corrupted data in the public folder. LUN 005PublicFolder is currently mounted on MailNode01. Given the scenario described, what should you do to restore the data with the least data loss?

    A. Revert to the 2 P.M. snapshot for LUN 005PublicFolder.

    B. Apply the backup from 8 P.M. from the night before and then revert to the 2 P.M. snapshot for LUN 005PublicFolder.

    C. Fail over LUN 005PublicFolder to MailNode02 and then reset the integrity error.

    D. Take MailNode01 out of the cluster.

20. A junior administrator accidentally deletes LUN 003 from the iSCSI storage array at 9 P.M. Given the scenario described, what should you do to restore the data with the least data loss?

    A. Revert to the 2 P.M. snapshot for LUN 003-MailDB01.

    B. Apply the backup from 8 P.M. from the night before and then revert to the 2 P.M. snapshot for LUN 003-MailDB01.

    C. Create a new LUN 003-MailDB01 with the same size as the old LUN 003-MailDB01 and then restore the backup from 8 P.M. from the night before for LUN 003-MailDB01.

    D. Apply the backup from 8 P.M. from the same day for LUN 003-MailDB01.

21. You notice connectivity errors in the log for the second iSCSI NIC in each of the clustered servers. You verify the zone, and it is configured correctly. Given the scenario described, what might be the problem? (Choose all that apply.)

    A. The switch for the secondary iSCSI NICs is offline.

    B. The iSCSI storage array is in maintenance mode.

    C. The second controller on the iSCSI storage array lost its IP address.

    D. The iSCSI storage array lost power.

    E. The VLAN configuration on the switches is missing.

22. Which of the following is not an advantage of cable management?

    A. Cable management improves airflow in the rack.

    B. Cable management separates data and power cables to better prevent EMI.

    C. Cable management helps prevent cable stretching and snags.

    D. Cable management extends the life of rack equipment.

23. Which of the following is a benefit of a high cache hit ratio?

    A. Faster storage array response time

    B. Lower latency for storage replication

    C. Increased utilization of system cache

    D. Less storage used because of deduplication

24. Your company expands into a neighboring office space that already has Ethernet cabling installed using Cat5e. The cables terminate in a wiring closet. Your users require 1 Gbps connections to the network, and the wiring closet must support 10GigE to the storage system in your server room. The server room is 75 meters away from the wiring closet. What cabling should you add or replace in this situation? Keep costs to a minimum.

   A. Replace the Cat5e cables with Cat6 and add Cat6 cabling from the wiring closet to the server room.

   B. Add Cat6 cabling from the wiring closet to the server room.

   C. Add multimode fiber between the wiring closet and the server room.

   D. Replace the Cat5e cables with Cat6 and multimode fiber from the wiring closet to the server room.

   E. Add Cat6a cabling from the wiring closet to the server room.

25. You are a storage administrator responsible for backups on the storage network. Backups must be sent to tape each day using a single tape drive, and the duration of backup jobs on the storage systems must be kept to a minimum. Which backup design would best fit this situation?

   A. D2T

   B. D2D2T

   C. NDMP

   D. D2D

26. Which of the following is an advantage of storage tiering?

   A. Data is migrated to another site for disaster recovery.

   B. Duplicate files are suppressed.

   C. Data retention policies are enforced.

   D. Most frequently used files can be accessed faster.

27. What is the most frequent backup performed in a GFS rotation?

   A. Hourly

   B. Daily

   C. Incremental

   D. Transactional

   E. Weekly

28. Which technology encapsulates FC data over Ethernet but does not use IP?

   A. iSCSI

   B. FCoE

   C. FCIP

   D. iFCP

29. If you configure seven 400GB drives in a RAID6, how much usable space will you have?

    A. 2,800GB

    B. 2,400GB

    C. 2,000GB

    D. 1,600GB

30. Technicians at your company remotely manage the SAN fabric using Telnet. Port 23 is open on the firewall to allow the technicians to connect remotely. What changes should you make to encrypt this traffic?

    A. Disallow port 23 on the firewall. Configure an SSL VPN and allow port 443 on the firewall. Instruct technicians to connect to the network using the VPN and then to use Telnet within the VPN.

    B. Configure the SAN fabric to use SSH instead. Instruct technicians to connect using SSH rather than Telnet.

    C. Enable "require encryption" on the Telnet configuration on the SAN fabric. Instruct technicians to utilize the encryption option when connecting.

    D. Disable Telnet and require technicians to use a serial cable to manage the SAN fabric.

31. What is the primary requirement for a system to be considered high availability?

    A. 24/7 monitoring

    B. Higher SLAs

    C. Offsite backups

    D. Redundant components

32. How do hot and cold aisles enhance airflow in a data center?

    A. Hot and cold aisles keep hot air flowing away from computing equipment and toward cooling equipment while cold air is directed toward computing equipment.

    B. Hot aisles and cold aisles allow for high-density racks to be placed where they will receive the most cooling.

    C. Hot aisles and cold aisles aid in emergency evacuation.

    D. Hot and cold aisles allow for better capacity planning

33. Users in the finance, accounting, and administration departments need access to the quarterly reports. You would like to create a central location to store the files and allow concurrent access to users in the departments. Which protocol would be best suited for the task?

    A. SNMP

    B. CIFS

    C. Telnet

    D. iSCSI

    E. FC

34. A system that has three LUNs formatted with the EXT3 file system crashes overnight. Web developers need access to the LUNs immediately while the crashed system is being rebuilt. Which type of system should the LUNs be mounted to?

   A. Windows 98

   B. Windows Server 2008 R2

   C. Ubuntu Linux

   D. AS/400

   E. Apple iOS

35. A multipathed server is connected to a storage array, but it is experiencing higher latency on some traffic and low latency on other traffic. You check the configuration of the HBAs, and they are configured in an active/passive load-balanced team. After analyzing the switches, you find that the ISL between two redundant switches has periods of high utilization that correspond to the higher latency. How might you solve the problem? (Choose the best answer.)

   A. Add more links to the ISL between the switches.

   B. Map the LUNs to the server using a file-level architecture rather than a block-level architecture.

   C. Increase the buffer-to-buffer credits.

   D. Configure the multipathed HBAs to be active/active.

36. Which of the following topologies uses optical cables in a logical ring but is configured as a physical star?

   A. FC-AL

   B. FC-SW

   C. P2P

   D. Ethernet

37. Which device can make decisions based on information it receives from neighboring devices on where to send traffic most efficiently in a meshed or partially meshed network consisting of multiple potential paths from source to destination?

   A. Switch

   B. Director

   C. Repeater

   D. Router

   E. Transceiver

38. What role does iSNS play on a SAN?

   A. It provides attached devices with information on available storage resources.

   B. It notifies administrators when critical events occur on the SAN.

C. It registers new FC addresses when a device connects to the SAN.

D. It load-balances connections between multipathed adapters.

39. Which media would be best suited for archival storage at the lowest cost for 400GB of files on a periodic basis?

A. DVD

B. Flash media

C. Nearline storage

D. Tape

40. How do fiber switches connect to one another?

A. ISLs are created between two switches using E-ports.

B. ISLs are created between two switches using F-ports.

C. Fiber cables are connected to both switches on U-ports.

D. Fiber cables are connected to both switches on F-ports.

41. In a business continuity planning meeting, your manager asks you how the organization would continue business if a fire consumed the equipment in the server room. Which technology would be useful for business continuity in this situation?

A. Offsite tape backups

B. Hierarchical storage management

C. Snapshots

D. Remote replication

42. Users complain of slow performance on a key application. You calculate current performance metrics. What must you compare the metrics to in order to identify which component or system is slow?

A. Alerts

B. Baseline

C. Scope

D. Logs

43. Which technology would ensure that the same data is present on all devices before committing a transaction?

A. Snapshot

B. Replication

C. Consistency group

D. Integrity group

44. Which of the following statements is true?

   A. LTO3 tapes have a native capacity of 400GB and a compressed capacity of 800GB.

   B. LTO4 tapes have a native capacity of 400GB and a compressed capacity of 800GB.

   C. LTO5 tapes have a native capacity of 800GB and a compressed capacity of 1,600GB.

   D. LTO2 tapes have a native capacity of 100GB and a compressed capacity of 200GB.

45. Your organization plans to replicate data from a high-performance database in New York to Los Angeles. The link between sites has high latency, and performance must be only minimally impacted. What form of replication would be best suited to this situation?

   A. Synchronous replication

   B. Direct replication

   C. Asynchronous replication

   D. Host-based replication

46. A storage array has four front-end ports connected to four servers. A fifth server is added. What should be installed so that this device can connect to the storage array?

   A. Director

   B. Router

   C. Switch

   D. Repeater

47. How many heads are in a hard disk drive, and how are they situated?

   A. There is a head at the top and bottom of each platter with its own actuator arm.

   B. A single head runs between all of the platters on the hard drive.

   C. There is a head at the top and bottom of each platter. All heads are attached to the same actuator arm.

   D. The head runs along the surface of each disk and is used to read the hard drive.

48. Where is the controller board located, and what job does it perform?

   A. A controller board controls the movement of the actuator arm from below the disk.

   B. A controller is mounted to the base of the disk and contains an interface for sending and receiving data to a connected device. It controls the movement of the actuator arm and rotation of the spindle.

C. A controller board is mounted to the top of the disk and controls the physical components in the disk.

D. A controller board is attached to the top of the disk and causes the disk to spin.

49. While both solid-state and hard disk drives are used to store data, how do SSD and HDD differ in the way they organize data?

   A. SSD organizes data into blocks rather than tracks and selectors.

   B. In an HDD, blocks consist of multiple pages made up of 150 bytes.

   C. In SSD, pages consist of blocks, which are generally 128 bytes.

   D. An HDD uses logical bit addressing to reference a location on a disk, while SSD uses a master table.

50. How does Fibre Channel reference other devices on the network?

   A. A simple channel access system (SCAS)

   B. A reference ID

   C. A twofold security connection number

   D. A World Wide Name (WWN)

51. What is Fibre Channel layer 3 known as, and what does it do?

   A. It is known as the block layer, and it is the upper-layer protocol mapping. It is responsible for encapsulating upper-layer protocols.

   B. It is the processing layer, and it breaks data into smaller chunks called *frames*.

   C. It is the services layer, and it supports striping, hunt groups, and the spanning of multiple ports.

   D. It is the infrastructure layer used to ensure all pathways are planned for data to travel.

52. What is a World Wide Name (WWN)?

   A. A 16-bit or 32-bit identifier for a network communication port

   B. A computer's external IP address

   C. The main port identifier in a simple channel access system

   D. An 8-byte or 16-byte identifier for a network communication port on a Fibre Channel network

53. One of the most basic metrics used in measuring storage performance is called what?

   A. File Transfer Protocol

   B. System Storage Monitoring

   C. Input Output Operations per Second

   D. Send Receive Operations per Second

54. How do optical cables transmit data?

    A. Optical cables transmit data via long-range frequencies.

    B. Optical cables transmit data via light impulses.

    C. Optical cables transmit data via electromagnetic waves.

    D. Optical cables transmit data via electromagnetic impulses.

55. Which of the following best describes a converged network adapter?

    A. A device that connects an iSCSI host to storage

    B. A device that can be used for communication with non-storage-related equipment via a network

    C. An onboard device that connects two devices via copper cabling

    D. A device capable of connecting a host to storage with connections over FC, Ethernet, or twinax connections

56. Which of the following best describes a fiber director?

    A. A high-capacity modular switch with two or more hot-swappable power supplies and redundant routing engines, pathways, and processors.

    B. A layer 3 device that is used to connect network segments of differing topologies.

    C. A device that connects storage segments that traverse a WAN. The director performs encapsulation over the WAN of supported storage protocols and deencapsulation of data on the receiving end.

    D. A device that filters storage data at the application layer utilizing a wide array of software. Such devices are typically vendor updatable.

57. The condition known as *buffer underrun* refers to which of the following?

    A. When a disk is rendered unusable because of a failure during the write process

    B. When the scratches on a disk have rendered portions of the data unusable

    C. When the buffer is emptied during the process of burning information to a disk

    D. The condition where a disk drive cannot read a disk at the optimal speed

58. How does the Storage Networking Industry Association (SNIA) define storage virtualization?

    A. The application of virtualization to storage services or devices for the purposes of aggregating functions or devices, hiding complexity, or adding new capabilities to lower-level storage resources

    B. The abstraction of software and hardware used to provide storage services such that each can operate independently

C. Implementation of standards-based storage products that can be layered upon one another to provide functionality to meet business objectives

D. Utilizing virtualization in storage services to provide differing views to the data based on the level of virtual provisioning used

59. According to the Storage Networking Industry Association Shared Storage Model, what is the job of the file/record layer?

   A. This layer organizes the information required by the application and interfaces with the application.

   B. This layer uses virtualization to map logical addresses to physical addresses.

   C. This layer of virtualization is an abstraction of physical storage to logical partitions independent of storage structure, allowing several physical disks to be accessed through a single virtual/logical interface.

   D. This layer stores data on virtualized removable media, including virtual tapes (VTs), virtual tape libraries (VTLs), and tape library virtualization (TLV).

60. Which of the following is not a form of storage provisioning?

   A. Privileged provisioning

   B. LUN provisioning

   C. Thick provisioning

   D. Thin provisioning

61. Which of the following is shared by in-band and out-of-band virtualization?

   A. Optimization of SAN utilization and performance.

   B. Storage management is offloaded from the host.

   C. Latency is avoided by separating control functions from the paths where data travels.

   D. A consolidated virtual platform for network storage management.

62. Which of the following is not a type of storage virtualization?

   A. Disk virtualization

   B. Host virtualization

   C. Block virtualization

   D. Tape virtualization

63. What is a high-speed memory that can be used to service I/O requests faster than accessing the disk?

   A. Memory

   B. Logical disks

   C. Solid-state drives

   D. Cache

64. Which of the following best describes the Common Information Model?

   A. It is an object-oriented approach to organizing information where objects have attributes, and each is created from a class that describes the format of the object.

   B. It is a method used to allow multiple levels of abstraction to exist in the data path and to pool storage under the control of a domain manager.

   C. CIM is a method of creating a LU that can grow as needed. The LU appears to the host system as the maximum size it can grow to, but it consumes only the amount of space the host uses on the storage system.

   D. CIM is used to set warning and alarm thresholds in storage management tools that then compare the set values against real-time readings from the system.

65. What does it mean if in-band management is used for a storage network?

   A. Data as well as management and monitoring information travel over different paths.

   B. An appliance is used to manage and monitor data.

   C. An appliance is used to monitor data, but transfers occur over the front-end data path.

   D. Data as well as management and monitoring information travel over the same path.

66. Appliance-based data migration specifically refers to which of the following?

   A. A data migration in which stand-alone network appliances migrate files and volumes, interfacing with storage systems and providing a separate interface for managing the replication

   B. Migrating entire applications, referred to as appliances, from one site to another or from one redundant clustered node to another

   C. Migrating management data such as logs and configuration settings from network appliances for the purposes of centralized review and business continuity

   D. A data migration solution that can be plugged into a rack without additional customization or configuration

67. What amount of space do thick logical units take up? (Choose the best answer.)

   A. Only the amount of space consumed by files within the logical unit.

   B. The amount of space consumed by files in the logical unit plus 20 percent.

   C. Thick logical units are those that exceed 1TB.

   D. The same amount of space as is presented to the host operating system.

68. What best defines data integrity?

    A. Assurance that data remains unchanged after creating, modifying, copying, completing, or otherwise operating on data.

    B. Having a backup of every version of a data set since its creation.

    C. Encrypting a file or data set to prevent tampering.

    D. The data given is proven factual and is supported by other reports.

69. Which of the following is not a broad classification for the causes of system outages?

    A. Human error

    B. Intentional error

    C. Workflow error

    D. Systematic error

70. Which of the following is the primary objective of business continuity planning?

    A. Providing a proactive strategy to prevent or limit the impact of system failures and to rapidly restore operations should such events occur

    B. Outlining the essential activities required when a disaster occurs

    C. Leveraging redundancy in each aspect of the storage and networking environment to be better able to resist a failure of a single component

    D. Replicating duties such that the loss of a single employee, role, or division would not impact the ability of the organization to continue doing business

71. If malware infection potentially impacts the business by a loss of three hours of productivity on average and this is expected to happen once every other month, then the cost per year in hours is which of the following?

    A. 12 hours of lost productivity

    B. 18 hours of lost productivity

    C. 24 hours of lost productivity

    D. 36 hours of lost productivity

72. What is necessary to determine how much redundancy is needed?

    A. Knowing how available a system needs to be

    B. Logical block addressing

    C. How well the failover system works

    D. Whether the system is replicated

73. What does a risk assessment analyze?

   A. The threats that could impact the integrity, confidentiality, or availability of business systems

   B. The cost that a business could incur because of the exploitation of potential threats and the likelihood of such exploitation occurring

   C. Organizational security as a whole

   D. Both A and B

74. What does a business impact analysis estimate?

   A. The time, cost, and effort to respond to and contain a security incident

   B. The cost an organization could incur should systems be unavailable because of incident or disaster

   C. The amount of time it would take to bring business operations back to normal

   D. The controls required to bring risks below the organization's risk tolerance level

75. What is the main difference between remote and physical authentication?

   A. Remote authentication is used to access a system from offsite, while physical authentication is used to connect from another portion of the onsite network.

   B. In remote authentication, passwords are sent via the network, while physical authentication is done on the machine being logged into.

   C. Physical authentication is the type of authentication where a certain visual pattern is used, while a remote authentication is used to easily access devices via a network.

   D. Remote authentication is used when a system is accessed through another system, while physical authentication is used only to access a remote authentication service.

76. When services are transferred from one component to another in a redundant system, it is called what?

   A. Service redundancy

   B. Failover

   C. Overflow

   D. Component transfer

77. What is the name of a system that provides immediate response and high availability?

   A. Emergency system processing

   B. Online transaction processing

   C. Rapid response protocol

   D. Systemic fabrication principles

78. Which technology allows multiple N-ports to reside on the same physical N-port?

   A. VSAN

   B. SCR

   C. PLOGI

   D. NPIV

79. What is a result of a single configuration, a network, hardware, or software malfunctioning and causing the entire system or process to fail?

   A. Large-scale system failure

   B. A single point of failure

   C. Network failure

   D. Server-side power failure

80. What is a secondary risk?

   A. Risk caused by another risk response strategy

   B. Risk that is moderately likely to occur

   C. A risk that can occur when multiple other risks occur

   D. A risk computation obtained from an alternate methodology such as quantitative, if qualitative was used for the primary risk

81. Low humidity can create an environment where charges can build up, which can lead to what?

   A. Water damage

   B. Electrostatic discharge

   C. Overheating

   D. Electrical failure

82. Fire suppression systems that use gaseous agents remove components that fire needs to exist. Which of the following examples remove heat from fire?

   A. FSC-500

   B. HFC-125

   C. CFN-330

   D. HVAC

83. What does *rack density* refer to?

   A. The amount of heat generated by devices in a rack

   B. The number of cables running between devices on the rack

   C. The number of types of devices on the rack

   D. The number of devices in the rack

84. What is a form of storage management where data of varying formats is transferred between hosts or storage systems at periodic intervals?

 A. Transfer protocols

 B. Replication

 C. Data backup

 D. System support

85. What presents files and directories as a composite object with a single integrated file interface while optimizing their location?

 A. Block management architecture

 B. Hierarchical storage management

 C. Manual storage tiering

 D. Storage management system

86. What purpose does the alias serve on a fiber network?

 A. The alias is an alternate WWPN that can be used in case the first WWPN fails.

 B. The alias is used to identify ports that belong to a multicast or hunt group.

 C. The alias is a descriptive name given to a node so that it can be referred to by it instead of its WWN.

 D. The alias was used in FDDI ring implementations, but it is not used in modern fiber networks anymore.

87. What specifies that data potentially relevant to ongoing or expected lawsuits should be preserved?

 A. Mandatory preservation

 B. Litigation holds

 C. Trial backup requirements

 D. Litigation preservation

88. A technician notifies you that the tape drive at your data center is making noise. You investigate and find that the drive repeatedly stops, rewinds, and then writes again. What could be causing this issue?

 A. The tape drive needs cleaning.

 B. The drive is shoe-shining.

 C. The cable between the tape drive and the backup server is going bad.

 D. The backup system has mounted the tape drive for random reads.

89. Which controller technology breaks files up into segments to be stored on multiple nodes in a process known as *encoding*?

 A. Full mesh

 B. Cache

C. Grid

D. Dual

90. Which unit of measurement is used to describe the number of devices data must traverse from source to destination?

   A. Jump

   B. Hop

   C. Latency

   D. Ping

91. Which technology is used to prioritize traffic?

   A. Class of service

   B. Routing

   C. Link-level prioritization

   D. Switching

92. Your customer would like to implement a SAN over their existing Ethernet network. What solution should you recommend?

   A. FC on FC switches

   B. FC on the same LAN

   C. iSCSI on the same LAN

   D. iSCSI with VLANs

93. A server rack in your data center is configured with A/B power. Normal power levels are 25 percent on each link, and peak power is 60 percent. Do you recommend any changes? If so, which changes?

   A. No changes are required because the load is less than 80 percent.

   B. Reduce the load to bring each link below 50 percent.

   C. Add one more circuit and put 30 percent load on it.

   D. Two more circuits should be added to bring the load below 40 percent peak for each link.

94. Which of the following devices is not hot pluggable?

   A. Hard drive

   B. Power supply

   C. Switch module

   D. Motherboard

95. Which disk type can run at 15,000 rpm? (Choose all that apply.)

    A. IDE

    B. SCSI

    C. SATA

    D. SAS

    E. FC

96. Which device would be used by a host to connect to a Fiber Channel SAN?

    A. HBA

    B. NIC

    C. Modem

    D. TOE

97. Which piece of safety equipment can a person wear to protect against electrostatic discharge?

    A. Hard hat

    B. Lifting belt

    C. Wrist strap

    D. Aluminum gloves

98. A user needs to quickly transfer 10GB data from their workstation to a remote office. The user offers to bring the data to the remote office, but they need to store the data on some removable media. Which media would be best suited for transferring the data and be easiest for the user to utilize?

    A. DVD

    B. Flash drive

    C. CD

    D. Tape

99. Your company would like to implement a network to connect multiple disk arrays to servers. Which technology should they employ?

    A. NAS

    B. DAS

    C. LAN

    D. SAN

100. Which of the following could be used to send e-mails to administrators when storage resources are at or above 80 percent capacity?

    A. Baselines

    B. Thresholds

    C. Alerts

    D. Logs

101. Which type of drive would be best suited for a small office NAS with low I/O and utilization?

    A. Consumer drive

    B. Entry-level drive

    C. Midrange drive

    D. Enterprise drive

102. Fred is pricing out a new server that will be used to house development virtual machines for a variety of different departments. Each department is on its own VLAN, and developers require a dedicated NIC for their virtual machines. Fred determines that he needs to have 12 Ethernet connections, so he plans to purchase three quad-port Ethernet adapters. Which PCI bus should he utilize for the server and the expansion cards?

    A. PCI

    B. PCI-X

    C. PCIe

    D. PCI-M

103. Juan is the new storage administrator for his company, and he recently found that the company file shares are stored on a single 3TB SATA drive. The server does not have a RAID controller. Juan wants to implement RAID 5 using three identical 2TB drives he already has on hand to replace the current disk. Juan has no budget for other equipment. Which RAID controller should he implement?

    A. Host-based controller

    B. Software RAID

    C. Hardware RAID

    D. Software RAID using a hardware controller

104. Which cloud storage method is most vulnerable to latency?

    A. Cloud backup

    B. Locally mapped cloud storage

    C. Cloud synchronization

    D. Web-based cloud storage

105. Which of the following is an example of cloud storage?

    A. An application writes a transaction to a database, which then replicates to another database in another data center.

    B. A user modifies a file on their computer, and that modification is synchronized with another remote third-party source over the Internet and other replica sets that connect to the remote source.

    C. A user stores data on a share hosted on a file server, but the share is on a volume mounted through iSCSI to another storage device.

    D. An e-mail server stores user mailboxes on a volume that is mapped back to a number of nodes. The data is encoded, and portions of the data are spread across the nodes in the set.

106. Which of the following is an accurate definition of a hybrid cloud?

    A. A hybrid cloud is owned and operated by a third party and made available to customers over the Internet.

    B. A hybrid cloud is a proprietary system owned and operated by a single organization for its use.

    C. A hybrid cloud is a cloud that is owned and operated by a third party or jointly by its members.

    D. A hybrid cloud is a combination of a public cloud and a private cloud.

107. Which of the following is not an ITIL service change approach?

    A. Phased

    B. Push

    C. Big bang

    D. Core

108. Which information would be useful for properly sizing backup drives? (Choose all that apply.)

    A. Current size of backups

    B. Growth rates

    C. Storage location

    D. Backup frequency and retention

Quick Answer Key

1. A	28. B	55. D	82. B
2. B	29. C	56. A	83. D
3. A and B	30. A	57. C	84. B
4. B	31. D	58. A	85. B
5. D	32. A	59. A	86. B
6. C	33. B	60. A	87. B
7. A	34. C	61. D	88. B
8. C	35. D	62. B	89. C
9. B	36. A	63. D	90. B
10. A	37. D	64. A	91. A
11. A	38. A	65. D	92. D
12. C	39. D	66. A	93. D
13. A, C, and E	40. A	67. D	94. D
14. B	41. D	68. A	95. B, D, and E
15. A	42. B	69. C	96. A
16. C	43. C	70. A	97. C
17. C	44. A	71. B	98. B
18. D	45. C	72. A	99. D
19. A	46. C	73. D	100. C
20. C	47. C	74. B	101. C
21. A and C	48. B	75. B	102. C
22. D	49. A	76. B	103. B
23. A	50. D	77. B	104. B
24. E	51. C	78. D	105. B
25. B	52. D	79. B	106. D
26. D	53. C	80. A	107. D
27. B	54. B	81. B	108. A, B, and D

In-Depth Answers

1. ☑ **A** is the correct answer. Each HBA in a host is assigned a WWN that is unique to it. WWN zoning allows access to LUNs based on the WWN of the device. In this way, it does not matter which port the HBA is plugged into on the switch because the zone will still allow access based on the WWN of the HBA port, which would still reside in the host.

   ☒ **B** is incorrect because the SFP is simply a transceiver, and it does not contain port information or an identification number. The SFPs can be changed without impacting the zoning. **C** is incorrect because port zoning would map LUNs to switch ports, which would not change automatically if a device was moved from one port to another. **D** is incorrect because this problem did not occur because of a zoning change. Rather, it occurred because a change was made to the physical cable. A restriction on zoning would not prevent a technician from moving a cable.

   Chapter 8: Storage Visibility | Zoning
   SCSP objective 1.3, Identify storage mapping elements

2. ☑ **B** is the correct answer. TOE is a chip on a NIC that performs TCP/IP processing so that the computer processor does not have to. This would reduce the CPU utilization.

   ☒ **A** is incorrect because while it would result in more CPU, it would not do so with the least effort and cost. **C** is incorrect because fiber cables are not used with iSCSI for host connectivity and the problem is not one that can be solved with cables. **D** is also incorrect. Faster- or slower-speed cables will still require the CPU to perform TCP/IP computations.

   Chapter 4: Storage Networking Devices | NIC | TCP Offload Engine
   SCSP objective 1.6, Describe how to improve performance for host applications

3. ☑ **A** and **B** are the correct answers. Initiators send requests to targets. Targets are storage resources that can be utilized by initiators. An HBA and an iSCSI NIC both function as initiators.

   ☒ **C** is incorrect because a switch port cannot be a target or an initiator. **D** is incorrect because a storage controller would most likely host targets, not initiators.

   Chapter 3: iSCSI Storage Network | Initiator
   SCSP objective 2.3, Identify Ethernet/IP SAN components

4. ☑ **B** is the correct answer. The RPO is the recovery point objective, and it indicates how current the restore will be. The RPO relates to how much data would be lost. In this case, the RPO is 15 minutes because snapshots are taken every 15 minutes. Any data changed or added in the last 15 minutes would be lost.

   ☒ **A** is incorrect. It takes 2 minutes to restore from nearline storage, so 2 minutes is the recovery time objective (RTO) for restoring from nearline storage. **C** and **D** are incorrect because 45 minutes is the RTO for restoring from tape and 30 minutes is the shortest amount of time recovery from tape could be completed.

Chapter 7: Business Continuity Objectives | Recovery Point Objective
SCSP objective 4.3, Describe disaster recovery concepts

5. ☑ **D** is the correct answer. Given the choices provided, you are looking for a choice that increases the speed of transfers to tape. Possible solutions would include using faster tapes or utilizing multiple tapes at the same time. A tape library allows backup software to write to multiple tapes at a time so more data could be backed up in the same backup window.

☒ **A** is incorrect because a disk-to-disk solution would not archive to tape as required. **B** is incorrect because a tape autoloader has only one drive. **C** is incorrect because the same amount of data would still need to be backed up to tape with D2D2T.

Chapter 4: Removable Storage | Tape Media | Libraries and Autoloaders
SCSP objective 4.1, Identify backup technologies

6. ☑ **C** is the correct answer. The packet capture shows that FTP traffic is traversing the same network as iSCSI traffic. To segment this traffic, a VLAN is needed. The VLAN would allow iSCSI traffic to traverse its own network without impacting FTP traffic, and vice versa.

☒ **A** is incorrect because increasing the priority of iSCSI would impact the FTP transfers. **B** is incorrect because decreasing the FTP priority would also impact FTP transfers. **D** is incorrect because the problem is not with excessive CPU processing.

Chapter 5: Network Virtualization | Methods | VLAN
SCSP objective 1.4, Describe virtualization concepts and techniques

7. ☑ **A** is the correct answer. Call Home is a feature of computing equipment that allows the device to send relevant alerts to the equipment vendor so that the vendor can respond independently. This allows for quicker response to critical issues because local resources do not have to analyze the logs or contact support with a trouble ticket to begin the process of resolving the issue.

☒ **B** is incorrect because the storage vendor did not have to review event logs to receive the alert. **C** is incorrect because the vendor received the alert automatically and did not need to connect to the device to look through the logs. **D** is incorrect because SNMP traps are used locally and would not be delivered to the storage vendor.

Chapter 6: Storage Monitoring, Alerting, and Reporting | Alerting Methods
SCSP objective 5.2, Identify storage management technologies

8. ☑ **C** is the correct answer. Of the available choices, SSD offers much greater speeds than SCSI, SAS, or SATA, but SSD is not available in as large of a capacity as SATA disks.

☒ **A**, **B**, and **D** are incorrect because SSD is faster than SCSI, SAS, or SATA.

Chapter 1: Available Disk Interfaces and Their Characteristics
SCSP objective 3.4, Describe disk technologies

9. ☑ **B** is the correct answer. Domain IDs must be unique on the SAN, so two virtual SANs must be created to allow for the same domain ID.

☒ **A, C**, and **D** are incorrect; they are all imaginary concepts that sound similar to real concepts.

Chapter 5: Network Virtualization | Methods | VSAN
SCSP objective 1.4, Describe virtualization concepts and techniques

10. ☑ **A** is the correct answer. The multipathed server has two connections, but they are going to the same switch, and that is why both connections were lost when the switch died. Cabling each HBA to a different switch will guard against single switch failure.

☒ **B** is incorrect because the software is working fine. This is a physical cabling issue. **C** is incorrect because the ports should be on different switches, not in a LAG group. **D** is incorrect because failover is not configured on the zone level.

Chapter 9: Redundancy | Path/Bus | Multipath
SCSP objective 4.3, Describe disaster recovery concepts

11. ☑ **A** is the correct answer. The figure shows two cables on each storage array, but they are going to one switch each. For the systems to be configured for high availability, the storage arrays should have a connection to both switches to protect against a switch failure.

☒ **B** is incorrect because the switches have an ISL between them. **C** is incorrect because the hosts have redundant connections to both switches, and **D** is incorrect because the ISL connects all switches.

Chapter 9: Storage Architecture Components | High Availability
SCSP objective 4.3, Describe disaster recovery concepts

12. ☑ **C** is the correct answer. A NAS hosts shares using protocols such as NFS and CIFS.

☒ **A** is incorrect because iSCSI uses a block-level architecture and the iSCSI protocol, not NFS or CIFS. **B** is incorrect because SaaS is a cloud-based application, but this would require StaaS, cloud-based storage. **D** is incorrect because a DAS would provide access only to a locally attached device, and it would not support NFS or CIFS.

Chapter 2: Network Attached Storage
SCSP objective 2.1, Identify NAS components

13. ☑ **A, C**, and **E** are the correct answers. Answer **A** would increase the storage available in the pool, and then the share would expand as necessary to consume the space when it needs it. Answer **C** would work because this would increase the available space to that individual folder by mounting the extra space as a folder. **E** would work because it would utilize the same directory structure while pointing the folder that is running out of space to the new disks with available storage.

☒ **B** is incorrect because extending a volume works only within a single RAID set or storage pool. To extend the volume, both RAID sets would need to belong to the same storage pool. **D** is incorrect because RAID sets cannot be modified once they are created. To add more disks to a RAID set, the data would need to be migrated to alternate storage, and then the RAID set could be deleted and re-created as a larger RAID set.

Chapter 1: Hosts Interaction with Disks | File Systems
SCSP objective 1.2, Describe host-based functions for storage

14. ☑ **B** is the correct answer. Two hot spares are needed. One hot spare is needed to cover the 500GB SATA disk because a SAS disk cannot be a hot spare for a SATA, and vice versa. Another disk is needed to cover the SAS disks. A 400GB SAS 15k disk can be a hot spare for the 300 or 400GB SAS disk. Please note that a 300GB SAS 15k disk would not be able to function as a hot spare for both because it would not have enough capacity if a 400GB SAS disk failed.

☒ **A** is incorrect because a SAS disk cannot be used as a hot spare to a SATA disk. **C** is incorrect because a single SAS disk of at least 400GB can be used as a spare for all the SAS disks. **D** is incorrect because SSD cannot be used as a hot spare for SAS or SATA.

Chapter 1: Multiple Disks for Larger Storage and Fault Tolerance | RAID Levels
SCSP objective 3.3, Describe the different RAID levels

15. ☑ **A** is the correct answer. Each RAID 5 group will require one drive for parity, and the solution requires a drive for a hot spare, so that is three drives. To get 5TB of space using 500GB drives, 10 drives are required, so the solution requires 13 drives. This would be two 5+1 RAID sets and a hot spare.

☒ **B** is incorrect because this does not include the hot spare. **C** might seem right if you forgot that both RAID sets need a parity disk, but it is incorrect. **D** might seem right if you forgot that both RAID sets need a parity disk and that the solution requires a hot spare.

Chapter 1: Multiple Disks for Larger Storage and Fault Tolerance | RAID Levels
SCSP objective 3.3, Describe the different RAID levels

16. ☑ **C** is the correct answer. You would need to start with the full backup. Since the scenario is using incremental backups, you need to restore all incrementals since the last full backup, so this includes the Sunday 10 A.M., 10 P.M.; Monday 10 A.M., 10 P.M.; Tuesday 10 A.M., 10 P.M.; and Wednesday 10 A.M. backups.

☒ **A** is incorrect because a backup was not taken at 5 P.M. **B** is incorrect because incremental backups require that each incremental following the full backup be restored in sequence. This choice restores only the latest incremental, so it would not work. **D** is incorrect because a full backup needs to be restored before the incremental backups can be restored.

Chapter 7: Backup Reliability | Backup and Restore Methods | Incremental
SCSP objective 4.2, Describe backup types

17. ☑   **C** is the correct answer. A RAID 10 is a stripe of mirrors. The smallest stripe requires two sets, and each mirror set requires two drives. The math is $2 \times 2 = 4$, so you need four drives at minimum. RAID 10 sets will always have an even number of drives.

☒   **A** is incorrect because a single drive cannot make any of the RAID sets. **B** is incorrect because a RAID 10 is a stripe of mirrors, so it requires multiple mirrors, each consisting of two drives. This means that a RAID 10 set will be an even number. This also eliminates choice **D**.

Chapter 1: Multiple Disks for Larger Storage and Fault Tolerance | RAID Levels
SCSP objective 3.3, Describe the different RAID levels

18. ☑   **D** is the correct answer. Storage as a Service would present the files to users, but the files would be stored in the cloud.

☒   **A** is incorrect because SaaS is a cloud-based application. **B** is incorrect because PaaS is a cloud-based system and database. **C** is incorrect because CaaS is not a cloud solution. **E** is incorrect because IaaS is a cloud-based system with networking and computing resources.

Chapter 9: Storage Architecture Components | Cloud Services | Storage as a Service
SCSP objective 6.2, Identify cloud storage types

19. ☑   **A** is the correct answer. The 2 P.M. snapshot offers the latest backup, and it can be recovered quickly.

☒   **B** is incorrect because the snapshot can be applied without first applying other backups. **C** is incorrect because resetting the integrity error will not solve the problem. It will remove the error from sight only until it appears again. **D** is incorrect because taking the node out of the cluster would move the resource to another node, which would also report an integrity error.

Chapter 7: Backup Locations | Array-Based Backups | Snapshot
SCSP objective 4.2, Describe backup types

20. ☑   **C** is the correct answer. Since the LUN was deleted, the snapshot will not work since the snapshot stored only files that changed. A new LUN will need to be created, and then the full backup can be restored to it.

☒   **A** is incorrect because the snapshot would not work since it holds changes only to the LUN and the entire LUN has been deleted. **B** is incorrect because there is no LUN to restore to. Also, the snapshot is associated with a LUN, so the snapshot would be lost when the LUN was removed. **D** is incorrect because the LUN is not available to restore to.

Chapter 7: Backup Reliability | Backup and Restore Methods
SCSP objective 4.2, Describe backup types

21. ☑   **A** and **C** are the correct answers. Traffic that is directed on the second NIC is not going through because either the switch is offline or the second controller is not configured properly.

☒   **B** is incorrect because maintenance mode would restrict access to the unit entirely. **D** is incorrect because lost power would cause the entire unit to be unavailable. **E** is incorrect because a lack of VLAN configuration would result in the same experience on both switches if the solution worked at all. It would not result in the connectivity errors for just one NIC.

Chapter 12: Network Troubleshooting
SCSP objective 2.1, Identify NAS components

22. ☑ **D** is the correct answer. Cable management does not extend the life of rack equipment.
☒ **A** is incorrect because cable management can keep cables away from air intake and exhaust vents. **B** is incorrect because bundled data cables can be routed away from bundled power cables with cable management. **C** is incorrect because cable management keeps the cables together so that they are not easily bumped or pulled on. It is much more difficult to stretch a set of bundled cables that are attached to supporting structures than it would be to stretch a single cable hanging loose from the back of a rack.

Chapter 10: Facilities | Cable Management
SCSP objective 1.5, Describe data storage planning for various business applications

23. ☑ **A** is the correct answer. A high cache hit ratio means that more data is being returned directly from cache instead of having to seek from disk first.
☒ **B** is incorrect because latency is related to distance, so a high cache hit ratio would not impact this. **C** is incorrect because simple utilization of system cache is not an advantage. **D** is incorrect because deduplication is not performed in cache hits.

Chapter 12: Optimize Performance | Cache | Cache Hit and Miss
SCSP objective 1.6, Describe how to improve performance for host applications

24. ☑ **E** is the correct answer. The scenario requires 10GigE spanning 75 meters. Cat6a is the only solution that can meet both requirements.
☒ **A** is incorrect because the cables from the wiring closet to the rest of the office can handle the required 1Gbps, and Cat6 cables from the wiring closet to the server room would not provide the 10GigE connectivity because Cat6 only provides 10GigE at up to 55 meters. **B** is incorrect because Cat6 only provides 10GigE at up to 55 meters. **C** is incorrect because fiber cabling would not be able to provide Ethernet. **D** is incorrect because the Cat5e cables do not need to be replaced and fiber would not support Ethernet.

Chapter 4: Cables | Copper Cables | Cat6a
SCSP objective 1.1, Identify host connectivity components used in a support matrix

25. ☑ **B** is the correct answer. A disk-to-disk-to-tape solution allows for backups to be quickly written from the storage device to another disk, minimizing the duration of the backup job on the storage system. The data is then written to tape without impacting the production environment.
☒ **A** is incorrect because directly writing to tape would impact the storage systems for a longer period than writing to disk would. **C** is incorrect because NDMP would allow the storage devices to talk to the backup tapes directly, but this solution does not specify what else would be used to reduce the

backup window. **D** is incorrect because disk to disk would not result in the data being archived to tape.

Chapter 7: Backup Locations | Disk-to-Disk-to-Tape
SCSP objective 4.2, Describe backup types

26. ☑ **D** is the correct answer. With storage tiers, the data that is most frequently used is placed on the fastest disks.
☒ **A** is incorrect because storage tiering does not replicate to other sites. **B** is incorrect because storage tiering does not remove duplicates. Duplicates would be removed with deduplication software. **C** is incorrect because storage tiering does not necessarily implement or enforce retention policies. Retention policies would need to be enforced through additional software controls, but they could utilize archival tiers to store some data.

Chapter 11: Information Lifecycle Management | Storage Tiers
SCSP objective 5.2, Identify storage management technologies

27. ☑ **B** is the correct answer. GFS backup schedules use daily, weekly, and monthly backups. Daily backups are the sons, weekly the fathers, and monthly the grandfathers, so daily is the correct answer.
☒ **A** is incorrect because GFS backup schedules do not include hourly backups. **C** and **D** are incorrect because GFS specifies the backup intervals, not type. **E** is incorrect because daily backups occur more frequently than weekly backups.

Chapter 7: Backup Frequency | Rotation Schemes
SCSP objective 4.3, Describe disaster recovery concepts

28. ☑ **B** is the correct answer. FCoE uses Ethernet at layer 2, but higher layers are implemented with the FC protocol stack.
☒ **A** is incorrect because iSCSI does not utilize FC at any layer. **C** is incorrect because while FCIP does use Ethernet, it also uses IP. **D** is incorrect because it also uses IP.

Chapter 3: Fibre Channel Storage Network | Protocols | FCoE
SCSP objective 2.2, Identify Fibre Channel SAN components

29. ☑ **C** is the correct answer. If seven drives are in a RAID 6 (5 + 2), two drives are used for parity, and five are available for data: $5 \times 400 = 2,000$.
☒ **A** is incorrect because this assumes that all seven drives are used for data, but two are required for parity. **B** would be the right answer if this question asked about RAID 4, which uses only one drive for parity, but this question is using RAID 6. **D** is incorrect because only two drives are required for parity. The solution in choice D uses three drives for parity.

Chapter 1: Multiple Disks for Larger Storage and Fault Tolerance | RAID Levels
SCSP objective 3.3, Describe the different RAID levels

30. ☑ **A** is the correct answer. Telnet transmits data in plain text, so another solution is needed to encrypt the traffic. The first step is to remove access to Telnet by disabling port 23 on the firewall. Next, a VPN would allow for the Telnet traffic to be encapsulated in an encrypted channel.

☒ **B** is incorrect because the question states that Telnet must be used, not SSH. **C** is incorrect because Telnet does not support encryption. **D** is incorrect because a locally attached serial cable would require local access, not remote access.

Chapter 6: Storage Administration | CLI | Telnet
Chapter 8: Encryption | Data in Motion | VPN
SCSP objective 5.1, Describe storage security methods

31. ☑ **D** is the correct answer. High availability must be able to support the loss of a single component, so redundancy is necessary.
☒ **A** is incorrect because monitoring can alert staff to a failure but not prevent it. **B** is incorrect because a higher SLA just increases the burden on the organization but does nothing to implement high availability. **C** is incorrect because offsite backups offer business continuity but not high availability. The backups would need to be restored, and this would take time, during which the system would be unavailable.

Chapter 9: Storage Architecture Components | High Availability
SCSP objective 4.3, Describe disaster recovery concepts

32. ☑ **A** is the correct answer. Hot aisles are areas where hot air from computing equipment is expelled and directed back to cooling equipment, while computing equipment draws cool air from cold aisles.
☒ **B** is incorrect because high-density racks and low-density racks both would need to be directed so that their hot air flows into hot aisles. **C** and **D** are incorrect because hot and cold aisles do not aid in emergency evacuations, and neither do they aid in capacity planning.

Chapter 10: Facilities | Cooling
SCSP objective 1.5, Describe data storage planning for various business applications

33. ☑ **B** is the correct answer. To provide concurrent access, a share must be created so the CIFS or NFS protocols could be used.
☒ **A** is incorrect because SNMP is a monitoring protocol, not a file access protocol. **C** is incorrect because Telnet is a management protocol, not a file access protocol. **D** and **E** are incorrect because iSCSI and FC provide block-level access, and this would allow only one machine to access the storage at a time, and the solution requires for many users to have concurrent access.

Chapter 2: Network Attached Storage | NAS File System Protocols | CIFS
SCSP objective 2.1, Identify NAS components

34. ☑ **C** is the correct answer. The EXT3 file system is used on Linux.
☒ **A** is incorrect because Windows 98 supports only FAT16 and FAT32. **B** is incorrect because it supports only FAT and NTFS. **D** is incorrect because it uses the integrated file system, not EXT3. **E** is incorrect because Apple iOS uses the HFSX file system. Please note that the AS/400 and Apple iOS were not discussed in this book and will not be on the SCSP exam.

Chapter 1: Hosts Interaction with Disks | File Systems
SCSP objective 1.2, Describe host-based functions for storage

35. ☑ **D** is the correct answer. The storage array is configured for active/active, but the HBAs are active/passive. When the storage array sends data on the active connection that is sent to the passive connection on the host, the traffic must traverse the ISL and then be delivered to the active port. If you are using active/active in one place, try to use active/active everywhere else.

☒ **A** is incorrect because adding more ISLs solves the symptom, not the root issue. **B** is incorrect because a file-level architecture cannot be used to map LUNs. **C** is incorrect because buffer-to-buffer credits only need to be changed on links that extend over a long distance.

Chapter 9: Redundancy | Clustering | Active-Active
SCSP objective 4.3, Describe disaster recovery concepts

36. ☑ **A** is the correct answer. Fibre Channel Arbitrated Loop (FC-AL) is a loop or ring, but devices are connected to hubs that implement the loop inside them. The hubs are central devices that appear like a star configuration.

☒ **B** is incorrect because FC-SW, switch fabric, is not a logical ring. It is a logical star. **C** is incorrect because P2P is not a physical star. It is a bus. **D** is incorrect because Ethernet is not a topology.

Chapter 3: Fibre Channel Storage Network | Topologies | Arbitrated Loop
SCSP objective 2.2, Identify Fibre Channel SAN components

37. ☑ **D** is the correct answer. A router receives information from its neighbors on the networks that each device manages and on how many hops it takes to get to the destination through a device. If a connection fails, the routers update the number of hops to compensate so that they maintain accurate information on how to route packets through a network.

☒ **A** is incorrect because a switch does not receive information from its neighbors to make such decisions. It maintains a bridging table that it builds itself and makes only decisions on how to send data to local devices. **B** is incorrect because a director is just an upgraded switch. **C** is incorrect because a repeater just takes a signal and rebroadcasts it. It does not make a routing or forwarding decision. **E** is incorrect because transceivers convert one signal type to another but do not make routing or forwarding decisions.

Chapter 4: Storage Networking Devices | Router
SCSP objective 3.1, Identify host to SAN components

38. ☑ **A** is the correct answer. ISNS is a database of targets that can be queried by initiators.

☒ **B** is incorrect because iSNS does not perform monitoring or alerting functions. **C** is incorrect because FC addresses are registered by one of the FC services, not iSNS. **D** is incorrect because iSNS does not have any understanding of load balancing, nor can it configure it.

Chapter 8: Storage Visibility | iSCSI Security | iSCSI and iSNS Security
SCSP objective 1.3, Identify storage mapping elements

39. ☑ **D** is the correct answer. Tape is an inexpensive way to archive data, and it comes in large capacities.
☒ **A** is incorrect because it would take many DVDs to back up 400GB of data. **B** is incorrect because it would take many flash drives to archive this much data. **C** is incorrect because nearline storage is more expensive than tape.

Chapter 4: Removable Storage
SCSP objective 4.1, Identify backup technologies

40. ☑ **A** is the correct answer. ISLs link fiber switches together, and expansion ports (e-ports) are used to connect to other switches.
☒ **B** is incorrect because F-ports connect to N-ports on nodes. **C** is incorrect because an ISL is required. **D** is incorrect because an ISL is required and F-ports are not used for ISLs.

Chapter 3: Fibre Channel Storage Network | ISL
SCSP objective 2.2, Identify Fibre Channel SAN components

41. ☑ **D** is the correct answer. Remote replication would store the data at another site, and the data could be used there if the first site becomes unavailable.
☒ **A** is incorrect because offsite tapes would have to be restored to equipment, but the equipment in the scenario was consumed by the fire. **B** is incorrect because HSM organizes data into tiers but does not protect it against site loss. **C** is incorrect because snapshots are used within a storage array, and they would be lost along with the array in the fire.

Chapter 9: Replication | Scope | Remote
SCSP objective 1.5, Describe data storage planning for various business applications

42. ☑ **B** is the correct answer. A baseline is a record of metrics under normal load. Comparing current data to the baseline will help identify items that are slower than the baseline.
☒ **A** is incorrect because an alert would notify of an item that is in an error condition or exceeding a threshold, but it would not be compared to the current metrics. **C** is incorrect because the scope defines the area affected but could not be used to compare against current metrics. **D** is incorrect because the logs would contain a large amount of data that would not match up to the collected metrics.

Chapter 6: Storage Monitoring, Alerting, and Reporting | Recording a Baseline
SCSP objective 5.2, Identify storage management technologies

43. ☑ **C** is the correct answer. A consistency group ensures that a set of writes is performed on each member of the group. Items in a consistency group retain the same data, and writes that occur to one member of the group will not be fully committed until they have been implemented across all members of the consistency group.
☒ **A** is incorrect because a snapshot would track changes to data from a point in time. **B** is incorrect because replication alone would not ensure consistency because some data may not have been replicated yet. **D** is incorrect because

integrity groups were not discussed and are not related to replication or transaction commitment.

Chapter 7: Backup Locations | Array-Based Backups | Consistency Group
SCSP objective 4.2, Describe backup types

44. ☑ **A** is the correct answer. LTO3 tapes have a native capacity of 400GB and a compressed capacity of 800GB.

☒ **B** is incorrect because this is the capacity of an LTO3 tape, not an LTO4 tape. **C** is incorrect because this is the capacity of an LTO4 tape, not an LTO5 tape. **D** is incorrect because LTO2 tapes have a native capacity of 200GB and a compressed capacity of 400GB.

Chapter 4: Removable Storage | Tape Media | LTO Versions
SCSP objective 4.1, Identify backup technologies

45. ☑ **C** is the correct answer. Asynchronous replication would send data to the remote site when possible and would not wait to commit new transactions if data had not been replicated yet.

☒ **A** is incorrect because synchronous replication would make the main database wait to commit transactions until they had been committed at the remote site as well. Since the link between sites is high latency, this would reduce performance considerably. **B** is incorrect because direct replication is not a form of replication. **D** is incorrect because the question is concerned with consistency between sites and the impact this has on production, not on where the replication is managed.

Chapter 9: Replication | Continuous Replication
SCSP objective 1.5, Describe data storage planning for various business applications

46. ☑ **C** is the correct answer. A switch would connect the four front-end ports and the five host ports and allow communication between them.

☒ **A** is incorrect because a director is not needed in this simple situation. **B** is incorrect because a router would be needed only if the storage array was on a different network. **D** is incorrect because a repeater would only rebroadcast a signal, not allow additional connectivity.

Chapter 4: Storage Networking Devices
SCSP objective 3.1, Identify host to SAN components

47. ☑ **C** is the correct answer. There is a head at the top and bottom of each platter. All heads are attached to the same actuator arm.

☒ **A** is incorrect because each head does not have its own actuator arm. They are all on the same arm. **B** is incorrect because each head can read data only from a single platter. **D** is incorrect because it references disks, not platters. There is a head for each platter, not disk.

Chapter 1: How Disk Storage Systems Work | Physical Components | Head
SCSP objective 1.1, Identify host connectivity components used in a support matrix

48. ☑ **B** is the correct answer. A controller is mounted to the base of the disk and contains an interface for sending and receiving data to a connected device.
☒ **A** is incorrect because it is incomplete. The controller board operates more than just the movement of the actuator arm. **C** and **D** are incorrect because the controller board is not mounted to the top of the disk.

Chapter 1: How Disk Storage Systems Work | Physical Components | Controller Board
SCSP objective 1.1, Identify host connectivity components used in a support matrix

49. ☑ **A** is the correct answer. Solid state organizes data into blocks rather than tracks and selectors.
☒ **B** is incorrect because SSD consists of blocks made up of pages, not HDD. **C** is incorrect because SSD blocks are not 128 bytes. **D** is incorrect because logical bit addressing is not an addressing method, and SSDs do not use a master table.

Chapter 1: How Disk Storage Systems Work | Solid-State Drive
SCSP objective 1.1, Identify host connectivity components used in a support matrix

50. ☑ **D** is the correct answer. Fibre Channel references other devices on the network by using a World Wide Name (WWN).
☒ **A** is incorrect because SCAS is not a method of referencing other devices. **B** is incorrect because Fibre Channel does not use a reference ID. **C** is incorrect because a twofold security connection number is not an element of FC.

Chapter 3: Fibre Channel Storage Network | Components | World Wide Name
SCSP objective 2.1, Identify NAS components

51. ☑ **C** is the correct answer. Fibre Channel layer 3 is the services layer. This layer supports striping, hunt groups, and the spanning of multiple ports.
☒ **A** is incorrect because layer 3 is the services layer, not the block layer. **B** is incorrect because FC does not use frames, and layer 3 is the services layer, not the processing layer. **D** is incorrect because layer 3 is not the infrastructure layer.

Chapter 3: Fibre Channel Storage Network | Protocols | FCP
SCSP objective 2.2, Identify Fibre Channel SAN components

52. ☑ **D** is the correct answer. A WWN is an 8-byte or 16-byte identifier for a network communication port on a Fibre Channel network.
☒ **A** is incorrect because a WWN is 8 or 16 bytes, not 16 or 32 bytes. **B** is incorrect because WWNs are used on an FC network while IP addresses are used on an IP network. **C** is incorrect because WWNs are used in Fibre Channel, not simple channel access.

Chapter 3: Fibre Channel Storage Network | Components | World Wide Name
SCSP objective 2.2, Identify Fibre Channel SAN components

53. ☑ **C** is the correct answer. Input/output operations per second (IOPS) is one of the most basic metrics used in measuring storage performance.
☒ **A** is incorrect because FTP is used for sending and receiving files and is not a performance metric measurement method. **B** is incorrect because system storage

monitoring is not a specific metric. **D** is incorrect because send receive operations per second is not a metric that is used.

Chapter 12: Optimize Performance | Necessary IOPS
SCSP objective 1.6, Describe how to improve performance for host applications

54. ☑ **B** is the correct answer. Optical cables transmit data via light impulses.
☒ **A** is incorrect because optical cables transmit data via light, not long-range frequencies. **C** and **D** are incorrect because optical cables use light instead of electromagnetic waves or impulses. Copper cables conduct electromagnetic waves.

Chapter 4: Cables | Optical Cables
SCSP objective 1.1, Identify host connectivity components used in a support matrix

55. ☑ **D** is the correct answer. A converged network adapter (CNA) is a device capable of connecting a host to storage with connections over FC, Ethernet, or twinax connections.
☒ **A** is incorrect because CNAs are not used with iSCSI. **B** is incorrect because it is incomplete. This is only one thing that a CNA can do. **C** is incorrect because a CNA is a card that is added to a host rather than being built onboard.

Chapter 4: Storage Networking Devices | CNA
SCSP objective 2.2, Identify Fibre Channel SAN components

56. ☑ **A** is the correct answer. A fiber director is a high-capacity modular switch with two or more hot-swappable power supplies and redundant routing engines, pathways, and processors.
☒ **B** is incorrect because a director is not a layer 3 device. **C** is incorrect because a director is not used for WAN connections. **D** is incorrect because a director does not perform filtering.

Chapter 4: Storage Networking Devices | Director
SCSP objective 2.2, Identify Fibre Channel SAN components

57. ☑ **C** is the correct answer. Buffer underrun is a condition where the buffer is emptied during the process of burning information to a disk.
☒ **A** is incorrect because the buffer underrun is a specific failure when the buffer is empty during the burn process. There are many errors from the write process that would not be considered buffer underrun. **B** is incorrect because buffer underrun is not related to scratches on the disk. **D** is incorrect because a drive that cannot read a disk at the optimal speed is a speed mismatch, and this choice is related to reads rather than writes.

Chapter 4: Removable Storage | Optical Media
SCSP objective 4.1, Identify backup technologies

58. ☑ **A** is the correct answer. SNIA describes storage virtualization as the application of virtualization to storage services or devices for the purposes of aggregating functions or devices, hiding complexity, or adding new capabilities to lower-level storage resources.
☒ **B** is incorrect because storage virtualization virtualizes storage resources, not software. **C** is incorrect because with storage virtualization there are proprietary

storage virtualization technologies that do not offer interoperability. **D** is incorrect because storage virtualization is not used to limit data access.

Chapter 5: Types of Storage Virtualization
SCSP objective 1.4, Describe virtualization concepts and techniques

59. ☑   **A** is the correct answer. The file/record layer is the layer that organizes the information required by the application and interfaces with the application.
☒   **B** is incorrect because the mapping of logical addresses to physical addresses is how disks use virtualization. **C** is incorrect because this choice describes block virtualization. **D** is incorrect because this describes tape virtualization.

Chapter 5: Types of Storage Virtualization
SCSP objective 1.4, Describe virtualization concepts and techniques

60. ☑   **A** is the correct answer. Privileged provisioning is not a form of storage provisioning.
☒   **B** is incorrect because LUN provisioning is a form of provisioning of logical units. **C** is incorrect because thick provisioning creates a logical unit of a specified size. **D** is also incorrect because thin provisioning creates a logical unit that is variable in size.

Chapter 6: Storage Provisioning
SCSP objective 1.3, Identify storage mapping elements

61. ☑   **D** is the correct answer. In-band or out-of-band virtualization can consolidate the virtual platform for network storage management.
☒   **A** is incorrect because only out-of-band virtualization optimizes SAN utilization and performance. **B** is incorrect because only out-of-band virtualization offloads storage management from the host since the management device exists outside the host-to-SAN relationship. **C** is incorrect because only out-of-band virtualization avoids latency.

Chapter 5: Types of Storage Virtualization
SCSP objective 1.4, Describe virtualization concepts and techniques

62. ☑   **B** is the correct answer. Host virtualization is not a type of storage virtualization.
☒   **A**, **C**, and **D** are incorrect because disk, block, and tape virtualization are all types of storage virtualization.

Chapter 5: Types of Storage Virtualization
SCSP objective 1.4, Describe virtualization concepts and techniques

63. ☑   **D** is the correct answer. Cache is high-speed memory that can be used to service I/O requests faster than accessing the disk.
☒   **A** is incorrect. While memory is faster than disk, it is not used to service I/O requests. **B** is incorrect because logical disks are not faster than physical disks. **C** is incorrect because SSD is a form of physical disk.

Chapter 12: Optimize Performance | Cache
SCSP objective 1.6, Describe how to improve performance for host applications

64. ☑   **A** is the correct answer. The Common Information Model is an object-oriented approach to organizing information where objects have attributes and each is created from a class that describes the format of the object.
☒   **B** is incorrect because this describes in-band management. **C** is incorrect because it describes thin provisioning. **D** is incorrect because it describes setting thresholds.

Chapter 6: Management Protocols | WBEM
SCSP objective 5.2, Identify storage management technologies

65. ☑   **D** is the correct answer. When in-band storage management is utilized, data as well as management and monitoring information travel over the same path.
☒   **A** is incorrect because it describes out-of-band management. **B** is incorrect because in-band management is concerned with the path the data uses, not whether it is an appliance. Also, this answer has the management and monitoring of data occurring on the appliance, but the transfer of data is not mentioned. **C** is incorrect because this separates the data from the management and monitoring, as would be performed in out-of-band management.

Chapter 6: Management Protocols | In-Band vs. Out-of-Band Management
SCSP objective 5.2, Identify storage management technologies

66. ☑   **A** is the correct answer. Appliance-based data migration is data migration in which stand-alone network appliances migrate files and volumes, interfacing with storage systems and providing a separate interface for managing the replication.
☒   **B** is incorrect because appliance-based migration can operate on data or applications. It is not what is being moved, but how it is being moved that this question is concerned with. **C** is incorrect because the data on the appliances themselves is not being migrated in this situation. **D** is incorrect because an appliance would require configuration and possibly some customization for it to work.

Chapter 11: Deduplication and Compression | Deduplication Software and Appliances
SCSP objective 5.3, Describe data reduction techniques

67. ☑   **D** is the correct answer. Thick logical units take up the same amount of space as is presented to the host operating system.
☒   **A** is incorrect because thick logical units take up the assigned amount of space, so if 100GB is allocated, the logical unit will be 100GB even if only 20GB is stored in it. **B** is incorrect because thick logical units do not allocate additional space beyond what is assigned. **C** is incorrect because thick logical units can be any size.

Chapter 6: Storage Provisioning | Thick Provisioning
SCSP objective 1.3, Identify storage mapping elements

68. ☑   **A** is the correct answer. Data integrity is assurance that data remains unchanged after creating, modifying, copying, completing, or otherwise operating on data.

☒ **B** is incorrect because having backups does not mean you will know when to use them or when data has been changed or corrupted. **C** is incorrect because data tampering is only one way data integrity could be lost. Encryption is primarily used to protect confidentiality, not integrity. **D** is incorrect because integrity is not concerned with how the data is used, just that it remains unchanged in between authorized changes.

Chapter 7: Backup Reliability | Backup Reliability Methods | Data Integrity
SCSP objective 4.2, Describe backup types

69. ☑ **C** is the correct answer. Workflow error is much too specific to be considered a broad classification for a cause of system outages.
☒ **A**, **B**, and **D** are incorrect because human error, intentional error, and systematic error can all be considered a broad classification for the cause of system outages.

Chapter 9: Storage Architecture Components | High Availability
SCSP objective 4.3, Describe disaster recovery concepts

70. ☑ **A** is the correct answer. The primary objective of business continuity planning is to provide a proactive strategy to prevent or limit the impact of system failures and to rapidly restore operations should such events occur.
☒ **B** is incorrect because this describes disaster recovery. **C** and **D** are incorrect because these address only part of business continuity.

Chapter 7: Business Continuity Objectives
SCSP objective 4.3, Describe disaster recovery concepts

71. ☑ **B** is the correct answer. The cost per year in this case is 18 hours of lost productivity. Every other month means six times per year, and the loss is three hours per month: 6 × 3 = 18.
☒ **A**, **C**, and **D** are incorrect because 6 months × 3 hours = 18 hours of lost productivity, not 12, 24, or 36.

Chapter 7: Business Continuity Objectives | Data Value and Risk
SCSP objective 4.3, Describe disaster recovery concepts

72. ☑ **A** is the correct answer. You must first know how available the system should be in order to determine how much redundancy should be put in place to achieve that availability. This availability measurement is usually expressed as a percentage of uptime such as 99.9 percent.
☒ **B** is incorrect because logical block addressing will help locate data on disk, not identify how much redundancy is needed. **C** is incorrect because the failover system is a component of redundancy that might be put in place, but it is not a factor to determine what is needed. **D** is incorrect because replication is a method for achieving redundancy, so it should not be used to determine whether redundancy should be put in place. The decision should be based on a business decision on the required uptime.

Chapter 9: Storage Architecture Components | High Availability
SCSP objective 4.3, Describe disaster recovery concepts

73. ☑   **D** is the correct answer. A risk assessment analyzes the factors that could impact the integrity, confidentiality, or availability of business systems and their expected damage/likelihood.
☒   **A** is incorrect because it is incomplete. The threats alone do not provide enough information to make a decision on the security controls to implement. **B** is also incorrect because it is incomplete. Choice B is the other part that is required to make a decision. Both the threats and the damage/impact are used to calculate risk. **C** is incorrect because organizational security as a whole is too broad a scope for a risk assessment.

Chapter 7: Business Continuity Objectives | Data Value and Risk
SCSP objective 4.3, Describe disaster recovery concepts

74. ☑   **B** is the correct answer. A business impact analysis estimates the cost an organization could incur should systems be unavailable because of incident or disaster.
☒   **A** is incorrect because the BIA is also concerned with the cost to the business's image, sales, and competitive advantage, to name a few costs. **C** is incorrect because the BIA may include time as an input to the cost, but that is not the main concern. **D** is incorrect because the controls required to bring risks below the organization's risk tolerance level is part of the risk assessment.

Chapter 7: Business Continuity Objectives
SCSP objective 4.3, Describe disaster recovery concepts

75. ☑   **B** is the correct answer. In remote authentication, passwords are sent via the network, while physical authentication is done on the machine being logged into.
☒   **A** is incorrect because remote authentication could be used to connect to computers at the same site. **C** is incorrect because visual patterns are not used in authentication, and there are many types of physical authentication, even if this were an option. **D** is incorrect because physical authentication is used for devices you are directly interfacing with, not remote authenticators.

Chapter 8: Access Control | Authentication | Physical Authentication
SCSP objective 5.1, Describe storage security methods

76. ☑   **B** is the correct answer. Failover is the transfer of services in a redundant system from one device to another.
☒   **A** is incorrect because service redundancy can be achieved with or without failover. **C** and **D** are incorrect because overflow and component transfer are not storage concepts.

Chapter 9: Storage Architecture Components | High Availability | Failover
SCSP objective 4.3, Describe disaster recovery concepts

77. ☑   **B** is the correct answer. OLTP provides immediate response and high availability.
☒   **A**, **C**, and **D** are incorrect because these are made-up terms.

Chapter 9: Storage Architecture Components | Online Transaction Processing
SCSP Objective 1.5, Describe data storage planning for various business applications

78. ☑ **D** is the correct answer. N-port virtualization allows multiple N-ports to reside on the same physical N-port.

☒ **A** is incorrect because a VSAN is a way to logically partition a SAN into an isolated virtual storage area where network communication is restricted to a virtual domain. **B** is incorrect because state change notifications are used to inform fiber devices about the presence of devices on the fiber network. **C** is incorrect because PLOGI is a port logon.

Chapter 3: Fibre Channel Storage Network | Components | Addressing
SCSP objective 2.2, Identify Fibre Channel SAN components

79. ☑ **B** is the correct answer. A single point of failure is a single configuration, a network, hardware, or software malfunctioning and causing the entire system or process to fail.

☒ **A** is incorrect because a large-scale system failure indicates more than a single failure or a catastrophic failure, which may not be the case in all instances of a single device failure. **C** is incorrect because a network failure does not necessarily indicate a failure of a single component. **D** is incorrect because a server-side power failure is only one example of a component that could fail.

Chapter 9: Storage Architecture Components | High Availability | Single Point of Failure
SCSP objective 4.3, Describe disaster recovery concepts

80. ☑ **A** is the correct answer. Secondary risk is risk caused by another risk response strategy.

☒ **B** is incorrect because a risk that is moderately likely to occur is something risk managers would need to evaluate against the potential impact to determine reasonable controls. **C** is incorrect because a risk that can occur when multiple other risks occur is part of the impact of the risk. **D** is incorrect because the secondary risk is not a second opinion.

Chapter 7: Business Continuity Objectives | Data Value and Risk
SCSP objective 4.3, Describe disaster recovery concepts

81. ☑ **B** is the correct answer. Low humidity can lead to electrostatic discharge.

☒ **A** is incorrect because a charge does not create water damage. **C** is incorrect because the buildup of charge would not be sufficient enough to cause overheating. **D** is incorrect because electrical failure would be a byproduct of another failure.

Chapter 10: Facilities | Humidity Control
SCSP objective 1.5, Describe data storage planning for various business applications control

82. ☑ **B** is the correct answer. HFC-125 removes heat from fire. Other agents that remove heat from fire include FM-200 and HFC-237ea.

☒ **A** and **C** are incorrect because they are not real gaseous agents. **D** is incorrect because HVAC is the heating and cooling systems in place in an organization.

Chapter 10: Facilities | Fire Suppression
SCSP objective 1.5, Describe data storage planning for various business applications

83. ☑   **D** is the correct answer. Rack density refers to the number of devices in the rack.
☒   **A** is incorrect because heat is measured in BTUs. **B** is incorrect because cables do not have an impact on how dense the rack is. **C** is incorrect because the type of device is not a factor in determining density.

Chapter 10: Safety | Weight Considerations | Floor and Rack Loading
SCSP objective 1.5, Describe data storage planning for various business applications

84. ☑   **B** is the correct answer. Replication transfers data between hosts or storage systems.
☒   **A** is incorrect because a transfer protocol can be used for many data transmissions that are not periodic. **C** is incorrect because backups do not always occur between hosts or storage systems. **D** is incorrect because system support is the ongoing maintenance of a system, not the transference of data at periodic intervals.

Chapter 9: Replication
SCSP objective 1.5, Describe data storage planning for various business applications

85. ☑   **B** is the correct answer. Hierarchical storage management presents files and directories as a composite object with a single integrated file interface.
☒   **A** is incorrect because a block management architecture does not exist. A block-level architecture exists, but it is not concerned with files but rather the blocks that make up logical units. Files may or may not reside in these blocks. **C** is incorrect because manual storage tiering requires intervention to optimize the location of data. **D** is incorrect because a storage management system is much too broad a system to be described as presenting a composite object with a single integrated file interface.

Chapter 11: Information Lifecycle Management | HSM
SCSP objective 5.2, Identify storage management technologies

86. ☑   **B** is the correct answer. The alias directs traffic to a group of N-ports that are part of a multicast or hunt group.
☒   **A** is incorrect because the alias is not used for failover. **C** is incorrect because the alias is not a descriptive name. **D** is incorrect because the alias has not been removed from the FC protocol and it is still in use.

Chapter 3: Fibre Channel Storage Network | Components | Addressing
SCSP objective 2.2, Identify Fibre Channel SAN components

87. ☑   **B** is the correct answer. Litigation holds specify the data that should be preserved for potential or ongoing litigation.
☒   **A** is incorrect because a mandatory preservation is simply a requirement to preserve data but not necessarily related to lawsuits. **C** is incorrect because trial backup requirements is a made-up term. **D** is incorrect because the term is litigation hold, not litigation preservation.

Chapter 11: Compliance | Preservation and Litigation Holds
SCSP objective 1.5, Describe data storage planning for various business applications

88. ☑ **B** is the correct answer. Shoe-shining occurs when the device sending data to the tape does not send data fast enough so the tape has to stop and rewind so that the data will be written sequentially.

☒ **A** is incorrect because a dirty drive will cause data read and write errors. **C** is incorrect because a cable problem would result in communication loss or errors. **D** is incorrect because mounting a tape for random reads would not issue writes to the drive.

Chapter 4: Removable Storage | Tape Media | Shoe Shining/Backhitching
SCSP objective 4.1, Identify backup technologies

89. ☑ **C** is the correct answer. A grid breaks up files into segments, or it can store an entire file on a node in the grid. Files or segments are often replicated to other nodes for redundancy.

☒ **A** is incorrect because a full mesh controller does not exist. **B** is incorrect because the cache is used to store files that are waiting to be written to disk or that may be read from the array. **D** is incorrect because dual controllers do not break files into segments and they operate on only one node.

Chapter 2: Storage Arrays | Controller Head
SCSP objective 3.4, Describe disk technologies

90. ☑ **B** is the correct answer. A hop measures how many devices are traversed between source and destination.

☒ **A** is incorrect because a jump is not a networking term. **C** is incorrect because latency measures the time from source to destination. **D** is incorrect because ping measures whether connectivity exists.

Chapter 12: Performance Metrics and Tools | Switch | Hops
SCSP objective 1.6, Describe how to improve performance for host applications

91. ☑ **A** is the correct answer. Class of service is used to prioritize traffic.

☒ **B** is incorrect because routing delivers packets across networks. **C** is incorrect because this is a made-up term. **D** is incorrect because switching delivers frames to ports based on MAC addresses.

Chapter 3: iSCSI Storage Network | Ethernet Features | Class of Service
SCSP objective 2.3, Identify Ethernet/IP SAN components

92. ☑ **D** is the correct answer. iSCSI would take advantage of the Ethernet network, and VLANs would segment the iSCSI traffic from the normal LAN traffic.

☒ **A** and **B** are incorrect because FC would not utilize the Ethernet network. **C** is incorrect because it is better to segment the iSCSI traffic from the LAN traffic with VLANs.

Chapter 3: iSCSI Storage Network
SCSP objective 2.3, Identify Ethernet/IP SAN components

93. ☑ **D** is the correct answer. Since the power is A/B, each circuit must be able to handle the entire load. Since the peak load is 60 percent, this would translate to 120 percent in failover mode when 80 percent is the max recommended.
☒ **A** is incorrect because a single circuit could not handle the entire load if one circuit fails. **B** is incorrect because circuits do not always provide 100 percent of their available power, and reducing both links to 50 percent could result in a load that the circuit could not handle in failover. **C** is incorrect because a third circuit would not be on A/B power.

Chapter 10: Storage Power Requirements | Sufficient Capacity
SCSP objective 1.5, Describe data storage planning for various business applications

94. ☑ **D** is the correct answer. A motherboard is not hot swappable.
☒ **A**, **B**, and **C** are incorrect because they are all hot swappable.

Chapter 4: Storage Networking Devices | Hot-Swappable Network Components
SCSP objective 2.2, Identify Fibre Channel SAN components

95. ☑ **B**, **D**, and **E** are the correct answers. SCSI, SAS, and FC disks can all run at 15,000 rpm.
☒ **A** and **C** are incorrect because IDE and SATA have a maximum rpm of 7,200.

Chapter 1: Available Disk Interfaces and Their Characteristics
SCSP objective 3.4, Describe disk technologies

96. ☑ **A** is the correct answer. A host bus adapter is used to connect to a Fibre Channel SAN.
☒ **B** is incorrect because a NIC is used to connect to an Ethernet network or iSCSI SAN. **C** is incorrect because a modem is used to create a dial-up connection. **D** is incorrect because TOE is a function of a NIC that offloads the processing of TCP/IP to the NIC.

Chapter 4: Storage Networking Devices | HBA
SCSP objective 2.2, Identify Fibre Channel SAN components

97. ☑ **C** is the correct answer. A wrist strap can take excess electrostatic charge and direct it to a ground instead of sensitive components.
☒ **A** is incorrect because a hard hat protects against head injury. **B** is incorrect because a lifting belt protects against back injury. **D** is incorrect because aluminum is a conductor of electricity and could increase the chance of electrostatic discharge.

Chapter 10: Safety | Antistatic Devices
SCSP objective 1.1, Identify host connectivity components used in a support matrix

98. ☑ **B** is the correct answer. Many modern flash drives can hold 10GB of data, and they are easy to use.
☒ **A** and **C** are incorrect because a DVD or CD would not be able to hold 10GB of data. **D** is incorrect because a tape would require a tape drive capable of reading the tape at the user's desk and the remote office.

Chapter 10: Safety | Antistatic Devices
SCSP objective 1.1, Identify host connectivity components used in a support matrix

99. ☑ **D** is the correct answer. A storage area network (SAN) connects disk arrays, tape drives, and other storage components to servers and hosts.
☒ **A** is incorrect because a NAS connects servers to network shares. **B** is incorrect because a DAS can only connect to devices directly attached to it. **C** is incorrect because a LAN is used for communication between hosts and servers.

Chapter 2: Storage Area Networks
SCSP objective 3.1, Identify host to SAN components

100. ☑ **C** is the correct answer. Alerts can send e-mails or notify administrators in other ways when certain conditions are met.
☒ **A** is incorrect because a baseline is a measurement of normal activity. **B** is incorrect because a threshold is a limit that defines an error condition. **D** is incorrect because logs record activities performed on a device.

Chapter 6: Storage Monitoring, Alerting, and Reporting | Setting Alerts
SCSP objective 5.2, Identify storage management technologies

101. ☑ **C** is the correct answer. A midrange drive is ideal for business situations with low I/O requirements. Since this is a NAS device, somewhat higher reliability is needed than what an entry-level or consumer drive could offer.
☒ **A** is incorrect because a consumer drive does not offer the reliability needed for a business NAS. **B** is incorrect because this is just another name for a consumer drive. **D** is incorrect because an enterprise drive is best for high I/O requirements, and this is a low I/O situation.

Chapter 1: How Disk Storage Systems Work | Electrical and Mechanical Differences
SCSP objective 1.1, Identify host connectivity components used in a support matrix

102. ☑ **C** is the correct answer. Each of the quad-port Ethernet adapters will utilize a significant amount of bandwidth. PCIe is the only bus that can deliver dedicated bandwidth for each of the three cards.
☒ **A** is incorrect because PCI would not have sufficient bandwidth to support a quad-port Ethernet card. It is also a shared bus, so the cards would contend for bandwidth. **B** is incorrect as well. PCI-X would support a quad-port Fast Ethernet adapter, but it is a shard bus, so a single quad-port card would consume most of the bandwidth, leaving little for the other cards. **D** is incorrect because PCI-M is not a bus type.

Chapter 1: Available Disk Interfaces and Their Characteristics | PCI Versions | PCI
SCSP objective 3.4, Describe disk technologies

103. ☑ **B** is the correct answer. Juan wants to implement RAID 5, but he does not have other equipment besides the three 2TB SATA drives. The server does not have a RAID controller either. His only option is to use software RAID. This will provide the redundancy needed to protect the data, but the server processor will see increased utilization for parity computations.
☒ **A** and **C** are incorrect because there is no RAID controller available in the system. **D** is incorrect because software RAID is not configured in this way.

Chapter 1: Multiple Disks for Larger Storage and Fault Tolerance | Hardware, Host-Based, and Software Implementations
SCSP objective 3.3, Describe the different RAID levels

104. ☑ **B** is the correct answer. Cloud storage may be located far away from the user, in which case data transfers would need to traverse through many hops to reach the destination. This increases the latency for disk writes unless local caching is used. However, with local caching, there is risk of data loss if adequate redundancies have not been placed on local cache.
☒ **A** is incorrect. Latency could make a backup job take longer to run, but backup windows usually have a greater tolerance for fluctuations in backup times than production applications do. **C** is incorrect because cloud synchronization occurs behind the scenes while the user still works with their local copy of the data. **D** is incorrect because web-based cloud storage does not operate behind the scenes like other cloud storage methods. The user of a web-based cloud storage system knows when a transfer starts and when it ends. Also, only the file selected is downloaded, not all files on the storage system. Only information on the remaining files is displayed so latency can affect it much like it would other systems. The fact that the user is aware of the time it takes to transfer files and that those transfers are minimized makes latency less of an issue for web-based cloud storage.

Chapter 2: Cloud Storage | Cloud Storage Methods
SCSP objective 6.1, Identify cloud storage methods

105. ☑ **B** is the correct answer. This is an example of cloud synchronization. The Internet resource is owned by a third party, which describes a cloud resource.
☒ **A** is incorrect because this is an example of database replication. **C** is incorrect because this is an example of an iSCSI volume mount. **D** is incorrect because this is an example of a grid storage array.

Chapter 2: Cloud Storage | Cloud Storage Methods
SCSP objective 6.1, Identify cloud storage methods

106. ☑ **D** is the correct answer. A hybrid cloud combines elements of the public and private cloud models.
☒ **A** is incorrect because this definition describes a public cloud. **B** is incorrect because this definition describes a private cloud. **C** is incorrect because this describes a community cloud.

Chapter 2: Cloud Storage | Cloud Storage Types
SCSP objective 6.2, Identify cloud storage types

107. ☑ **D** is the correct answer. Core is not an ITIL service change approach. The ITIL change approaches are big bang, phased, push, and pull.
☒ **A**, **B**, and **C** are incorrect because they are ITIL service change approaches.

Chapter 6: Configuration Management | Information Technology Infrastructure Library
SCSP objective 5.2, Identify storage management technologies

108. ☑ **A**, **B**, and **D** are the correct answers. The current backup size can be used to establish the baseline. The growth rate allows the administrator to determine how much will be needed in the near future so that the backup drives do not have to be immediately replaced. It is also important to know the backup frequency and retention because each of these copies will consume space.

☒ **C** is incorrect because the backups will need to be an appropriate size no matter where they are stored.

Chapter 12: Backup Troubleshooting | Space Limitations
SCSP objective 4.1, Identify backup technologies

Analyzing Your Results

Now that you're done, let's analyze your results! First you will need to tally up the number of questions you answered correctly. With this information in hand, please consult the following table:

Number of Answers Correct	Recommended Course of Study
1–59	If this had been the actual SCSP exam, it's unlikely you would have passed. Considerable study is recommended before taking the exam. It is advised that you thoroughly review the content of this book again.
60–79	If this had been the actual SCSP exam, you likely wouldn't have passed. Additional study and targeted review is recommended. For your review purposes, it will be helpful to know which exam objectives are points of weakness in order to tailor your studies based on your needs. Use the objective references included in the "In-Depth Answers" section to determine which objectives correspond to the questions you answered incorrectly. Then use this information in conjunction with the Objective Map, which precedes Chapter 1, to determine which chapters should be the focus of your additional study.
80–100	Congratulations! You have passed this practice exam. Before sitting the actual exam, it is recommended that you read through the chapter summaries one last time and study the chapter review questions again.

Best of luck on your exam!

INDEX

References to figures are in italics.

10GigE (10GbE), 99

A

A/B power, 52
abstraction, 159
AC, 298–299
access control, 234
    authentication, 234–235
    authorization, 235–240
    interoperability, 240–241
access control entries (ACEs), 237
access control lists (ACLs), 236–237
ACLs. *See* access control lists (ACLs)
active tape libraries (ATLs), 131
active-active, 272
active/active controllers, 46
active-passive, 272
active/passive controllers, 45–46
actuator arms, 4
Address Resolution Protocol. *See* ARP
adequate share capacity, 349
Advanced Technology Attachment.
   See ATA
AFR. *See* annualized failure rate (AFR)
aggregation, 159
alerts, 187–188
    alerting methods, 194–195
    auditing log files, 193
    backup logs, 194
    setting, 191–193
algorithms, 241
   See also encryption
alternating current (AC), 298–299

amplifiers, 123
amplitude, 111
analog
    vs. digital, 111–113
    signals, *112*
annualized failure rate (AFR), 9–10
antistatic devices, 306
appliance-based data migration, 311
application verification, 222
application-specific integrated circuits
  (ASICs), 56
architecture
    block-level, 265
    cloud services, 267–271
    controllers, 273
    failover, 266, 272
    file-level, 265
    high availability, 265–267
    online transaction processing (OLTP), 267
    overview, 263–264
    power supplies, 273
    redundancy, 271–279
    replication, 279–284
    service level agreements (SLAs), 266
    single point of failure, 267
    types of storage architecture, 264–265
archive bits, 216
archiving, 317
area ID, 73–74
ARP, 101–102
array-based backups, 227–228
array-based data migration, 311
array-based virtualization, 157–158
arrays, 353
    redundant, 278

ASICs. *See* application-specific integrated circuits (ASICs)
asymmetric encryption, 242
  See also encryption
asynchronous replication, 281–282
ATA, 13
auditing log files, 193
authentication, 234–235
authorization, 235–236
  access control lists (ACLs), 236–237
autobypass, 124
autoloaders, 131–132
automated storage tiering (AST), 315–316
automatic failover, 272
availability, 207
  high availability, 265–267
average rotational latency, 2–3
average seek time, 4

B

baby giants, 96
baby-jumbo frames, 96
backbone fabrics, 162
backhitching, 128
backup frequency, 210–211
  contention of media, 213–214
  continuous data protection, 212–213
  impact on production, 214
  rotation schemes, 211–212
backup implementation methods, 219
  LAN-free backups, 219
  server-based backups, 220
  serverless backups, 219–220
backup locations, 222
  array-based backups, 227–228
  disk-to-disk (D2D) backups, 222–223
  disk-to-disk-to-tape (D2D2T) backups, 224
  disk-to-tape (D2T) backups, 223
  offsite tape storage, 225–226
  vaulting and e-vaulting, 224–225
  virtual tape libraries (VTLs), 223
backup logs, 194
backup methods, 216
  differential backups, 217, *218*
  full backups, 216

incremental backups, 217–218
  progressive backups, 219
backup reliability, 220
  application verification, 222
  checksums, 221–222
  data integrity, 220–221
  overview, 214–216
backup troubleshooting, 370–371
  open files, 372–373
  permissions, 374–375
  space limitations, 371–372
  virus scanning, 373–374
bad frames, 89
bandwidth, 342, 353, 355
  bus and loop, 342–343
  cable speeds, 343
  disk throughput vs. network bandwidth vs. cache, 343–344
  embedded switch port speed, 344–346
  network device bandwidth, 347–349
  shared vs. dedicated, 348
  WAN, 102–103
baselines, 190–191
BCP. *See* business continuity planning (BCP)
bilingual network management, 179
BitLocker, 244–245
block mode, 53, 93
block virtualization, 145, 150–151, 256
block-level architecture, 265
block-level deduplication, 319–320
Blu-ray Disc File System (BDFS), 136
Blu-ray discs (BDs), 134–135
B-ports, 163
broadcast storm, 99
buffer underrun, 133
buffering, 125
buffer-to-buffer credits (BB_Credits), 104
buses, 277
business continuity, offsite storage for, 226
business continuity planning (BCP)
  availability, 207
  backup frequency, 210–214
  backup locations, 222–228
  backup reliability, 214–222
  data integrity, 207
  data value and risk, 208–209

objectives, 206–210
overview, 205–206
reliability, 207–208
business impact analysis (BIA), 209

C

cable select, 14
cables
    colored and labeled, 120
    copper, 116–120
    crossover cable, 117
    failed cable, 361
    management, 293–294
    optical, 113–116
    overview, 111
    PATA, 13–15
    SAS, 18, 119, 120
    SATA, 16
    SCSI, 17
    serial cables, 118–119
    speeds, 343
    troubleshooting cable failure, 367
    twisted pair cabling, 116
cache, 47–48, 335
    battery backup, 279
    de-staging, 336, *338*
    disk throughput vs. network bandwidth vs.
        cache, 343–344
    hit and miss, 337
    hit rate, 354
    mirroring, 279
    read vs. write, 335–336
    redundancy, 278–279
cache read hit, 47
capacity planning, 189–190
CAS. *See* content-addressable storage (CAS)
CDP. *See* continuous data protection
CD-ROMs, reliability, 215
channels, 7
checksums, 10, 221–222
CHS, 6, 34, 145
    LBA to CHS mapping, *150*
CIFS, 59–60, 239
cipher text, 242
circuit limitations, 302
class of service (CoS), 97–98, 349

CLI, 181–182
clock synchronization update (CSU), 75
clones, 227–228
cloud services, 267–268
    Infrastructure as a Service (IaaS), 270
    Platform as a Service (PaaS), 269–270
    Software as a Service (SaaS), 268–269
    Storage as a Service (StaaS), 270–271
cloud storage, 41–42
    backup, 62–63
    community clouds, 61–62
    hybrid clouds, 62
    locally mapped, 63
    methods, 62
    overview, 60–61
    private clouds, 61
    public clouds, 61
    synchronization, 64
    web-based, 64
cluster size, 33
clustered file systems (CFS), 152–153
clustering, 271–272
    incorrect settings, 369–370
coarse wavelength division multiplexing
    (CWDM), 114
command processors, 182
command queuing, 16
command-line interface. *See* CLI
command-line interpreters, 182
Common Information Model (CIM), 179
Common Internet File System. *See* CIFS
community clouds, 61–62
Compact Disc File System (CDFS), 135
compact discs (CDs), 133
    CD transfer speeds, 134
compliance, 316–318
compression
    deduplication, 319–321
    Linear Tape-Open (LTO), 129–130
computation replication, 279
concurrency, 340
configuration management, 185–187
Congestion Notification (CN), 99
connections, 75
    physical vs. logical, 76
    troubleshooting bad connectors, 365–366

consistency groups, 227
consumer drives, 11
    operating environment, 11
    performance, 9
    reliability, 9
content-addressable storage (CAS), 318
contention of media, 213–214
continuity. *See* business continuity
    planning (BCP)
continuous data protection, 212–213, 282
continuous replication, 280–281
controller boards, 6
controller heads, 44–46
controllers, 273
converged network adapter (CNA), 123
convergence enhanced Ethernet, 98
cooling, 294–295
copper cables
    care, 119–120
    Cat5, 117
    Cat5e, 117
    Cat6, 117–118
    Cat6a, 118
    noise, 117
    overview, 116
    serial cables, 118–119
    twinax, 119
copy-on-write, 227
CPU load, 354–355
critical load, 300
crossover cable, 117
crosstalk, 116
culling, 318
cyclic redundancy checks (CRCs), 90, 351
cylinder, head and sector. *See* CHS
cylinders, 3–4

D

D2D backups, 222–223
D2D2T backups, 224
D2T backups, 223
data bus width, 13, 19–20
data center bridging, 98–99
data center Ethernet (DCE), 98
data integrity, 207, 220–221
    in data migration, 311

Data Linear Tape (DLT), 128
data migration, 311–313
data replication, 279
data valuation, 208–209
    based on frequency of access, 313
database management systems (DBMSs), 42
DC, 299
DCB. *See* data center bridging
DDR. *See* Double Data Rate (DDR)
DDs. *See* discovery domains
decode errors, 90
dedicated bandwidth, vs. shared
    bandwidth, 348
dedicated storage, vs. shared storage, 346
deduplication, 319–321
defragmentation, 333–334
    impact of, 334
    schedules, 335
dense wavelength division multiplexing
    (DWDM), 114
deny permissions, 240
    See also permissions
desktop drives. *See* consumer drives
differential backups, 217, *218*
digital
    vs. analog, 111–113
    signals, *113*
direct attach (DA) twinax, 119
direct attached storage (DAS), 41–42
    and array-based virtualization, 157–158
    eSATA, 55
    Fibre Channel (FC), 55
    overview, 54
    SAS, 55
    SCSI, 54–55
direct current (DC), 299
dirty bits, 47, 335
disaster recovery, offsite storage for,
    225–226
disc burning, 132–133
discovery domains, 94, 255
disk encryption, 244–245
    See also encryption
disk rpm, 2
disk virtualization, 149–150
disk-buffered replication, 283

disks
    capacity vs. speed, 12–13
    electrical and mechanical differences,
        8–9
    external disk speeds by type, 16
    floppy disks, 1
    hard disk drives (HDDs), 1–6
    hosts interaction with, 32–34
    I/O vs. throughput, 11–12
    operating environment, 11
    overview, 1
    PATA, 13, 15
    performance, 9
    reliability, 9–11
disk-to-disk (D2D) backups, 222–223
disk-to-disk-to-tape (D2D2T) backups, 224
distributed file systems (DFS), 152, 153
Distributed Management Task Force
    (DMTF), 179
domain ID, 73
Double Data Rate (DDR), 20
D-ports, 163
dual active, 272
DVDs, 134
dynamic multipathing (DMP), 159

E

ears, 291
electromagnetic interference (EMI), 15,
    113, 294
electronic vaulting, 224–225
electrostatic discharge (ESD), 306
e-mail, alerts, 195
encapsulation, 79
encoding, 46
Encrypting File System (EFS), 246
encryption
    asymmetric encryption, 242
    data at rest, 243–246
    data in motion, 246–249
    disk encryption, 244–245
    file encryption, 246
    host encryption, 249
    IPSec, 248
    keys, 241, 242–243
    Linear Tape-Open (LTO), 129–130

network encryption, 247–248
    overview, 241–242
    symmetric-key encryption, 242
    tape encryption, 246
    virtual private networks (VPNs),
        248–249
end-to-end credits (EE_Credits), 105
Enhanced Transmission Selection (ETS), 99
enterprise drives
    operating environment, 11
    performance, 9
    reliability, 9–11
entry-level drives. See consumer drives
E-ports, 79, 87, 125–126, 163
equipment
    antistatic devices, 306
    floor and rack loading, 304
    proper lifting techniques, 304–305
    rack stabilization, 304
    weight considerations, 304
    See also facilities
eSATA, 15, 55
Ethernet switches, 94–96, 123–124
Ethernet-based storage, 60
e-vaulting, 224–225
execute permissions, 237
    See also permissions
expansion ports, 79
EX-ports, 163
extents, 155
external hard drives, reliability, 215
external interfaces, 13
    See also interfaces

F

fabric, 53
    backbone fabrics, 162
    logical fabric, 162, 164
    redundant fabric, 85
    switched fabric, 83–84
fabric busy events, 90
facilities, 291–292
    cable management, 293–294
    cooling, 294–295
    ears, 291
    fire suppression, 295–296

facilities (*cont.*)
    gaseous agent fire suppression
      systems, 297
    humidity control, 295, *296*
    power requirements, 298–303
    safety, 304–306
    U, 291
    water sprinklers, 297
failover, 266, 272
failover clustering, 272
FC. *See* Fibre Channel (FC)
FC addressing, 73–75
FC arbitrated loop (FC-AL), 82–83
FC Extended Link Service (ELS), 90
FC fabric, 83–84
FC point-to-point (FC-P2P), 81
FC switched fabric (FC-SW), 83–84
FC-0, 76, 78
FC-1, 78
FC-2, 77
FC-3, 77
FC-4, 76
FCIP, 79–80
FCoE, 80, *81*
FCoE Forwarder (FCF), 80
FCoE Initialization Protocol (FIP), 80
FCP, 76–78
fcping, 90–91
fiber directors, 126
fiber hubs, 124
    ports, 125
fiber switch ports, 125–126
fiber switches, 125
Fibre Channel arbitrated loop (FC-AL)
  topology, 124
Fibre Channel (FC), 18, 52, 55
    addressing, 73–75
    components, 71–75
    connections, 75, 76
    links, 75
    misconfigured Fibre Channel cable, 362
    overview, 71
    port channel, 85–86
    port types, 86–88, 163
    protocols, 76–81
    service classes, 72–73
    tools, 88–92
    topologies, 81–85
    trunking, 86
    World Wide Name (WWN), 71–72
Fibre Channel over Ethernet. *See* FCoE
Fibre Channel over IP. *See* FCIP
Fibre Channel Protocol. *See* FCP
field terminating, 119
file encryption, 246
    See also encryption
file hashing, 311
file permissions, 237
    See also permissions
file servers, 55
file system ACLs, 237
file system virtualization, 146, 152–153
file systems, 32, 33–34, 135–136
    on host, 53–54
file virtualization, 146, 151–154, 256
file-level architecture, 265
file-level deduplication, 319
FileVault 2, 245
fire suppression, 295–296
    gaseous agent fire suppression systems, 297
    water sprinklers, 297
firewall settings, 369
first-in-first-out (FIFIO) backup scheme,
    211–212
flash drives, 7
    See also solid-state drives (SSDs)
flash media, 136
flash-based add-in cards, 136
floating gates, 8, 333
FLOGI, 87
floppy disks, 1
flow control, 104–105
FL-ports, 88, *89*, 163
flux transition, 5
forecasting, 189–190
F-ports, 87, 125, 163
frame check sequence (FCS), 351, 355
frames, 77, 78
    baby-jumbo frames, 96
    bad frames, 89
    jumbo frames, 95–96
    short frames, 90

frequency, 111
front-end ports, 48–49
full backups, 216
full disk encryption (FDE), 244–245
    See also encryption
full rotational latency, 2
full stroke seek time, 4

G

gaseous agent fire suppression systems, 297
gateways, 352
GBIC, 124
    failed, 362
Gigabit Interface Converter. *See* GBIC
G-ports, 88, 125–126, 163
grandfather-father-son (GFS) backup
    scheme, 211
graphical user interfaces. *See* GUIs
grid storage, 46
grounding, 299
groups, 24
GUIs, 181

H

hard disk drives (HDDs), 1
    controller boards, 6
    cylinders, 3–4
    head disk assembly (HDA), 1
    heads, 4–5
    overview of physical components,
        1–2
    platters, 2
    vs. solid-state drives (SSDs), 7
    spindles, 2–3
hard zoning, 253
hardware, troubleshooting, 365
hardware fault tolerance, 207
hashing, 311
HDDs. *See* hard disk drives (HDDs)
head crash, 4–5
head disk assembly (HDA), 1
heads, 4–5
hierarchical storage management (HSM),
    313–314
hops, 352

host bus adapters (HBAs), 89, 122, 278
    failed, 362
    intermittent HBA connectivity, 362–363
host encryption, 249
    See also encryption
host issues, troubleshooting, 364–370
host protected area (HPA), 17
host tools, 357–360
host virtualization, 154–156
host-based data migration, 311
hot spares, 275–276
hot-pluggable/hot-swappable interfaces, 16
hot-swappable network components,
    126–127, 276
HPA. *See* host protected area (HPA)
HSM. *See* hierarchical storage management
    (HSM)
HTTP/S, 181
humidity control, 295, *296*
HVAC systems, 294–295
hybrid clouds, 62
Hypertext Transfer Protocol Secure.
    See HTTP/S

I

IEEE 802.1AB, 98
IEEE 802.1aq, 98–99
IEEE 802.1Qau, 99
IEEE 802.1Qaz, 99
IEEE 802.1Qbb, 99
IEEE 802.3bd, 99
IETF Transparent Interconnection of Lots of
    Links (TRILL), 99
iFCP, 80
in-band management, vs. out-of-band
    management, 180
incremental backups, 217–218
information lifecycle management,
    311–316
Information Technology Infrastructure
    Library (ITIL), 186–187
Infrastructure as a Service (IaaS), 270
initiators, 93
inline deduplication, 320
input queue, 350–351

Integrated Drive Electronics (IDE). *See* PATA
interfaces
    ATA, 13
    CLI, 181–182
    Fibre Channel (FC), 18
    overview, 13
    PATA, 13–15
    PCI versions, 18–19
    SAS, 18
    SATA, 15–17
    SCSI, 17–18
internal interfaces, 13
    See also interfaces
Internet Fibre Channel Protocol. *See* iFCP
Internet Storage Name Server. *See* iSNS
interoperability issues, troubleshooting, 364
interswitch links (ISLs), 73, 85, 353
invalid CRC, 90
invalid destination address, 90
I/O
    latency, 356–357
    random vs. sequential, 329–330
    vs. throughput, 11–12
IOPS, 11–12
    necessary, 328–329
    random vs. sequential I/O, 329–330
    standard IOPS ratings for SATA, SAS,
        and SSD disks, 12
IOstat, 359–360
ipconfig/ifconfig, 100–101, 365, *366*
IPSec, 248
    See also encryption
iSCSI protocol, 53
iSCSI security, 253–255
iSCSI storage network
    block mode, 93
    Ethernet features, 96–99
    Ethernet switching, 94–96
    initiators, 93
    overview, 93
    targets, 93–94
    tools, 99–102
iSCSI VLANs, 254
ISLs. *See* interswitch links (ISLs)
iSNS, 94
    security, 254

ISO, 135
isolation, 159
ITIL. *See* Information Technology
  Infrastructure Library (ITIL)

J

JBOD, 31
    See also RAID
journaling, 54
jumbo frames, 95–96
jumpers, 14
Just a Bunch of Disks. *See* JBOD

K

key pairs, 243
keys, 241
    See also encryption

L

landing zone, 4
LAN-free backups, 219
LANs, 97
latency, 63, 103, 339, 356–357
LBA. *See* logical block addressing (LBA)
least privilege, 240
least recently used (LRU), 48
leaves, 86
legal holds, 317–318
libraries, 131–132
linear mapping, 156
Linear Tape File System (LTFS), 130–131
Linear Tape-Open (LTO), 128, 246
    compression and encryption, 129–130
    size vs. speed, 130
    versions, 129
link aggregation, 278, 348
link command frames, 78
link failover, 276
Link Layer Discovery Protocol (LLDP), 98
links, 75
litigation holds, 317–318
load balancing, 251–252, 276
    multipathing for, 346
load/unload cycle, 11
local area networks. *See* LANs

local connectors (LC), 115
local replication, 282
log shipping, 283
logical block addressing (LBA), 7, 34, 145,
    150–151
    LBA to CHS mapping, *150*
logical disk file systems, 152
logical extents, 155
logical fabric, 162, 164
logical groups (LGs), 155
logical storage area networks. *See* LSANs
logical switches, 162
logical unit numbers (LUNs), 150–151, 172
    load balancing, 251–252
    masking, 250, 251
    provisioning, 171, 172
    sharing, 250–251
logical units (LUs), 18, 172
    thick, 173–174
    See also provisioning
logical volume managers (LVMs),
    154–155, 282
logical volumes, 32–33, 155
logs, 54
    auditing log files, 193
    backup, 194
low-level formatting, 3
LSANs, 162–163
LUN masking, 250, 251
LUN provisioning, 171, 172
LUN sharing, 250–251

M

magazines, 131
management applications, 181
management protocols, 177–180
MANs, 97
manual failover, 272
manual storage tiering, 315
mean time between failure (MTBF),
    9–10, 210
mean time to failure (MTTF), 210
mean time to repair (MTTR), 360
mesh, 85
metropolitan area networks. *See* MANs

midrange drives
    operating environment, 11
    performance, 9
mirroring, 24–25, 27
    cache, 279
modal dispersion, 114
modem alerts, 195
molex connectors, 15
most recently used (MRU), 48
mounted disks, 238
MTBF. *See* mean time between
    failure (MTBF)
multicast groups, 74
multipath connections, 277
multipath I/O (MPIO), 276
multipathing
    incorrect settings, 369–370
    for load balancing, 346
multiple-level cell (MLC), 7, 8
multiplexing, 128
    coarse wavelength division multiplexing
        (CWDM), 114
    dense wavelength division multiplexing
        (DWDM), 114
    in optical cable, 114
    wavelength division multiplexing
        (WDM), 113
multistreaming, 128

N

name servers, 91
name zoning, 252–253
NAND flash, 7, 136
NAS. *See* network attached storage (NAS)
nearline storage, 210
    reliability, 216
negated AND (NAND) flash.
    See NAND flash
network attached storage (NAS), 41–42
    components, 57
    Ethernet-based storage, 60
    file system protocols, 58–60
    overview, 55–57
    TCP/IP-based storage, 58
    UNC-addressable storage, 57–58

Network Data Management Protocol
   (NDMP), 131, 148
network encryption, 247–248
   See also encryption
Network File System. *See* NFS
network interface cards (NICs), 122, 278
   troubleshooting, 362, 365, 368–369
network resiliency, 207
network virtualization, 159–164
networking ACLs, 237
NFS, 58–59
NFS3, 238
NFS4, 239
NL-ports, 87, *88*, 163
node ports, 72–73, 163
nonrepudiation, 243
NPIV, 164
N-port ID, 86
N-port ID virtualization. *See* NPIV
N-ports, 72–73, 86–87, 163
nslookup, 101

O

object-oriented storage (OOS), 319
offsite tape storage, 225–226
OLTP. *See* online transaction processing
   (OLTP)
online backup services, reliability, 216
online transaction processing (OLTP), 267
OOS. *See* object-oriented storage (OOS)
optical cables
   cable care, 115–116
   connectors, 115
   limitations, 115
   multimode fiber (MMF), 114
   multiplexing in, 114
   overview, 113–114
   single-mode fiber (SMF), 114
optical media, 132–136
organizationally unique identifiers (OUIs), 72
out-of-band management, vs. in-band
   management, 180
output queue, 351, 355
overburning, 133
overhead, 112
oversubscription, 177

P

pages, 47
Parallel ATA. *See* PATA
parity, 31–32, 332–333, 351
partitioning, 159
partitions, 32
   alignment, 340–341
passive replication, 280
passwords, hard disk passwords, 16–17
PATA, 13–15
   versions, 15
paths, 277
payload, 78
PCI
   overview, 19–20
   versions, 18–19, 20
PCI Ethernet card, 18, *19*
PCI Express. *See* PCIe
PCIe, 18, 22–23
   bandwidth by slot type and version, 23
PCI-eXtended. *See* PCI-X
PCI-X, 18, 19, 20–21
perfmon. *See* Performance Monitor
performance
   adequate share capacity, 349
   cache, 335–337
   and capacity implications, 321
   concurrency, 340
   defragmentation, 333–335
   impact of replication, 337–339
   latency, 339
   metrics and tools, 349–360
   necessary IOPS, 328–329
   network device bandwidth,
      347–349
   optimizing, 327
   partition alignment, 340–341
   queue depth, 341–342
   RAID, 330–333
   random vs. sequential I/O, 329–330
   storage device bandwidth, 342–346
   synchronization time, 340
   throughput, 339
Performance Monitor, 192, 358–359
Peripheral Component Interconnect.
   See PCI

permissions, 236
  access control lists (ACLs), 236–237
  best practices, 239–240
  file permissions, 237
  share permissions, 237–239
  troubleshooting, 374–375
phone alerts, 195
physical access, 235
physical authentication, 235
physical extents, 155
physical volumes, 155
ping, 99
plain text, 183, 242
Platform as a Service (PaaS), 269–270
platters, 2
PLOGI, 87
pointers, 319
point-in-time replication, 280
polarization, 5
port error counters, 89–90
port groups, 352–353
port statistics, 350–351, 355
port types, 86–88
port zoning, 252
ports, troubleshooting, 367–368
postprocess deduplication, 320
power distribution units (PDUs),
  52, 300, *301*
power requirements
  AC, 298–299
  circuit limitations, 302
  DC, 299
  division of circuits, 301
  grounding, 299
  hardwiring, 302
  overview, 298
  spikes and lulls, 301
  sufficient capacity, 299–301
  uninterruptable power supplies (UPSs),
    301–303
power supplies, 273
preservation, 317–318
priority tagging, 98
Priority-based Flow Control (PFC), 99
private clouds, 61
private keys, 243

progressive backups, 219
protocols
  management, 177–180
  See also specific protocols
provisioning
  best practices, 176–177
  overview, 171–172
public clouds, 61
public keys, 243
purging, 317

Q

QDR. *See* Quad Data Rate (QDR)
Quad Data Rate (QDR), 20
quality of service (QoS), 73
queue depth, 341–342

R

radio frequency interference (RFI), 113
RAID
  and automated storage tiering (AST), 315
  groups, 24
  hardware, 31
  host-based implementations, 31
  mirroring, 24–25, 27
  number of disks, 331–333
  overview, 24
  parity, 31–32, 332–333
  performance, 330–333
  RAID 0, 24, *25*
  RAID 0+1, 28–29, *30*
  RAID 1, 24–25, *26*
  RAID 10 (1+0), 27–28, *29*
  RAID 5, 25–27
  RAID 50, 29–30
  RAID 51, 30–31
  RAID 6, 27, *28*
  read, modify, write, 32
  rebuild, 32
  software-based implementations,
    31–32
  and storage arrays, 43–44
  striping, 24, 28, 332
  strips, 332
  type and size, 330–331
  See also JBOD

random read IOPS, 12, 330
random reads, 4
random write IOPS, 12, 330
read miss, 47
read permissions, 237
   See also permissions
read-ahead cache, 47, 335
record virtualization, 146
recovery point objective (RPO), 209–210
recovery time objective (RTO), 209, 210
reduction ratios, 321
   See also deduplication
redundancy, 271
   active-active, 272
   active-passive, 272
   arrays, 278
   cache battery backup, 279
   cache mirroring, 279
   cache redundancy, 278–279
   clustering, 271–272
   host bus adapters (HBAs), 278
   hot spares, 275–276
   hot-swap, 276
   link aggregation, 278
   link failover, 276
   load balancing, 276
   multipath I/O (MPIO), 276
   network interface cards (NICs), 278
   paths and buses, 277
   redundant paths to disks, 274–275
   site redundancy, 283–284
   switches, 278
Redundant Array of Independent Disks.
  See RAID
redundant fabric, 85
reliability, 207–208
   backup reliability, 214–222
remote authentication, 235
remote replication, 283
removable storage
   flash media, 136
   optical media, 132–136
   overview, 127
   tape media, 127–132

repeaters, 123
replication
   asynchronous, 281–282
   computation replication, 279
   consistency, 284
   continuous, 280–281
   data replication, 279
   disk-buffered replication, 283
   impact of, 337–339
   in-band management, 280
   local, 282
   log shipping, 283
   out-of-band management, 280
   overview, 279–280
   passive replication, 280
   point-in-time replication, 280
   remote, 283
   scope, 282
   site redundancy, 283–284
   storage array remote replication, 283
   synchronous, 281, 282
reports, 187–188
rescans, 91–92
retention policies, 316–317
risk assessment, 209
RLL. *See* run length limited (RLL)
rotation schemes, 211–212
rotational latency, 2–3
rotational vibration, 11
Rotational Vibration Feed Forward (RVFF), 11
routers, 126
Routing Bridges (RBridges), 99
RPO. *See* recovery point objective (RPO)
RTO. *See* recovery time objective (RTO)
run length limited (RLL), 5
runt counters, 351, 355
RVFF. *See* Rotational Vibration Feed Forward
  (RVFF)

S

safety, 304–306
SAN arrays, reliability, 216
SAN file systems, 152
SANs. *See* storage area networks (SANs)

SAS, 18, 55
    cables, 119, 120
SATA, 15–17
    versions, 16
scale-out storage. *See* grid storage
scope entry, 94
SCSI, 17–18, 54–55
    versions, 17
SDS. *See* software-defined storage
Secure Shell. *See* SSH
security
    access control, 234–241
    authentication, 234–235
    authorization, 235–240
    encryption, 241–249
    overview, 233–234
    storage visibility, 249–256
seek time, 4
segmentation, 255–256
sequential read IOPS, 12, 330
sequential reads, 4
sequential write IOPS, 12, 330
Serial ATA. *See* SATA
Serial Attached SCSI. *See* SAS
serial communication, 182–183
Server Manager, 92
server-based backups, 220
serverless backups, 219–220
service classes, 72–73
service level agreements (SLAs), 266
Service Location Protocol (SLP), 93–94
services layer, 77
SFP, 125
share permissions, 237–239
    See also permissions
shared access, 237–239
shared bandwidth, vs. dedicated
    bandwidth, 348
shared disks, 238
shared documents, 238
shared drive volumes, 238
shared files, 238
shared folders, 238
shared printers, 238

shared scanners, 238
shared storage, vs. dedicated storage, 346
Shared Storage Model (SSM), 144–145
shares, 55, 56–57
shells, 182
shoe shining, 128
short frames, 90
Short Message Service (SMS), 195
Shortest Path Bridging (SPB), 98–99
Simple Network Management Protocol.
    See SNMP
Single Connector Attachment (SCA), 17
single point of failure, 267
single-instance storage (SIS), 319
single-level cell (SLC), 7–8
single-path connections, 277
site redundancy, 283–284
SLAs. *See* service level agreements (SLAs)
Small Computer System Interface. *See* SCSI
small form-factor pluggable (SFP)
    transceivers, 125
    failed, 362
SMI-S, 180, 350
snapshots, 156, 227
sneakernet, 55, 136
SNIA Storage Virtualization Taxonomy,
    145–146
SNMP, 177–179, 350
    alerts, 195
soft zoning, 253
software, troubleshooting, 365
Software as a Service (SaaS), 268–269
software-defined storage, 196–197
solid-state drives (SSDs), 1, 7
    and partition alignment, 340–341
    See also flash drives
source deduplication, 320
spindles, 2–3, 331
split-mirror, 227
spoliation, 317
SQL implementations, 237
SSDs. *See* solid-state drives (SSDs)
SSH, 183–185
SSH2, 184

standard connectors, 115
storage, overview, 41–42
storage administration, 181–185
storage architecture. *See* architecture
storage area networks (SANs), 41–42
   and array-based virtualization, 157–158
   block mode, 53
   fabric, 53
   FC or iSCSI protocol, 53
   Fibre Channel (FC), 52
   file system on host, 53–54
   overview, 52
storage array remote replication, 283
storage arrays, 41–44
   array port types and cabling, 48–49
   cabling, 52
   cache, 47–48
   controller heads, 44–46
   disk enclosure, 49–51
   dual-controller, 45–46
   enclosure addressing, 51–52
   enclosure controllers, 51
   expansion adapters, 48
   grid storage, 46
   hot-swap, 52
   monitoring cards, 51
   overview, 42–44
   single-controller, 45
Storage as a Service (StaaS), 270–271
Storage Management Initiative (SMI), 179
Storage Management Initiative-Specification.
  See SMI-S
storage monitoring, 187–188
   auditing log files, 193
   backup logs, 194
   displaying performance data in Windows
    with Performance Monitor, 192
   forecasting and capacity planning,
    189–190
   recording a baseline, 190–191
   settings thresholds, 188
   trending, 189
   See also alerts
storage networking devices
   amplifiers, 123
   converged network adapter (CNA), 123

Ethernet switches, 94–96, 123–124
fiber directors, 126
fiber hub ports, 125
fiber hubs, 124
fiber switch ports, 125–126
fiber switches, 125
GBIC, 124
host bus adapters (HBAs), 89, 122
hot-swappable network components,
  126–127
network interface cards (NICs), 122
overview, 121–122
repeaters, 123
routers, 126
small form-factor pluggable (SFP)
  transceivers, 125
TCP Offload Engine (TOE), 122
storage pools, 147
storage provisioning. *See* provisioning
storage replication. *See* replication
storage tiers, 314–316
storage virtualization
  array-based virtualization, 157–158
  block virtualization, 145, 150–151, 256
  defined, 144
  file systems, 151–154
  file virtualization, 146, 256
  host virtualization, 154–156
  network virtualization, 159–164
  overview, 143–144
  Shared Storage Model (SSM), 144–145
  SNIA Storage Virtualization Taxonomy,
   145–146
  types of, 144–154
storage visibility
  iSCSI security, 253–255
  LUN security, 250–252
  overview, 249
  segmentation, 255–256
  zoning, 252–253
straight tip (ST) connectors, 115
stripe size, 33
striped mapping, 156
striping, 24, 28, 332
subfile deduplication, 320
subscriber connectors, 115

sufficient capacity, 299–301
switch blades, 125
switched fabric, 83–84
switches, 278, 350
symmetric-key encryption, 242
    See also encryption
synchronization time, 340
synchronous replication, 281, 282
sysmon, 357–358
system outages, causes for, 205

T

tape encryption, 246
    See also encryption
tape jukeboxes, 131
tape library virtualization (TLV), 145
tape media, 127–132
    reliability, 214–215
    tape care, 130
tape virtualization, 145, 146–149
target deduplication, 320
TCP Offload Engine (TOE), 122
TCP/IP-based storage, 58
teaming, 278, 348
Telnet, 183
TE-ports, 163
thick provisioning, 172, 173–174
thin provisioning, 172, 174–176
thresholds, 188, 352, 355, *356*
throughput, 339, 355–356
    disk throughput vs. network bandwidth vs.
        cache, 343–344
    vs. I/O, 11–12
time-limited error recovery, 10
total load, 300
Tower of Hanoi rotation scheme, 212, *213*
tracert/traceroute, 100, 352
tracks, 3
track-to-track seek time, 4
transfer rate, 6
trending, 189
troubleshooting
    backups, 370–375
    bad cables, 367
    bad connectors, 365–366

bad ports, 367–368
connectivity issues, 361–363
hardware or software incompatibility, 365
host issues, 364–370
incorrect cluster or multipath settings,
    369–370
incorrect firewall settings, 369
incorrect NIC configuration, 365
interoperability issues, 364
outdated firmware or drivers, 365
overview, 360–361
VLAN issues, 363
zoning issues, 363–364
trunking, 86
Trusted Platform Module (TPM), 244
twinax cables, 119
twisted pair cabling, 116
    See also copper cables

U

U (racks), 291
uniform naming convention (UNC) path,
    57–58
uninterruptable power supplies (UPSs),
    301–303
Universal Disc Format (UDF), 136
U-ports, 88, 163
UPSs. *See* uninterruptable power supplies
    (UPSs)

V

vaulting, 224–225
VE-ports, 163
VEX-ports, 163
virtual circuits (VCs), 73
virtual controllers, 46
virtual local area networks. *See* VLANs
virtual private networks (VPNs), 248–249
virtual provisioning, 156, 158
virtual SANs. *See* VSANs
virtual tape libraries (VTLs), 145, 146,
    147, 223
virtual tape servers, 146, 147–148, *149*
virtual tapes (VTs), 145, 146–147
virtualization. *See* storage virtualization

virus scanning, 373–374
VLANs, 95, 163–164
    iSCSI, 254
    troubleshooting, 363
volume groups, 32–33, 155
VPNs. *See* virtual private networks (VPNs)
VSANs, 161–162
    and trunking, 86

W

WANs, 97
    connections and their speeds, 343
    storage over, 102–105
water sprinklers, 297
wavelength division multiplexing
    (WDM), 113
WBEM, 179–180
Web-Based Enterprise Management.
    See WBEM

wide area networks. *See* WANs
Windows Disk Defragmenter, 333, *334*
World Wide Name (WWN), 52, 71–72
    zoning, 252–253
World Wide Node Name (WWNN),
    72, 253
World Wide Port Names (WWPNs),
    164, 253
write penalty, 332
write permissions, 237
    See also permissions
write-back cache, 47, 335
write-through cache, 47, 336

Z

zone sets, 252
zoning, 252–253
    best practices, 253
    troubleshooting, 363–364

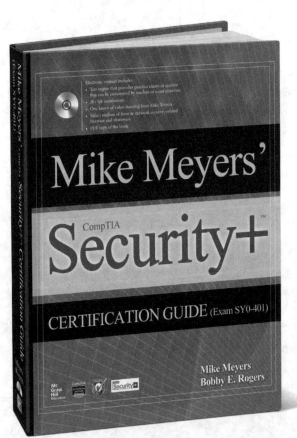